# The Changing Landscape of Work and Family in the American Middle Class

# The Changing Landscape of Work and Family in the American Middle Class

## Reports from the Field

Edited by Elizabeth Rudd
and Lara Descartes

LEXINGTON BOOKS

A division of
ROWMAN & LITTLEFIELD PUBLISHERS, INC.
Lanham • Boulder • New York • Toronto • Plymouth, UK

LEXINGTON BOOKS

A division of Rowman & Littlefield Publishers, Inc.
A wholly owned subsidiary of The Rowman & Littlefield Publishing Group, Inc.
4501 Forbes Boulevard, Suite 200
Lanham, MD 20706

Estover Road
Plymouth PL6 7PY
United Kingdom

British Library Cataloguing in Publication Information Available

**Library of Congress Cataloging-in-Publication Data**

The changing landscape of work and family in the American middle class : reports
from the field / edited by Elizabeth Rudd and Lara Descartes.
    p. cm.
 ISBN-13: 978-0-7391-1739-2 (cloth : alk. paper)
 ISBN-10: 0-7391-1739-4 (cloth : alk. paper)
 ISBN-13: 978-0-7391-1740-8 (pbk. : alk. paper)
 ISBN-10: 0-7391-1740-8 (pbk. : alk. paper)
 1. Work and family—United States. 2. Middle class families—United States. I.
Rudd, Elizabeth, 1963- II. Descartes, Lara, 1968-  HD4904.25.C448 2008
 306.3'60973--dc22          2007045422

Printed in the United States of America

⊗™ The paper used in this publication meets the minimum requirements of
American National Standard for Information Sciences—Permanence of Paper
for Printed Library Materials, ANSI/NISO Z39.48-1992.

For all the children in our lives from A to Z, including:
Alexa, Andre, Elina, Geramey, Irene, Jason, and Zeaira

# Contents

Acknowledgments        ix

Foreword        xi

1   Changing Landscapes of Work and Family        1
    *Lara Descartes and Elizabeth Rudd*

**Part I: Intersections of Work and Family**

2   Working Selves, Moral Selves: Crafting the Good Person
    in the Northern Plains        17
    *Tom Fricke*

3   Kitchen Conferences and Garage Cubicles: The Merger of
    Home and Work in a 24-7 Global Economy        41
    *Alesia F. Montgomery*

4   "We Pass the Baby Off at the Factory Gates": Work and Family
    in the Manufacturing Midwest        61
    *Elizabeth Rudd and Lawrence S. Root*

5   The Work-Family Divide for Low-Income African Americans        87
    *Alford A. Young, Jr.*

6   American Dreaming: Refugees from Corporate Work Seek
    the Good Life        117
    *Brian A. Hoey*

7　Patrolling the Boundaries of Childhood in Middle-Class
　"Ruburbia"　　　　　　　　　　　　　　　　　　　141
　*Lara Descartes and Conrad P. Kottak*

**Part II: The (Not So) Standard North American Family**

8　Gay Family Values: Gay Co-Father Families in Straight
　Communities　　　　　　　　　　　　　　　　　159
　*Diana M. Pash*

9　Black Women Have Always Worked: Is There a Work-
　Family Conflict Among the Black Middle Class?　　　189
　*Riché Jeneen Daniel Barnes*

10　"It's Like Arming Them": African American Mothers' Views on
　Racial Socialization　　　　　　　　　　　　　211
　*Erin N. Winkler*

11　Seeing the Baby in the Belly: Family and Kinship at the
　Ultrasound Scan　　　　　　　　　　　　　　243
　*Sallie Han*

12　Stabilizing Influence: Cultural Expectations of Fatherhood　265
　*Todd L. Goodsell*

13　Focused on the Chinese American Family: Chinese
　Immigrant Churches and Childrearing　　　　　　281
　*Carolyn Chen*

14　Choosing Chastity: Redefining the Sexual Double Standard
　in the Language of Choice　　　　　　　　　　　301
　*M. Eugenia Deerman*

**Afterword**

15　What Is a Family?　　　　　　　　　　　　　　319
　*Kathryn M. Dudley*

About the Contributors　　　　　　　　　　　　　327

# Acknowledgments

We are pleased to acknowledge the intellectual community and financial support provided by the Center for the Ethnography of Everyday Life (CEEL) at the University of Michigan, where this book got its start, and the encouragement of CEEL Director Tom Fricke. CEEL was generously funded by the Alfred P. Sloan Foundation's program on Workplace, Work Force, and Working Families, and we are indebted to the vision of the program director, Kathleen Christensen. We thank Rebecca Upton for key contributions at early stages, and Kathryn Dudley and Carrie Lane for constructive criticism of complete drafts of the manuscript. For thoughtful feedback on selected chapters, we thank Sarah Bland, Gene Deerman, Sallie Han, and Rebecca Rudd.

—Elizabeth Rudd and Lara Descartes

I would like to thank Elizabeth Rudd for conceiving of this volume, inviting me to participate as co-editor, and being a wonderful and thoughtful friend and colleague, and Conrad Kottak for including me in the CEEL program and for our collaboration since.

—Lara Descartes

I would like to thank Lara Descartes for making completion of this book possible and fun and for always being a constructive critic and supportive friend. Many thanks also to Tom and Anna Rudd for the basement office with a window full of mint plants, to Kerry Nelson for coaching, to Lissa Bell for Toulouse and Panajachel, to David Fathi for being so happy about this, and to Randy Deshazo for being part of my life.

—Elizabeth Rudd

# Foreword

Since the latter part of the twentieth century, we in the United States have lived through a period of major social change as middle-class mothers have entered and remained in the workforce in record numbers. This development has resulted in the rise of dual-earner parents and single-earner single parents; and a concomitant challenge to most of them in figuring out how to balance the demands of their work and family. Much of our understanding of these changes has been premised on statistical profiles comprising facts and figures. Behind these statistics, however, are real families who vary tremendously in the type of work they do, in the resources they have available to them, and in their ideas—passed down from their own parents as well as society at large—as to what is a good mother, a good father, and a successful family. Yet, we have substantially less understanding of how families vary in these ideas that guide them in forming their families and living out their lives on a day-by-day basis.

In *The Changing Landscape of Work and Family in the American Middle Class*, Lara Descartes and Elizabeth Rudd provide us with rich and compelling ethnographies of how families of various races, incomes, aspirations, and sexual orientations come to terms with the traditional middle-class family ideal of a nuclear family comprising a male breadwinner and a female homemaker/caregiver. While this ideal continues to exercise a powerful hold on our imaginations and actions regarding making a family, it cannot—as this volume so eloquently shows—ultimately undermine the resiliency and determination of parents to build families that reflect their personal values and ideals.

I am particularly pleased that Lara Descartes and Elizabeth Rudd have published this important volume. They and most of the chapter authors have been affiliated with the University Michigan Center on the Ethnography of Everyday Life (CEEL), which was one of six original centers on working families funded by the Alfred P. Sloan Foundation in the mid- to late-1990s. It was the first of our centers to bring the rich insights of anthropologists, working with other social scientists, to bear on understanding the daily lives of middle-class working families. Through the work of these scholars, no longer could any of us ever again conceive of the "middle class" as a monolithic set of norms or ideas. Nor could we ever think of working families except in their diversity.

Kathleen Christensen
Alfred P. Sloan Foundation
New York City
July 2007

# 1

## Changing Landscapes of Work and Family

*Lara Descartes and Elizabeth Rudd*

> "He perceived that he had blundered into falseness by living in the midst of ideas about people, instead of among people themselves."
>
> —Czeslaw Milosz (2001, 116–17)

Talk of failing families is a staple of contemporary mass media. Yet we rarely stop to consider how we know what makes families "good" or "bad." We also tend to think of work and family as two separate and opposed domains, with one stealing time from the other. This book is based on the premise that what makes a good family is a cultural question and that family and work lives are two sides of the same coin—the experience of being a family and the meanings of family life cannot be understood separately from the qualities of the jobs that support families. In this volume, we think of individual families as being part of a landscape of work and family. This landscape has some natural features: Babies are conceived when egg and sperm unite, women birth them, infants and small children remain helpless for a long while, and in general, all humans need to procure food and shelter. But this landscape is also culturally shaped, with widespread and well-recognized ways of being a family and meanings attributed to work and family life. Just as we create and change our physical surroundings by transforming nature, we also shape and alter the work-family landscape through how we structure employment and caregiving, combine work and family, and make sense of our work and family lives. And, as this landscape changes, opportunities for new kinds of families may arise, and what we value in work and family life may be transformed. The chapters in this book can be thought of as reports from various field sites throughout this ever-shifting, yet patterned, landscape of work and family.

In the recent history of the United States, one particular idealized image of the family has been especially influential: a mother and father and children living together in a single-family home that they own, largely supported financially by the father's income while the mother takes responsibility for caregiving and homemaking. Historically, this family model has been most attainable by middle-class, white families. Today, economic changes, shifting gender roles and race relations, and the social realities of divorce, remarriage, and single-parent and gay-couple families are challenging this specific image of the nuclear family as a cultural ideal and making it lose ground as social reality. The studies in this book shed light on how shifting ideologies and social realities of middle-class families look and feel to ordinary Americans. Perspectives presented range from those of farming families coping with sea changes in their livelihoods to stay-home mothers forging new paths in the African American community to modern-day pioneers who have left corporate jobs to move to rural locations to lead what they see as more ethical lives.

This book does not try to provide a comprehensive treatment of trends in middle-class work and family life, a catalog of middle-class family types, or a statistical portrait of the situation of middle-class families. Instead, this volume explores the intersections of work and family lives and the roles and relationships within families from the perspectives of people situated differently in relation to the idealized middle-class family. With two exceptions, each chapter is based on an original, ethnographic study of middle-class family life. The exceptions include one on representations of family and gender roles in popular magazines; this chapter highlights the media as key players in disseminating and interpreting images of family life. The second exception is an ethnographic study of the struggles of families who lack middle-class economic security. This chapter focuses on those whose labor helps make middle-class comfort possible and underscores the difficulties in combining work and family for those whose labor is not well compensated. As a whole, the collection reveals the continuing power of symbols of middle-class family life rooted in now-vanishing socioeconomic contexts, even as people forge new ways of making and being family.

## WHY ETHNOGRAPHY?

Ethnography is a research methodology that brings unique contributions to the study of family and work life. Methodologies are underlying ideas about research. These ideas, in turn, motivate the research methods, the actual procedures by which data are collected. The methodology of ethnography is phenomenological (Bernard 1994), premised on the idea that reality is constructed through social interaction, and therefore that reality means different things to different people. Ethnography's goal is to depict research participants' realities as fully as possible, through investigating beliefs and values as well as behaviors. This is a subjective process—the ethnographer seeks to understand the way the research participant sees the world. So to investigate people's family and work lives ethnographically involves trying to understand who those individuals are and how they experience, feel about, and make meaning of being members of their families and of their roles as workers. Agar (1985) describes the ethnographer's role as one of a learner: The role of the researcher is to let the research participant teach her about the participant's culture. Ethnographic research methods aim to capture the complexity of people's lives, in part by paying attention to context, whether that is the historical background, the social structure, the cultural value system, or a combination of these that frames people's everyday experiences.

A great deal of ethnographic research on families in the United States has been carried out among racial/ethnic minority families (Descartes, Kottak, and Kelly 2007). A famous example is Stack's 1974 study of African American families coping with economic hardship. The middle class, however, has remained relatively unexamined ethnographically. Perhaps ethnographers, often middle-class themselves, did not think to study cultural groups they were so familiar with. Recently, however, researchers have begun to make the familiar "strange" by turning the ethnographic lens on their own kind (e.g., Townsend 2002, Lareau 2003). The research in this volume was motivated partly by an interest in the contributions ethnography could make to understanding the diverse situations and world-views of American middle-class families (Overbey and Dudley 2000).

Ethnographic studies of family life are especially useful at a time when patterns of combining work and family are in flux, and the cultural ideals representing the best way to combine work and family are also changing. When social relations are evolving and the meanings of key symbols—such as work and family—in a society are being questioned, it is impossible to study these relationships with preconceived categories and concepts. A survey might ask respondents about their "family," for example. If "family" means children and spouse to the researcher, but to the respondent it means parents and siblings, or same-sex partner and children, the interpretation of findings will be flawed. Similarly, a male factory worker might indicate that he works overtime hours for "family reasons" while his wife offers "family reasons" to explain her part-time work schedule. Obviously the meanings of work and family are different for these two people—but these meanings are not simply individual differences, they also reflect ways of thinking rooted in conventional family gender roles. The very existence of and meanings of differences like these can be discovered through ethnographic research.

## Ethnographic Research Methods

There are two primary ethnographic methods. One is ethnographic interviewing. These are interviews that encourage research participants to talk at length, using their own words to describe events, feelings, and meanings in detail. Ethnographic interviews use open-ended questions to allow the interviewees to discuss topics in ways that are relevant to them rather than in ways that fit the researcher's own preconceptions of what is important. The ethnographer needs highly developed listening skills, allowing the respondent to follow her own thought processes. Simultaneously the ethnographer must listen with an analytic ear, thinking ahead to pertinent follow-up questions as ideas and concepts emerge. Interviews are typically audiotaped and transcribed for subsequent systematic analysis, and researchers usually write detailed notes (known as "field notes") about the interview experience and context.

A second important ethnographic method is participant observation, which is sometimes called ethnographic observation. This method entails the researcher spending time with the research participants in their own environment, doing what they do in order to experience what they experience. Ethnographers can directly observe the milieux in which events take place and, through engaging in those events themselves, may, over time, approach understanding them from an insider's point of view, while keeping an outsider's more analytic perspective. Ethnographic researchers not only participate in the activities of people they are studying but also spend hours writing detailed field notes documenting their observations and experiences. Field notes then form the basis for analysis of observations and reflection upon the researcher's own experiences in the field site.

## Subjectivity and Identity

All social science methods and analyses are shaped by the subjective positions of the researchers themselves. This observation holds true in multiple ways—for instance, the choice of topics, research questions, and methods as well as the interpretation of data are influenced by the researcher's own identity, including her social position, personal experiences, and background. However, these factors may be more obvious with ethnographic methods because ethnographers are engaged in direct face-to-face interactions with people in the contexts of their daily lives. An ethnographer's ability to study a group depends upon his ability to establish relationships with them such that he is able to be present in the times and places he would like to observe and is able to engage with the people with whom he is working. In in-depth, face-to-face interviews and participant observation, the ethnographer herself is her most central data collection tool. Some social science methodologies view interactions between researchers and participants in studies as "contaminating" the research findings. In contrast, ethnographers focus on what their presence may reveal about the culture of the group they are investigating. Ethnographers try to use their centrality in the research process to their advantage by reflecting upon their roles in the field sites and interviews, and upon their relationships to the people whose worlds they are trying to understand.

Because of the centrality to the research of the ethnographer's relationships with the people being studied, we asked each author in this book to write a short afterword reflecting on his or her experiences while conducting the fieldwork presented in the chapter. These afterwords provide the reader with information about the subjective perspectives of the authors and their connections to their field sites and topics of study. We feel these reflections offer important insight into the conditions of the research and simultaneously illuminate the ethnographic process in a way that the chapters alone could not. We allowed each author to craft his or her afterword with few guidelines so that it would be a reflection of the author's own concerns and experiences. Each author took a slightly different tack. Some wrote mostly of how and why they became interested in the topic, some about how their identities affected data collection and/or analysis, and some about leaving the field and future directions.

## STUDYING THE CHANGING LANDSCAPES
## OF WORK AND FAMILY

Each of the authors in this book explores aspects of the changing *cultural* landscapes of work and family. In everyday usage "culture" refers to the characteristics of other people that make them different from us (whoever that *us* is), whether it be their clothing, food, language, religion, values, and so on. Social scientists, however, define culture in a way that stresses that *all* human groups have culture. Culture is what we make, eat, think, do, feel, learn, and teach. Culture is all-encompassing: It permeates every aspect of our lives at every moment. Culture is shared among group members: We learn it from others—our language, our religion, how to act, what to believe, what is good, what is bad, what is tasteful, what is tacky, and so on.

Examples of American culture are Western dress—items such as business suits, blue jeans, tee shirts, and halter tops; our foods, which include hamburgers and apple pie; and our values of independence and hard work. Our culture also encompasses our ideas about family structure and relationships between family members. If you say the word *family*, for example, certain images come to most people's minds. In the United States, those images are often of a two-parent family with children, living in a private home, with a husband who is the main breadwinner and a wife who is the main home-maker and family caregiver. This nuclear family image represents a middle-class family ideal, which historically also has been heterosexual and white. It presumes that male-female unions are the only way, certainly the only proper way, to form families. It also assumes that family relationships are supposed to be based on love and companionship.

The nuclear family is the normative model, and it stands relatively un-challenged as an ideology. In other words, the idea of a family like this frames our thinking about how families *should* be. It is a powerful, persua-sive, and all-permeating idea, reinforced by everything from childhood sto-ries, to contemporary films, to federal law. One researcher (Smith 1993) has labeled this model the "SNAF": the "Standard North American Family." This representation of family life, she notes, is so powerful that other fam-ily forms are judged against it and found lacking and even deviant if they don't conform to it. Single-mother families, for example, are seen as in-complete and broken versions of *real* families (cf. Nelson 2006).

For those who have fewer financial resources or those who face structural barriers, such as institutionalized racism, the middle-class ideal has not al-ways been within reach (DeVault 1999). In working-class families, for ex-ample, both parents may need to be breadwinners in order to keep the fam-ily afloat. This situation is more common among non-white families since class is conflated with race in the United States (minorities have been kept, sometimes forcibly, from the opportunities that lead to middle-class jobs and security). Increasingly, the middle-class ideal is out of reach of even the middle class. In 1970, this type of family made up 40 percent of all Ameri-can households; in 2003 that number had dropped to 23 percent (U.S. Cen-sus 2006).

Although we contend that the SNAF model is still culturally powerful, clearly the conditions that sustained it are changing. The exclusive claim of whites to middle-class respectability has been contested by the civil rights movement and its consequences. Even the previously completely taken-for-granted heterosexuality of marriage and parenting is being challenged by same-sex couples who are having children and leading otherwise conven-tional, visible, middle-class family lives. The middle-class family's relation-ship to the workplace also has altered dramatically. Barriers to the employ-ment of non-whites and white women in good middle-class jobs have lessened, but at the same time the availability has decreased of the secure jobs with middle-class incomes that supported the Standard North Ameri-can Family.

The SNAF model of a breadwinning husband and stay-home wife and mother was made possible for many white middle-class families by the work-family system developed in the United States after World War II. This system was based on the economic dominance of U.S. companies and women's roles as unpaid family caregivers. Growing U.S. corporations tried to create economic security for their male, white-collar, professional and managerial employees by providing job security, regular increases in pay, and benefits such as health and disability insurance (Osterman 1999). Employers relied on the wives of male workers to care for home and children so that men were free to put in long hours on the job, travel, and move as needed by the company (Kanter 1977, Vogel 1993, Williams 2000). Union organizing captured some of the success of U.S. firms for many blue-collar workers too, creating the "blue-collar middle class." This system made it possible for working-class men with good union jobs to achieve the traditional middle-class status markers of owning a home and supporting a non-working, stay-home wife (Chinoy 1955, Halle 1984, Rubin 1976, Zavella 1987).

This system began to break down in the 1970s when U.S. firms faced increasing international competition. To compete with foreign production, American companies moved to lower-wage regions in the United States, and then overseas (Bluestone and Harrison 1982). In addition to laying off employees (downsizing), firms also began restructuring, that is, devising ways of producing more with fewer workers. Jobs for both less-skilled workers and professional employees in the manufacturing industries dwindled, and employment in service and knowledge-based industries increased. Throughout the economy, employment practices became more flexible: Use of temporary workers increased, employer commitment to worker job security was rejected, and, for the first time after World War II, men in professional and managerial jobs were affected in large numbers by lay-offs (Newman 1988, Osterman 1999, Uchitelle 2006).

As the economy changed, middle-class women entered the workforce to help maintain their families' standards of living. In the 1970s, women's work rates began to rise especially quickly such that between 1950 and 1998 their labor force participation rose from 34 to 60 percent (Fullerton 1999). The work rates of mothers of young children rose particularly sharply (Hayghe 1997), and attitudes toward working mothers became much more accepting (Thornton and Young-Demarco 2001). The work rates of white women lagged behind women of color, though. Historically, the notion that mothers should stay home and be full-time homemakers applied mostly to white women, especially to middle-class white women. African Americans often viewed women's paid work as an important contribution to their communities (Barnes this volume, Hine 1989). Only in the last few decades have white women's work rates come near the traditionally much higher work rates of black women (Amott and Matthaie 1996).

Women's rising work rates and the increasingly taken-for-granted full-time employment of middle-class mothers, the spread of flexible employment practices, and the historic shift away from an industrial and toward a postindustrial economy are trends that have profound implications for the experience of being in a family and the meanings of family life. Understanding how families are positioned in relation to the changing nature of work and employment in the United States today is central in the chapters in part I of this book. Part II shifts perspective to look more closely at roles and relationships within families.

## Part I: Intersections of Work and Family

The chapters in part I highlight multiple connections between work and family, including connections between work identities and family roles, the demands of jobs and the quality of family life, and the meanings of work and the cultural identities of families. In chapter 2, Tom Fricke writes about work, family, and identity in a community of family farmers. "Fewer than two percent of Americans work at farming these days," he notes, "yet most people feel a connection beyond experience" to images of life on a farm. Fricke's ethnography of a farming community in North Dakota describes how farming is not just a way to make a living but a deeply meaningful way of life. For some couples, being together as a family means working together. One farmer explained, "A lot of people can't imagine working with your wife day in and day out like I do but that's what, one of the strongest things that keeps us together." This chapter also highlights the importance of intergenerational relations for understanding the meanings of family life. Parents hope to instill a strong work ethic, self-reliance, and character in their children by raising them on a working farm—even though they know their children are unlikely to become farmers themselves. For Americans who don't farm, the family farm is still an important symbol of a harmonious melding of work and family life.

Echoes of older patterns of overlapping work and family spheres can be seen in the new postindustrial economy, as Alesia Montgomery shows in chapter 3, which focuses on a post-modern, job-sharing family in the high-tech labor market of Silicon Valley. Steve and Marjaneh, a married couple, live with Marjaneh's immigrant parents in one household. Everyone works full-time and they all support each other's paid work, using the family home as a workshop and workspace, in a way evocative of now largely bygone family farms. Marjaneh works mostly from home. When not at work, Steve and his father-in-law share the garage as a place to tinker with computer hardware. Marjaneh helps her mother with accounting for the family business in the kitchen. Montgomery traces the ups and downs of daily family relations during the dot-com boom when the family could hope to become very rich almost instantly, to the let-down of the 2000–2001 crash when internet stocks rapidly lost value.

Chapter 4, by Elizabeth Rudd and Larry Root, follows two young mothers who belong to the shrinking blue-collar middle class through the course of a typical working day. The women, Melanie and Jenny, have high-paying factory jobs in a unionized auto parts factory but their factory schedules conflict with family time. Most of the time that Melanie and her husband have together is spent sleeping. Jenny worries she won't be able to help her children enough with school work. Yet both women found their way into factory work through family connections, and they stick with their jobs so they can provide materially for their children. The chapter shows how jobs designed for men with stay-home wives force parents into very long work hours and compress family time to a minimum.

For workers left behind when the factories went away, there are few good alternatives. In chapter 5, Alford Young, Jr., analyzes community, family, and work among a group of low-income African Americans in Ypsilanti, Michigan, a small city formerly sustained by union factory work. The people Young spoke to might have held well-paying factory jobs if such jobs were available. The jobs that they actually have don't support their families adequately even when they work very long hours. One man told Young that he couldn't understand how his parents had created economic stability for him and his siblings. "I have to work more and more and harder and it's not enough time in the day for me," he commented. Their employment also interferes with caring for family members. A young mother emphasized that finding affordable childcare was the main barrier she faced when trying to get a job that would allow her to save some money. In the community Young studied, work and family roles are not mutually supportive but instead interfere with each other.

Compared to the less-skilled workers Young studied, professional and managerial employees affected by corporate downsizing and restructuring have more options. In chapter 6, Brian Hoey introduces us to former corporate employees who chose to leave their jobs and seek ways of bringing their families and their working lives closer together. In response to changing workplace values that took away employees' job security, these people left and moved their families to a rural Michigan town to start different lives. These "lifestyle migrants," Hoey argues, "are part of a larger moral story of what constitutes the good life in America." Their stories are "part of a shared cultural process of change in the historical context of economic restructuring."

In chapter 7, Lara Descartes and Conrad Kottak offer insight into the lives of people very much like Brian Hoey's respondents, who, however, have chosen to stay in corporate America. These families have high incomes, and they can afford to live far away from the urban blight left behind by the exodus of industry from the American Midwest. They live in socially homogenous "ruburbia"—a term for the subdivisions sprouting up beyond the older suburbs on the edge of rural areas—to protect themselves and their children from the dangers they associate with cities. These white, middle-class, heterosexual couples form the most SNAF-like families in this volume. The mothers stay home or work only part-time, and they spend hours a day driving children between home, school, and after-school activities. Fathers are the breadwinners and they tend to be absent from the home because of the very long hours they spend working and commuting. Mothers can closely control their children's environments and activities and live out ideologies of "intensive mothering" (Hays 1996) and "concerted cultivation" (Lareau 2003).

## Part II: The "Standard North American Family" (SNAF)

Part II of this volume, while not ignoring work, focuses more on family roles and relationships. Three of the authors report on families for whom, historically, the SNAF has not been easily attainable. The first is Diana Pash in chapter 8. The men in Pash's study are homosexual, in clear violation of the central symbol of the conventional family unit: the married, heterosexual couple. Bespeaking the power of the ideal, however, these men form SNAF-like configurations. They are members of couples and bring children into their families. Do these families challenge the SNAF because they are male-male instead of male-female? Or do they conform to the SNAF because their families are based on the nuclear model? Or do they do both simultaneously? Other questions this chapter raises revolve around class. How did the men's class status affect their ability to form their families and live their lives the way they do? How might their family lives have developed if they were working poor, for example?

The women Riché Barnes interviewed for chapter 9 are also from a group that historically has faced barriers in attaining the conventional middle-class family ideal. Her informants are African American women. Throughout the history of the United States, black women have worked. Due to institutionalized racism, it has been more difficult for African Americans than Euro-Americans to enter the middle class and families have needed the income of all able-bodied adults to get by. But now the black middle class is growing, and some black women can choose to stay home full-time. These families challenge the SNAF because they are not white, yet simultaneously buttress it by adopting it as the model of appropriate family life.

Erin Winkler's chapter, 10, shares with Barnes's a lesson about how history shapes the present day realities of family life. Winkler's informants are also African American, and due to the trenchant racism in the United States, face issues that whites do not. Her interviews show that to deal with this racism, African American mothers define good mothering in terms of the

SNAF but in a more culturally specific way. For them, to be a mother of an African American child is to be responsible for socializing that child about race and racism. The conventional middle-class nuclear model and its roles cannot encompass these families' daily realities, even if they conform to its other elements. It is interesting, however, to note how Winkler frames racial socialization as care work, in light of the fact that it was specifically mothers, rather than fathers, who responded to her interview requests. Despite cultural variation in its specifics, the SNAF still shapes the familial division of labor in this way: Care is women's domain.

In chapter 11, Sallie Han also examines motherhood, specifically the role of the "good mother." The fetal ultrasound provides the lens with which to view a woman's first performances in her new role as a mother. Han's interviews show how sonographers rate women as fit or unfit mothers before their babies are even born, and how women start to shape themselves into culturally acceptable mothers as they relate to the images of their fetus produced by ultrasound technology. The women first must get the ultrasound, showing by their participation in this medical rite of motherhood that they are concerned, responsible mothers-to-be. These judgments revolve around notions of maternal caretaking, women's primary responsibility in the SNAF. Han's chapter raises the issue of the relative inflexibility of the good mother role. To avoid the ultrasound entirely would be bad mothering, as doing so would indicate unconcern for the child's health. To not cherish the images, to be too interested in "cute" images, to not be interested enough . . . all may indicate bad mothering and all illustrate the very narrow criteria by which women are judged as mothers in American culture.

Todd Goodsell focuses on fathers in chapter 12, examining ideas of what it means to be a good father. His informants use stories created from events in their own pasts to provide models for good fatherhood. Goodsell illustrates some of the tensions inherent in the SNAF. Mothers, not fathers, are responsible for families' emotional lives. How then do men learn to conduct the emotional work of being fathers, given its presumed secondary status in their family roles? Through combinations of positive and negative examples, the men in Goodsell's study grapple with this question.

Carolyn Chen's work with Taiwanese immigrants in the United States, described in chapter 13, reflects on family ideology and family roles, how they vary cross-culturally, and what happens when cultures come into contact through immigration. Chen's fieldwork reveals how Taiwanese parents cope with finding their traditional power challenged as they raise their children in the more individualistic, less authoritarian American culture. They consciously strategize to reinforce their parental status through the Christ-based model of family life provided by Evangelical religion. Through her interviews, Chen reveals a key part of the SNAF: that the American nuclear family is supposed to be bound by love rather than obedience. Moreover, its roles are to be fulfilled out of willingness rather than obligation. Part of what her informants must adjust to is the friendly parent-child relations dictated by American norms. This observation helps illustrate the wide range of possible familial relations and helps make the SNAF transparent. It is not natural, universal, or inevitable. Instead, it is a cultural product of a certain moment in history.

Chapter 14 by Gene Deerman presents a textual analysis of magazine stories about young adults who align themselves with an ideology of virginity in preparation for their future heterosexual marital unions. All kinds of stories about family life are circulated in public media, including magazine articles like the ones Deerman analyzes, radio programs such as those of Dr. Laura and Dr. Joy Brown, and news coverage of the most recent sociological studies on topics such as marriage, divorce, and children in day care. The virginity stories Deerman explores are undergirded by assumptions about what makes a good family, assumptions predicated upon the SNAF. The hopes and fears of the young people that are conveyed in the stories Deerman discusses are very real, yet these narratives reinforce a moral order in which it is acceptable for men to have multiple sexual partners, but there is only one proper context for women's sexuality: The heterosexual, marital bed.

The final chapter, 15, of this volume reflects on this book as a whole. It was contributed by Kathryn Dudley, an anthropologist who has devoted decades to the study of social class and economic stratification in contemporary American culture. Dudley's commentary emphasizes the enormous economic and symbolic significance to American society of the nuclear family, which is simultaneously expected to care for the young, old, and infirm and also support each individual's efforts at self-fulfillment. Viewing the ethnographies as providing evidence of "tension between the kind of family people aspire to have and the kind of family they are able to achieve," she questions whether "the cultural ideal American families aspire to can be realized by anyone at all." Our anxieties about threats to the family today, Dudley argues, often lead us to misidentify dangers: We ignore powerful forces that undermine the capacity of a family to care for its members and focus instead on notions like the "breakdown of moral values." Her analysis reminds us that the reports from the field contained in this volume reflect a cultural landscape that although changing in some ways, remains strongly constrained by socioeconomic factors.

## REFERENCES

Agar, Michael H. 1985. *Speaking of ethnography*. Beverly Hills, CA: Sage.
Amott, Teresa, and Julie Matthaei. 1996. *Race, gender, and work: A multi-cultural economic history of women in the United States*. Boston: South End Press.

Barnes, Riché. This volume. Black women have always worked: Is there a work-family conflict among the black middle class?

Bernard, H. Russell. (1994). *Research methods in anthropology: Qualitative and quantitative approaches,* 2nd ed. Thousand Oaks, CA: Sage.

Bluestone, Barry, and Bennett Harrison. 1982. *The deindustrialization of America.* New York: Basic Books, Inc.

Chinoy, Ely. 1955. *Automobile workers and the American dream.* Boston: Beacon Press.

Descartes, Lara, Conrad P. Kottak, and Autumn Kelly. 2007. "Chauffeuring and commuting: A story of work, family, class, and community." *Community, Work, and Family* 10: 161–78.

DeVault, Marjorie L. 1999. "Comfort and struggle: Emotion work in family life." *Annals of the American Academy of Political and Social Science* 561: 52–63.

Fullerton, Howard N. 1999. "Labor Force Participation: 75 Years of Change, 1950–1998 and 1998–2025." *Monthly Labor Review* December: 3–12.

Halle, David. 1984. *America's working man.* Chicago and London: University of Chicago Press.

Hayghe, Howard V. 1997. "Developments in Women's Labor Force Participation." *Monthly Labor Review* September: 41–46.

Hays, Sharon 1996. *The cultural contradictions of motherhood.* New Haven, CT: Yale University Press.

Hine, Darlene Clark. 1989. *Black women in white: Racial conflict and cooperation in the nursing profession 1890–1950.* Blacks in the Diaspora Series. Bloomington and Indianapolis, IN: University of Indiana Press.

Kanter, Rosabeth M. 1977. *Work and family in the United States: A critical review and agenda for research and policy.* New York: Russell Sage Foundation.

Lareau, Annette. 2003. *Unequal childhoods: Class, race, and family life.* Berkeley, CA: University of California Press.

Milosz, Czeslaw. 2001. "Alpha the moralist." In *To begin where I am: Selected essays,* ed. Bogdana Carpenter and Madeline G. Levine, 116–41. New York: Farrar, Straus and Giroux.

Nelson, Margaret K. 2006. "Single mothers 'do' family." *Journal of Marriage and Family* 68: 781–95.

Newman, Katherine S. 1988. *Falling from grace: Downward mobility in the age of affluence.* Berkeley and Los Angeles, CA: University of California Press.

Osterman, Paul. 1999. *Securing prosperity.* Princeton, NJ: Princeton University Press.

Overbey, Mary Margaret, and Kathryn Marie Dudley. 2000. *Anthropology and middle class working families: A research agenda.* Arlington, VA: American Anthropological Association.

Rubin, Lillian. 1976. *Worlds of pain: Life in the working-class family.* New York: Basic Books.

Smith, Dorothy E. 1993. "The standard North American family." *Journal of Family Issues* 14: 50–65.

Stack, Carol. 1974. *All our kin: Strategies for survival in a Black community.* New York: Harper and Row.

Thornton, Arland, and Linda Young-DeMarco. 2001. "Four Decades of Trends in Attitudes Toward Family Issues in the United States: The 1960s Through the 1990s." *Journal of Marriage and Family* 63:1009–37.

Townsend, Nicholas. 2002. *The package deal: Marriage, work, and fatherhood in men's lives*. Philadelphia: Temple University Press.

Uchitelle, Louis. 2006. *The disposable American: Layoffs and their consequences*. New York: Alfred A. Knopf.

U.S. Census. 2006. *Families and living arrangements in 2003*. Accessed on January 5, 2006 from www.census.gov/population/pop-profile/dynamic/FamiliesLA.pdf.

Vogel, Lise. 1993. *Mothers on the job: Maternity policy in the U.S. workplace*. New Brunswick, NJ: Rutgers University Press.

Williams, Joan. 2000. *Unbending gender: Why family and work conflict and what to do about it*. Oxford and New York: Oxford University Press.

Zavella, Patricia. 1987. *Women's work and Chicano families: Cannery workers of the Santa Clara valley*. Ithaca, NY and London: Cornell University Press.

# I

## INTERSECTIONS OF WORK AND FAMILY

# 2

# Working Selves, Moral Selves

## Crafting the Good Person
## in the Northern Plains

*Tom Fricke*

The ordinary person does not, unless corrupted by philosophy, believe
that he creates value by his choices. He thinks that some things really are
better than others and that he is capable of getting it wrong. We are usually not in doubt about the direction in which Good lies.

—Iris Murdoch, *The Sovereignty of the Good* (1970, 95)

There's a whole bunch of everything. It's growing things. Raising the cattle, and just doing things like that. Just being out here. It's just . . . farming isn't out there, it's in you. It's not in your head. And it has to be a business anymore, more than it was when my dad was farming. But there's
something that's more than the business of farming. If it was just a business I wouldn't be here. There's easier businesses than this to work at.

—Joe Bauer, *West River Farmer*

One Monday night in August, under the pan-sized harvest moon over Joe
Bauer's Dunn County wheat fields, two tired men eased their huge red machines into the shadows of an abandoned farmstead marked by a shelter-
belt and a single weather-beaten shed. Joe and his wife, Marie, had hauled
their last load of the day. Their son Will had just taken his full load of grain
back to the yard after working his magic under the old Ford's hood. I'd
hung back with the service van and the gas tank trailer to feel the cooling
air and watch the play of combine lights against the sharp edge where stub-
ble meets standing grain. Joe's cousin Craig and brother Wayne gentled
their combines into position, swung their augers out, and pumped the
sweet fullness of new wheat into the last truck's groaning box. They'd been
out here all day running three trucks through their paces. Two combines

17

**Figure 2.1.**    Anthropological research often involves "participant observation" and this can mean working alongside the people being studied. But even in the field in the United States, office duties can beckon. Here, Tom Fricke takes a break from work on the Bauer farm to call his office at the University of Michigan. He's on the tractor to get up higher so he can catch a signal on his cell phone.
Photo by Julie Hoff for Tom Fricke

bring surrender to a field more quickly than seems reasonable. Nobody gets much chance to rest.

I went to the world of farms and ranches near the North Dakota town I call West River with questions about how the culture of work and family gets shaped by a place and its history. I was interested, too, in how changes in work and career choices might affect relations between those who stay and those who leave. My work concentrates on how enculturation in a rural world structures the responses of people to American work and family changes. This chapter looks especially at notions of character and the good in that light.

The uses of rural and farm life turn on the cultural idea we call character, a notion which has fascinated Americans throughout their history and which bears important connections to that sense of individualism first diagnosed and named by Tocqueville in the 1830s. Our sense of the play of character in our lives has always carried an ambivalence. On the one hand, its qualities seem to emphasize its instrumental role in achieving material advantage, as though a person's quality must inevitably be revealed in exterior circumstance. But another stream emphasizes more interior elements of selfhood where the measure of character is less public, less inscribed in material markers of success. For farmers in particular the thing they call character is as rooted in community history, the physical nature of place, and the rhythm of everyday life as in the things they can put into words.

My discussion here is based on sharing that everyday life, along with conversation, with about a hundred people in West River and its surrounding landscape. Although most of the quotes come from transcriptions of taped interviews, the experiences and conversations of my fieldwork are still fresh enough to remember the sound of voice, the quality of the day, and the details of setting in ways that get lost once these things get hardened into data. I go through my fieldnotes thinking of the reluctance of Brother Ambrose Vettel, a Benedictine monk, to talk to me when I first walked down the hill to where he was cleaning out a grain bin. "Can't have you at the barn," he said, "you'll scare the cows with that hair of yours." I told him I'd put it up under my cap if it would make them feel better. He laughed and told me to come on over.

There's an advantage to writing from within this freshness. If I wait longer, I might find myself concentrating on that part of our interview that I taped and had transcribed rather than on the laugh preceding it. I might forget how Ambrose hummed to himself while sweeping up the old grain. Or that his jeans were patched a few times over. Or that his work boots had holes worn into their scuffed leather. I might forget, too, how the cool morning of that August day was sliding toward heat and late afternoon thunderheads. How the oats needed harvesting while we talked.

Sharing lives is the most classic of ethnographic methods. In my case, it meant sleeping in the Bauer family's spare room and rising at five a.m. to start the day with them. It meant driving tractor and combine, breaking machinery, and helping with repairs. It meant walking fence line and being bit by deer flies in a high, hot wind. It meant pulling calves when cows needed help with a birth, watching who calls whom in an emergency, and learning how to tie chains around those delicate hooves, attach them to a pulley, and avoid the pour of afterbirth when the newborn calf yanks free. And it meant staying in the fields until the red sun crossed the western buttes at ten p.m. and we could all go home to eat supper.

Fewer than 2 percent of Americans work at farming these days, yet most people feel a connection beyond experience to these scenes. The family farm signifies a core element of our self-understanding. From the Jeffersonian image of a democratic republic resting on its landed and independent citizenry to more current images linking the good life, a living work ethic, and strong family values to the countryside, farming holds an especially virtuous place in the American imagination. Writing about Britain, Raymond Williams could have easily had the United States in mind when he noted the almost "inverse proportion, in the twentieth century, between the relative importance of the working rural economy and the cultural importance of rural ideas" (1973, 248). The rural continues as a contemporary icon of the past.

Much of what these images have in common has to do with the connections among work, character, and family. Couched in a language that emphasizes farming as a way of life, our understanding of farm life too easily treats it as the last redoubt of integrated family and work life before "capitalists took production out of the household and collectivized it, under their own supervision, in the factory" (Lasch 1979, xx). Even when the story is less than idyllic, we nevertheless hold farmers up as an idealized contrast to the sense that something is missing in our own "modern" temperament.

Of course, this denial of the present tense to farming simplifies a complex reality (see, for example, Davidson 1996 or Dudley 2000). Farmers are as subject to globalized markets as any other worker. Joe's satellite feed is one indication of this. Despite the family economy of husband, wife, son, and cousin, he tracks the potential impact of American grain sales to Pakistan and the long-term probability of drought in grain-producing regions of Texas or Argentina as closely as any other producer eyes the competition.

Even as they continue to see it as a privileged way of life that instills a particular set of values, most people in West River acknowledge that farming has changed. Joe mentions that things were different for his father and uncle who farmed about 1,000 acres together and made do without the FHA loans that Joe's own family requires to get their over 2,000 acres into seed. The pressure to produce and sell grain at a level that will repay those loans and leave a margin grinds without relief at both Craig and Joe from the spring seeding through the harvest.

The paradox of farming, and its relevance to understanding wider American life, is precisely that its symbolic role in our cultural imagination more explicitly acknowledges its interweaving of work, family, and character. Both Joe and Craig see farming as a partnership that involves the commitment of their wives and families. It requires an array of skills to be done right and instills a special set of virtues in their children. At the same time, it connects them to a set of worries that encumber the free exercise of the spirit. Craig put that tension into words:

> Oh, I love to drive combine. That part of it I could do all the time. But when it comes to managing this stuff, watching the markets bounce back and forth, back and forth, a penny, a dime, a nickel, I can't take that crap. It's too much stress. I won't do it. As far as the marketing part of it, the older people don't watch the markets that close because it's too stressful. The markets never used to vary much. If they varied a dime in a year that was a lot. But now it's so off the wall.

The business of farming is based on explicit assumptions about idealized family relationships, gendered categories, and work. These are the avenues that link domestic and public worlds. The countervailing myth of the American middle-class family has, on the other hand, pretended to a separation of these same domains. As scholarly attention shifts to the dynamic relationship that has always characterized these intersections among the majority of Americans (Hochschild 2001, Newman 1999, Schor 1993), a reconsideration of this powerful symbol places us on firmer comparative ground. The poet Thomas McGrath, a native North Dakotan, wrote "Dakota is everywhere" (1997). His meaning points to the value of ethnography—wherever we live and whatever we do, the stories we hear about a single place tell us something about ourselves.

## IDENTITIES OF FAMILY, PLACE, AND CHARACTER

West River residents hold their own private geographies, a composite of the moral and physical landscapes they call home. There's no avoiding the drama of place in West River Country. Where in more humid and forested places the trees seem to spike the sky and hold it out of reach, the West River skies seem to brush the grass. One day's aching blue gives way to thunderhead or the green shimmer of the northern lights. The space and distance are all around and acknowledged by people like the school principal who uses the perception of outsiders to make his point. He talked about coming on some students from a nearby college. "They were from New York or New Jersey and sitting on a hillside looking out over the prairie to the north. I said, 'Isn't that a beautiful sight?' and one of them said, 'Not particularly.' He was staring off into the distance and said, 'I just didn't think a person could see this far.'"

But that sense of space is also personalized. I first noticed it in the drive to find the site of a once thriving community that no longer exists even as a ghost town. It lives on only in the cemetery where people still bring their dead though their families moved on years ago. But it wasn't the practice of burying the dead at the former site of a family's living that alerted me to the connection of family and place. It was the long drive south from West River with the school principal, his wife, and the monk who held the maps for finding our lost town.

We couldn't pass an abandoned farmstead or any other building, strangely shaped tree, creek, or butte without a story being attached to it and linked to a person or a family. The principal gave running commentary the whole way. "See that place—that's where the old woman who used to cook for the Abbey lives—all her kids are gone and she's still getting around at ninety-three. Looks like the house could use some work, she must be slowing down some. Wonder how much longer she'll be able to live out here alone. Her son moved out to Fargo and the daughters are all gone, too, with marrying. I don't think this place will stay in the family much longer."

Even after a family leaves, its memory stays tethered. Huthmacher Hill lies four miles north of West River and marks the site of a homestead where no Huthmacher has lived since 1960. This identity of place and family was marked in a conversation I had with one of ten siblings born in West River and now the only remaining member of his family in town:

> They said we have to have another reunion in West River because that's home. We still own fourteen acres of land sort of behind that house, my brothers and sisters. We are hanging onto it because what if one wants to come back? We talked about this. One of them could come back here and build a house there if they wanted to though we sold the house that's still there.

Place is a matter of both character and location. Great Plains people see themselves as distinctive. The geographer James Shortridge presents a table (1989, 79) that, with a little tweaking, gets at some of this self-image. Although it doesn't allow a contrast with Great Plains views of outsiders, it makes it clear that people in the plains states are far more likely to view *themselves* in the positive terms of Thomas Jefferson's original vision for the American experiment. Fully 93 percent of his respondents were likely to mention the character traits such as friendly, hard-working, honest, and thoughtful that Jefferson associated with the robust democracy based on a farming citizenry. Only 35 percent of the people from outside this region were likely to characterize its inhabitants in such positive terms.

West River residents share that self-image and contrast themselves with outsiders in ways that redound to their own credit. George Gleit, a retired contractor and mason, put it like this:

> A lot of your people in the business sector, they're always interested in hiring a North Dakota guy. Well, the work ethic. I mean, they've proven themselves. When you get one of them they work continuously. And the rest of 'em never show up for work. Doesn't worry them that they're tardy or anything like that. One of the young guys went to work for Boeing Aircraft. He went out there and he was hired and within a couple of weeks, why, he was appointed the foreman. He couldn't believe what happened. And they says, "He was the only guy that showed up for work every day and he was there before time to go to work," you know? And then he was still there at the close-up time where the rest of them were, you know, goldbrickers.

His thoughts were echoed by Frank Falkenstein, president of the town's farm machinery manufacturing company, who also elaborated on the conditions leading to this difference:

> If you go back to the time I'm talking about—fifties, sixties—you not only had a good, hard, strong work ethic but honesty, courtesy, concern for the other

person, that was all just built in. I mean, that was just assumed and expected. It wasn't even things that people talked about or discussed. Everybody just sort of had a high moral caliber. I think there's a lot of factors contributing to that. Maybe being from a small town had something to do with it. Maybe being from a large family where there were responsibilities of taking care of the younger ones had something to do with it. But the younger ones also had that same quality so it wasn't like the older ones had more responsibility and, therefore, had better characters.

But he finished his comment with a note of concern. For him, the good things of character that set Great Plains people apart were passing. In contrast to West River today, he saw himself growing up in isolation. "Do you know," he said, "that when I was ten years old we lived basically fifty-five miles from Glendive following the road and seventy-five miles from Dickinson following the road. That's not very far away and yet if I was in Dickinson and Glendive combined four times a year that would have probably been a lot."

Now, kids will jump in a car in Beach and go to a movie in Dickinson. The world is coming in and the morality that is presented to children through television or through the magazines or in the newspapers or on billboards has eroded. Everyone is becoming homogenized.

Frank's comments bring relief to the dilemma of character faced by all West River farmers. On the one hand, their sense of the good derives from a history of community separateness where character "was all just built in," growing out of everyday expectations and obligations in the manner of habits that required no comment. In one sense, "being good" was no more than an unconscious outcome of living a life without alternative. The hope of the grandparents and parents of today's West River farmers was that their way of living would continue unchanged as their children and grandchildren followed the same life. But the reality of farming in the semi-arid plains introduced the need to prepare for other worlds. Children leave and, for those who stay, "the world is coming in." The need to confront these new circumstances introduces a more conscious reflection on instilling character into generations who may go elsewhere.

## THE MORAL CHARACTER OF A SETTLEMENT FRONTIER

The area of North Dakota west of the Missouri River was one of the last to be settled in the state. The land is more rugged than in those eastern portions that shape the popular perception of a relentlessly featureless expanse. Just east of Bismarck, the land begins its westward slope into the high plains, the broken badlands country, and the scattered buttes with names like Eagle's Nest, Rainy, Sentinel, and the Virgin's Breasts. And it's where the later immigrants to the United States after the closing of the frontier could still find open land. As Brother Ambrose put it, "The German-Russians were farmers . . . . They wanted to be nothing else but farmers and they were willing to work hard. They were willing to settle on the poorest land because they just figured that, you know, that they can make it."

These German-Russians are the descendants of immigrants whose ancestors had moved from Germany to Russia at the invitation of Catherine the Great and who began to leave the Black Sea areas of Russia in the latter part of the nineteenth century and early twentieth century. Although people whose families came to the area between 1890 and 1910 dominate West River today, the country opened to intensive settlement with the Northern Pacific Railroad's crossing of the Missouri River at Bismarck in 1879. The earliest settlers were Yankees and Scandinavians who had far less attachment to the place and who tended to leave more quickly in hard times. Before and between those hard times that seemed to come every decade or so, the West River Country was promoted as a land of infinite possibility—a huge empire of emptiness ringed with sky, awaiting only the application of labor before being converted into wealth and the seat of new metropolises rivaling those of the east. Much of the hype better served the ends of real estate speculators and the railroads who wished to convert the unfilled Jeffersonian grid into dollars. But the hype also settled into the imaginations of those who came to the region. In 1908, the Dickinson Commercial Club published a pamphlet intended to bring more people west:

> [N]owhere upon this broad planet can the young, middle aged or old man, landowner or renter of the older states, or any woman, more easily gain a competence than by becoming a resident of this region. Thousands of people with less earthly possession than would fill a box car have . . . in three years established themselves in comfortable homes, have good crops and a few head of stock and are on the way to permanent prosperity and affluence. In this country a man's wealth as a rule is measured by the time he has resided in it—the longer he stays and attends to his business the more he is worth.

West River was one of these towns. Located on the ridge forming the watersheds for the Heart and Knife Rivers, regular rail service commenced in 1882. Its post office was established in 1883, the same year that the town was platted and lots began to be sold. Town growth was slow until the turn of the century, speeding up in 1899 when the Benedictine Abbot Vincent Wehrle relocated his monastery from the northeastern part of the state to the town of West River, which he projected to become the center of a thriving German Catholic community that would dominate the region. The Abbey became its own attraction for Catholic immigrants. West River became an almost entirely Catholic town, its skyline cut by the grain elevators on the south and, after 1908, by the twin spires of its Bavarian Romanesque abbey church on the north.

By the early 1930s the public school closed for lack of attendance because most people in town were sending their children to the parochial school. The small group of non-Catholics living in town either sent their children to Catholic school or transported them five miles west to the next non-Catholic town. Nearly every person above forty years old was educated in the Abbey or parish schools by Benedictine teachers. The renewed public school system opened in the early 1960s after a combination of legal battles threatened the unusual system in Catholic-dominated towns in which public school money supported parochial school teachers.

The halting increase of settlement during those earliest years may account for some of the breathless reports of land sales, expansion, and the business of farming in the local papers. It's as though town merchants were shouldering a simultaneous burden of enticing newcomers while convincing those who had come to remain. The newspaper reports for the families around Joe Bauer's farmstead follow the script of progress and success:

June 25, 1909: "Peter Gress claims to have received $855.00 for two wagon loads of wool this week and Lee Hoff $810.18 for one load. That's going some. The past week has been a lively one for wool growers."

April 22, 1910: "Peter Gress has purchased a new Reeves steam plow rig and Tom Armstrong will run it this summer."

Feb. 10, 1911: "Peter Gress is remodeling the building at the west end of the lot on which the R. P. Gress residence stands, and will make a double house of it. The house will be modern, with bath and sewer and has already been rented to two families."

Even the undercurrent of failure when a family is forced out of farming from years of unpaid debt is whitewashed in the language of success. This same Peter Gress sold his farm just a few years later to Joe Bauer's grandfather, the private account of the transaction—in which John Bauer agreed to take care of the accumulated debt—differing markedly from the newspaper's story:

October 10, 1918: "Peter Gress sold 1038 acres, the largest portion of his land, to John Bauer who has recently moved here from Texas. On October 21st Mr. Gress will hold one of the largest auction sales in the history of Richardton and then he thinks he'll come to live in the city as a retired and wealthy private citizen. He has kept a half section of land for the time being."

## STORIES OF DECLINE

In contrast to the boosterism that began the century, the refrain a hundred years later is one of decline. It is a fitting historical parallel that European

American settlers with their different motivations—setting up religious commonwealths, ethnic homelands, healthy farmsteads—shared something with the people that preceded them. West River sits in the middle of old Hidatsa and Mandan eagle-trapping territory, the place where young men sought their visions on isolated buttes. The ancestors of today's West River people were moved by their own visions and dream quests that have been frayed by a few generations of hard reality.

In August, Joe Bauer and I walked his wheat field after an evening's random hail storm had turned its bumper crop to near total loss. Kicking through the broken stems and shattered heads, he spoke the slow cadences of resignation. I had wondered why, just a week before, he was reluctant to speculate about his harvest and here was the answer at our feet. It was a beautiful cloudless morning with a touch of coming fall weather, almost crisp. The grain would have been ready for harvest in just one more week. Joe was already saying that next year might be better and then he stopped and looked around at the hills and sky and his broken wheat. "Sometimes I ask myself," he said, "just why they stopped here. Why'd my grandpa think this was the place? Was it a broken axle on the wagon or what?" And then he laughed and we kept on walking.

Joe was half-joking out there in that field, but his joke turned on an inescapable story for all residents of the northern plains. Headlines from the area's two largest papers make this a more general tale of decline and concern that I think of as a litany of despair. Excerpts from a single month's worth of newspaper headlines during one part of my time in the field are a kind of found poem of packing up the landscape. "Small Towns Shrink," they announce; "Continuing to Dwindle," they proclaim; "Farm Sales Like Funerals," they close.

Today the entire southwestern region of North Dakota, an area 250 miles by 120 miles, is served by a single phone book about half the size of the one we use in the Michigan university town where I live. Most of these people continue to live in towns strung along the original Northern Pacific Railway line, now the Interstate 94 corridor. Nearly all these communities reached their peak populations twenty years and more ago and have been in steady decline since. Those further off the corridor began their declines earlier.

The results of population loss are the topic of daily conversation and are written in the physical space of closing schools, churches, hospitals, and businesses throughout the region. The high school principal gives his own account of these changes:

> You look at the business: When I came to town thirty years ago we had two auto dealers. They're both gone. Two major implement dealers. One of those is gone and the other one will be closing up in September. There was a little clothing store, of course, and the grocery has really struggled and he has to compete with those two big stores in Dickinson. When I first came to town we

had three in town. We had three service stations, and now we're down to one that doesn't even sell premium gas so I have to fill in Dickinson or Bismarck. Well, let's see what else did we have when I first came to town? There were three bars and now they're down to one. And there was a bar and a restaurant in the bowling alley. So that's another thing, the restaurants. There were three of them. And now it's down to one. And that struggles too.

One little remarked upon change in the character of the county since the earliest population figures in 1910 is an almost complete reversal of the urban-rural distribution of its population. Sixty-five percent of the population lived on farmsteads and 35 percent in towns at that earliest year of record. Where section roads passed by a dense network of farmsteads and families in past years, today's countryside is littered with abandoned homesteads. Farm sizes have increased and the percentage of people living in the largest city today almost exactly tracks the percentage that once distributed itself across the countryside.

West River's history is mostly a history of leaving. By 1970, it began its steady loss of young people and population decline after edging up to its Census peak of 799. Its 1990 population was 625. I looked at the graduating classes of 1973–1975, people in their mid-forties, and found that of the one hundred (out of 116) people for whom I could find addresses only a quarter still lived in West River or on its neighboring farms. When the high school principal assigned an essay to the graduating seniors of the class of 2000, only three out of twenty-five thought they would be living in the area five years from now.

While decline is partly a material event linked to the thinning population and poor farm economy, the way people talk about it goes beyond a simple recounting of the inevitable. Decline has a moral component, too. Just as the early booster literature emphasized that anybody of a certain character could make it in this country, West River people also link economic circumstances to character. The shrinking population base and the hollowed out main streets are taken to be indicators of moral failure.

## FARMING AS A WAY OF LIFE

Robert Bellah and his colleagues write of the ways Americans think of work and its relation to the self in a culture of individualism. They distinguish work as a job, as a career, and as a calling along a continuum defined by its intersection with character. "In the strongest sense of a 'calling,' work constitutes a practical ideal of activity and character that makes a person's work morally inseparable from his or her life" (1996, 66). Such work as calling joins the person to a larger community in which the meaning and value of work goes beyond profit or production.

Farming shares these attributes, but also goes beyond them. When we finished seeding one of his fields late at night, the two of us alone on hillside
that once hummed with the shared labor and banter of six crews, Joe and I
stood under the stars talking about the thinning out of the countryside. We
were quiet for a while taking in the chill and the damp, when he turned to
me and spoke. "I know the Lord made me for this. I just want to do it right
is all." Joe's simple statement fills the criteria for work as calling, but where
Bellah and his colleagues were concerned with individual commitments,
farming goes beyond them to include a whole culture of relationships. It
widens to encompass a shared way of life where the virtues of family and
work are apparent to all.

These wider commitments introduce an embattled and contentious note
to West River. The extent to which doing right is limited to the direct tasks
of farming or to a wider universe of being and the content of farming as a
way of life are sources of a dispute that runs along generational lines in
West River. A fair description of the community must make note of changes
that parallel those in the world beyond the plains. Marriages break down.
Children grapple with the law and other problems. Single women in town
openly raise their out-of-wedlock children. When Frank Falkenstein talked
in the words quoted above of the "good, hard, strong work ethic" and the
"honesty, courtesy, and concern for the other person" that he uses to characterize North Dakotans, he was quick to add that he was talking about the
past, to the 1950s and 1960s. The problem as he sees it is that outside influences are making their way into West River and changing the culture.

While all agree that farming has changed, it's the older generation that
makes the link between the business and production sides and the decline
in character. Brother Ambrose was emphatic about the farming requiring a
whole bundle of commitments that characterize a way of life:

> Farming has never been easy. It's always been very, very tough but in the earlier
> days farmers were willing to be poor. Farmers used to be able to make a living
> because they were willing to go without the luxuries and nowadays people are
> not willing to go without the luxuries. I mean, nowadays they have to have
> everything. You know, they go hunting in the fall, they go skiing in the winter
> and they take trips. And they have the biggest TV available and carpets wall-to-
> wall in the house and they have central air conditioning in the house and they
> have everything that anybody else has. I think that they should stop com-
> plaining. If they can't make it on the farm they should quit the farm and go to
> town and get a job. Go to the West Coast or whatever they have to do.

At the same time, even those younger farmers who might quibble about
what counts as luxury regard themselves as having no less a commitment to
a way of life distinguished from that of wage and salary workers in towns
and cities. Growing up, Joe's reference point turned around the neighbor-

ing farms; today it's the whole United States. Although Joe and Marie live in a house with carpeting, have a fairly large color TV (but no cable), and a window air-conditioner that they set up every summer, they are as adamant as Brother Ambrose and Frank Falkenstein that farming confers a special character on its practitioners. Throughout the area, parents of Joe's generation say that a compelling reason for them remaining behind when so many have left is that their children will profit by being raised here. The sources of that conviction are in their own experience, as Craig made clear:

> Every since I was this high I wanted to raise my kids up on the farm because I knew what it was like. I grew up on the farm. We had horses, we had cows, we had sheep, we had pigs, chickens, geese. I mean, you name it, that place had it. And we never had no money but we had the experience of working with all this stuff. And that was very important to me to raise my kids that way. And we've made a lot of sacrifices to do this but it's worth it to us. Our kids will be able to go out in the world and do any dang thing they want and they won't be afraid to do it.

Even those who talk about farming as a job, as a way to make a living, emphasize that in spite of the low pay, they can't imagine working for wages to another person's schedule.

## CONSTRUCTING A WAY OF LIFE

The elements of a way of life go beyond a single set of technical skills. Farming is notorious for its variety of tasks, some sequenced by season and others fit into the gaps between more time-laden jobs. West River's high school secretary grew up on a farm and continues to work with her husband in addition to her salaried work in town. She spoke about that punctuated variety:

> Living on the farm as we do now there's such a swing of things. It's not like you're doing the same thing day in and day out every day of the year. And with our four seasons, every few months you're changing. It's like changing a job in what is required of you, so, I don't know, it's kind of, I have to say I enjoy it.

And beyond that, a feeling of belonging. As Craig expressed it:

> After working in town and being there all the time and then getting out in the country, it was like a picnic. It was great. What we are doing today, and I'm sure you feel that, it gets to you. Maybe it's just the appreciation that other people get out of you helping them. When you'd come out, they were glad to see you, happy you were there, and you couldn't screw up. No matter what you did there they were glad you were there because they were getting things done and you enjoyed being there.

The pieces that go into constructing a way of life include a set of ideas that link behavior, relationships, and internal virtues. In West River, people speak of these in terms of work, family, and the character defined by having a work ethic. These ingredients exist within a shared context that we can think of as a family farm culture. They depict internally necessary orientations within West River.

## Work

Regardless of age or gender, the people I talked with rooted things in work. Not only is life unimaginable without working at something, but the absence of work signifies a kind of death. "I think work is very important and not just to have something to do. But I think work—for me, for anybody—work is life," as one man put it. Another man told me, "There's a time for work and a time for play. When it's time to work, you work, and when it's time to play, you play. I believe, dinking around, I can't handle that." And a woman put it similarly, "I think, you know, your life is your work."

But there are ways of talking about work, too, that suggest the special place it has in West River culture. My transcripts are rich in discussions of the topic, sometimes obliquely and sometimes head on. In all the different ways it gets discussed it is clear there are few better indicators of character. At one level, it's something that has to be done, a condition of being alive. The same man who talked about his family retaining a symbolic membership in West River by holding onto fourteen acres out of 1,920 acres, went on about the subject of work, too:

> People who think they don't have to work . . . I mean, I can't comprehend that. Who just want to exist or just want to read novels or something like that. I get very impatient with that and as you know there are people in the community who would be very content to just read novels all day. I think life demands work in some form or another. I'm not just talking physical work. There's all kinds of work, mental work, and writing, or whatever—I have no problem with that as work. But work is very important and I personally don't think people tend to be balanced or happy without it.

Another man, one who moved his family back to North Dakota after time away from the state working in the finance offices of Boeing Aircraft in Seattle, gives another side of that inevitability of work. His comments followed an earlier discussion of his moving back and the realization that his children would be marked by the place they spent their early years:

> I think it does stand the North Dakotans in good stead because you learn. You are expected to accomplish, you have goals, you have demands placed on you

and it's not like it's negotiable. You're eight years old and you drive the truck to town, for example. Well, there's no negotiating there; you just do it. Or, we've got this truck and the hoist is broke so you shovel the truck off if it's loaded with wheat. You don't shovel it half off. You just shovel it off because you have to meet a combine. You've got a deadline and people just have a good, strong work ethic.

These reflections suggest a possibility that the way work is viewed in this place grows out of its agricultural history. I think of the task orientation I saw repeatedly in the short time I was there. Haying needed to be done when the grass was ready and not before. Once started, it needed to be finished. The oat harvest followed close on its heels. And then the wheat. No bucking the schedule and, once begun, whole families were out in the fields until it was finished.

The task orientation co-exists with others, though, and there's plenty of evidence of change. The orientation exists within a whole way of life and so another piece of the work story is whether it's viewed as a means to an end or something on the order of vocation. Younger farmers seemed to be struggling with that, to the extent that one young family I grew close to were talking in terms of pay-per-hours worked and calculating their annual take in those terms. This is a controversial way to do it, one that creates some tension between generations as the following reflections by an older farmer show:

> And then others want to farm because it's a good place to raise kids. Well, that's true it's a good place to raise kids but what about the other ninety-eight percent of the people who don't raise their kids on the farm? How did they do it? If the other ninety-eight percent are able to survive in town I think this two percent could also survive in town. So, I don't think it's worth the struggle they go through just to raise their kids on the farm.

These sentiments become physical in the posture of West River people at rest, no more evident than on Sundays and Holy Days of Obligation when the farming population takes enforced respite from action at the Abbey Church that dominates the town. Men, especially, sit uncomfortably immobile during the Mass, their big hands held open as if in need of a wrench. At such moments, the Catholic practice of frequent rising, sitting, and kneeling appears to be a blessing.

There's no need to look far for the origins of this strong feeling about work. Every person I spoke with talked about its importance in setting the character of their lives. Whether they grew up in town or on the farm, nearly every person had the experience of farm work because of the overlapping kin and labor-sharing networks that tied townspeople to farm relatives. It's easy to see that most people grew up in a world that lacked room for idleness and the comments of older people are hard to distinguish from those in Joe's generation. For some, the sheer amount of activity was a source of humor, as with a retired seventy-two-year-old carpenter:

> You grew up working all the time. I think my father stayed awake at night, you know, thinking of things for us to do. Oh, there was no such thing as hours! I mean, you just worked continuous—daylight to nightfall, you know?

Another man, now a medical doctor who lives in the small city near West River, and who grew up on a farm north of West River was similarly emphatic. He had gone away to medical school and had more opportunities than most to live a comfortable life away from the region, but returned to live as close to his home as he could because he felt more comfortable there. Even with the high income and free time of his profession, he takes on special tasks like building a porch that "kept getting bigger and bigger and bigger" to keep active. His memories of growing up were memories of work:

> Anytime you weren't eating or sleeping, you worked. Very labor intensive, as farming was back in those days. Very labor intensive. We had a diversified farm so we raised pigs, we raised chickens, we had a few sheep every once in awhile, that was very unusual to keep them back then. We did grain farming, raised hay, and everything was very laborious. Our machinery was never top-of-the-line, modern machinery. It was always older. In fact I can only remember a couple vacations when I was a kid. You just didn't do that.

Craig's wife, Renae, a notably independent and competent member of the community, wakes up every day at four thirty a.m. to have quiet time to get work done and think by herself. I remember sitting down to a late dinner at Joe and Marie's only to be interrupted by a phone call from Renae. One of her cows was having trouble calving and she needed help. Joe set down his fork without taking a bite and we rushed over together to give her a hand. "Renae never calls for help unless she means it," was Joe's explanation, "She hates taking help on little things." I asked her once about how work became so central for West River farmers.

> Well, you don't know a different life. When your parents told you this is something you have to do, then this is what you do because if you don't do it then the rest doesn't function. Everything that happens there is important in one way or another. And my dad's philosophy was, just because I was a girl didn't mean I couldn't do what the boys did. If I wanted to learn whatever, I mean I roped and did whatever the boys did because he felt that he didn't want me to ever have to rely on a man, and that's how we trained our daughter too. We taught her the same way.

Renae's comment begins to supply a reason for the emphasis on hard work beyond its self-evident value: Work was a part of an economy of relations. It also broaches the subject of gender in a way indicative of changes in a local culture that involved clearly identified and separate roles for men and women.

## The Working Family

Although it took city scholars a longer while to recognize the family nature of farm work and the central role women play in the farm economy, West River farmers are quick to point to the collective nature of the enterprise. Craig is especially aware of the impossibility of relying on one person:

> I honestly don't know how we've been doing it. There's a lot of luck there and a lot of hard work. Otherwise we wouldn't be here. And we both have to want to be doing it. Oh, God. If one of us wanted to quit it would be done. There's no way you could stay. You see that time and time again. As soon as one of the two doesn't want to do it anymore the place either falls apart or there's a divorce or they just up and leave, they're just done. Because you can't do it alone. It's a partnership.

Joe's vision of the partnership of work and relationship is similarly expressed, but he links it directly to the quality of their family relationship, too, by contrasting their current relationship with the way it was during the time Marie supplemented the family income with a job at a community bank. When she was at the bank, he felt a distance because they couldn't share conversation about the content of their daily work:

> And a lot of people can't imagine working with your wife day in and day out like I do but that's what, one of the strongest things that keeps us together. It's a great way to do things I think . . . . Here we consult and talk about everything we do.

Marie follows up by emphasizing the inseparability of family and work and the complementary roles they fill in the farm economy:

> When you're living this life it's a family thing or it doesn't work. We respect each other's territory, mostly. I do the household decisions, no doubt. That's obvious. And I let Joe make the decisions on the cropping, the insurance work, all those things. He just has a feel for it where I don't quite understand all of it. Although I'm learning more, I'm getting better at that. But he just has that, he just knows that stuff, and I just trust he'll make the right decision. And he doesn't step on my toes here either. He lets me do the management part how I want within the household, plus the business management, too. He sees that as, he doesn't care to even start looking at that.

Marie and Joe's comments point to the heavy reliance of the family farm way of life on gendered divisions of labor. As adept at the work of driving trucks and tractors, feeding cattle, and handling the calving as Marie and Renae are, they take these tasks on as additions to their other responsibilities within the household. Both of them bake for their families. Both of them handle the book work. Both of them also handle the emotional economy of the family enterprise. It's Marie who makes regular visits to Joe's grandmother at the hospital in West River, who surprises Joe on his birthday with a few days off a grueling schedule in a rented cabin in the Badlands, who is alert to the needs of smoothing family tensions.

Early on in West River I asked Joe if there were any women farmer-operators in the area. His response was a quiet double take and a look of wonderment as though he had never imagined such a thing. Still, although many West River residents point to a strongly held patriarchal culture that they call "German," it's no longer unusual to see women driving equipment. Men are as proud of their daughters' abilities in the field as they are of their sons'. Craig's comments serve as an example of both a growing acceptance of women in the field and of the relative novelty that makes it worth remarking:

> [My daughter's] an equal, just like me and you. Just because she's a girl doesn't mean she can't do anything. She was driving pickup when she was six years old. She would drive alongside, I had an automatic pickup and we'd fix fence. Me and her would go out together and fix fence. She'd put it in drive or in low and she'd idle along the fence and I'd walk and do whatever I needed to do. And I told her if she gets in trouble, you turn the key off. And that's what she would do. She'd turn the key off. And to start it she'd just turn it back on. Not a big deal. But that girl's got a lot of confidence. She'll go a long ways.

### The Work Ethic

When farmers drive the section line roads and highways of West River, their eyes drink up the landscape the way most people read a newspaper. Nothing is more revealing of a person's character than the neat lines of a well-tilled field, the missed crop rows where a seeder was plugged, or the pockets of discoloration caused by weeds missed in the spraying. A sloppy field is a headline announcing a sloppy character.

A failed field is called a wreck and everybody gets a pass for one. Bob, nodding to our left from the pick-up toward a field overrun with the sturdy weed called kocia, said, "This is my wreck for the year." Craig's wreck that year displayed itself to the world in the field by the highway and every neighbor saw it on the trip back from town. Reading fields after seeding, Joe would joke about a missed row or a plugged line in the air seeder in those holes where black earth pooled like oil in an otherwise green field. There's no stealth to farming, no covering your tracks, where every crooked line and every gap with a sprayer gets inscribed for later reflection and casual commentary. This is one of the reasons that Joe experiments with unfamiliar crops in a back quarter bordering little-used roads.

This concrete relationship between character and work encourages a special emphasis on the quality of work that West River people see as the presence of a work ethic. Although the classic American notion of the work ethic links it to Protestant and upper-class virtues of hard work for self and community, its treatment as the unique property of a single class or culture is probably overdone. West River residents clearly speak of it in terms that connote the original spiritual goods that redound to individual and community.

On the one hand, the work ethic is a latent quality of character that will express itself as an internal virtue made public by action, as when Joe commented on his daughter's drive:

> And I told her that once when were talking—she was always working—and I said, "Some day that German work ethic's going to kick in on you and you're not going to be able to stop it. You're going to hate it but you're going to keep doing it." And it has. She's driven now. When she got in school, it was overwhelming for her and just to the point she couldn't take it. And she got through that first year and announced that she was taking summer classes. And now she has a job on the side and married and everything else and she's going for a music minor. It's in her whether she likes it or not. And I knew it would happen to her. Just knowing the type of person she is and where she came from, she's going to work.

On the other, it has to do with relationships between people that connote unstated obligations of quality, as the West River doctor implies:

> Oh, I think work ethic, in my mind, means that if you have accepted the job, if you've accepted the responsibility, even if there's not a written contract, or even a verbal contract, there is an unwritten and unverbal agreement that you will do as good a job as you can. In return the person or employer will treat you fairly, too. I guess that's what I'm thinking. It's kind of like what I would hope would be an optimal physician-patient contract. Even though you never speak about these things, you in a sense agree to take the best care of the patient that you can and they agree to follow your advice, take your medications that you prescribe, and go through with what your recommendations are.

A very similar definition comes from another former West River resident in the professional world:

> I guess to me it's just a standard of excellence, of doing above and beyond what people expect you to do. I guess if somebody expects you to do a certain level

of work for them, or their client expects a certain level you do something the next level above that. If you're doing something extra that's going to be good for you in the long term. In the short run it keeps your client happy, it gives you repeat business, it gives you referrals. Just do above and beyond and do the best that you can. That's kind of how I approach it. You treat people like they're the most important person on earth. That's how you treat them. Because that's how you would expect to be treated if you were them. That's kind of how I approach it.

Both of these different emphases have in common a sense of something internal made concrete in action—in short a connection between character and work.

*Crafting the Good Person in the Context of Change*

Those were the last years of the Agrarian City
City of swapped labor
Communitas
Circle of warmth and work
Frontier's end and last wood-chopping bee
The last collectivity stamping its feet in the cold.

Thomas McGrath, *Letter to an Imaginary Friend*

When Joe and Craig were growing up, it was more or less assumed that some of the kids would stay to take over the farm. Working in the family economy was an unstated apprenticeship for a way of life. Contemporary life makes that a far less certain prospect. It isn't just West River that's losing people. The entire county loses population with every census. Farms grow bigger as the population thins. School districts consolidate. Businesses close. Joe watches quietly as yet another farmer shuts down and leaves the land and wonders, "Will I be next?"

Today, parents are compelled toward a more consciously planned upbringing for their children. Where Joe and Marie never went to college, they made a point of encouraging their own son and daughter to attend. Their son, Will, one of the three people in his high school graduating class who intends to be in West River and can't imagine anything else but farming, is a reluctant conscript at the nearby regional college where he studies agricultural economics. Joe and Marie tried hard to get him to go to a college further from home, but compromised on his choice to stay near West River, happy that he was giving it a try at all.

I opened this chapter with a quote from Iris Murdoch to emphasize the connection between everyday life and the ideas about "the good" that, though often unstated, give meaning to life. Unlike so many other forms of work in the United States, our image of farming comes to us as a complete package where individual character, family, and community join seamlessly to define how work and the good are one thing. In the face of threats to this way of life, the farmers I worked and talked with have more explicitly separated person and context. The good becomes something that is internalized and portable. Frank Falkenstein expressed some of this separation:

> You asked me if it had bothered me that people leave West River. To leave West River just for the sake of West River doesn't have any meaning but the fact that they've got an education and they've gotten involved in different occupations that they're interested in, that they find fulfillment from, is important. The work itself, is not important. The fact that the work is part of what helps them grow as an individual in their overall development and their walk through life is what's important and wherever that occupation takes them to is fine. You know, I really don't care where it is if it's helping them grow as a person.

In the changing world of West River, farming gets viewed as an advantaged preparation for a probable life away. Renae spoke for a widely shared view that incorporates that note of preparation with an air of sacrifice:

> So we're telling the kids, see, we're giving you something that lots of kids will never ever have. And I don't want them to feel like they owe me for that, but we have sacrificed a lot for those kids to have this life. And I think they have thrived by doing this. They can go out in the world and do anything. They know so many things. Town people, no offense to town people but, a lot of them have such a narrow idea of what the world really is. If it isn't in a book or it isn't this way, they don't understand that and my kids have the best of both worlds because they know what it's like to work harder or farm or have . . . . I don't know, it's just a whole different way of life. You know so many things. You know the reaction of one thing to the other. You're aware of the weather, not because, "Well, it's raining today, I can't play softball." That just doesn't happen here. They're more aware of what the real world is like. And I think when they go out into the world they will be able to relate to so many different things because they've had this.

Growing up on a farm becomes valuable for the virtues of realism, practicality, and internal character that it instills. Renae continued:

> I want them to be able to go out in the world and not be afraid to work for what they want. I want them to know honesty. That's a big thing in this household. I would rather hear an ugly truth than a fantasy. Fairy tale just doesn't get it. And the kids have, as far as I know, have been very honest. And loyal and committed to what they do. We're very committed to this or we wouldn't be doing this. So I think by them seeing how committed we are that they can be committed to something when they go off into the world, too. And whatever that is, that's their choice. I don't care what my children decide to do. Just so that they go out and work hard at it. Apply themselves. Don't think that you can go out and just get paid for looking at the stars. I'm sure people get paid to do that but my children probably aren't going to. The real world. So I want

them to go out and be able to make themselves a living. And be good people. Go into a community, if it's not this one, go into a community and be good people.

I asked her about this idea of the good, the word that brings us full circle to Iris Murdoch. Renae didn't miss a beat in her reply:

Good people. Someone who works hard, someone who's honest, probably those two major things. Someone who doesn't think about themselves all the time. They're willing to help someone out or give of themselves and not be afraid that they're not getting anything back.

This new world of preparation has its continuities with the way of life in West River, but the focus is on internal qualities that are not necessarily shared by others. Nor will character be so easily reflected in the concrete ways that West River fields can reveal to the attuned eye. Where all farmers share the same modes of work and are better or worse at it, those who leave West River will pursue different careers and will live in a more varied context.

Anthropologists are reluctant retailers of solutions. We see everyday life and document it, observe change, and avoid judgment. Nevertheless, any discussion of people's lives in the depopulating northern plains is a discussion with a genealogy going back to the original soul of America. Thomas Jefferson had an idea that he was sure would give solidity to American democracy. Part of that idea involved the very elements of character expressed by the people of West River. To talk of these people is to talk of a cultural tradition that has fed America's ethic throughout its history. This is not a simple question of economics. These are cultural questions for which we have, as yet, few established traditions of approach.

## AFTERWORD

The first thing to catch the eye of most visitors to my office at the University of Michigan is a large rock, about the size of a misshapen and slightly deflated soccer ball. It sits on my desk balanced on a tripod constructed of the bent and welded steel fingers from the inside of a combine's header. It isn't so much the rock that catches the eye as the bold inscription, "Tom, You Suck!" inked onto the side. The rock arrived in a heavy UPS package a few months after one of my returns to Ann Arbor from West River. I had no idea what could be in a box with that kind of heft but pulled it open and recognized it right away. It was the rock I picked up with Joe's combine when we harvested Craig's wheat just east of town. Joe made the stand in his shop using the same fingers I managed to bust in the field. They must have looked hard to find that rock because I heaved it as far into the weeds along the fence line as I could. Will's first words to me when I pulled out of the field for repairs are those very ones inked onto the rock. It holds a place of honor in my office, signed by the whole crew I worked with that day, reminding me that anthropology isn't just reading the classics.

## NOTE

Thanks to Lara Descartes, Brian Hoey, and Elizabeth Rudd for helpful comments on earlier drafts of this chapter. And many thanks to Callen, Julie, and Casey Hoff for their companionship and patient teaching. Not a word of this could have been written without these friends.

## REFERENCES

Bellah, Robert, Richard Madsen, William Sullivan, Ann Swidler, and Steven Tipton. 1996. *Habits of the heart: Individualism and commitment in American life.* New ed. Berkeley, CA: University of California Press.

Davidson, Osha Gray. 1996. *Broken heartland: The rise of America's rural ghetto.* Exp. ed. Iowa City, IA: University of Iowa Press.

Dudley, Kathryn Marie. 2000. *Debt and dispossession: Farm loss in America's heartland.* Chicago: University of Chicago Press.

Hochschild, Arlie. 2001. *The time bind.* 2nd ed. New York: Owl Books.

Lasch, Christopher. 1979. *Haven in a heartless world: The family besieged.* New York: W.W. Norton.

McGrath, Thomas. 1997. *Letter to an imaginary friend.* Port Townsend, WA: Copper Canyon Press.

Murdoch, Iris. 1970. *The sovereignty of the good.* London: Routledge and Kegan Paul.

Newman, Katherine S. 1999. *Falling from grace: Downward mobility in the age of affluence.* 2nd ed. Berkeley, CA: University of California Press.

Schor, Juliet. 1993. *The overworked American.* New York: Basic Books.

Shortridge, James R. 1989. *The middle West: Its meaning in American culture.* Lawrence, KS: University Press of Kansas.

Williams, Raymond. 1973. *The country and the city.* Oxford: Oxford University Press.

# 3

# Kitchen Conferences and Garage Cubicles

## The Merger of Home and Work in a 24-7 Global Economy

*Alesia F. Montgomery*

> This is the true nature of home—it is the place of Peace; the shelter . . . so far as the anxieties of the outer life penetrate into it . . . it ceases to be home; it is then only a part of that outer world which you have roofed over, and lighted fire in.
>
> —John Ruskin, 1865, *Sesame and Lilies*

As I began studying their mergers of paid work and family life in February 2000, Marjaneh and Steve—a married couple in their thirties—and Marjaneh's parents had just bought a home in an affluent Silicon Valley neighborhood.[1] Marjaneh and her parents were Iranian immigrants. Steve was American-born, with roots in Eastern Europe. Their new surroundings seemed idyllic. Beyond their window, squirrels played in fruit trees, birds darted from dangling feeders, and a golden retriever bounded down the quiet street to catch a Frisbee tossed by children.

The view from the family's window did not completely reveal the setting of their home lives. Email, faxes, and phone calls linked their home to high-tech firms within Silicon Valley and around the world. Although there were no parking lots or numbered suites, their pleasant neighborhood with its rose gardens and fruit trees was, in some sense, a busy industrial park. During the high-tech boom of the late 1990s, the family and some of their neighbors converted their garages and lofts into offices that enabled their homes to serve as "branches" of Silicon Valley firms. Marjaneh, her husband, and her father all had demanding high-tech jobs, and they collaborated on job tasks at home to meet these demands even though they had different employers. A business cycle (the high-tech boom and bust) and a cultural calendar (most notably, observance of the Iranian New Year,

*Norouz*) clashed in the home. Ancient seasonal celebrations organized around the cycles of agricultural work are not easily sustained in a 24-7 work world. Marjaneh's mother, a store manager, was the only family member who did not work in high-tech. She struggled to get the family to maintain "normal" patterns of family time, room use, and guest entertainment.

Does opening the home to job demands and work anxieties threaten the "true nature of the home," as nineteenth-century writer John Ruskin warned? In this chapter I argue that contemporary gender relations, management strategies, and technological practices enable diverse family and work forms—including work collaborations at home between husbands and wives and among parents and their adult children. Far from weakening family bonds, these mergers of home and work foster family cohesion. Unlike relations in the old middle class of shopkeepers, these mergers are not necessarily male-dominated—in Marjaneh's home, *she* led work collaborations. Yet similar to shopkeeping, the collaborations of Marjaneh and her family increased family togetherness and interdependence. Paid work and family life often are described as competing for time—an accurate description of time conflicts when work and home are separate spheres (Hochschild 1989, 1997, Perlow 1997). However, for Marjaneh's family and similar households in which work and home merge, the problem is not so much that job demands usurp family time, but rather that the home does not buffer job pressures.

## THE TRANSFORMATION OF FAMILY LABOR
## FROM AGRARIAN TO HIGH-TECH WORK

The separation of family life and paid work has not always been the norm. The industrial transformations of the eighteenth and nineteenth centuries in the United States and Europe increasingly removed production from the home, while cultural transformations valorized the home as a haven from the harsh work world. John Ruskin (1865) and other writers encouraged the rising middle class to embrace this new domestic ideal, but the separation of spheres was neither decisive nor abrupt. Employers relied upon fathers to discipline family work units in some early factories (Tilly and Scott 1989), and kin were sources of capital and labor for big industrialists and small shopkeepers (Segalen 1996). The baker's wife iced cakes a few steps from her husband, the butcher and his son chopped meat on the same counter, and for the family of grocers who lived in their shop, work and home merged. Until the early twentieth century, even scientists drew their households into their work (Pycior, Slack, and Abir-Am 1996). To gain access to their fields, the few women in science collaborated at home with their male relatives.

In the early twentieth century, corporations supplanted many family firms (Winder 1995), credentialed engineers replaced informally trained mechanics (Noble 1977), and "big science"—large projects that required numerous researchers and massive facilities—rose to prominence (Galison and Hevly 1992). Paid work became increasingly impersonal in its staffing and site. Based on his study of engineering firms in the 1970s, Robert Zussman (1987) describes engineering as the "prototypical occupation" of the "new middle class." The men in his study did not draw their wives into their work lives, and their wives did not involve them in family care. At the time of Zussman's study, some stay-at-home wives did "invisible work" such as typing that helped their husbands' careers (Kanter 1977, Papanek 1973, Smith 1987), but few wives of engineers had sufficient technical skills to help their husbands with work.

A move toward egalitarian marriages (Scanzoni, Polonko, Teachman, and Thompson 1989) and an easing of barriers to women's education and employment have expanded the possibilities for spousal collaborations in technical professions. Over the past few decades, women in the United States have increased their education in science and technology. For example, women held 17.9 percent of bachelor's degrees in engineering by 1996, compared to only 0.4 percent in 1966 (National Science Foundation 2000). In those years, the percentages of women with bachelor's degrees in the physical sciences and computer science also rose (from 14 percent to 37 percent and from 14.6 percent to 27.6 percent, respectively).

As the possibilities for spouses to collaborate increase, new management strategies encourage collaborations across firms. Compared to firms in the 1950s, employers today offer less job security and fewer job ladders; professionals use their personal ties to update their skills, find jobs, and advance their "boundaryless careers" across firms (Arthur and Rousseau 1996). Firms also have become less bounded. To deal with increased competition in the global economy, business is increasingly organized as a "network enterprise" that comprises shifting project alliances within and across firms and nations (Castells 1996).

The high-tech industry exemplifies trends toward boundaryless careers and firms. Researchers note the challenges of job insecurity, long work hours, and transnational work processes in high-tech (Barley and Kunda 2004, Benner 2002, Ó Riáin 2000), and they trace the inter-firm and personal ties that enhance careers and the bottom line of high-tech firms (Saxenian 1994, 1996). Employers sometimes demand that managers and professionals make themselves available twenty-four hours a day, seven days a week, to collaborate with distant colleagues on far-flung projects.

New communication tools facilitate these 24-7 work flows. Economic historian Joel Mokyr (2001) speculates that the benefits of moving production from households to centralized workplaces during the Industrial

Revolution may be changing today with the advent of new technologies. The barriers to organizing workers and information across different places and times have decreased. Mokyr predicts that centralized workplaces will continue to exist for aspects of production that require face-to-face coordination, but many workers increasingly will work from home.

In 2002, approximately 61 percent of U.S. employees reportedly used email on the job, and almost half of these work emailers also reportedly checked their work email from home (Fallows 2002). Between 2001 and 2002, more than a third of workers (38 percent) in the California Workforce Study (CWS) stated that they used pagers or cell phones on the job (Fligstein and Sharone 2002). Managers (65 percent) and professionals (44 percent) were most likely to use these devices. Among those who used these devices, 88 percent of managers and 68 percent of professionals reportedly used them for work after work hours. Compared to others in the CWS study, managers and professionals reportedly worked longer hours and were most likely to report that they had difficulty finding time for both family and work. The CWS study did not address how work and family time overlap. New technologies increase the possibilities for families to stay in contact during paid work (English-Lueck 2002), yet new technological practices also may facilitate exploitation: Studying teleworkers, Janet Salaff (2002) expresses concern that telework shifts burdens such as technical support from co-workers to families.

## MERGERS OF HOME AND WORK IN A "JOB-SHARING" FAMILY

Marjaneh's family exemplifies how new technologies, management strategies, and gender relations are changing the possibilities for work collaborations within households. As a teenager, Marjaneh had helped out in her father's shop after her family emigrated to the United States. Similarly, Steve had done assembly work in the small side business that his father had run from the family garage. As family members switched from being shopkeepers to salaried professionals, they still worked together, but the nature of their collaborations changed. In line with Judith Stacey (1996), I describe Marjaneh's family as "postmodern"—that is, a family that diverges from modern ideals of separate spheres and from modern realities in which wives gave "invisible" help that supported the businesses and careers of their husbands. Marjaneh's family mixed feminist sensibilities, a superficially modern spatial divide (Steve drove to work; Marjaneh worked at home), and a form of household labor (they collaborated on job tasks) that was almost pre-modern. They were a *job-sharing family* as opposed to a shopkeeping family. The gender relations, management strategies, and communication technologies of postmodernity do not support an infinite array of family and work forms, but these forms are elastic and diverse.

## FROM SHOPKEEPING TO JOB-SHARING

A decade before my study, Marjaneh and Steve had shared an apartment with Marjaneh's parents while the newlyweds worked as counter clerks at her father's hardware shop. The pace of the work had been slow, with plenty of time to buy coffee from a nearby café or read a newspaper. Marjaneh and Steve had just graduated from college, and they were waiting for responses to their resumes. As an undergraduate, Marjaneh started off majoring in the social sciences. After she met Steve, she began to take computer science courses. From chats with Steve and reading magazines, she believed that a high-tech career would be exciting and lucrative. Steve aided her to make the transition, assisting with her math homework. In exchange, Marjaneh helped Steve write papers for his courses.

After a few months at the shop of Marjaneh's father, the couple landed jobs as programmers at the same firm, and they got their own apartment. Marjaneh switched from programming to high-tech marketing. Although the couple no longer had the same employer, they helped each other with job tasks at home. Their educational and work histories had primed them for collaboration, and their shared technical expertise and industry knowledge were useful to each other. When they bought a home with Marjaneh's parents, their collaborations once again became intergenerational.

## HIGH-TECH BOOM, BUST, AND REVIVAL

Between February and May 2000, I spent ten to fifteen hours per week observing Marjaneh's home life, and I interviewed Steve and Marjaneh (my main focus) before and after my four months of observations. To see a range of family activities, I varied the time of day and week of my visits. By chance, my observations began before the Iranian New Year in March and the high-tech downturn in April—events that affected their practices. After my observations in 2000, I kept in touch by phone, and I returned to their home for a few days each year between 2001 and 2005 to track changes.

### Domestic Spaces as Job Cubicles

Before the high-tech downturn of April 2000, I made a diagram of the family's use of domestic space for job tasks (Figure 3.1). Marjaneh

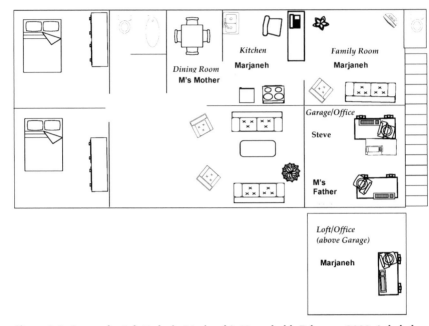

**Figure 3.1. Spaces for Job Tasks in Marjaneh's Household, February 2000. Labeled areas indicate the family member who most often used room as a space to do job tasks.**

telecommuted as a high-tech marketing manager. Occasionally she had to make business trips in and beyond the United States, but usually she worked from home. Her main office was her loft, yet other rooms gradually filled with her files and reports. When she first moved into her new home, Marjaneh had planned to contain her work in her loft/office, but she said that she found it lonely. She often worked with her laptop on the kitchen counter while watching TV and talking to Steve and her parents.

Marjaneh had thought telecommuting would give her more control over her day, but job demands increasingly dictated her use of household space and her family interactions. Business calls interrupted chats with family members and their viewing of TV shows in the evenings and on weekends. When the phone rang, Marjaneh's dog would bark and she had to run from the room or shush it. Also, she had to move away from the fountain in the kitchen. Her father had placed a small stone fountain on the counter among the flowers as a gift to Marjaneh. The water made splashing and tinkling noises. She said that she found the sound soothing, but she worried that callers might think that she was in the bathroom. In addition, she had to shush or escape from family members who called each other loudly or broke into laughter. Her parents sometimes seemed hurt or confused when she motioned for them to be quiet or to go away while she was on the phone, but she didn't feel that she had a choice. She also worried about awakening her family. She chose the loft as her office so she wouldn't disturb her family when she had to make calls at odd hours to the East Coast, Europe, or Asia.

Marjaneh had to constantly manage sounds. When she made business calls, she could be calling from anywhere—her home, her car, an airport, a regional office, a client's site, San Francisco, New York, London. . . . Not all of these places sounded "professional." A few times she took business calls in a local restaurant's parking lot. While her husband ate inside the noisy restaurant, she ran with her cell phone to the quiet of her car. When I began studying the family, Marjaneh did not have a cell phone—she was anxious about the possible brain cancer risks of holding a cell phone near her head. However, she got one after colleagues expressed surprise that she was not always accessible by phone. As a compromise, she bought a headset to distance the cell phone from her head.

Her husband, Steve, a software developer at a different firm, usually got his job done at his workplace. Both Marjaneh and her mother voiced concern that his long hours at his workplace were bad for his health, and they worried that it was dangerous for him to come home late at night. To pacify them, Steve sometimes used his garage/office for job tasks such as writing technical documentation. Marjaneh proofread his documentation (similar to their college days when she had helped with his papers). Occasionally at home he would get a call or email from a colleague in Silicon Valley or elsewhere about a problem with a program that his project team had written. Most of the time he would go to his workplace to deal with crises, but he increasingly dealt with crises from home, getting access to programs through a secure server.

Almost every night and weekend, Steve helped Marjaneh with her work reports. He spent at least ten hours each week on her projects, drawing upon his technical and industry knowledge. Marjaneh said that she often felt guilty asking him for help because he was tired and stressed from his own job. Steve helped Marjaneh to get her job done so that she could come to bed or watch TV. Marjaneh's mumblings that she could lose her job if she did not meet job demands also spurred his help. When they completed a project, he enjoyed her praise, and they often would go out to a restaurant to celebrate. However, when Marjaneh felt that Steve was not working quickly enough on her projects—or when Marjaneh had not proofread Steve's technical documentation—they would argue or not speak. Marjaneh noted that there were strong incentives for them to "make up" quickly whenever they had a falling out: They depended on each other's practical and emotional support to cope with work. Employer demands were displaced onto their personal relations, complicating their interactions.

While the job demands of Marjaneh and Steve often involved responding to crises, the job demands of Marjaneh's parents were usually routine and contained within their workplaces. However, the older couple also did some work at home. Marjaneh's father, an engineer at a high-tech firm, shared the garage/office with Steve, engaging in various work activities (for example, searching the web to find needed information). A hardware engineer, Marjaneh's father served as technical support for the family, fixing their computers and peripherals. This support was useful for Marjaneh, who had difficulty getting timely technical support from her employer.

Marjaneh's mother, a department store manager, used the dining room table as a workspace a couple of times each week for a few hours to fill out paperwork by hand. She often asked Marjaneh to double-check her calculations or to help filling out forms. Unlike Marjaneh's erratic job demands and requests for help with work, her mother's work was predictable. At the end of each month and around certain holidays, she had more paperwork, and thus she brought more work home and desired more help.

The bathrooms were motivational retreats for Marjaneh and Steve, stocked with business journals that saluted the "dot-com revolution." When their energies flagged, Marjaneh and Steve reminded each other about the success stories they had read. In an ethnography of a high-tech firm, Gideon Kunda (1992) describes how senior managers use meetings to make ideological points and inculcate corporate culture. Business journals served a similar function within Marjaneh and Steve's home, but these journals fostered allegiance to high-tech business culture, not to a specific firm.

Proximity facilitated their collaborations. While Marjaneh's mother did paperwork at the dining table, Marjaneh might go to the kitchen and pour herself a cup of tea; her mother would call out for Marjaneh to double-check her calculations. And while Steve and Marjaneh watched TV, Marjaneh might get a business call; Steve would ask about the call and get drawn into giving help. Or while Steve and his father-in-law sat in the garage/office, his father-in-law might ask Steve a work question.

On Saturdays, everyone in the house often was engaged in paid work or family support of paid work. While Marjaneh and her family worked on their own job tasks or helped each other with work, Latina immigrants—a mother and a daughter—helped each other to clean the house. The "hired help" enabled Marjaneh's family to devote more of their time to their jobs. Marjaneh served as a kind of office manager. She would get up from her desk and move from loft to family room, family room to garage, garage to living room, directing the house cleaners. . . . checking up on her husband's progress doing research for her. . . . seeking out her father if she had a computer problem . . . helping her mother with paperwork from her job.

Throughout the week, Steve did much of the cooking. Praised as the family "chef," he had honed his skills by watching cooking shows and buying cookbooks. On the weekends he prepared and froze meals for the week. The family also often ate at restaurants and bought fast food. Marjaneh rarely cooked. Although she was at home all day, she did not want to be viewed as a housewife. Since the days when they were students, Steve had agreed that placing her in that role would be sexist and unfair, so he had accepted cooking as his chore.

The family's labor divisions defied conventions of the breadwinner husband and the homemaker wife, yet their use of domestic space was to some extent gendered. Steve and his father-in-law never used the kitchen or dining areas for their job tasks, and Marjaneh and her mother rarely used the garage. Marjaneh found the garage cold and gloomy. Her father and husband left the cases off their computers after tinkering on them, exposing the metal and wire "innards" (as Marjaneh called them). Ripped-out innards were scattered on the floors, desks, and shelves. The innards made Marjaneh uncomfortable. Perhaps there are gendered computing aesthetics, influenced by cultural taboos against women tinkering with machines (Turkle 1995).

These gendered spaces made it more likely that Marjaneh would be drawn into helping her mother, and Steve would be drawn into collaborations with his father-in-law. Intergenerational exchanges about the nuts-and-bolts of computer hardware flowed between Marjaneh's father and Steve rather than between father and daughter. Steve became back-up technical support for the family, tinkering on their machines.

### Self-marketing and Workloads

During one of my visits, Marjaneh had a nine-thirty a.m. conference call: a nationwide company meeting. The meeting included employees at regional offices as well as telecommuters such as Marjaneh. The rapidly expanding company enabled telecommuting in part to reduce the cost of office space.

Marjaneh put the call on speaker phone. After a cheery greeting, the CEO asked, "If everyone could look at the new organizational chart . . ." Marjaneh clicked open the chart on her laptop, frowning, "Where am I?" Although she was in senior management, she was not on the chart. The CEO referred to the chart with brisk enthusiasm:

> Anybody you see on this chart is a resource for you to go get help. . . . It shows the individual responsibilities at each office. . . . It also shows recent promotions. . . . However, nothing you see is written in stone. . . . We have to stay flexible so that we can respond effectively to the market. . . . People will have to wear many hats. . . . Well, that's the organization. . . . To give you an impression of who does what and who you can go to for help and where you fit in . . .

After the teleconference, Marjaneh expressed hurt, confusion, and worry. Hurt because she longed for recognition of her hard work and talents; her long hours were not as obvious as the hours of her co-workers who went into the office. Confusion because she didn't understand the new organization chart. Despite the reassurances in the teleconference, she didn't have a clue "who she could go to for help" and "where she fit in." Worry because her invisibility as a telecommuter might make her job vulnerable. During the high-tech boom, Marjaneh felt that she could get another job, but she worried that the gap between jobs would make it hard to meet her huge house payments.

Marjaneh's work hours increased over the time of my observations as she tried to enhance her visibility within the firm by intensifying her work effort. She'd get up before dawn to call clients and co-workers in other time zones, and she often worked until ten or eleven at night doing analyses and preparing presentations. Rather than resting during lulls in employer demands, she would call the head office with ideas for additional assignments that she could complete. Marjaneh became an "entrepreneur," marketing herself to her employer.

Beyond the omission of Marjaneh, the neat boxes and arrows of the organizational chart did not account for Steve's growing entanglement in the company's projects. To meet job demands, Marjaneh increasingly drew upon her husband for help. Given that they had no children, the couple had few domestic responsibilities that opposed their escalating commitment to job tasks.

Marjaneh's strategy eventually paid off. She got recognition for huge, well-executed projects. At a subsequent teleconference she was called "bright" and "sharp." However, the hard work took its toll on her and Steve, and she was never sure how long the spotlight would last. "I don't have a life," Marjaneh complained. "I'm so tired."

## Entrepreneurial Orientation and Acceptance of Job Demands

Marjaneh and Steve seemed to accept their heavy job demands as necessary for the success of their employers and themselves. Occasionally they collaborated on an idea for a high-tech start-up of their own. They viewed their business plans, their stock portfolios, *and* their jobs as investment opportunities. If their employers went "public" (sold stocks to the public), and the stocks did well, they could cash in and get rich. Or if the stocks they held in other high-tech companies (which they incessantly checked online) continued to shoot up, they could become millionaires. Or if they cofounded a start-up, and the start-up did well, they could sell it and get rich. If they worked hard now, on their jobs, on their business plans, and on managing their stocks, perhaps one day they wouldn't have to work. They often talked about their dreams of becoming rich before they turned forty. If they got rich, they could travel to exotic places. Spend their weekends making pottery. Go to the opera or spa whenever they wanted. Sleep.

### Domestic Spaces for Leisure

Only two domestic spaces never were used for job tasks: the living room and the backyard garden. When family members entered these spaces, they left their laptops and cell phones behind. The living room was kept pristine for guests, decorated with beautiful flowers from the garden and supplied with glass bowls of nuts, fruits, and tiny, golden rocks of sugar for tea. Persian carpets, family photographs, and the Koran were displayed here. Marjaneh said the room's ornate French furnishings reflected the cosmopolitan tastes of her parents' generation in Iran. Oil paintings decorated the walls—a family feeding their farm animals at dawn . . . an urban street with black-coated pedestrians and horse-drawn carriages hurrying past amber-lit shops at dusk. The family dog was not allowed in the living room because she had an alarming, *najes* (unclean) habit of chewing the carpets, gorging herself on the treats in the bowls, sniffing the body parts of guests, and biting her own. The living room was reserved for the guests of Marjaneh's parents, mostly other Iranian immigrants of their generation. Marjaneh's mother served tea to them on a golden platter.

In contrast to the living room, which was the space for formal manners and clothing, the garden was the family's space for "acting naturally" in "natural" surroundings. When they found time in their schedules, one or two family members would come to the garden to pick mint or flowers, or to sip tea and fall asleep in a lawn chair. A pottery wheel sat in a corner of the patio, unused, a reminder to Marjaneh and Steve of their dreams of having time to indulge in idle creations. When the couple invited their friends (mostly co-workers and former co-workers around their age from diverse countries) to a backyard barbecue, the family dog was not only allowed to hover around the grill, she also was called upon to do tricks for chunks of meat—dancing on her hind legs, spinning in a circle—to the applause and amusement of guests.

The living room and garden differed sharply in appearance, yet they had somewhat similar functions. Unlike the garage/office and the loft/office, which were conduits to the ahistorical, depersonalized "timeless time" (Castells 1996) of never-ending global work processes, the garden and living room were thresholds to the personalized, preserved time of places of leisure—not simply to the immediate surroundings but also to the old country and an old world cosmopolitanism (in the case of the living room) and to ideals of "nature" and the "natural" (in the case of the garden). In the living room and the garden, the family could return to (or pursue) a lost time and the free time lost in 24-7 work flows. During their waking hours, family members were more likely to share time with each other in domestic spaces of work than domestic spaces in which work was forbidden. While Marjaneh and Steve felt compelled to work, they usually felt little or no compulsion (beyond biological demands) to relax.

### Cultural Calendars vs. "Timeless Time"

Despite their compulsions to work, it was hard for Marjaneh and Steve to resist cultural pressures to celebrate special days such as *Norouz*, the Iranian New Year. *Norouz* marks the spring equinox. Traditionally, several days before *Norouz*, the house is cleaned, special foods are cooked, new clothes are purchased, and an elaborate display—the *sofreh haft-seen*—is prepared on a table. On "Red Wednesday" (*Chahar Shanbeh Suri*) before *Norouz*, a fire ceremony is held in yards, and on the day of Norouz, at the moment of *tahvil* (the equinox), the well-wishing and sharing of treats begins. For two weeks afterwards, family and friends socialize at each others' homes.

Marjaneh had fond childhood memories of *Norouz*, but she felt that she had little time for it now. Time spent growing sprouts, painting eggs, and buying goldfish for the table display could be time spent getting her job done. Her job demands were particularly fierce that March as her company battled competitors. Steve also faced huge job stresses—his team had to meet a deadline for a product release, there were bugs in the program, and there were rumors of lay-offs in the not-so-distant future. In retrospect, the high-tech stock market crash was about to occur (spring 2000), and their companies were battling to stay afloat.

The family's *haft-seen* table display was small that year. Marjaneh's parents prepared the display, yet with Marjaneh and Steve too busy to share in the preparations, the parents felt little enthusiasm for it. At *tahvil* (the equinox) Marjaneh was on a business call. At the risk of missed work deadlines, she and Steve made time for a *Norouz* party with guests that Marjaneh's mother invited, but they were too stressed to enjoy it. At her mother's insistence, Marjaneh also made time to exchange New Year's pleasantries by phone with relatives in Iran, but her eye was on her watch—she expected a business call from abroad.

### The Crash and Its Aftermath

In April 2000, the high-tech bubble burst. High-tech stocks crashed on the NASDAQ, and many companies eventually closed their doors. Marjaneh and Steve's stocks tanked. Venture capital dried up. Their employers were on shaky financial ground, and there was less work for Marjaneh and Steve to do.

During the bleak days of 2001 and 2002, Marjaneh kept her laptop open on the kitchen counter so that she and Steve could check online job postings and send resumes to firms that seemed more solvent than their own. They rarely collaborated on job tasks during this period. Their collaborations shifted from help with work to help holding on to work: How should they word their resumes? At their jobs, how should they handle office politics to get on projects that were unlikely to be cut? The computers gathered cobwebs in the garage/office; it became a storage space for cost-saving bulk foods. To cut costs, they also eliminated weekly restaurant meals and shopping binges, and they cut back their use of housecleaners from weekly to biweekly. With less frequent international business calls, the loft/office was largely unused. Journals saluting dot-coms disappeared from the bathrooms.

Ironically, although Marjaneh and Steve had not "struck gold" during the boom—and they were constantly afraid of getting laid off—they now engaged in activities that they had dreamed they would be able to do if they became wealthy. With some of the money that they saved, they took a modest vacation. They spent their weekends making pottery. They went to the opera and the spa. They slept. The high-tech slowdown enabled them to engage in the affluent lifestyle that had been out of their reach during the boom because they never had enough time to indulge themselves.

Yet during the boom, the family had spent more of their waking hours together (and they had more waking hours) because they often had worked at home. Now Marjaneh and Steve spent time away from each other, hanging out with friends. Although the couple enjoyed more time for parties thrown by Marjaneh's parents, they spent less time at home with the older couple on an everyday basis. There were grand *Norouz* celebrations, but less mundane communication. Marjaneh's parents began to travel frequently: In the face of lay-offs at his company, her father had retired.

Gradually, business conditions improved. Marjaneh's company had folded, but she found a new job that allowed her to divide her time between working in the office and at home. Steve's company also had closed its doors, but he got a better job—his salary now was comparable with Marjaneh's salary.

When I visited their home in 2005, I was struck by the changes there. Steve had installed a wireless network so that he and Marjaneh could use their laptops in any room. I was shocked to see Marjaneh working on her laptop in the formerly sacrosanct living room. The family dog slept nearby, rotating her position on the Persian carpet as the day advanced in response to changes in the light—an animate sundial. A bellwether of the family's domestic order, the dog now had the run of the house; the boundaries between clean and unclean, sacred and profane were vanishing. Marjaneh's parents had become fond of the dog, and she had lost her taste for carpet as she matured. At any rate, Marjaneh's parents were rarely home to protest the dog's presence. Marjaneh began to work in the living room because she sought out the dog's company as she worked alone in the house; she rarely barked now when Marjaneh had a business call. On cold days, Marjaneh called the dog onto the ornate couch to nap next to her when she took a break, calling the dog her "little hot water bottle."

I was equally shocked to find Steve working on his laptop at the dining table in the old spot of Marjaneh's mother during one of my visits. His new job was farther away than his old job, so he often worked from home, although not as much as Marjaneh. He did not resume using the garage/office. Now that Marjaneh's father no longer used it, Steve did not want to work there by himself.

I was most shocked to find Marjaneh in the kitchen—cooking!—during one of my visits; she said that she felt that she should help out by cooking meals on the days that Steve was really busy with job demands. Marjaneh said that she was now open to changing the allocation of chores in response to changes in their job demands. Yet she still seemed somewhat uneasy that others might perceive her as a traditional homemaker. When their friends visited, she insisted that Steve cook and serve.

In short, the symbolic and spatial order of their home no longer preserved distinctions that structured roles and separated spheres. In the frequent absence of Marjaneh's parents—and in response to the pick-up in job demands—Steve and Marjaneh seemed on a trajectory to erase gendered spaces as well as boundaries between work and leisure in their home. In the process, their schedules became increasingly erratic—there were no fixed times for work or leisure. The backyard garden was the only domestic space of leisure that seemed relatively preserved, but perhaps that would change: The couple did not use their laptops in the garden, but Marjaneh had begun to take calls on her cell phone while relaxing there.

Calls and emails from co-workers began to follow them home again. While Steve participated in a teleconference in one room, Marjaneh might be on a business call in another room. When a call from work interrupted their TV shows, they would put their TV show on hold, then re-start it: They now had TiVo (that technology *par excellence* for managing disruptions).[2] They were less enthusiastic (at first) about another technological "advance": Some younger co-workers now used instant messaging (IM) to monitor each other's presence online and to continuously keep in touch. Her co-workers asked Marjaneh to IM, but she always changed the subject. She told me that she had no desire to constantly be "visible" and available to her co-workers when she went online, and she hoped that IM would not become as ubiquitous as cell phone use in the business world. Given her vehement opposition to IM, I was startled a couple months later when Marjaneh told me that—at the persistent urging of co-workers—she had finally downloaded the IM application, and she had become an avid user of IM. Although she did not always like being drawn into IM chitchat, she said that she found it useful to see if her co-workers were online and available to discuss work matters when something urgent came up in the evenings and on weekends. She also liked that IM gave her a cheap means to keep in touch with Steve when she went on business trips out of the country.

As their job demands picked up and the business climate in Silicon Valley improved, Marjaneh and Steve began to help each other with work again, and they began to collaborate on a new idea for a start-up. Maybe this new start-up would be successful, and they could sell it for big bucks and escape the stress of work . . . yet they were more doubtful now about their prospects.

I asked the couple whether their house "ceased to be a home" during the high-tech boom, and how they would feel about a return to those days. Steve said that during the boom, he often felt that he had lost his home because he had no control over the time and space that he shared with Marjaneh. A call or email from a co-worker could disrupt the couple's plans. He did not wish to see a return to those days.

Marjaneh expressed ambivalence. She said that there is a difference between the ideal of what one wants home to be and the reality of what home must be to care for those who live in it. Jobs are a large, unavoidable part of the lives of family members, and if you keep paid work and home life separate, you miss out on that part of your family members' lives. In Marjaneh's estimation, you don't really know a person unless you share their work lives with them. She mused that if she and Steve neither discussed nor got involved in each other's paid work at home, then a distance might grow between them. They might become strangers to each other, or at least strangers to that part of each other which was an employee somewhere. So home wouldn't feel like home. Yet she felt that there was an opposite danger—for example, when job demands became overwhelming during the boom—of becoming a stranger to that part of one's self or that part of your loved one which was more than an employee. For Marjaneh, neither home as a workplace nor home as a refuge was ideal.

## CONCLUSION

Often when one listens to researchers discuss the effects of paid work on family life, one gets the impression that work time limits family time. Researchers should pay more attention to the plethora of family and work forms. While some families "juggle" home and work, others combine spheres. In this chapter I have shown how transformations in gender relations, management strategies, and technological practices enable some professionals to merge work and home in quasi-entrepreneurial ways that recall pre-industrial agrarian households and modern shopkeeping families. This merger can have positive influences on family togetherness and interdependence—separate spheres are not necessarily the most desirable family and work forms.

I do not mean to suggest that merging home and work has no downsides. For Marjaneh and Steve, combining home and work had mixed consequences. On the one hand, working on job tasks at home increased their family cohesion. On the other hand, this merger reduced the degree to which their home served as a refuge from job pressures. Marjaneh and Steve were exhausted by long work hours at their home, and they got into fights over their work collaborations. Mergers of home and work did not reduce their time together, but these mergers restricted the time that they had for preserving cultural calendars, entertaining guests, and relaxing with each other. Similar to the old middle class of shopkeepers, they collaborated to meet heavy job demands. Unlike shopkeeping families, they faced erratic demands that were driven by global processes. These global processes were "sped up" and made more invasive by the use of innovative communication technologies in a "new economy."

As Steve observed, job demands *limited the control* that they had over the time and space of family life; family time was not so much cut as *depersonalized*. In the process, there was the danger (as Marjaneh suggested) that they might become strangers to that part of themselves and each other that was unrelated to the demands of work in a 24-7 global economy. Marjaneh and Steve "chose" to engage in work collaborations, yet their work practices were structured by employer expectations and work cultures that pushed them to be continuously connected to 24-7 work flows. They did not perceive many options. If they wished to hold onto their insecure yet lucrative jobs, their "choice" seemed to be between long work hours together or apart.

## AFTERWORD

Identities and backgrounds matter in ethnographic research (as in any social interaction), but the subsets of our identities and experiences that matter change from situation to situation, and they are not always obvious.

This ethnography would have been different if I had shared the same ethnic background as Marjaneh and her parents. If I were a native Farsi speaker (instead of someone who had acquired a toddler-level grasp of the language from a workbook and tapes), I would have been better able to follow their conversations when they mixed English with Farsi. If I had been born in Iran and made a similar journey to the United States (instead of being someone who had merely read about Iran and its immigrants), I would have had a richer, felt understanding of the meanings of time, space, and sociality for them. Indeed, if my focus of study were the older couple instead of Marjaneh and Steve (who did not speak Farsi to each other), I would not have undertaken this project.

Yet I believe that one can make useful sociological observations about people even if one does not share their ethnicity. Born and raised in South L.A., I am an African American ethnographer who sometimes studies people with whom I seem to have little in common. Years ago, I acquired my taste for ethnography in a high school program that encouraged students to use the entire L.A. metropolis as a classroom—not just the region's many museums and libraries but also its diverse streets and people. The program helped me to see that people and places that seem very insular and strange at first glance often have interesting links to or similarities with familiar people and places.

Once while I was walking down Venice Boulevard carrying out some independent study or another for this high school project (I dimly remember I wanted to map changes in people and shops from working-class Arlington Boulevard down to bohemian Venice Beach), a friend from my neighborhood (who was also in the program) pulled up to the curb: She was on her way to interview the Hare Krishna. Did I want to come along? I said "Sure" and hopped in the car. The Hare Krishna temple was just a few blocks away. If memory serves, the young guy whom we met was named Mario Karma (Chicano? Italian?); he had grown up in L.A.'s urban core, and he mentioned various places that we knew. As he gave us a tour, I was struck by how familiar things seemed. As a child, I had been taken to Catholic and Pentecostal churches, and the sights, sounds, and smells of the Hare Krishna temple reminded me of these experiences: The incense, the statues, the chants (Catholic), the tambourines and ecstatic dancing (Pentecostal). I do not mean to suggest anything as saccharine as "people are the same wherever you go"—it is unwise to ignore the ways in which the interests and beliefs of groups clash with each other—yet the forms by which divergent groups express themselves around and through their bodies often have interesting convergences. These convergences enable a level of empathy that facilitates the interpretation of experiences.

As a teenager, I simply wanted to document diverse forms or ways of being in the world. Today, as a sociologist, I am interested in how and why particular forms—enabled by societal structures and global developments—emerge at particular historical moments among certain types of people in specific places. In the case of Marjaneh and Steve, I traced the ways in which their work form was enabled and structured by social, economic, and technological transformations. I strongly empathized with them. At the time of my study, I was a graduate student. Although different processes, relations, and ideologies structured my 24-7 work demands, I too longed for time to sleep.

## NOTES

This research was made possible by a predoctoral fellowship from the UC Berkeley Center on Working Families, funded by the Alfred P. Sloan Foundation's program in Workplace, Workforce and Working Families.

1. Names and other identifying information have been altered to preserve confidentiality.
2. TiVo is a brand of digital video device that allows users to store television programs. When the user presses "pause" on the TiVo remote control, the action stops on the television screen but the device continues to save the television program on its hard disk. The user can resume viewing the television program whenever she wants.

## REFERENCES

Arthur, Michael B., and Denise M. Rousseau, eds. 1996. *The boundaryless career: A new employment principle for a new employment era.* New York: Oxford University Press.

Barley, Stephen R., and Gideon Kunda. 2004. *Gurus, hired guns, and warm bodies: Itinerant experts in a knowledge economy.* Princeton, NJ: Princeton University Press.

Benner, Chris. 2002. *Work in the new economy: Flexible labor markets in Silicon Valley.* Cambridge, MA: Blackwell.

Castells, Manuel. 1996. *The rise of the network society.* Cambridge, MA: Blackwell.

English-Lueck, Jan A. 2002. *Cultures@SiliconValley.* Stanford, CA: Stanford University Press.

Fallows, Deborah. 2002. *Email at work.* Washington, DC: Pew Internet and American Life Project.

Fligstein, Neil, and Ofer Sharone. 2002. *Work in the postindustrial economy of California.* Berkeley, CA: Institute for Labor and Employment, University of California.

Galison, Peter, and Bruce Hevly, eds. 1992. *Big science: The growth of large scale research.* Stanford, CA: Stanford University Press.

Hochschild, Arlie. 1989. *The second shift.* New York: Viking.

———. 1997. *The time bind: When work becomes home and home becomes work.* New York: Metropolitan Books.

Kanter, Rosabeth M. 1977. *Men and women of the corporation.* New York: Basic Books.

Kunda, Gideon. 1992. *Engineering culture: Control and commitment in a high-tech corporation.* Philadelphia: Temple University Press.

Mokyr, Joel. 2001. "The rise and fall of the factory system: technology, firms, and households since the Industrial Revolution." www.faculty.econ.northwestern.edu/faculty/mokyr/pittsburgh.PDF.

National Science Foundation. 2000. "Women as a percentage of all bachelor's degree recipients, by field: 1966–1996." In *Women, minorities, and persons with disabilities in science and engineering: 2000.* Arlington, VA: National Science Foundation (NSF 00-327).

Noble, David F. 1977. *America by design: Science, technology, and the rise of corporate capitalism.* Oxford: Oxford University Press.

Ó Riain, Seán. 2000. "Net-working for a living: Irish software developers in the global workplace." In *Global Ethnography,* ed. Michael Burawoy, Joseph A. Blum, Sheba George, Zsuzsa Gille, Millie Thayer, Teresa Gowan, Lynne Haney, Maren Klawiter, Steve H. Lopez, and Seán Ó Riáin, 175–202. Berkeley, CA: University of California Press.

Papanek, Hanna. 1973. "Men, women, and work: Reflections on the two-person career." *American Journal of Sociology* 78 (4): 852–72.

Perlow, Leslie A. 1997. *Finding time: how corporations, individuals, and families can benefit from new work practices.* Ithaca, NY: Cornell University Press.

Pycior, Helena M., Nancy G. Slack, and Pnina G. Abir-Am, eds. 1996. *Creative couples in the sciences.* New Brunswick, NJ: Rutgers University Press.

Ruskin, John. [1865] 1998. *Sesame and lilies.* www.gutenberg.org/etext/1293

Salaff, Janet W. 2002. "Where home is the office: The new form of flexible work." In *The internet in everyday life,* ed. Barry Wellman and Caroline Haythornwaite, 464–95. Oxford: Blackwell.

Saxenian, Annalee. 1994. *Regional advantage: Culture and competition in Silicon Valley and Route 128.* Cambridge, MA: Harvard University Press.

———. 1996. Beyond boundaries: Open labor markets and learning in Silicon Valley. In *The boundaryless career: A new employment principle for a new organizational era,* ed. Michael B. Arthur and Denise M. Rousseau, 23–39. New York: Oxford University Press.

Scanzoni, John, Karen Polonko, Jay D. Teachman, and Linda Thompson. 1989. *The sexual bond: rethinking families and close relationships.* Newbury Park, CA: Sage.

Segalen, Martine. 1996. "The Industrial Revolution: From proletariat to bourgeoisie." In *A history of the family, volume II: The impact of modernity,* ed. Andre Burguiere, Christiane Klapisch-Zuber, Martine Segalen, and Francoise Zonabend, 377–415. Cambridge, MA: Harvard University Press.

Smith, Dorothy. 1987. "Women's inequality in the family." In *Families and work,* ed. Naomi Gerstel and Harriet Engel Gross, 23–54. Philadelphia: Temple University Press.

Stacey, Judith. 1996. *In the name of the family: Rethinking family values in the postmodern age.* Boston: Beacon Press.

Tilly, Louise, and Scott, Jason 1989. *Women, work, and family.* New York: Routledge.

Turkle, Sherry. 1995. *Life on the screen: Identity in the age of the internet.* New York: Simon & Schuster.

Winder, Gordon. 1995. "Before the corporation and mass production: the licensing regime in the manufacture of North American harvesting machinery, 1830–1910." *Annals of the Association of American Geographers* 85(3): 521–552.

Zussman, Robert. 1987. "Work and family in the new middle class." In *Families and Work,* ed. Naomi Gerstel and Harriet Engel Gross, 338–46. Philadelphia: Temple University Press.

# 4

# "We Pass the Baby Off at the Factory Gates"

## Work and Family in the Manufacturing Midwest

*Elizabeth Rudd and Lawrence S. Root*

During a brief tour of the loading dock at the "Sylvania" auto parts factory, I was introduced to the then-pregnant Maureen. The dock office, a glassed-in space within the big, windowless factory, had hardly a whisper of daylight to soften the dinginess. In the middle of the office was a long table mostly covered with piles of paper; on one end there was a roast, which people seemed to be sharing.[1] Learning that I was studying how people combine work and family, Maureen burst forth with her plan to get out of the factory and stay home with her children. She spoke approvingly of German cousins who had several years of maternity leave.[2] To the general agreement of co-workers, Maureen's supervisor countered that she had NO IDEA how good she had it at the plant. He had worked in other kinds of jobs, he noted, and anyone who had never worked "in the real world" just could not know how good they had it in the Sylvania parts plant. As if to make her supervisor's point, as I was leaving, Maureen was calling her school-aged son and could be heard throughout the office discussing his day with him. Some time later when I returned to the dock, she was on the phone instructing her son in detail about how to arrange pizza dinner with Grandma.

The "real world" Maureen's supervisor had referred to was the labor market outside the unionized sector of the auto industry. In that labor market the jobs available to many workers were low-paid and insecure. Sylvania workers, in contrast, were protected by the union contract negotiated between the United Auto Workers (UAW) and the "Big Three" car companies, Ford, General Motors (GM), and Daimler-Chrysler (formerly Chrysler). This contract guaranteed high wages, health insurance, retirement pensions, and job security. The economic security enjoyed by Sylvania workers was a legacy of the emergence of the blue-collar middle class after World War II. Economic growth and the global dominance of U.S. car companies in the 1950s and 1960s had created tens of thousands of jobs in manufacturing for men (and some women) with little education or job training. Because the UAW in the 1930s and 1940s had organized strong labor unions, workers shared in the spectacular success of the American auto companies and became members of an expanding blue-collar middle class—factory workers who earned enough to buy homes, send their children to college, enjoy a secure retirement, and, if they were men, support a stay-home wife at least for a while (Chinoy 1955, Dudley 1994, Milkman 1987, 1997).

Beginning in the 1970s, however, union jobs in manufacturing began disappearing from the United States. Jobs that offered economic security for less-skilled workers dwindled, leaving more and more people to struggle in the cold, hard "real world" of insecure, low-wage jobs with few or no benefits. Maureen and her co-workers knew people with jobs that did not pay enough to support a family, and some had been there themselves before landing a job at Sylvania. By 2000 global competition and direct challenges to union power in the U.S. auto industry had been steadily eroding the supply of union factory jobs for three decades (Bluestone and Harrison 1982, Farley, Danziger, and Holzer 2000). Union factory workers were acutely aware of their privileged situation. They were in the ambiguous position of being working class, while earning upper-middle-class incomes, at a time when it was becoming more and more difficult for anyone to find a job that provided economic security. This context of dwindling good jobs and economic insecurity framed the workers' commitment to factory work, and shaped how mothers like Maureen juggled demands of factory work and family life.

This chapter takes a close look at how Maureen and Jenny, two women who worked at the Sylvania auto parts plant, combined their jobs with their family responsibilities, and what working in the factory meant to them. Maureen, introduced earlier, is a young, white mother of three married to a white, working-class man. Jenny is a young, African American mother of four married to an African American man from a working-class family. The challenges Maureen and Jenny faced combining work and family are typical for Sylvania factory workers with young children. Their stories illustrate the grueling schedules factory workers embrace to support their families. To put the women's stories in context, we begin by describing the Sylvania parts plant. Then we depict Maureen's and Jenny's schedules in detail, before turning to the meanings of factory work for family life. Even though workers at Sylvania earned enough money to support middle-class family lives, being blue-collar still carried a social stigma. We explore this cultural contradiction of the blue-collar middle class by looking closely at how Maureen and Jenny struggled to reconcile the low social status of factory work with their self-identities as workers and mothers.

## WORK AND FAMILY IN AN AUTO PARTS PLANT

The auto parts plant we call "Sylvania" was the site of an ethnographic research project beginning in 2001 that investigated constraints on family life
imposed by the factory system and how workers viewed their work and family lives ("Sylvania" and all the names of individuals used in this chapter are
pseudonyms). The research involved observations at the plant and union
meetings, semi-structured interviews with a randomly selected sample of
fifty-two employees (including blue-collar workers and white-collar and
professional employees) and seven key informants, and participation in
union and factory events and meetings. We initiated this research, and the
evidence presented is drawn from interviews we conducted, participant observation by the second author on production lines, as well as two in-depth
studies of individual women workers conducted by the first author that included observations and multiple interviews.

## FIELD SITE "SYLVANIA"

Sylvania is located in the historical heart of the auto industry, southeast
Michigan. The factory is part of the regional economy described by Young
(this volume). It was built in the 1930s as part of a network of plants owned
by one of the "Big Three" car makers. It supplies components such as
starters, brakes, and ignition systems for cars and trucks. In the late 1990s
Sylvania's parent company spun off its parts plants, creating a new, independent corporation. Compared to assembly plants, where cars are put together into their final form, the parts sector of the auto industry generally
pays lower wages. By spinning off its parts plants, the parent company
hoped to lower its costs for parts and make these factories more competitive with independent parts manufacturers. This strategy has proven difficult. At the time of our research Sylvania's primary customer was still its parent company and the future of the factory was uncertain.

We chose Sylvania as a research site because it was one of a shrinking
number of plants of its kind—a union parts plant in North America, specifically in Michigan, the birthplace of the blue-collar middle class. After
lengthy negotiations with union leadership and management, they granted
us access to the plant and its workers. We were allowed to attend union
meetings, observe workers in the plant, and interview workers at the plant
on work time. This made it easier to schedule interviews, and the chance to
get paid for time off the assembly line was an incentive for some to participate in the study.

The manufacturing workforce in the United States has been steadily de-
creasing and Sylvania is an example. In its heyday the factory ran three shifts

and employed more than 3,000 workers. By 2001, when our research started, the plant had only two production shifts a day, employing about 1,000 hourly workers and 120 salaried employees. By the beginning of 2006 the plant employed only about 650 hourly workers. About three-quarters of the workforce are white, with most of the rest African American. About 20 percent are women.[3] Like other Big Three auto plants, few new workers were hired at Sylvania during the 1980s and early 1990s. Thus, the age distribution at Sylvania is bi-modal, with some younger workers who were hired in the last ten years, but mainly older workers who have worked in the auto industry for a long time. In 2006, more than one-third of the hourly workers were eligible for retirement.

Pay for union auto workers is high compared both to manufacturing and income generally. Based on a forty-hour work-week, workers at Sylvania would earn about $50,000 annually. Most Sylvania workers, however, earned much more by working overtime, which was paid at time and a half or double time (on Sundays and holidays).[4] The union contract limited mandatory overtime to nine hours a day, six days a week, for a total of fifty-four hours. Workers could not be required to work on Sundays or more than two Saturdays in a row. In some departments the fifty-four-hour week was the norm and many workers sought even more overtime to raise their take-home pay. During most of the period of our research, workers routinely earned over $70,000 a year and often as much as $100,000—over twice the $45,893 median *household* income in 2003–2004 (U.S. Census Bureau 2005). In addition, auto workers typically enjoy comprehensive health insurance and pensions, as well as supplemental unemployment benefits, dental care, vision care, and legal benefits. These benefits are under discussion, as the auto companies seek to reduce their employment costs in face of stiff competition from foreign automakers and independent parts suppliers. But the benefits at Sylvania remained substantially more generous than in most other jobs.

## WORKING IN THE PARTS PLANT

There were a variety of blue-collar jobs at Sylvania, including: keeping track of production inputs and outputs, keeping machinery in working order, cleaning machines, cleaning the factory, and performing quality control. Most workers, however, were involved in direct production and this activity was organized in a variety of ways. Production could take place on assembly lines, in which the pace of the line dictated the pace of each worker's task, or at individual work stations, where the worker might have more control over each task within the parameters of overall expectations for production output. Specific tasks usually had an expected cycle-time, such as six seconds, which was the basis of determining assembly-line speed and production goals. In some cases, several work stations were part of a team while others were freestanding operations, in which the output of an individual worker was the end product. On assembly lines, rows of workers sat along a moving conveyor belt putting pieces together as parts flowed by. In team production, workers moved between separate work stations. Still other production work was so fully automated that workers simply tended the machines, feeding in parts, removing the finished part, and making adjustments when necessary to keep the machine going.

Production workers mostly stayed in one place and they were under pressure to keep up with the assembly line or to produce enough parts to meet demand for the day. Breaks were allowed, but in some jobs workers had to wait for the relief worker to take over their position before they could leave their station. All the jobs were tedious and repetitive. An excerpt from the second author's field notes described his experiences working in production at Sylvania, in a job involving testing parts and correcting flaws.

> Day 1: My job was to take each bracket, thread a nut onto each of the three bolts and if it didn't go all the way on by hand, then to hand-thread a die to re-cut/clean up the threads. This job lasted for the full eight-hour shift. I checked 367 brackets. . . . That meant threading 1,101 bolts. . . . I am hoping that tomorrow I'll be assigned to a line job. . . . Day 2: My second day . . . started with my arrival at five forty-five a.m. Although I had hoped to have seen the last of my job of yesterday—testing the bolts on hundreds of . . . brackets . . . as it turned out I stayed on the screwing, unscrewing, correcting, and loading of . . . brackets. . . . Over the last forty-eight hours, I have tested over 2,200 bolts. I feel like Charlie Chaplin in *Modern Times*.

A subsequent work assignment presented the researcher with the challenge of keeping up with production goals. The job was inserting a spring into a rubber casing, placing it and an electrical head part onto a machine press, pushing a button to activate the press that joined the parts, and then tossing the completed part into a little chute to the conveyor belt. Then doing it all over again. Training for the job took less than ten minutes. The cycle-time was 7.2 seconds, so that a worker could, theoretically, complete 500 parts an hour. Excerpts from the researcher's field notes reflected his difficulties keeping up this pace. In his ten-hour day, he should have completed 5,000 parts but only achieved 2,468.

> 5:00 a.m.: I arrived about one or two minutes after five a.m.
> 6:00 a.m.: Starting to get the hang of it—upper back starting to get tight.
> 7:40 a.m.: I asked [the supervisor] when there were breaks and whether there was some water nearby. He said that the break was at eight and then went off.
> 8:00 a.m.: Break time—915 parts completed.

9:38 a.m.: Glancing resentfully at the young salaried guys, in their chinos and knit shirts who wander around making jokes among themselves—what are THEY producing!

10:45–11:30 a.m.: 1569 completed parts—breaking for lunch.

12:30 p.m.: 1830 parts completed . . . in the last hour I only did about 260.

1:30 p.m.: 2165 parts (335/hour, with some slowdowns because of machine problems).

3:10 p.m.: My final count is 2468 parts completed . . . [the supervisors] joked about my pace . . . said that it wasn't bad for the first day, but the next day, they would stand over me with a baseball bat to make sure I got my speed up. . . .

Keeping up the pace of production may be a challenge, but most jobs at the Sylvania parts plant were less physically demanding than jobs on an auto assembly line, jobs that require heavy lifting, working in awkward positions, or climbing in and out of cars.

## FAMILY WORK AND FACTORY LIFE

For younger workers at Sylvania, the problem of combining work and family loomed large, especially for women. The challenges faced by mothers like Maureen and Jenny are rooted in the legacies of industrialization and have been shaped by more recent changes in attitudes about working mothers. Industrialization separated work from home and brought with it the "cult of domesticity," an ideology that defined a mother who worked for pay outside the home as a bad mother and a disreputable woman (Matthaie 1982, Rothman 1978). This ideal held the most force for white women (Amott and Matthaie 1996). For instance, as Barnes (this volume) discusses, African Americans traditionally saw women working as a way to contribute to the advancement of their communities. Yet the ideal of the stay-home mother influenced the development of job structures in the auto industry. Jobs were designed for men who could leave family work to their wives. Reflecting the times—and his wish for his workers to conform to middle-class standards of living—Henry Ford (1863–1947) advocated the "family wage" for male workers.[5] In his 1922 autobiography, he wrote:

[The worker] is a householder. He is perhaps a father with children who must be reared to usefulness on what he is able to earn. We must reckon with all these facts. How are you going to figure the contribution of the home to the day's work? You pay the man for his work, but how much does that work owe to his home? How much to his position as a citizen? How much to his position as a father? The man does the work in the shop, but his wife does the work in the home. The shop must pay them both. (www.gutenberg.org/etext/7213).

By the end of the twentieth century talk of a "family wage" was a thing of the past. In the years following World War II, women's labor force participation rose rapidly, with 34 percent of women working in 1950 and 60 percent in 1998 (Fullerton 1999). Even upper-class women began to view working for pay as highly desirable, or simply natural. Changing attitudes about working mothers were captured in a 1998 survey that found that more than 80 percent of women felt that working mothers were as capable as stay-home mothers of having warm, supportive relationships with their children (Thornton and Young-DeMarco 2001). The expectation for middle-class mothers to work bolstered political attacks on Aid to Families with Dependent Children, a program that had supported poor, single mothers because they were caring for children. The welfare reforms of 1988 and 1996 redefined welfare mothers as failed breadwinners who needed jobs (Little 2002, Naples 1997).

Maureen's and Jenny's lives were shaped by the expectation that mothers should work. Both of them, for instance, were married to men who worked full time and wanted their wives to work full time as well. When Maureen became pregnant unexpectedly at nineteen, her father saw this as a reason for her to *start* working in the factory. Jenny also had her first child in her late teens, but with the help of her parents she finished college and got a job in a hospital social work department. When interviewed for this project, Jenny had four children and everyone in Jenny's family expected her to work, including herself, her husband, her parents, her in-laws, and her children. But the jobs that Maureen and Jenny held were still designed for men with stay-home wives. Older, blue-collar men at Sylvania often reported they had experienced no problems with childcare because their wives had been home with the kids. But younger workers—both men and women—with children at home at the time of our research were either single parents or had partners who also held full-time jobs. The time left over for family life was minimal.

Work at Sylvania both supported and challenged family responsibilities. The jobs there required long and sometimes unpredictable hours so the timing of production largely defined the parameters of life outside the factory. On the other hand, the high pay provided the resources needed to sustain a middle-class standard of living. Maureen's and Jenny's stories illustrate two common arrangements for married factory workers with children. Maureen and her husband, Danny, worked different shifts, which is a common arrangement among dual-earner couples, practiced by more than a quarter of dual-earner couples with children under age thirteen (Presser 2003). Jenny and her husband, Forrest, both worked day shifts, but their shifts did not overlap exactly. Forrest was also taking college classes in the evenings. The complex and constantly evolving arrangements for combining work and family that Maureen and Jenny described were typical among Sylvania workers caring for children.

## Maureen and Danny: We Pass the Baby Off at the Factory Gates

About a year after I met Maureen on the dock at Sylvania, I interviewed her at home about her maternity leave and return to work. She had returned to work shortly after the birth of her daughter, Jill. She was living with Danny, Jill, and Luke, her ten-year-old son, in a small house about a ten-minute drive from the plant. Maureen and Danny were engaged and planned to marry soon. They shared housework and childcare and they both worked in production jobs at the factory. Maureen worked the day shift and Danny worked the afternoon shift. Maureen and Danny earned enough money to afford quality childcare, but they preferred family care, and Maureen wanted Danny to share parenting. Danny worked ten-hour or twelve-hour days. His afternoon shift typically started around three or four p.m. and ended in the middle of the night, sometime between one and three a.m. He often worked six days and sometimes even seven days a week. Maureen worked the day shift, often six days a week. Because of their split shift schedule, Danny could take ten-year-old Luke to school in the mornings and look after the baby during the day, and Maureen could be home when Danny was at work. If Maureen ended her day shift around three p.m. as scheduled, she could be home when Luke got back from school.

To arrange this schedule, Maureen had given up her job on the loading dock and taken a much less desirable job on a production line. On the dock Maureen had been involved in keeping track of the movement of goods in and out of the plant. She had worked in an office and been able to move around freely. She had been able to call her son at home from her workspace. On the production line, she stayed at her station and did the same thing over and over again all day long. Maureen had moved to a production line because she had been "bumped" from her day shift on the dock by someone who had more "seniority," that is, more years working for the company. At Sylvania, as in most union plants, seniority was a key determinant in the assignment to jobs and shifts.[6] A dock worker on the afternoon shift with more seniority had asked to work on the day shift, so Maureen had been bumped to an afternoon shift. Danny had considered requesting a transfer to days, but he preferred the more relaxed atmosphere of afternoon shifts when fewer supervisors and managers were in the plant. So Maureen had applied to work the day shift on a production line making small engine parts. Many of the workers on this line had low seniority, so Maureen could "hold days." She was not in danger of being bumped to an afternoon shift by someone with more seniority.

Maureen's new job was on one of the more profitable production lines at the plant. Steady demand for the small parts it produced meant the line usually was working overtime. Under the union contract, workers could be required to work up to fifty-four hours a week, that is, up to nine hours a day, six days a week. At time and a half for overtime and double time for holidays, many workers were eager to work overtime. But Maureen was pregnant again and did not want to work more than eight hours a day. Maureen's doctor wrote a "work restriction" for her stating that to protect her health during the pregnancy Maureen should work no more than eight hours a day, five days a week, for a total of forty hours a week. Thus, Maureen's supervisor could not require her to work more than eight hours a day or forty hours a week. Maureen chose not to work more than eight hours a day, usually from about seven a.m. to three-thirty p.m., but she ignored the forty hours a week restriction and worked six days a week, for a total of forty-eight hours a week. Maureen and Danny had little time together.

On a typical day, Maureen got up around five a.m. She woke her ten-year-old son, Luke, and fed him breakfast before leaving for work at about six-forty-five a.m. She drove to the factory in Danny's car. After getting home between one and three a.m., Danny got up around eight a.m. to see Luke off to school, which was a few blocks from the house. Then Danny tried to sleep, but he could only sleep if the baby slept. Around three p.m. Danny strapped the baby into the car seat in Maureen's minivan and drove to the plant. Maureen waited at the factory gates to take the minivan and the baby home when Danny went to work. Later, Danny found his car where Maureen had parked it that morning. Danny worked from three-thirty p.m. to the end of his shift, but he came home for a lunch break between seven-fifty and eight-twenty p.m. Maureen went to bed between nine and ten p.m. and

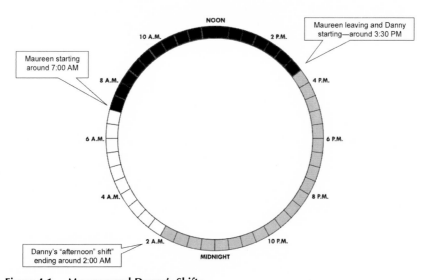

**Figure 4.1.   Maureen and Danny's Shifts**

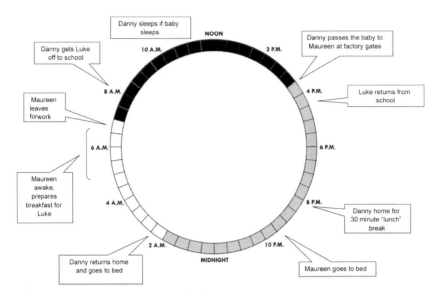

**Figure 4.2.    Maureen and Danny's Childcare**

Danny got home some time between one and three-thirty a.m. They followed this schedule six days a week. Danny often worked Sundays too.

Their schedule depended on Maureen and Danny getting particular jobs and shifts. Maureen needed to "hold days," but she also needed to be able to refuse overtime hours. Needing to hold days led her to take a job on a production line with mostly low-seniority workers, which, as it turned out, was also a production line with lots of overtime. Maureen could avoid overtime when working this particular line during her pregnancy because of the work restriction her doctor ordered. Maureen and Danny also depended on help from their extended families, including Maureen's parents and brother, and Danny's parents and brother. For instance, when Maureen first returned from maternity leave after Jill was born, she was erroneously scheduled for the midnight shift. Before this error was corrected, she had to work a week of midnights, starting work around eleven p.m. and getting home around eight a.m. With Danny working three-thirty p.m. to one a.m. (or longer) and Maureen working eleven p.m. to eight a.m., how could they cover those midnight hours? Danny's brother, a nurse, was working afternoons and got off work around eleven p.m. He agreed to stay at the house between the time when Maureen left for her midnight shift and when Danny got home from his afternoon shift.

Although their schedule was stressful and Maureen and Danny had little time together, the arrangement met two important goals for Maureen. It kept her children out of day care and made her husband share childcare. Maureen was adamant that her husband should be an equally involved parent. In discussions with her husband, she had used some of their friends as a bad example. These friends, Maureen explained, also worked split shifts—she worked days, and he worked afternoons—but they hired a babysitter during the days when she was at work even though he was home! This was Maureen's opportunity to drive her position home to Danny before they had a baby together, she explained, leaning forward and speaking rapidly: "I had told Danny, I said, I said, I will not allow that, I said . . . if you think that's a good plan, you need to let me know now 'cause I will not agree, I won't agree to it!" If Danny needed sleep, she noted, then they could bring someone in to look after the baby for a few hours now and then, but only as an emergency measure. She continued,

> . . . this whole idea that we're gonna have kids and I'm gonna be the number one person, I just dis, I disagree with it, I . . . guess I wouldn't consider myself a feminist, but I definitely believe in the feminist notion that it's not just the mother and you're [the father is] more than just the breadwinner.

### Jenny: I Have Four Hours to Do Homework and Dinner

Jenny was another hourly employee at the Sylvania parts plant. Her husband, Forrest, played a supportive role at home but was working and going to college, so Jenny was responsible for the household and children. Jenny worked as a "cleaner" rather than in a production job. Her job involved mopping twice a day in the areas where oil slicks formed, sweeping stairways and floors, cleaning grime and oil off tables and surfaces, cleaning the bathrooms and drinking fountains, scrubbing floors, placing "oil socks" around machines that leaked oil all day, as well as taking out garbage and cleaning out the industrial-sized trash compactor that served the whole factory. What with hoisting industrial strength mops and buckets of soapy water, carrying around oil socks and heavy brooms, scrubbing soaked-in oil and grime off wooden floors, and bending and crouching to clean fountains and bathrooms, Jenny's work was considerably more strenuous and physically demanding than production line work.

But Jenny preferred being a cleaner because the job was flexible and varied. When she started in the factory, she already knew she did not want to be on a production line. "I thought—I can't sit on the line and put a screw in—that was just all I knew," she remembered. As a cleaner Jenny was not chained to a production line. She was responsible for large areas of the factory and not directly supervised. She avoided the gossip and friction she felt would exist on a production line. She was also less likely to be required to work overtime. She could not work much overtime because she needed to be home for her children. She could not rely on her husband to take over if she got scheduled for overtime because he was working and taking classes in the evenings. "When I found out [about being pregnant]," she related, "I said,"

> I'm not gettin off clean-up, I'm gonna stay on clean-up because I still need the flexibility because I still have three other kids and a husband and a house and all that stuff, so I had just set in my mind that I would do whatever it took to continue to do my job [cleaning], as hard as it was on my body.

Jenny did worry about the danger of cleaners being outsourced. When I interviewed her, cleaners were UAW members covered by the UAW contract. If cleaners were outsourced, Sylvania would hire an outside company to clean the factory. The employees of the contractor would earn much less than the UAW workers and have limited or no benefits. If cleaners were outsourced, Jenny could lose her job or be moved to another plant, one in a location that made it impossible for her to combine her full-time job with caring for her family.

On the day I followed Jenny at work, I met her at the start of her shift at seven a.m. She began by emptying garbage cans, sweeping several areas of the factory, and picking up strewn-about debris, including cigarette butts. Then she filled up the "scrubber," a big machine shaped like a snowmobile with wheels, with a heavy-duty round scrubber on the front and, on the back, a squeegee and vacuum that sucked up the dirty water. She filled the scrubber up with water and added soap from an industrial-sized container, a three-foot by three-foot cube. As she pushed the scrubber forward, pressing down to keep the brush at the front tightly on the floor, the machine spewed clean, soapy water in front and sucked up the dirty water behind. After scrubbing for about an hour, Jenny mopped the floors. We had to find a mop and bucket, which she generally hid so that others would not appropriate them. She actually padlocked one mop bucket to a post. She also found it useful to hide oil socks in unused metal cabinets so that she would have them if they ran out at the supply room. Jenny wore gloves because everything in the factory was oily. Some time after ten a.m. Jenny noted that because she had removed immediate safety hazards—oil slicks—we could take a short break. At this morning break, she said, she often drinks tea and reads her Bible.

After a few more hours of scrubbing and cleaning we took a lunch break. Jenny described the onsite cafeteria as "too expensive and not very tasty." She had brought fresh carrots and strawberries, yogurt and a pre-packaged tuna fish sandwich. She and her friends in the factory had come to realize how important it was for their stamina and health to eat fresh, healthy foods. While we ate, a friend stopped by and invited Jenny to her wedding.

Jenny checked in with the day care provider to see if her baby's ear infection had flared again. Reassured that it had not, she went upstairs to the area designated for breast-pumping. (This lactation station was a policy of the parent company, instituted in response to activism by women engineers.) She returned happy with the eight ounces she had pumped despite difficulties relaxing enough to coax adequate milk letdown; she pumped again on her afternoon break. Later, another cleaner stopped by. He offered gossip about re-assignments among production superintendents and suggested that upcoming contract negotiations meant people should be "stacking away money," to be ready for a strike.

Jenny's schedule left little time for self or family. She depended on a combination of extended family and professional care givers, improvising on-the-fly when contingencies arose like a child's illness or changes in her husband's schedule. After getting up at four-thirty a.m., she fixed lunches and ate breakfast with her children, dropped her baby off at a family day care provider, took her school-aged sons to the bus stop, and left her toddler at a day care center near the factory, a day care center sponsored by a joint union-management initiative. She arrived at work about seven a.m. If Jenny worked an eight-hour shift, her work day ended at three-thirty p.m., but her two older boys got out of school before she could meet them. So, the oldest boy would meet his younger brother and together they would go to Jenny's mother's classroom. Jenny picked up the boys as soon as she could, and then she picked up the toddler and the baby. She got home around four or four-thirty p.m.

During the four hours between getting home and going to bed she made dinner, helped the boys with homework, and attended to household tasks like laundry, cleaning, and grocery shopping. Her boys helped out. In fact, she was not sure whether it actually eased her workload when her in-laws took the boys on a week's vacation to give Jenny a break. About her schedule, Jenny said, "At least I'm there in the evening to do homework and dinner and stuff." But she felt intense time pressure as she walked in the door after work with her children in tow. She gave herself a pep talk as they were getting out of the car and going into the apartment, telling herself she could do what needed to be done. ". . . I just hafta just, just okay, I get home, okay, it's four o'clock, I have FOUR hours, I can do this." Jenny tried to get to bed by eight-thirty p.m. She often put the younger children to bed, and then went to bed herself while her twelve-year-old stayed up a bit later.

When I first spoke with Jenny, her husband, Forrest, was working in a temporary position. Next time we spoke, he had been laid off. Consequently, Jenny started "hustling" to get overtime hours. She said her supervisor "knows I do a good job, [so] he got, arranged [overtime hours] for me." When she worked twelve-hour shifts, from seven a.m. to seven p.m., Forrest picked up the girls from day care. On days when he had class, the children went to Jenny's mother's house. Jenny's mother cooked dinner for the children and Jenny joined them later. If Forrest could not pick up the girls from day care, Jenny took her lunch break late in the day and used the time to pick up the children and put them to bed, then grab dinner from her mother and go back to work. If Jenny's overtime hours started before her usual starting time of seven a.m.—which was common in the plant—she would get up at two a.m. and go to work for several hours. She would then use her break time to go home, wake and feed the children, leave the boys with her mother or a neighbor, and drop the girls at day care before returning to work.

Despite Jenny's long and physically exhausting work days, her identity remained anchored in her family roles. She explained, "When I get home my real work starts."

## CONTRADICTIONS OF THE BLUE-COLLAR MIDDLE CLASS

In the next section of this chapter, we examine how Maureen and Jenny described the circumstances that led to working in the factory, and how they felt about holding blue-collar jobs. Like their co-workers, Maureen and Jenny valued the economic security provided by their jobs, but they were also acutely aware of the low social status of factory work. Workers made ironic comments about this and pointed to their high earnings to counteract the social stigma of being blue collar. "We jokingly called ourselves factory rats," Henry Sharpe, a skilled tradesman, reported, "because we viewed that other people viewed us that way." He continued: "It didn't bother me because the benefits were so good. The money was so good . . . if you worked all the overtime . . . we were making as much as the engineers." The high incomes earned in long hours of overtime work also countered social stigma for Dwayne Bateson and his wife. "One time my wife made a comment to one of her co-workers because she asked about my job title," Dwayne remembered, "She [Dwayne's wife] said, 'He doesn't have a title but he makes over $100,000 a year. Does that qualify?'"

Union wages enabled workers to take good care of their families, and this was a common justification for working in a blue-collar job at Sylvania. Despite its low social status, factory work enabled middle-class family lives, including home ownership, private schools, stay-home moms in some cases, help for children to go to college or start a business, and so on. Insecure and low-paid jobs without benefits, as Young (this volume) shows, interfere with parenting without providing enough money to sustain a family. Although factory work left little time for family life, union jobs offered families economic security, and factory workers at Sylvania found that their jobs supported their families very well.

Kathie Mannheim, for instance, a forty-seven-year-old single mother of two, had worked in low-skilled service jobs for many years while taking care of her daughter and autistic son. When she started working at Sylvania, her children were old enough to be left alone, so childcare was not a problem. She knew that she and her kids would never again have to sleep wrapped up in blankets together because she lacked the money to pay the heating bill. She was able to buy a house. She felt that her work in the factory had "never really interfered with my family life so much, as I was able to give them [her children] more." Ben Boxer, a twenty-six-year-old married father of a four-year-old, took a job at Sylvania so he could take care of his son: "I have a—at the time I hired in, I had a son. So to take care of me and him, insurance and things like that. At that point I kinda thought it'd be a good idea." He explained further: "So that way [working at Sylvania] I knew if he—my son—ever got sick or anything, he'd always be taken care of, and myself too."

Maureen and Jenny shared their co-workers' feelings about the value of union jobs for supporting middle-class family lives, and they also felt the stigma of factory work. As they talked about getting their jobs at Sylvania and how they felt about working in a factory, both women articulated what they saw as important social differences between blue- and white-collar workers. Yet they also revealed different ways of understanding their situations as blue-collar mothers. Maureen focused on her identity as a worker, while Jenny's concerns revolved around her identity as a mother.

## Maureen: "I Don't Like Being Blue-Collar"

Maureen drew a bold picture of differences between the white-collar and blue-collar worlds as she spoke about how she started working in a factory and why she wanted to leave. Blue-collar workers, according to Maureen, were not as smart, educated, or into reading and school; they were often rude and uncouth; they had low social status; and their work was meaningful to them only as a means to make more money. The physical layout of the Sylvania plant mapped Maureen's ideas of class differences. The offices for white-collar employees were on the floors *above* the production areas. Here the offices had windows and the people wore shirts and slacks; women sometimes wore skirts and pumps. In the production areas, safety glasses were required; men often wore jeans and t-shirts or coveralls, while women often wore sweat suits and athletic shoes. Production areas were dark and dingy and there were no windows to the outside world. In the plant, the differences in lighting and atmosphere and the practice of donning safety glasses upon leaving the white-collar areas and entering the production floor ritualized the distinction between blue- and white-collar worlds.

Maureen viewed the white-collar world as better and she identified herself with it in several ways. She mentioned several times that she had earned a scholarship to college. She described herself as a "serious, avid reader," referring to her "dozen Rubbermaid tubs full of books," and that she loved to read for fun. Furthermore, Maureen related that she had started working in the factory as a means to finish college, noting that her employer offered educational benefits, including tuition assistance. Even her co-workers could see that she did not really belong in the blue-collar world, she noted. "I've actually had people say to me that I work with, 'You're so intelligent, what are you doing here?'" She also valued education highly, saying:

> Like maybe some people . . . when they look at a Lexus, they're like ooooooooooooh so-and-so drives a Lexus—Me, I'm just like, well, they drive a Honda, but ooooooooooooooh they have a Ph.D.

For a while Maureen's job had put her in close contact with white-collar workers who worked upstairs in the plant. She used her personal experiences to define differences between "blue-collared" and "white-collared" worlds. For instance, she said that professional and other white-collar workers in the plant had made her feel they could relate to her pregnancy. But on the production floor, she felt the comments offered were impersonal or rude. People said things like, "How are you feeling?" or "You didn't have that baby yet?" She remembered,

> I actually had a woman who asked me, "Are both a yer children by the same husband?" . . . I couldn't even believe it that the lady had asked me that! . . . And it's different because when I talk to the people that I still talk to occasionally on the white-collared side, they don't ask questions like that.

Maureen explicitly rejected identification with the blue-collar world. She explained:

> I personally . . . don't like being blue-collar, it's a problem for me . . . I don't have a problem with Danny [her husband] . . . if I finished school and I was white-collar I would not *not* speak to him—but for me personally, for my own self-esteem, I do have a problem and I don't . . . like it [being blue-collar].

She expressed her sense of shame with an ironic aside, posing the question: "What do I say when people say 'What do you do'?" She then answered herself in a mock whisper that suggested she was imparting a dirty secret: "I'm a college drop-out, and now I'm blue-collar."

Going into the factory when she did, Maureen explained, had been a form of selling out. She had gone "for the dollars," instead of using her brain. She hoped, in fact, to quit her job and go back to school, but Danny was skeptical. She described their impasse.

> He says, "Okay, Maureen, so yer gonna go to school, do you know what you wanna do?" "No, not really" . . . He said, "All right, so yer gonna go to school, yer gonna take these four, five, six years, however long it's going to take you and then what?" And I said, "Well, then maybe I'll get a teaching job?" And he says "And then yer gonna make what? Eighteen thousand dollars a year? . . . down from . . . seventy, eighty thousand dollars . . . "

"And," Maureen concluded, "that's how he looks at it, he doesn't look at it as I personally need that, I look at it as a self-esteem issue for me."

Maureen emphasized as well that she and Danny hardly had any time together or with the children, and that if one of them quit working, their everyday lives would be easier and more satisfying. To gain more family time, she noted, it could be Danny who stayed home. She had even suggested that to him, pointing out that at the plant they have equal pay for equal work, so that she could make as much money as he could. "But," she reported, "he said, 'I'd go crazy, I couldn't stay home all day long.'"

In sum, Maureen had little basis for getting Danny to support her desire to quit the factory and go back to school. She could not appeal to his investment in a traditional gender division of labor. Maureen wanted her partner to share fully in parenting and Danny wanted to be an involved father. Likewise, Danny expected Maureen to earn a substantial portion of the family income. While men in an earlier generation would have found the notion of a stay-home wife attractive, for Maureen and Danny's generation this was not the case. Even women in middle-class and professional families were no longer staying home but were pursuing careers. Indeed, Maureen did not want to be a stay-home wife and mother. She wanted to go back to college and become a *white-collar* working mother.

### Jenny: "It Just Depends on Everybody's Needs"

Jenny also struggled with the low social status of factory work. She focused on differences between blue- and white-collar worlds in family lifestyles, in particular on the role of mothers. At different points throughout our discussions she drew comparisons between the values with which her husband was raised in a family of factory workers, and the values that her parents, a teacher and a social worker, transmitted to her. She felt that his (blue-collar) family had placed too much value on money, and not enough on supervision and education. Although her husband and his siblings had had a "telephone in every room" (in Jenny's view a pointless thing), her own (white-collar) parents had "made life good for us on a teacher's and a social worker's salary."

Before Jenny started factory work she had already earned a bachelor's degree in social work and married Forrest. When Jenny learned she could get a job at Sylvania, she was initially reluctant for several reasons, all of which related to her identity as a woman and mother. She characterized the factory as masculine, and probably not a good place for a woman. Her husband had expressed reservations about her working at Sylvania based on his own experiences in factory work, and "because of the way guys can be." Jenny's mother recalled touring a factory once and being disturbed by catcalls from the production floor. Jenny also mentioned conflicts she had had with men while working in the factory. Jenny's gendering of the factory as masculine was reasonable considering the proportion of women in the auto industry historically has hovered around 15 percent or less (Milkman 1987, 1997), and at Sylvania the workforce was about 80 percent male. However, Jenny's view was not inevitable. Maureen, for example, seemed to view the factory as a place with gender equality. She never mentioned any conflicts with men at work. She did not report feeling uncomfortable about being a woman in the factory. And she emphasized that "in the factory we have equal pay for equal work," a situation she contrasted to the outside world in which women earned fifty-nine cents for every dollar a man earned.

Jenny worried that factory work would interfere with her capacity to be a good mother. She did not want her children to be raised the way her husband had been raised. Both of his parents had worked in the factory and they had made a lot of money. But in Jenny's view her husband "didn't have a mother." She said,

> My husband grew up with parents who worked at GM and Ford, so he had no parental supervision—they were at work or asleep . . . I want to tell her what a disservice she did them—they were hands-off parents, and so my husband barely graduated from high school because he had no supervision.

Further, she noted she had learned a different work ethic. About her husband she said, "If he doesn't feel good, he'll come home early." In contrast, she said,

> For me, the rule is, and this is just how I grew up, if you don't have diarrhea or yer not throwin' up and you go into work, you stay or you go show yer face at least and then if you just can't make it cause you got a migraine or something, THEN you come home. And he doesn't push hisself like that, soooo I don't know if that's a good or bad thing.

Paradoxically, the factory job that threatened her ability to be as involved in her children's lives as she wanted to be provided her with the financial resources for taking care of her family in other important ways. In particular, Jenny and her husband were shopping for a house. They were able to buy largely on the strength of Jenny's income. Jenny said, "Y'know my son, Allan, he says, Moooooom, we prob'ly won't have a house 'til I get ready ta graduate!" For Jenny this observation was a motivation to work.

> I'm glad that he says stuff like that, 'cause it keeps me motivated, THAT brings me in at three o'clock in the morning, because I DON'T want him to NOT have, I, y'know, I had a house, I never lived in an apartment, my parents, my Dad . . . had been in the military and been to school and was still pursuing his education and she [Jenny's mother] moved into a house that my Dad had.

Despite her initial reservations about taking the factory job, Jenny said,

> But I AM so grateful for my job, because . . . the benefits ALONE and the income, it's steady, I know it's there, I can count on it, so I, we are just so blessed that at least THAT we can count on.

Jenny's discomfort with being a factory worker stemmed from her feeling that women did not really belong in the factory. She was not sure that a factory was a good place for a woman, and she worried that the job might threaten her ability to fulfill her notions of good mothering. The difference between the blue- and white-collar worlds was as important for her as it was for Maureen, but she distinguished them differently. Jenny saw differences in childrearing—and more particularly, mothering—between her own family and her husband's family of origin. In her (white-collar) family, supervision, education, and a good work ethic were important. In her husband's (blue-collar) family, she suggested, there was not enough emphasis on care and supervision and too much importance on having things, often meaningless things, like a telephone for each child. Nonetheless, Jenny accepted working in the factory as a way to help meet the needs of each of her family members. She wanted her children to live in a house she owned. She wanted her husband to finish college. Whether or not she pursued her own dream of becoming a nurse, she explained, "just depends on everybody's needs."

## After the Blue-Collar Middle Class

Maureen and Danny agreed that both should be involved parents and both should earn a substantial portion of family income. Jenny, too, although she was less adamant about having her husband share childcare responsibilities, wanted to work full time and contribute to her family financially. As an African American family, Jenny and Forrest's arrangements reflected greater continuity with historical family roles of African American women. Maureen and Danny's arrangements reflected shifts in family values among whites that have moved away from valorizing a strict division of labor that keeps women in the home and men at work. The "cult of domesticity" with its ideal of feminine identity anchored in homemaking and raising children has been laid to rest. Today even middle-class and upper middle-class women want to work for pay and often work full time. Women's labor force participation increased after WWII, and since 1970 the work rates of mothers of young children have risen most rapidly (Fullerton 1999, Hayghe 1997). There is little political support for welfare programs designed to help mothers of young children stay home to care for their infants and toddlers.

With most mothers working, jobs based on the notion of male breadwinners with stay-home wives do not fit families today. Yet, at Sylvania, as in other factories, shifting production schedules, unpredictable overtime, and job assignment based on seniority tightly constrained workers' family involvements. Workers could make only small adjustments within the factory system. Jenny, for example, avoided overtime, until her husband got laid off, and she shifted some of the family work to him and to her mother so that she could work ten or twelve hour days six days a week to make up for his lost earnings. Maureen moved to a tedious job on an assembly line to stay on days so that she and Danny could take turns being home with their baby. Coming home was very stressful for Jenny because she had just four hours to feed the children, help with homework, get chores like shopping and laundry done, and put the children to bed before she went to bed. Most of the time that Danny and Maureen were together was spent sleeping.

Jenny's stress and Danny and Maureen's sleeping relationship were partly due to work schedules that minimized family life, but also due to a labor market that offered few attractive alternatives. Despite the physical demands of their tedious jobs, their chronic lack of sleep and harried family lives, Maureen and Jenny and their co-workers were lucky to have union manufacturing jobs. Despite the stigma of factory work, and the lack of opportunities for self-development or advancement in production work, their jobs supported a comfortable, middle-class standard of living. They could afford to buy homes and take good care of their kids; they had health insurance and pensions, and they earned enough to save for retirement. They were among a small and dwindling group of workers in union manufacturing jobs.

In a process known as "deindustrialization," manufacturing jobs as a proportion of all U.S. jobs have been declining steadily for decades. In 1960, manufacturing accounted for 31 percent of all non-agricultural jobs in the United States (Jacobs 1998), a proportion that had declined in 2000 to 14.6 percent and in 2004 to 12 percent (U.S. Census Bureau 2006a). The Sylvania parts plant reflected this decline. Its workforce fell during the course of our research from 1,000 to 650 hourly workers and the future of the factory itself was in doubt. Workers left through transfer, retirement, and buy-outs. Similarly, union membership is declining. In the early 1980s almost one out of four workers were covered by a union contract, but in 2004 union contracts covered only 13.8 percent of workers (U.S. Census Bureau 2006b). As the factories leave regions with a history of strong unions, the jobs that do not require specific training or credentials but still pay well enough to support a middle-class family life also disappear. For workers in the manufacturing Midwest, and especially for workers with less education, labor market alternatives to union factory work are bleak.

Workers who participated in our study were acutely aware of the difficulty of finding jobs that support a family well. Before working in the factory, Jenny held a job in a hospital that paid much less than her job at Sylvania. Maureen knew that becoming a teacher would mean a significant drop in income. Other respondents had worked in retail stores for low pay and no health insurance, in hospitals and schools in very stressful environments for low wages and minimal benefits, and in non-union factories for half the pay and sometimes in unsafe conditions. Low-income workers often have the worst of both worlds: Their jobs interfere with caring for family members but nevertheless do not pay enough to sustain a family materially (Chaudry 2004, Young this volume).

Maureen's and Jenny's situations were typical of Sylvania workers with young children. Their stories show that a high income does not in itself ameliorate the impact of working very long hours on families. Even workers who earn well above the median family income are so tightly squeezed that they barely have time to see their spouses and their children. This situation indicates that the future well-being of American families will depend on reorganizing the time demands of jobs to help both men and women take care of their families, while also earning enough to support their families financially. At the same time the proliferation of jobs that neither support a family materially nor allow adequate time for caregiving suggests that the future well-being of American families will also depend on redistributing wealth to better support the working class. In the United States, many of the social supports that characterize public policies in other developed countries have been left to individuals, families, and the workplace. In the face of increasing global competition and the wholesale loss of manufacturing jobs, we need to revisit our basic assumptions about how to address the inherent tensions between work requirements and family lives.

## AFTERWORD

The hardest thing about this research was getting up so early. To observe a full day shift on the production line Maureen worked on, for instance, I had to arrive at the factory by five a.m. (and I ended up staying until five p.m.). A few days in advance of early appointments I would try to switch over to a schedule like Jenny's—going to bed before nine p.m. and getting up before five in the morning. But when I arrived at Maureen's production line her supervisor was already marking down stragglers as "late" (workers' time was tracked in six-minute increments). At one seven a.m. interview, my respondent was worried that I wasn't quite awake and kindly insisted on buying me coffee before we started talking. This was how I learned about the skilled tradesmen selling coffee in the factory. We had to schedule a few interviews before seven a.m. to catch people coming off the night shift or before they started early day shifts, and I let my co-author do those.

As a sociologist doing qualitative fieldwork, I'd like to be a welcome guest and an exceptionally good listener. I think it means people are more likely to explain to me "obvious" things that "everybody" knows, so I don't mind being seen as somewhat ignorant and maybe a little naïve about the topics under study. In the factory in Michigan, this was easy and a role I felt comfortable with. I was an outsider in so many ways. I had never worked in a factory. I had no children. I was a woman from the university. I was from the West Coast. I obviously wasn't used to factory work schedules. My previous research had been in Germany.

My sociological interests in Sylvania grew out of my dissertation, which investigated problems of combining work and family in German postsocialism. Studying how people coped with capitalism in formerly socialist Germany led to my interest in how people conceptualize and make sense of trade-offs between work and family lives. As socialism collapsed, I learned, economic security gave way to rising stratification and economic insecurity. These experiences changed the way people balanced work and family lives, making it harder to place a high priority on family caregiving and more urgent to place a very high priority on keeping a job. Pressures to put work first at Sylvania, it turned out, were enormously stronger than anything I had come across in my research in Germany. This, I think, is partly due to the more extreme forms of social inequality in the United States today.
—Elizabeth Rudd

I always experience a sense of trepidation when entering a new field site. How will I be perceived as an outsider? Will I be seen as a voyeur? Will my presence engender self-consciousness or embarrassment? Early visits to the union hall had all of these elements, combined with the potential of class tensions. As a "professor," will I look down on those with less education? Workers sometimes refer to themselves as "factory rats." I take this as a self-deprecatory way of "beating you to the punch"—so that *you* know that *they* know how others may view them. For my part, I want to be seen as a "regular guy," not an aloof academic who puts people into categories rather than listening to what they have to say. In a factory setting, a political element is added. Management wonders whether the research will make the plant look good or look bad. Union leaders have the same thoughts plus concern that their cooperation might hurt them in the next union election.

But these initial issues soon fade into the background. Like dogs that have sniffed and accepted each other, the field researcher becomes a more or less normal part of the environment and, perhaps, a welcome break from humdrum routines. For most respondents, a researcher interested in them and their work provides a kind of validation. Most enjoy the opportunity to reflect on their lives, their experiences, their perspectives. At Sylvania, workers are often proud of their place in the economic order.

But the future of the plant is in doubt. At the beginning of our research, workers often remarked that there have always been rumors that the plant was going to close, but twenty years later, it was still there. Toward the end of our time in the field, we no longer heard such reassuring comments. Now the talk is of buyouts, transfers, and job loss—and the end of an era.
—Lawrence S. Root

## NOTES

This research was supported by funding from the Center for the Ethnography of Everyday Life, one of the Alfred P. Sloan Foundation's centers on working families. The authors thank the plant management and the local union for permission to attend meetings and spend time in the factory, as well as their assistance contacting and scheduling workers for interviews. We are especially indebted to the people from the factory we call "Sylvania" who generously shared with us their knowledge, their perspectives, and their daily lives.

1. Later I learned that the woman who brought the roast was selling pieces to co-workers. The roast certainly looked more appetizing than anything in the cafeteria, which also had limited hours. Selling food and drink was a lucrative sideline in the factory. One group of skilled tradesmen sold coffee. Another group sold snacks, keeping large inventories in metal cabinets near their workspaces.

2. Actually at that time German women got fourteen weeks of paid maternity leave by law. The legally allowable three years of family care leave (available to both parents to share) was remunerated on a means-tested basis only. Although a leave-taker was supposed to be able to return to her job after three years, the law allowed the company to restructure the job out of existence in the meantime (Helwig and Nickel 1993).

3. Official data were not available. These are estimates based on review of union membership lists and observations in the plant.

4. Overtime is a topic of central importance in the factory, see Rudd, Root, and Young (2002).

5. Henry Ford founded the Ford Motor Company and, beginning in the early 1900s, pioneered the use of mass-production techniques.

6. At Sylvania workers had a chance to move quarterly. They could only move to jobs for which they were qualified and supervisors could reject an application.

# REFERENCES

Amott, Teresa, and Julie Matthaei. 1996. *Race, gender, and work: A multi-cultural economic history of women in the United States*. Boston: South End Press.

Barnes, Riché. This volume. "Black women have always worked: Is there a work-family conflict among the black middle class?"

Bluestone, Barry, and Bennett Harrison. 1982. *The deindustrialization of America*. New York: Basic Books, Inc.

Chaudry, Ajay. 2004. *Putting children first*. New York: Russell Sage Foundation.

Chinoy, Ely. 1955. *Automobile workers and the American dream*. Boston: Beacon Press.

Dudley, Kathryn M. 1994. *The end of the line: Lost jobs, new lives in postindustrial America*. Chicago and London: University of Chicago Press.

Farley, Reynolds, Sheldon Danziger, and Harry J. Holzer. 2000. *Detroit divided*. New York: Russell Sage Foundation.

Ford, Henry. 1922. "My life and work." Accessed at www.gutenberg.org/etext/7213.

Fullerton, Howard N. 1999. "Labor force participation: 75 years of change, 1950–1998 and 1998–2025." *Monthly Labor Review* December: 3–12.

Hayghe, Howard V. 1997. Developments in women's labor force participation. *Monthly Labor Review* September: 41–6.

Helwig, Gisela, and Hildegard Maria Nickel, eds. 1993. *Frauen in Deutschland 1945–1992*. Berlin: Akademie Verlag.

Jacobs, Eva E. ed. 1998. *Handbook of labor statistics* (2nd edition). Lanham, MD: Bernan Press.

Little, Debra. 2002. "'But they're helping us because we're taking care of kids': Struggles over need at welfare's end." Paper presented at the Qualitative Research Forum, University of Michigan, Institute for Social Research, November 21, 2002, Ann Arbor, Michigan.

Matthaei, Julie A. 1982. *An economic history of women in America: Women's work, the sexual division of labor, and the development of capitalism*. New York: Schocken Books.

Milkman, Ruth. 1987. *Gender at work*. Urbana, IL: University of Illinois Press.

———. 1997. *Farewell to the factory*. Urbana, IL: University of Illinois Press.

Naples, Nancy A. 1997. "The 'new consensus' on the gendered 'social contract': the 1987-1988 U.S. Congressional hearings on welfare reform." *Signs: Journal of Women in Culture and Society* 22 (4): 907–45.

Presser, Harriet. 2003. *Working in a 24/7 economy*. New York: Russell Sage Foundation.

Rothman, Sheila M. 1978. *Woman's proper place: A history of changing ideals and practices, 1870 to the present*. New York: Basic Books, Inc.

Rudd, Elizabeth, Lawrence S. Root, and Alford Young, Jr. 2002. "The taste of overtime." CEEL Working Paper 040-02, Ann Arbor, MI: Center for the Ethnography of Everyday Life, University of Michigan.

Thornton, Arland, and Linda Young-DeMarco. 2001. "Four decades of trends in attitudes toward family issues in the United States: The 1960s through the 1990s." *Journal of Marriage and Family* 63:1009–37.

U.S. Census Bureau 2005. "Two-year-average median household income by state: 2003-2005." Accessed at www.census.gov/hhes/www/income/income05/ statemhi2.html.

——. 2006a. *Statistical abstract of the United States 2006.* Table 608.

——. 2006b. *Statistical abstract of the United States 2006.* Table 649.

Young, Alford, Jr. This volume. "The work-family divide for low-income African Americans."

# 5

## The Work-Family Divide for Low-Income African Americans

*Alford A. Young, Jr.*

The pressures resulting from the often-conflicting demands and expectations of the workplace and the household affect people across the socioeconomic divides in American society. For white-collar professional families these pressures appear as mother and fathers struggle to commit to the long and often tedious hours necessary for success, if not survival, in the modern business world (Bailyn 1993, Blair-Loy 2005, Hochschild 1997, Perlow 1997, Presser 2003). Households in this category may be quite secure in terms of the degree to which a spacious home, modern appliances, and expensive cars have been acquired. However, what is at stake in continuing to face the pressures of balancing work and family demands is preserving and enhancing one's status at work, or putting forth the kind of hours and work performances that ensure promotion, power, and influence in the workplace. Hence, despite having the means to a relatively good life at home, the steep climb of that corporate ladder means confronting and carefully balancing time committed to work with that given to family.

For working-class families (consisting of parents or adults that work in skilled or semi-skilled employment capacities and who bring home consistent wages and fringe benefits) the quest to balance both demands is pursued, in part, for the same reasons that pertain to white-collar professional families. For members of these families, promotion, power, and influence at work are equally important. However, adult members of these working-class families also are considerably more focused than are professional-class members on success at work leading to the capacity to advance the socioeconomic standing of the family. This advance enables these families to acquire some of the accouterments and resources that delineate white-collar professional life, otherwise known as the "good life" (Chaudry 2004, Heymann 2000).[1]

For many low-income families, however, a different sort of relationship between work and family comes to surface. At the top end, these families include people who are marginally connected to secure employment. They may make hourly wages at or near the legally mandated minimum of $5.15 per hour, or work in jobs that do not provide health or other benefits, nor retirement plans. Of course, those low-income families consisting of adults who maintain steady employment may function much like working-class families. At the bottom end, however, are families that have no secure or consistent connection to the world of work. Hence, their primary challenge is to immerse themselves into that world so that the basic needs and interests of family members—daily meals, clothing, and shelter—can be met. In looking carefully at how such adults think about the world of work and work opportunity, the emphasis falls on how these people make sense of work prospects that may allow them to meet basic needs (even if those work prospects appear to be distant or dim given their circumstances), how they evaluate them as meaningful or relevant to their lives and family life situations, and how they conceive of the means of access or entry into such work opportunities. Accordingly, this chapter will look at the work-family relationship as it pertains to three issues relevant to low-income families whose adult members remain at the margins of the world of work. The first is their vision of the quality of family life in their communities. The second is their sense of the quality of employment prospects available to them. The third is how their status as parents affects and inspires their approach to job-seeking and maintaining employment. Included here is attention to what they will not pursue or commit to (at least not for very long) in the world of work and why they feel as they do.

Each of these issues will be examined in an illustrative manner. That is, this chapter will not offer conclusive or theoretically saturated arguments about any of these matters. Instead, the objective here is to provide some portraits of how each domain of concern is addressed by people who do not directly engage the tensions of the work-family divide in the ways that white-collar professional parents, or those in highly skilled and stable working-class occupations, do. Instead, these people struggle to find secure and materially rewarding work opportunities that allow them to maintain a consistent and meaningful daily presence in their children's lives. Consequently, because the individuals discussed in the following pages are so tenuously linked to work, they constitute a unique category of actors in the larger discussion of the tensions between commitments to work and to family in American society. The unique quality of their situation is that rather than face the kind of work-family divide experienced by more privileged families, they must balance family demands with the challenge of trying to find secure work. Consequently, family demands often alter, if not corrupt all together, the project of finding and maintaining secure employment. The core point of inquiry for these kinds of families, then, is how the best possible work prospects can be conceived of and pursued while parents strive to serve the interests of their families and maintain households that are healthy, and emotionally and socially secure.

## SMALL-CITY, LOW-INCOME AFRICAN AMERICANS

In order to draw out with sufficient depth and detail the kinds of views offered by low-income African Americans this chapter will focus on four individuals who represent particular social types of disadvantaged African Americans. These four illustrative cases are from Ypsilanti, Michigan, which is a small city located approximately twenty-five miles from downtown Detroit. Its residential population consists of 22,362 people, of which 6,838, or about 31 percent, are African American. Its population base also is largely low-income or working-class, meaning that many of its residents who are in stable employment work in blue-collar sectors, retail, or lower-skilled service delivery. Others simply function without regular work opportunities.

Ypsilanti is separated from its larger neighbor, Detroit, by a series of small towns that constitute Detroit's western suburban core. Throughout the early and middle part of the twentieth century, Ypsilanti, like much of Michigan, benefitted from the manufacturing plants established by the major American automobile manufacturers, the Ford Motor Company, the Chrysler Corporation (which became the DaimlerChrysler Corporation in 1998), and the General Motors Corporation. Ypsilanti residents benefitted from the proliferation of manufacturing plants in or nearby the city. In fact, Ford's Willow Run Bomber Plant, located immediately north of Ypsilanti, was built for the creation of the B-24 bomber used in World War II and employed over 100,000 people in the 1940s. It was during the middle of the twentieth century that migrants from the South and the Appalachian region came to Ypsilanti and its surrounding communities in order to cement themselves in secure blue-collar work in the automobile industry.

Sixty years later there exists no manufacturing sector of this magnitude in Ypsilanti. Consequently, rather than being an economically vibrant small city, Ypsilanti has come to appear as a small city that strives to become vibrant once again. According to 2000 measures 4,767 people, or 26 percent of the population of Ypsilanti, whose income status could be determined by the U.S. Census Bureau (which is 18,507 of Ypsilanti's approximately 22,362 people), were living below the poverty level (U.S. Census Bureau 2000). Additionally, the median household income for the year 2000 (measured in 1999 dollars) was $28,610 and 24 percent of the households in Ypsilanti (2,054 households) functioned at or below poverty (Southeast Michigan Council of Governments 2006).

As is the case for much of southeastern Michigan, the residents of Ypsilanti, especially its low-income and working-class segments, have been affected by the economic transformations that have impacted Detroit. Ypsilanti has often served as a feeder community for employment in that municipality. Hence, Ypsilanti's fortune resembles that of its larger eastern neighbor. Ypsilanti is separated from Detroit by a small number of suburbs that largely consist of working-class individuals and families (almost all of Detroit's more privileged suburbs are north and south of the line connecting Ypsilanti to Detroit). As has been well-documented in prior research, the city of Detroit and the surrounding communities have been severely impacted by job loss and socioeconomic despair (Farley, Danziger, and Holzer 2000, Sugrue 1996). The declining employment opportunities in the auto industry have been pivotal factors in this unfolding.[2] The socio-economic decline experienced by central Detroit residents has affected the residents of Ypsilanti. Consequently, many residents of this town—especially people like those who are the focus of this analysis—have been trapped in and are fluctuating between unstable working-class status and poverty. As Ypsilanti is within a thirty- to forty-minute drive of downtown Detroit, its residents are affected by the diminishing employment opportunities in the Detroit metropolitan area.

To the west of Ypsilanti is the city of Ann Arbor, Michigan (population 114,000), home of the University of Michigan, and one of the most liveable cities in America, according to a popular magazine that focuses on economic and quality of life issues (CNNMoney.com 2006). The spacious parks, and numerous research and development firms located throughout Ann Arbor, offer a contrast to much of Ypsilanti, which maintains a considerably smaller downtown region, housing of lesser quality than available in Ann Arbor (except for select neighborhoods, many of which are mostly located on the western edge of Ypsilanti, close to Ann Arbor), and a sequence of census tracts just south of the downtown area that are populated by low-income African Americans who live in public housing or somewhat dilapidated homes. As Ypsilanti and Ann Arbor share a public transportation system, access to the latter is much easier than to Detroit. Yet, the research project that this chapter draws from indicates that Detroit's blue-collar manufacturing-sector image fits much better with what Ypsilanti's low-income African Americans understand to be the kind of work milieu that is most appropriate for them.[3] For that reason, Detroit consistently looms in the background of what many low-income African American residents of Ypsilanti have to say about the world of work and work opportunity.

## A PORTRAIT OF FOUR LOW-INCOME AFRICAN AMERICANS

The men and women introduced in the following pages were participants in a research project that aimed to counter the paucity of information about how African Americans conceive of the world of work and how they believe that people navigate that environment. It came together because there has been little effort to document more broadly how these individuals conceptualize the occupational sphere in American life, including the types of jobs that may be available in specific geographical contexts, or the relevant skills and capacities needed to find and perform in such occupational milieux. Instead, prior research on this population tends to focus on the specific jobs that do or do not appeal to lower-income African Americans, and the types of benefits they desire from work. In pursuing these issues the larger project involves documenting what they consider to be "good" jobs in American society (including why they hold those views, and what they understand to be the means of accessing these jobs), what they believe is accessible work for African Americans of their class standing (including how those beliefs compare with their ideas about good jobs in American society), their sense of their own work ethic (including how that compares with their vision of the general work ethic in American society), their assessment of their own skills and resources relevant to finding good work, and their understanding of how to employ those skills and resources in order to find such work.[4]

It has especially been the case that issues concerning how African American low-income individuals conceptualize the world of work have gone unexplored within the context of individuals who reside in small cities. Much of the story concerning the socioeconomic tribulations of black Americans in the last fifty years took place in urban America. As the story of black Americans in urban society turned from the pursuit of possibility to the decline into blight and despair, the large urban arena endured as the terrain to pay attention to when assessing the status and fate of black America. That is because African Americans have become a constituency associated with large metropolitan areas since the middle of the twentieth century (Grossman 1989). It was in such larger regions that they found work opportunities in manufacturing, and for a significantly smaller group, later on in the white-collar professional sector. However, black Americans also have lived in suburbs and small cities throughout this period of time (Wiese 2004). Often, the situations affecting black Americans in larger cities also impacted those who lived in nearby suburbs and small towns, yet their story, which seems less intriguing and portentous in the age of the urban underclass, has garnered less attention.

The four cases considered here (two men and two women) reflect the particular kinds of issues and struggles that many low-income African Americans confront in trying to reconcile the pressures of meeting family needs and interests in securing good work. Hence, the challenge at hand is to more closely examine a selection of people as they explain their views on this relationship, and by doing so help make a case for the distinctive quality of the work-family divide for people who have little security at work, and who have achieved much less than they hoped that they would for their families. The four cases are Karen Andrews, Brian Collins, Carl Fuller, and Ellen Martin.[5] We now turn to a synopsis of the life situation of each.

At the time that she was interviewed in 2000, Karen Andrews was a twenty-five-year-old woman who was living with her boyfriend and three children (two boys, aged eight and seven, and a four-year-old girl). All of her children were produced through involvements with men prior to her boyfriend. However, as her boyfriend resided with her and helped her provide for her three children, her household took the form of a two-parent one. She has lived in Ypsilanti for all of her life, never residing outside of walking distance from where she was raised, and on the same city block for the past eighteen years.[6]

Karen was raised in Ypsilanti by her two parents, who worked in blue-collar sectors throughout her life (her father was a porter for much of his adult life and her mother was a floor manager at a short-order restaurant for much of hers). Her parents experienced periods of unemployment, which resulted in the family having to rely on public assistance at various points throughout Karen's upbringing. She has three brothers, and of the sibling set she is the only one who has attended some college. She withdrew from college in order to care for her children. Her boyfriend is a high school graduate who brings home a paycheck as a laborer (she did not care to state more specifically what he does for a living). At the time of her interview Karen was working as a machine operator for a book-binding company. In her past she has held one other job, serving as a cashier at a donut shop.

Brian Collins, who was interviewed in 2002, is a young man with a troubled past. He was twenty-six years old when interviewed, and has a general equivalency diploma (GED) acquired while he was in prison. He and his fiancé care for two daughters. One, aged two, is the product of his fiancé's relationship with another partner. The second, who is two months old, is his and his fiancé's biological daughter. Brian was raised by his mother and grew up in Ypsilanti. She worked for temporary employment agencies doing menial labor when she was not receiving public assistance. Brian did not know much about his father. He explained that his father was abusive toward him and his two sisters while growing up (all of whom have different fathers). As Brian's father was a long-term convict he was not a consistent presence in the household. In fact, the presence was so minimal that Brian could not recall anything about his father's employment history, schooling, or even his age.

Brian, himself, has served five years in a juvenile detention center for stealing an automobile and he reported that he sold drugs in his past. In talking about his turbulent personal history he said, "I mean, I felt like I had to do things for myself . . . I mean, as I got older, I felt like I never really got a chance to be a child . . . like most kids who normally get a chance to do. . . . At ten [I was doing things] I shouldn't have even been thinking about, you know."

Brian made parole in March of 2001 and got engaged shortly after he was released. In 2002 he became interested in stabilizing his work situation so that he could be a good father to his daughters. He found work through a temporary employment agency that placed him with a landscaping company. He was interviewed for this project when he was two months into his employment with the company. Since his parole he also has worked as a dietary aid for a health care service center.

Although finding better and more secure employment was a priority for him, so was the effort to keep his family together as child protective services was investigating his fiancé and him for negligence after the youngest daughter was accidentally burned with hot water by the oldest. Brian explained that the hot water in their small apartment was measured at 156 degrees, and that the older child had been running the water when she accidentally spilled some on her half-sister. Determining that parental negligence had occurred, the court took their children out of the home. In the weeks prior to being interviewed, Brian and his fiancé were working on getting the children back home with them.

Carl Fuller is a forty-one-year-old man who lives with his girlfriend, a three-year-old daughter, and a twelve-year-old stepdaughter. He grew up in Indianapolis, Indiana, in a working-class, racially mixed neighborhood. His mother worked on an assembly line in a cookie-making factory and his father worked as a photographer and an insurance salesman. His parents had twelve children. Thus, while his mother was gainfully employed throughout his life and his father worked in stable, lower-tier, white-collar-sector employment, the number of children at home resulted in a quality of life that resembled the blue-collar-sector working-class families that resided in his childhood neighborhood.

Except for a few years as a machine operator, Carl has always worked in construction, plumbing, or home repair. After being laid off from work as a home remodeler five years before his interview, Carl moved from Indianapolis to Ypsilanti, following one of his brothers who previously had relocated there. Carl was working as a repair man for an apartment complex in Ypsilanti, and his girlfriend was not employed. Although he explained that he was no longer in a state of extreme employment crisis, he hoped to soon move into more stable work that would allow him to be closer to home.

Ellen Martin, aged twenty-three and a high school graduate, was raised by her grandmother in Detroit. There was no male adult figure at home. Shortly after her mother gave birth, she was literally dropped her off at her grandmother's doorstep, who by the time was retired and sharing a household with her own sister, an employee with the Ford Motor Company. Ellen lives in Ypsilanti with her husband of eight years and their two daughters, aged two and one.

Up until about a month prior to her interview, Ellen worked as a food preparer for an adult care center. In the past five years she has worked as a cashier, security guard, and day care staffer. Her husband was in a minimally skilled area of construction, making approximately $15.00 an hour. Up until a year before she was interviewed in 2002, Ellen and her husband were in a childless, two-income household. That situation placed them squarely in the kind of working-class status defined at the beginning of this chapter. However, in 1999 her husband was severely injured in a shooting. Ellen reported that the hospital doctors discovered about fifteen bullet holes in his body. Each child was born at some point in the midst of his recovery. Consequently, the burden of support for the family fell solely on Ellen. She began rearing the children as well as tending to the medical and emotional needs of her husband, thus adding significantly to the normal pressures involved with caring for family. As she explained:

> At first, we didn't have no kids. I had the kids the last two years. And, um, you know, we had gas in the car, rent paid up for the whole year, vacations, everything. But when we started having kids, that's when everything started going bad. He couldn't work no more. Um, I had to work—I had to work two jobs for my last child in order to maintain. We were living in Canton for, I would say, five years, and then we had to move to Ypsilanti the last year because we couldn't maintain the rent that we were . . . He's unable (to work), so he'll just have to get Social Security or something like that to help out, though. He's working on that right now. They're [federal government services agencies] constantly denying him and I'm tired of that, you know, because we have every thing proved, that, you know, he got rods in his neck, he got bullets in him and he can't hold a job, you know, and they're giving us a hard time. So, that'll be income right there [when he begins receiving government aid], but until then, he's helping out with the kids. He's doing what he can do, which is not much, but he's trying, so that's a good thing.

Ellen gave up her job a month prior to the interview because she had no support in caring for her children while her husband was recovering. She was in the midst of finding a job that would be closer to her home, and that had some hourly flexibility, when she agreed to participate in the research project that this chapter is based upon.[7]

Each of the four individuals reflects a particular situation in the social milieu circumscribing disadvantaged African Americans. While none explained themselves as experiencing ideal work situations at the time of their interviews, all were employed. Moreover, each of them also lived in a nuclear-family-style household. Aside from these similarities, their life histories and current situations are distinct. Carl and Ellen are experienced workers who come from slightly more privileged backgrounds than did Karen and Brian, although Ellen had recently fallen down the socioeconomic ladder due to a family crisis. Karen and Brian are from much more humble backgrounds. However, while Karen has maintained some connection to work as an adult, Brian has encountered some trouble with the law.

All of them also were experiencing tensions at home, either in terms of trying to keep immediate family members in the household (Brian) or balance commitments relating to employment with interest in spending more quality time with children (Karen, Carl, and Ellen). Hence, each was struggling with navigating the work-family divide when neither work nor family was a site for the kind of emotional or material security that Americans generally desire from them. Accordingly, each of the four cases presented here represents ideal-type, gender-specific depictions of socioeconomically challenged African Americans. With a basic understanding of their life circumstances having been established, we can now turn to how each considered work and family in the small working-class city that is their home.

## VISIONS OF FAMILY AND COMMUNITY IN A DOWNTRODDEN SMALL CITY

Despite some differences in family patterns and general life experiences, all four of these people reside in one of the more socioeconomically deprived sections of Ypsilanti. These sections, in the southwestern part of the city, constitute the poorest areas of Ypsilanti. They contain a series of gated public housing developments made up of three-story buildings, each divided into apartments. These developments are separated by streets that contain small one- and two-story private houses, many in need of structural repair. Weeds grow out of the cracks in the sidewalks that circumscribe each block, and abandoned vehicles and debris can be found on many of the streets in this part of the city.

On the western edge of this part of town is Michigan Avenue, which southbound leads to an interstate highway that going west leads directly to Ann Arbor. Going east that interstate highway takes travelers through a range of suburbs and small towns before ending up in Detroit about thirty miles in that direction. On the eastern edge of that same part of town is a main southbound thoroughfare that also leads to the interstate highway, but goes into Ypsilanti Township and small communities where it is less expensive to live than in Ann Arbor. The preceding commentary should make clear that rather than being immersed in social networks of people who work during the week, each of the four people discussed in this chapter is immediately surrounded by blight and despair. They reside in isolated neighborhoods where unemployment is rampant and where there is little going on that stimulates thoughts or actions that promote upward mobility.

In talking about the neighborhood, and the tribulations that it causes for people to stay focused on employment opportunity, Karen, who has resided on her block for the past eighteen years, said:

> I can about name on a couple of hands how many [children] with mommas and daddies here. You know what I mean? Even if daddy came by, he wasn't staying. So, you know, it's tough . . . And a lot of people get here and they get comfortable with the, with the rent and they get comfortable with, you know, because in the "hood" everybody close. And if somebody come in here that we don't know, you gonna know about it . . . And they don't let too many people bother each other, you know. Even though it's a lot of stuff, I don't hear that happening. It's real close as far as, you know, getting along . . . People looking out for each other.

Karen's point is that her neighbors grew comfortable with living in a place, and in social circumstances, that were familiar. Her neighbors knew full well what kinds of conditions and challenges they faced in the neighborhood, and that they had the means to handle at least some of them (such as the amount of money needed to pay the rent). They also had the comfort of knowing who else was in their social space, at least much of the time, and what those people were capable of doing. Thus, this kind of habituation brought forth at least some measure of security and stability even if the situation may appear to outsiders to be anything but secure and stable.

For Karen and her neighbors, familiarity meant the virtual absence of men in the household, and the capacity to put together the money necessary to maintain a residence in subsidized public housing among people who, in her mind, were not capable of acquiring anything better for themselves because what they saw around them was all they could imagine as accessible to them. She went on to say, "And they don't understand that this is a stepping stone. You step in, you step your ass out. Because it's nowhere for kids to live at all. You know. So some people get, just get comfortable . . . "

Of course, the neighborhood had its problems, and these were not unlike the kind found in any low-income community. Karen shared her views about living amid these problems as well:

> It's not the people here, it's just the environment itself. The people that come. Because most of the people who shoot, who sell dope, who gamble . . . they

don't live here. Okay? But they come here . . . Because they ain't gonna do it [make trouble] at they momma house . . . And you gotta remember, this is the "hood." It's been like this. It ain't just started this year. It's been here for years and years and years. People have always came and stopped and did they thing. So it's just handed down from generation to generation.

For Karen, the sense of fatalism that penetrated life in the neighborhood around matters of socioeconomic mobility was also applicable to the ways in which people responded to crime and delinquency:

Now we all sit here and we complain about this. We complain about that. But ain't nobody goin' go and do nothing because see they afraid of what's gone happen. It's um, you know, when you speak out, you get threw out. You know what I mean? . . . And where else you gone go, you know, paying this much rent or whatever or on a limited budget, you know, when the average two-bedroom is five, six hundred, and the three-bedroom, don't even speak about houses. You know. What are you gonna do? So you keep your mouth shut. Hope it get better. If it don't, you still shut up.

While Karen put it more directly and succinctly than the other three, the point shared by all of them was that life in low-income Ypsilanti was as if many people lived in a closed off part of the world, where there was little motivation to leave because people did not know what to expect from living in other places, and in many cases did not know how to move themselves to other places. For Karen, as well as many other residents of this community, life amid despair and deprivation resulted in a worldview about the neighborhood and its inhabitants that seems to be contradictory, if not confusing.[8] Yet, when approached analytically, the lucidity and consistency in her remarks is more apparent. Like her neighbors, Karen knows her block, and knows much about the people on it. Hence, she speaks quite freely of how familiarity, even in the social turbulence and anxiety caused by life in poverty, breeds some level of comfort because those that experience this condition grow used to what they encounter. They also learn how to read and best respond to threats, such as violence, even if they cannot control when or how these occurrences unfold, nor what their ultimate outcome may be. The argument that outsiders are the source of many problems becomes the manner by which the unpredictability and capriciousness of life in disadvantaged communities gets addressed. That is, people in such environments have no difficulty explaining what they understand about their local community. However, they also know that they often have little personal control of that space. Hence, that which is beyond their realm of control is explained as resulting from some notion of outside influences. Of course, one other aspect of what can be controlled by the residents is how, why, and what they choose to complain about to institutional authorities.

Karen made clear that as a resident of public housing, too much complaining, or the wrong kind of it, can result in being put out of such housing by the authorities (whether one's removal is by legitimate means or not is another matter).

In essence, then, safety, stability, and a vision of how to secure upward mobility were the guiding interests of the four people discussed in this chapter, and many of their neighbors as well. A great deal stood in the way of those objectives, and most of it concerned the quality of life in their community. Access to a good job was discussed as the principal means of achieving the desired ends. As we shall see, the effort to access such jobs meant having to negotiate and manage family issues that were particularly trying for socioeconomically disadvantaged people.

## TRYING TO MAKE WORK AND FAMILY WORK TOGETHER

The absence of work, especially the blue-collar kind that was the trademark preference for Ypsilanti residents, left people with little hope for a better life and little knowledge of how to make it so. Karen went on to say:

> Some people may feel like they can't get out. . . . You know what I mean? They stay forever. Anybody can get out. . . . All it takes, is a job, you know . . . Well, not any job. You can't have any job, but some job is better than no job. But what it takes is we gotta get our childcare issues together. We gotta be able to get a job that's gonna, even, even starting here, you know, a job that's gonna get you a little extra money so that you can start saving. Then we gotta get us a car. And then we're gonna look for a better job, maybe somethin, and then we can save one or two classes.

Again, in terms that reflected the sentiments of others, Karen spoke about the lack of quality job prospects in Ypsilanti as the root of the social problems. Families like hers were subjected to risks such as drug dealers and violence because the ticket to a better life—"a job that's gonna get you a little extra money so that you can start saving"—was unavailable. That meant that issues of family security and well-being were not restricted to emotional matters such as the amount and quality of interactive time between children and parents, but also included matters such as physical safety and access to people and resources that provided support for upward mobility.

Indeed, it was not just the residential community, but the workplace where each drew considerable attention to the well-being and security of family in talking about hopes and dreams for the future. It is to that area that I now turn.

The reasonably secure positions that many middle-class and upper-income parents depend on were not available to Karen, Brian, Carl, or

Ellen. Many middle-class and upper-income parents, whether in white-collar or blue-collar occupations, find themselves in reasonably secure positions of employment while trying to get more control of their involvement at home. Neither Karen, Brian, Carl, nor Ellen were in that position. In fact, each was struggling to achieve a sense of security concerning their work lives so that they could begin to think about healthier involvements at home. This is the nature of the work-family divide for struggling working-class and low-income families. Consequently, all four had thoughts about work opportunities that were better than they currently had, and those thoughts were grounded in how such work would enable them to stabilize their family lives.

With his daughters not at home with him and his recent release from jail leaving him with an extraordinarily brief post-release work history, Brian was in the most precarious situation of the four. He explained that he had not yet established specific career goals for himself because he was first trying to get his family situation resolved (recall that his children were removed from his home by child-welfare officials). He said that his fiancé was near completion of her studies to become a nurse's assistant, and he was working for the landscaping company until he could land a permanent job.

Brian had a car, which put him in a position of privilege relative to many low-income individuals who seek employment. That car was his principal resource for getting to work and seeking out better work opportunities. However, he explained that he had to be very careful about how he goes about finding work because he was not in possession of a valid driver's license. It was suspended due to his inability to pay fines for violations that he incurred. He and his fiancé also were behind in rent by about a thousand dollars, and this was a motivating factor as well for finding a better job. In assessing his current situation he said:

> I don't have any money, but I got a job, she's got a job, so we do have income coming in. . . . I got a friend that does landscaping, and I'm trying to work some with him. I can work on the weekends because I don't work weekends (with the landscaping company). She (his fiancé) might be getting a second job just until we get the girls back.

Brian and his fiance's primary goal was getting their children back home and creating a positive household environment for the family. Accordingly, even though they were in extreme debt, Brian said that any additional work that his fiancé might find would have to end when the children came home. He believed that the cost of childcare would outweigh any income that her second job could accrue. As he said after being asked about childcare possibilities, "So, we can't afford a babysitter. . . . We're not even going to bother with that."

Brian's desire to get a permanent job and create a stable work history was initially mandated by the terms of his parole. Yet, the crisis that came upon him with his children, coupled with the financial problems, forced him to determine that, at least for the short-term future, all of his energy had to be put into work such that his fiancé would be the central presence at home once the children came back. In explaining how he thought about balancing the effort concerning work with his interest in being a consistently visible father at home he said:

> I might be a little more tired. But that's about it . . . I kind of use it as motivation because I want my children to have more than I had. That's why . . . probably the reason I try to work and try to work more hours. One week I had worked like sixteen hours, three days in a row just so I could . . . this is before we had the youngest one, just so I could get her a little stuff for Christmas. I guess I want them to have more than I had . . . I just use it as motivation. I mean, and I want to try to get . . . do more things and get more things.

In essence, Brian has made the kind of commitment that men usually make when the household and the workplace serve as simultaneous sources of tension—he chose to commit to going to work (Hochschild 1997, Kanter 1977, Nelson and Smith 1999, Townsend 2002). In his case, however, that choice was made without having the same degrees of freedom available to more privileged people. In Brian's case, he believed that he had to demonstrate a capacity to be a consistent wage earner and a dependable employee, given his criminal record. He also had to resolve his debt in order for him and his fiancé to maintain a household. Consequently, Brian did not perceive that he had a choice in terms of reconfiguring the time divide between work and home. For now, work would always have to get the attention.

Carl certainly did not face the same kinds of pressures that confronted Brian. Carl had no criminal record, and his children lived at home with him and his partner. What Carl was lacking, however, was the time to commit to being a part of his children's lives in the way that he hoped he could. He said that he accepted whatever extra work opportunities became available at his job because he wanted to someday reproduce the kind of family life for his children that he experienced as a child, which meant having meals at home with his siblings and parents, and enjoying quality time with his parents despite the fact that they had eleven other children to care for. As he explained:

> (I) have to work more and more and harder and it's not enough time in the day for me. . . . I've gotten super-hyper and it got to a point to where I was, to me I was like having a, not a nervous breakdown, but there's not enough time

for me to do anything. It's not enough time for me to even think, and that's what I can't understand, how my mother and father had twelve kids [and were able to achieve a sense of economic and social stability at home].

As far as how his children serve as a motivating factor for him, Carl went on to say:

> I wanted more stuff for them. Everything for them. . . . And I'd say, "Man I gotta get more money and get more stuff." I want them to be happy. I want happy, happy. "I want you all to be happy. I want you to have things that I never had." I want you to have everything that I always wanted." And it's, I can't, I can't do it. I have to change my thinking. But right now if I could just make enough money to get these apartments [to one day buy some property]. Ooh. I want to stay home.

For Carl, staying home did not mean never going back to work (later on we shall see how much he values and desires the kind of work that he does). Instead, he wanted the chance to control his capacity to be at home regularly with his children; a situation that he was far from experiencing in his life. Like Brian, Carl clearly saw his role in the family as the core material provider (although, like Brian, he fully supported his partner's right, and actual necessity, to go to work). Hence, he did go to work on as many assignments as he could get in addition to his regular duties. However, the desire to be at home was a salient part of his quest for a better life as well.

Ellen also preferred to narrow the distance, temporally as well as geographically, between work and home. However, as her husband was recovering from his near-life-ending situation, her interest in doing so was for reasons that drastically differ from Carl's and Brian's. Although Ellen's husband was fully into his recovery from the shooting, she explained that he still had limited capacity to function in the household. This meant that Ellen had to serve as the primary material provider as well as the caretaker of the home, even though she was part of a two-parent household. In explaining the unique way in which she was faced with having to manage the work-family divide, Ellen said:

> Because sometimes if he's not well or something like that, he cannot watch them (the children), and then I barely have a babysitter because I moved out here, and I have no family out here but him. So, that's the hard thing. It's really hard having a baby. Right now, that's what I'm going through. I had to quit my job because I didn't have nobody to watch them for four hours, and this was a good job.

Although the reasons differ, the stress that Ellen felt was shared by Karen, who was insistent that good work for parents who care about their children had to include provisions for being able to respond to family emergencies whenever necessary. As she said:

> I mean, when they sick, they sick. You gotta stay home. Sometimes you can't help it . . . Even when you want to go to work, if they sick you just can't go. . . . You have to worry about, you know, who's gonna babysit. Who's gonna pay the babysitter? Where can you get a babysitter for cheap? So you have to go through all that, so childcare's a major issue. . . . It would be much easier to say, okay, I can work this shift or that shift because then you have to limit what you do, you have to limit what shift you can work because you got, you know, a family.

Unlike more privileged people, who can afford to turn to professional support mechanisms in times of crisis or unexpected emergencies, people like Karen, Brian, and Carl have no one other than themselves and their partners to turn to for help, and Ellen barely had that option available to her. For people like these four, the problem is exacerbated by the fact that the kinds of work opportunities often available to them are those least likely to provide flexibility when family crises emerge. Karen has had extensive personal experience with jobs that do not allow much leeway for handling family crises. She explained what happened at one job as an example:

> It was just to the point where this job was, um, they give you like an eight, eight occurrences a year [to be late or absent, irrespective of the reasons why]. . . . If you're late one minute, it don't matter. Or, if you totally missed a day or whatever. So you got eight per year and even if say your child got sick. I worked midnights. If your child got sick at four o'clock in the afternoon and you was in emergency room till eleven-thirty and you brought in this note, it don't matter. It still counts against you for the simple fact you was not there. And so, you know, it comes to a point in time where you gotta say, okay, it's either this job or my kids.

In discussing how she has handled the constraints that have emerged in trying to keep a job while dealing with family emergencies she said:

> I've had jobs where, where my kids was up at work with me. . . . I didn't have a babysitter . . . and some of 'em who don't have kids don't understand. Some with kids do, but a lot without don't. . . . And so it makes it kind of harder to deal with them since they don't really know.

As people who are situated as being no higher than lower-tier working-class, Karen, Brian, Carl, and Ellen are most familiar with jobs that pay by the hour and contain little, if any, flexibility if problems outside of work emerge. This means that rather than simply experiencing a sense of consternation or disappointment about being unable to commit to their families as much as they would like to, such people must, quite literally, risk losing their jobs in order to deal with family pressures. Clearly, the two men have explained that, at least thus far in their lives, they have committed to going to work in order to provide for their families rather than to spending more time with their families. However, both men have the luxury of having partners or spouses who are able to respond to family pressures first. In contrast, Ellen cannot effectively rely on her partner to handle the family needs (at least not at present) and Karen has decided to commit to what she believes is crucial time with her children rather than to finding good-quality work, which often means having less involvement in and awareness of the events and circumstances in her children's daily lives.

We have looked carefully at how these four people handle the tension between work and family responsibilities and interests. What we have not explored in significant detail is the larger social and geographical context in which they do so. Turning to those concerns also helps establish a basis for exploring what they hope to achieve in the future and why. It also helps in understanding what they will not accept and their reasons for not doing so.

## THE QUALITY OF WORK OPPORTUNITY IN YPSILANTI

Although Karen, Brian, Carl, and Ellen lived in communities where, at least according to them, many of their neighbors had minimal work experience, each had some past history of employment, and each was employed when interviewed. Thus, each could talk about the world of work by drawing from personal experience and observations, rather than by speculating or making inferences. In fact, they had much to say about the structure of Ypsilanti's world of work and how one could best manage that environment. Each spoke quite extensively about what that world could offer them, and what they wanted to acquire from it. One of the most consistent points of emphasis across these four people was the conviction that the modern world of work in Ypsilanti was not devoid of work, just vacant of the kind of employment opportunities that would allow them to effectively provide for their families. As Carl said:

> It is so easy to find a job nowdays. You could walk out the door and people will just, "What are you doing, man? You want to work?" You can find it. It may not be the job you want. . . . I can walk to a fast food restaurant and say, "Hey, how you doing, blah, blah, blah, my name is Carl," you know, "I'm looking for some part-time work." "What do you want to do?" "Just wash the dishes." "Okay." See you can find a job. Jobs are plentiful out there right now. . . . It's easy to find even menial jobs.

But his view on finding good jobs was bleak, Carl said, "Oh, it's hard. That's hard."

And Ellen said this about the kind of jobs that she believed existed, "Really, nothing. Sales jobs. Um, telemarketing jobs, the ones I was applying for. Day care. Jobs, but no career, you know what I'm saying? You can't carry it on for the rest of your life. You can't get nowhere."

In making a point that is commonly made by people who function at the margins of the world of work (Young 2004), Ellen stressed that a career was much more meaningful than simply going to work. In her mind, a career included a secure job that provided opportunities for promotion, for an increase in responsibilities and duties, and for the enhancement and application of the kinds of skills and abilities that are associated with basic notions of good jobs. Simple labor opportunities like house cleaning and janitorial servicing were not within her landscape picture (nor any of the others') when discussing the kinds of jobs that could allow a person to function effectively as a head of household and a caretaker of children and possibly other family members.

As each of them explained, then, work could be found, and each testified to the fact that jobs existed in Ypsilanti. The problem remained in trying to find work that provided the kind of employment security and monetary return that would allow them to support their families. The kinds of jobs that each believed to be available were situated in per diem or short-term arrangements, or else provided no fringe benefits or promotion opportunities. Consequently, each of them made clear that the problem was not the absence of work but the absence of employment opportunities that allowed an adult to function as an effective provider for his or her family. Like many people who are gainfully employed, these individuals argued that meaningful work meant more than having a job, but of having job security and the prospect of getting promoted. Each also argued that the current quality of work prospects was the result of increases in technology that reduced the need for workers in sectors that provided "good" jobs.

In discussing the matter Karen said quite assertively:

There is no such thing as job security. You understand what I'm saying? No such thing, because you can always be replaced with somebody better, somebody younger, somebody older, somebody smarter. You can always be replaced. And then with technology in, we may all as far as humans be replaced. . . . We could never have a total, you know, robotic world, but . . . it could cause a major crisis if companies you know, started to use more modern technology, started to do these robot things, there could be a crisis for lots of people.

And although Carl said that jobs are available in Ypsilanti, he also said the following about whether job security is reality:

Not at all. Not at all. I could walk in and feel like any minute I'm gonna be terminated. At every job that I've had. At every one of them. I think, uh, people try to make you feel inferior and also a lot of, a lot of white guys will make you feel like, you know, we can get rid of you any time we want. They won't say it, but . . . if their buddy come up in there, you gone. You know, I don't care what kind of credentials you got, Mr. Black Man, you can be gone. We can make something up to make sure you leave, or just piss you off to where you say, "Look I got to go."

And Brian said, "I don't think too secure just because of the way things are going. People are laid off here and there."

These sentiments make sense in the context of the changing nature of work opportunity in Ypsilanti. Recall that these people reside in a small town that established itself by the proliferation of the factory. Factory jobs were virtually gone, and much of what was done in the factory on the assembly line now was done by machines. Hence, the proliferation of technology in the workplace meant that a consistent threat to work stability and security was an ever-present concern for many blue-collar workers in Ypsilanti.

Despite the challenges standing in the way of good jobs, each of the four maintained clear ideas about what kind of income was necessary in order to provide appropriate material resources for a family. As Karen explained:

I think, in order to, to probably live comfortably with a job with your expenses, and me with three kids, I mean, you have to be making, uh, like I'm talking probably fifty to seventy-five thousand a year, you know, really to be comfortable as far as owning not renting. Uh, having nice things, uh, then it, then able to just enjoy life. I mean, fifty to seventy-five thousand a year, and when you break it down, it's not a lot of money at all, especially with four people, four kids, even, I mean, to just live a decent life. You know, so.

As parents, each of the four discussed the importance of jobs that allowed each to function effectively in their families as much as at work. Although there was a considerable need for each to increase and stabilize his or her income, each also realized that a commitment to work and an increase in income would not necessarily benefit the well-being of the family. In expressing her views on the matter Karen said:

A lot of jobs, it needs to be more family oriented. . . . They need to be more helpful towards parents, you know, people with kids. Especially single parents, because there's so many of us out here, you know, that don't have kids with 'em. So they need to be more compassionate and they need to, you know, find out what the needs are for their employees. Such as people, you know, singles coming in with, you know, single families and stuff like that. And, and then I think it'll be much better because it's like issues like the childcare and you know, the attendance, and stuff like that. That, that all revolves around family. So they need to work on those type of issues.

Each also stressed the importance of fringe benefits. Carl said the following while discussing the importance of health care benefits, "That is like the number one thing. Oh, man, because I got a doctor bill for $3,500 for one day. Oh, God! And my Blue Cross/Blue Shield didn't cover it. Health insurance I think is the number one issue in my life."

Carl elaborated upon this point by talking about how employers prevent workers from being able to garner health coverage:

You got jobs now days will not give you any health coverage for ninety days. You could die in ninety days. And then most of the places are only going to let you work up to eighty-nine days so they don't have to cover you on the health care and then re-hire you. Or either they're gonna be temporary services where they don't have to pay hardly no health insurance on you if you do get hurt. You should be covered from day one when you get your job. No matter what the government, our own government should say you're gonna be covered from day one. What if you trip and fall and hurt your leg and you have no health insurance because they say, "Well you didn't work here for ninety days." What are you gonna do? You gonna have to go to the ADC [(sic) Aid to Families With Dependent Children, or AFDC] system and then they're gonna say, well you should a came here before this happened to you. So health coverage is a big issue and it's gone to the point to where it's gone to the extent to silly.

And Ellen said that a job that pays well is more crucial than a job that one might enjoy, and that it needs to come with benefits and flexibility. As she put it:

Because income is more important than what you enjoy. You're not going to enjoy everything you do because you're not working for yourself, so how can you enjoy that? . . . Um, if I found a job that paid at least $10.50 an hour, or at least $10 at the most, and you get paid every week with benefits. I would be happy, you know, with that. . . . I just like the straight-hours shift. I don't like the swing shift. That's what I just got off of. I don't like that, because the kids. If I didn't have the kids, it wouldn't matter. . . . It needs to be nearby. At least, I would say, twenty minutes (away) at the most.

Karen shared this sentiment:

I'd rather take a less, less money with good benefits than a job with you know, a lot more money but shitty benefits. Cause that's what you need, that health insurance, that you know, life insurance, whatever. You need those things, you know, and that's more important when, when you got uh, you know, a $10,000 hospital bill and your insurance only paying, well I don't know, fifty percent or whatever. Five thousand dollars is a lot of money to come up with.

So I think when you've got a good plan, a good insurance plan . . . (the job is) much better. . . . The location is important 'cause I want to be able, you know, to get there, you know, on time, and get home to my kids quickly. And of course if something happens, I wouldn't be able to get there within an ample amount of time. So I ain't goin' to take nothing down in Detroit, not right now. . . . I ain't about to you know, take a job down there, and somethin' happen and I got to get back here . . . I ain't about to do that.

Each of the four was equally clear about what constitutes a bad job or what kind of work that they would not accept. These were jobs that were short-term, like handing out flyers or running errands for local merchants, or otherwise paid low wages, which for these individuals meant jobs at or near the minimum wage. The rationale for not accepting work that did not pay what they believed was an acceptable wage was that there were ways of making that income without having to report to a job that provided a taxable income. As Karen said in discussing minimum-wage jobs:

I think it's $5.25. And, hell no. I will not (accept that). . . . I will pick up some cans all day (instead). I would, I ain't taking $5.00. You know, I'm just, now I know I can get something better than $5.00. I mean, if, if I was in, if I was fourteen, and I didn't have a family and bills, you know, $5.00 is a lot of money. I mean, a $200.00 check is a lot of money when you're twelve and, and you ain't got shit to do with it. But, come on now, you can't do it. I would nev, no, I ain't going to say never, cause a check is better than no check. But no, uh uh . . . Some employers know that there's people out there with not many skills, not a lot, that will settle for that, because nobody else would hire them. So it's always going to be people out there with . . . who didn't graduate from college, who didn't graduate from high school, who don't know how to read real good, who don't know how to write real good . . . that they can get for $5.50, and some people that settle for that, 'cause they feel like that's all they can do . . . Abuse, okay?

Brian made the same argument about minimum wage jobs:

I won't work for minimum wage. Not like that . . . As long as there's temp services around, I would get another one (job). I mean, I've got a custodial certificate, doing carpet, you know, cleaning upholstery, buffing, and waxing . . . stripping. So if I, probably if I tried to find something like that, I might be able to [get another job].

Karen, Brian, Carl, and Ellen were caught in a world of deprivation—not simply in terms of their family's material situation, but in terms of the social environment circumscribing their lives. The kinds of jobs that not only were sought after but were regarded as essential if family stability and security were going to be achieved, were those most plentiful in a by-gone era in Ypsilanti—the kinds with fringe benefits and union membership.[9] The kinds of jobs that they believed were easily accessible provided minimal material reward, little job security, and no fringe support. If good work was not immediately available, family-based problems and crises certainly were. For each of them, then, this meant that some kind of work had to be avoided because the returns on investing in it did not help circumvent or minimize family problems. Accordingly, when low-income African Americans are considered with respect to issues concerning the work-family divide, the solution is not simply work first, but how the available work options mesh with the kind of family situation that one is experiencing. Depending on the quality of that situation, some kinds of work—that which involved extensive travel away from home, that which paid wages so low that travel to work and other work-related expenses severely reduced one's income, or that which was short-term and thus of the kind that prevented effective long-term planning for family security—had to be avoided all together.

Now that we have explored the kinds of circumstances these four individuals encounter and try to reconcile during their everyday lives, we can turn to what they dream about for the future.

## LOOKING TOWARD THE FUTURE
## IN TERMS OF WORK AND FAMILY

Not surprisingly, Karen, Brian, Carl, and Ellen each looked toward the future with the hope that stability could be achieved in terms of both family and work life. Each also spoke about finding themselves in a field that was not far from what they experienced or were trained to do. Thus, nobody strongly embraced any ideas about achieving a state of extreme financial security or complete satisfaction with their place in the world of work, probably because none of them had the time or inclination to adopt such ideas given the attention devoted to handling the pressures already extant in their lives.

When asked to comment about what she hoped for the future, Karen presented a vision that contrasted with much of what her work history had been about thus far. As she explained, she wanted to work in an office setting where she could help people solve their problems. She also stated, though, that she had to earn a good income while doing so:

> It's gonna be some money though. It's got to be offering me some money. So that could be computers. Because I done went to school for computers at the college, Washtenaw (Community College). . . . So computers or whatever. So that can be from anything like that to, um, to being an advisor or counseling young people who, you know . . . who's not there yet. You know, twelve, thirteen, fourteen. Because at them ages, you know, by the time I was twenty, I had three kids. You understand what I'm saying? So I want to catch 'em before that

and let 'em know (about what to do better with their lives) so, I'd like to deal with young people or something like that.

Carl imagined working in a small apartment complex that he also owned, thus allowing him complete freedom of control at work and immediate access to his family. For him this would allow him to maximize the joys of work and home life. In order to make his dream become reality, he wanted to remain in construction or physical plant care, as those were the fields that he felt he was best suited for. As he said:

I like the maintenance field. . . . The great jobs are the ones to where you can get up in the morning and it doesn't feel like a job. You just feel like, "Oh, I gotta go in and take care of this." Like working for, working for the apartment complex where I live. This don't feel like a job to me. My kids are here, she's here, everything is right here. Uh, the apartments are here. I don't have to go nowhere.[10]

He continued to explain:

Uh, once I get my four-unit apartment building, I'm through. I'm not gonna work (for anybody else) no more. After I get these four units, I'm gonna live in one and rent out the other three and then I'm gonna go look for some more property. And that there, I'm only gonna, I'll be my own maintenance man and own management staff and I am gonna be through.

In what is the case for so many other Americans, what stands in the way of his achieving his dream is debt and opportunity. He said, "I'm like about ten grand in debt right now. And I haven't been able to pay off any of it because I'm so busy trying to make money to survive. And take care of my family and of myself." Realizing his constraints, Carl said that he is willing to settle for a job that will allow him to have some control over his hours and some access to his children. As he put it:

I like what I'm doing now. I don't even want to work full time. But if, um, if a maintenance job happened to come up for that twelve, fifteen dollars an hour, I'm not, I'm not gonna turn it down. I'm not really looking for a job. . . . Right now I just want to work the least amount of hours that I can. That sounds really sick (but) I want to spend more time with my family. . . . I want some more children.

Like many Americans, Brian's goal in life is to be financially secure and the owner of his own home. While achieving family stability was his utmost goal, in the most literal sense of the term given the situation that he was experiencing with his children, he also said:

I want to own a house. And I got a goal. I want to have . . . like landscaping-lawn care business, snow removal thing. But I just can't do right now. I'm going through too much stuff and, I'm not really sure yet, because I mean, like I said, we're right behind our goals and stuff, but once we get everything paid up, everything situated, you know, because she's got a bank account. Put some money away. I'm going to talk to my brother, see if . . . because he also wanted to . . . he was thinking about getting into the lawn care thing.

Finally, Ellen talked about becoming a white-collar professional, which for her implied the kind of employment sector that would generate the level of income that she desired as well as the capacity for personal control. She said:

Well, right now, I want to go back to school, but I have two kids and, you know, my husband, in the position the way he is right now, my kids, no babysitter, so the only thing I can do is work and go ahead and get my real estate license and day care license and try to get my own twenty-four-hour day care so I don't have to worry about nobody watching my kids for me. And then, I'll save up some money and get my own house and rent it out.

## CONCLUSION

Like other low-income African Americans, Karen, Brian, Carl, and Ellen desired not simply work opportunities, but employment prospects that would allow them to achieve some stability in the workplace, the chance to develop and apply some meaningful skills on the job, and the chance to move up in the workplace through promotion and the acquisition of greater responsibility (Young 2004, 2006). Moreover, each wanted a work situation that would allow them to commit to family needs and interests, especially given the often critical nature of such needs. Each believed that a good job for both men and women is a job that stabilizes family life by paying enough money, by accommodating caregiving (family time), by being flexible enough to allow responding to family crises, and by allowing people to provide well for their children/give their children "more" than they had. In contrast, jobs that are not worth taking are jobs that prevent family care without providing enough income to meet basic needs.

Karen, Brian, Carl, and Ellen understood that the social environment in which they lived did not provide easy access to these kinds of positions. Accordingly, none of them had any pretensions that the good job would come about any time in the immediate future. Professional and working-class families may commit to work either through overtime or for career advancement in order to attain status-rich material standards of living. For low-income families without a consistent connection to work, however, the primary challenge is to work enough to meet basic needs.

What is especially important to keep in mind about their testimonies, however, is that although the good job was far from their grasp, none was so driven to attain higher-quality employment that attention to the family was neglected. This is a critical point to consider as family life takes place in residential settings that lack provisions for physical safety and that are cut off from access to good jobs. Hence, security and safety are crucial family challenges that are compounded with the quest to gain access to people and resources needed for upward mobility.

Yet, all things considered, it is important to note that those who function on the margins of the world of work and work opportunity do not necessarily abandon thoughts about and commitments to family when they try to engage that world. The fact that family crises abound in low-income households, which are so defined precisely because work is either scarce or problematic, means that individuals who belong to such households cannot easily withdraw to the workplace in order to buffer themselves from the tensions in family life.[11] Indeed, these tensions are reinforcing. Undoubtedly, many of those who live on the margins of the world of work are committed to both family and work. Despite their marginal work situation they do not give up family for work, partly because they are in a situation where the jobs they see as options will not stabilize their families. This means that when low-income African Americans are considered with respect to issues concerning the work-family divide, the solution is not simply work first, but how the available work options mesh with the kind of family situation that one is experiencing. Depending on the quality of that situation, some kinds of work had to be avoided all together.

Accordingly, when public discussion and debate about the work-family divide is explored in the context of socioeconomically disadvantaged families, the stakes are much more severe, and finding a means of generating a healthier balance in American life is essential for the survival of the people in such families.

## AFTERWORD

As an African American male who was born and raised in the East Harlem section of New York City, it has always seemed natural to me to be interested in the views and opinions of men who share my racial categorization and geographical background. It was in East Harlem that I first began to ponder questions concerning what everyday life must be like for socially marginalized people. After all, despair and destitution were common, if not defining, features of this urban community throughout the last decades of the twentieth century. To be clear, my thinking about marginalized people was not a wholly narcissistic endeavor. That is because, unlike many of my neighbors, I was raised in a solidly middle-class family. My father was a college graduate and a certified public accountant, and my mother worked as a legal secretary for much of my childhood. I was among the first children that I knew of from my neighborhood to leave it in order to help integrate a Catholic elementary school in the considerably more elite midtown section of Manhattan. By the time that I attended college I knew quite well that my life chances exceeded those of many that I grew up with in East Harlem. Hence, I did not experience, but rather intimately witnessed, everyday life in socio-economic constraint, and what I saw and thought about became a basis for what I now study as a sociologist.

It was my deep intrigue into what allowed people to make sense of their life situations, as well as to possibly come to some understanding of how people unlike themselves might think about everyday life, that motivated my pursuits of academia and a research agenda of low-income African Americans. At the time that I committed to sociology I knew that I wanted to have conversations with low-income African Americans (especially men) about how they made sense of their lives and the social contexts that circumscribed them. My goal, in essence, was to represent and promote the humanity of people that, like my peers and neighbors in East Harlem, were easily depicted as flawed or maladjusted, rather than thoughtful, contemplative, and complex.

I first ventured into serious research concerning this agenda in the mid-1990s, where I explored the views and opinions of a range of African American men from Chicago's Near West Side, a community area that was quite similar in poverty measures and the presence of various social ills to that which was my place of rearing, East Harlem. My first book, *The Minds of Marginalized Black Men*, told the story of how twenty-six such men thought about social inequality, social mobility, opportunity structures, and the world of work and work prospects. One of the lessons that I learned from this endeavor is that people have a lot to say about that which may seem so common or basic that it deserves little formal inquiry. For instance, while anyone can imagine that people living in socioeconomic constraint may find life to be hard or unfair, there is still much to be learned about precisely what is hard for them, and the degree to which they argue that various aspects of their lives are unfair. It is not so much the basic design of their stories, then, that interests me, but how and why they choose to tell it (at least what version of the "why" they choose to tell me). My interviews in the field, then, become moments for me to think about and try to examine what kind of person is sharing their words with me, and how that person may be different from another who chooses to do so, even though they both share the same condition of deprivation or limited prospects.

I find that interviewing is an exciting and provocative way of exploring these matters. Rather than providing me with a list of short responses from people that involve some scaleable measure of how good or bad they feel, I acquire a rich and complex set of narratives that provides a basis for assessing the uniqueness of each person, even if that uniqueness rests in the particular ways in which they speak in contradictions, or without having full grasp of or belief in what they are saying to me. Having pursued this interest in Chicago, Boston, Detroit, and Indianapolis, I have turned to the situation of low-income African Americans in a small city, Ypsilanti, Michigan, to produce the chapter included in this volume. In doing this work I have found that the smallness of the environment does not reduce the complexity of the views that low-income people have of themselves and their social worlds. It only means that points of reference may be different, and contact with different kinds of social spaces are sometimes fewer, than for those who reside in larger cities. Otherwise, and unfortunately, the situations are quite similar.

## NOTES

1. In this case, the pressure often appears in the form of extensive commitment to overtime at work so that income can rise such that materials and resources can be acquired that embellish the household even if such workers cannot spend enough time at home with family to enjoy these acquisitions (Jacobs and Gerson 2004, Rubin 1994, Rudd, Root, and Young 2002, Schor 1991).

2. Despite some broad patterns of economic decline in this region, there remain some privileged Detroit suburbs and small cities in Michigan that house white-collar professionals in the automobile sector as well as in financial and service sectors (i.e., law, medicine, etc.). Descartes and Kottak, this volume, provide an investigation of how families in one such community confront work-family challenges and pressures.

3. This larger research project is explored in a manuscript entitled *From the Edge of the Ghetto: Low-Income African Americans and the World of Work* (Young forthcoming). This project consists of an examination of the views of over one hundred low-income African Americans from the small city of Ypsilanti, Michigan.

4. The interviews were conducted between 1999 and 2002 in the homes of the participants or in publicly accessible places in Ypsilanti. All of these individuals are men and women between the ages of twenty and forty-one. Participants were paid a fee for participating in the study, which consisted of one-time, audiotape-recorded interviews with the author of this chapter, the co-principal investigator for the project (Sandra S. Smith, Assistant Professor of Sociology at the University of California, Berkeley), or one member of a team of graduate student research assistants working on the project.

5. Each name is a pseudonym.

6. Any reference to time in this chapter takes the year of the interview for each person as the contemporary moment. Thus, for instance, Karen has lived on that block from 1972 through 2000.

7. A blossoming area of research has emerged in the past two decades on the benefits to the family of flexible work schedules (see Dalton and Mesch 1990, Hill et. al 2001).

8. The evidence about other residents of the community is provided in the manuscript drawn from the larger research project (Young forthcoming).

9. These jobs and the family lives enabled by them are described by Rudd and Root, this volume.

10. An extensive commentary on the value of bringing work and home life together such that less emotional energy and time is given to traveling to a job and being away from family is provided in Hoey, this volume.

11. The fact that some adults in families do so, and that doing so has consequences for how family life evolves, is explored in detail by sociologist Arlie Hochschild (1997).

## REFERENCES

Bailyn, Lotte. 1993. *Breaking the mold: Women, men, and time in the new corporate world*. New York: Free Press.

Blair-Loy, Mary. 2005. *Competing devotions: Career and family among women executives*. Cambridge, MA: Harvard University Press.

Chaudry, Ajay. 2004. *Putting children first: How low-wage working mothers manage childcare*. New York: Russell Sage Foundation.

CNNMoney.com. 2006. "The Best Places to Live in America." money.cnn.com/magazines/moneymag/bplive/2006/index.html.

Dalton, Dan R., and Debra Mesch J. 1990. The impact of flexible scheduling on Employee attendance and turnover. *Administrative Science Quarterly* 35: 370–387.

Descartes, Lara and Conrad Kottak. This volume. "Patrolling the boundaries of childhood in middle-class ruburbia."

Farley, Reynolds, Sheldon Danziger, and Harry J. Holzer. 2000 *Detroit divided*. New York: Russell Sage Foundation Press.

Grossman, James R. 1989. *Land of hope: Chicago, black Southerners, and the great migration*. Chicago: University of Chicago Press.

Heymann, Jody. 2000. *The widening gap: Why America's working families are in jeopardy and what can be done about it*. New York: Basic Books.

Hill, E. Jeffrey, Alan J. Hawkins, Maria Ferris, and Michelle Weitzman. 2001. "Finding an extra day a week: The positive influence of perceived job flexibility and work family life balance." *Family Relations* 50(1): 49–58.

Hochschild, Arlie. 1997. *The time bind: When work becomes home and home becomes work*. New York: Metropolitan Books.

Hoey, Brian A. This volume. "American dreaming: Refugess from corporate work seek the good life."

Jacobs, Jerry, and Kathleen Gerson. 2004. *The time divide: Work, family and gender inequality*. Cambridge, MA: Harvard University Press.

Nelson, Margaret K., and Joan Smith. 1999. *Working hard and making do: Surviving in small town America.* Berkeley, CA: University of California Press.

Perlow, Leslie. 1997. *Finding time: How corporations, individuals and families can benefit from new work practices.* Ithaca, NY: Cornell University Press.

Presser, Harriet. 2003. *Working in a 24/7 economy: Challenges for American families.* New York: Russell Sage Foundation.

Rubin, Lillian B. 1994. *Families on the fault line: America's working-class speaks about the family, the economy, race, and ethnicity.* New York: HarperCollins.

Rudd, Elizabeth and Lawrence Root. This volume. "'We pass the baby off at the factory gates': Work and family in the manufacturing midwest."

Rudd, Elizabeth, Lawrence Root, and Alford Young, Jr. 2002. "The taste of overtime." CEEL Working Paper 040-02, Ann Arbor, MI: Center for the Ethnography of Everyday Life, University of Michigan.

Schor, Juliet B. 1991. *The overworked American: The unexpected decline in leisure.* New York: Basic Books.

Southeast Michigan Council of Governments (SEMCOG). 2006. Community profile for Ypsilanti City, Michigan.

Sugrue, Thomas J. 1996. *The origins of the urban crisis.* Princeton, NJ: Princeton University Press.

Townsend, Nicholas W. 2002. *The package deal: Marriage, work, and fatherhood in men's lives.* Philadelphia: Temple University Press.

U.S. Census Bureau. 2000. "Poverty status in 1999 of individuals: Ypsilanti City, Washtenaw County, Michigan." Census 2000 Summary File 3 (SF 3)—Sample Data.

Wiese, Andrew. 2004. *Places of their own: African American suburbanization in the twentieth century.* Chicago: University of Chicago Press.

Young, Alford, Jr. 2004. *The minds of marginalized black men: Making sense of mobility, opportunity, and future life chances.* Princeton, NJ: Princeton University Press.

———. 2006. "Low-income black men on work opportunity, work resources, and job training programs." In *Black males left behind,* ed. Ronald Mincy, 147–84, Washington, DC: Urban Institute Press.

———. Forthcoming. *From the edge of the ghetto: Low-income African Americans and the world of work.* Boulder, CO: Rowman and Littlefield Press.

# 6

# American Dreaming

## Refugees from Corporate Work
## Seek the Good Life

*Brian A. Hoey*

"Do you get told what the good life is or do you figure it out for yourself?" Alan poses the question rhetorically, but I can see that he is considering how he might answer it. His query comes in the course of animated conversation as we drink strong coffee at his kitchen table. We sit bathed in the glow of light reflected off deep drifts of snow blown in from Lake Michigan during one of many sudden squalls that blanket these northern Michigan communities during long, cold winters. It is the kind of weather that keeps the area's population from even higher rates of in-migration. A former Towncar-driving, suit-wearing, corporate manager who became a Carhartt canvas- and flannel-clad, pick-up-truck-driving jack-of-all-trades, Alan is a former self-professed "professional people hater."

After a few moments have passed sitting in thoughtful silence, Alan leans forward over his steaming cup for emphasis and answers his own question. "In corporate America I started getting told." Pausing briefly, he continues. "I look back now and I was told what the good life was: a four-bedroom colonial house in the suburbs and working for a main company, dressing in a suit every day, going to the job, weekends off, and getting to go someplace on the weekend. But I wasn't happy. I just didn't know it at the time."

I first met Alan when my wife and I were looking for a place to live while I conducted the two years of ethnographic fieldwork on which this chapter is based. Although we eventually chose to rent elsewhere, early in our search we saw an inexpensive apartment located in the broad glacial plains above Grand Traverse Bay, a long blue arm of Lake Michigan. Answering the realtor's questions in polite conversation, I described my reason for moving to the area. As I spoke, a man emerged gradually from behind the kitchen counter where he quietly was making repairs. In paint-splattered coveralls, he stood gripping a putty knife with an expectant stare. The rapt attention was unnerving and I took a step toward the door. Why would this disheveled handyman show such interest in my research? As it turned out, he and our realtor were husband and wife. They had moved here only a few years earlier when both left jobs in metropolitan Detroit. Alan and Beth were two of many urban-to-rural migrants moving to my study area in the Grand Traverse region.

## INTRODUCTION—LIFESTYLE MIGRATION AS A QUEST FOR THE GOOD

Alan felt that he underwent a kind of self-transformation that allowed him to claim what he described as a "second chance" in life. Alan claimed this in his decision to leave a self-destructive personal and professional past and move from an upscale, middle-class neighborhood 250 miles to the south. He now lives in the rural, northwestern part of Michigan's Lower Peninsula. He became one of the growing numbers of what some call "corporate refugees" (e.g., Luban 2001). Corporate refugees relocate as a way of starting over. Like Alan, they tell a story of travel made in physical and psychical worlds to find personal refuge.

Their stories are constructed in a manner akin to those of people who have undergone religious conversion.[1] When applied to non-religious phenomena or experiences, "conversion" refers to a far-reaching personal change related to adopting a new interpretive framework within which individuals structure their actions and experience them as purposeful. Conversion stories are a special form of autobiographical narrative where individuals distinguish a "real self" from an inauthentic self. This self-transformation entails the creation of a new vision of one's self when long-time social roles and self-presentations are challenged and eventually stripped away.

My research with "lifestyle migrants" examines the travel and conversion stories of corporate refugees who start over, as they move not only outwardly on asphalt roads to new places but also on the less tangible psychical paths of introspection and self-discovery that negotiations among work, family, and self blaze. I refer to these urban-to-rural migrants as lifestyle migrants to emphasize their use of relocation as a way of redefining their relationship to work and family through changes in lifestyle, the patterns of everyday life. The expression lifestyle migrant is intended to emphasize the growing importance in American lives of consumption behavior, including individual choices about how and where to live relative to production activities, such as income-generating work. Anthropologist Dean MacCannell (1999) suggests that as a term, lifestyle should be understood as "combinations of work and leisure . . . replacing 'occupation' as the basis of social relationship formation, social status and social action" (6). As MacCannell reasons, lifestyle migrants may be a sign that the "affirmation of basic social values is departing the world of work and *seeking refuge* in the realm of leisure" (ibid, emphasis added). That is, seeking refuge in areas such as personal lifestyle, where the individual is thought to have greater discretion (cf. Putnam 2000, Weiss 1999, Zukin 1991). Lifestyle migrants seek personally meaningful places of refuge that they can call home, which they believe will resonate with inspiring visions of self—what I refer to as the *potential self*.

As revealed in work by sociologist Arlie Hochschild (1997), the potential self resides in some idealized, future point in time, set apart from an everyday self living in the hustle and bustle of the present. In her study of workers at a Midwestern company she calls "Americo," Hochschild found the potential self to be a set of imagined, future possibilities. These served as a substitute for, rather than preparation for, action in the lives of overscheduled individuals coping with the time squeeze of increasingly complicated work and family commitments. Removed from the uncertainties and conflicts of everyday life, imagining a potential self is one way individuals may cope with the demands of busy, self-consuming schedules. Lifestyle migration involves individuals and families who choose relocation as a way of attempting to actualize this potential self through reordering work, family, and personal priorities. Lifestyle migrants seek a kind of moral re-orientation to questions about what gives meaning, fulfillment, dignity, and self-respect to a life. In their stories, we see how individual identity and the moral dimension are profoundly intertwined in the unfolding narrative account of a personal "quest" to make sense of that life through culturally informed questions about what constitutes the good life (MacIntyre 1984, Taylor 1989). Lifestyle migrants seek to define themselves according to their own "moral narratives of self" (Hoey 2005). In these narratives, they describe their transition from one kind of life to another and their reorientation to basic life questions as a kind of self-transformative conversion experience (Taylor 1997). And, as life stories grow out of the activities of everyday life in a sequence of lived events and one's literal as well as figurative movement through both time and space, they are naturally stories of travel (de Certeau 1984).

Both voluntarily downshifted and involuntarily displaced corporate workers, or "refugees," may attempt to redefine themselves and renegotiate work and family obligations. By moving to places they believe possess qualities likely to support a more balanced and integrated life, they try to harmonize material and practical domains with their own moral and spiritual needs. Lifestyle migration entails the quest made by people like Alan and Beth for refuge. They hope to explore a more authentic, inner self through pursuing different, more deliberate work and family arrangements enacted in new geographic and social surroundings. For those in my research, choosing to relocate to a *rural* place, with perceived elements of greater authenticity and a slower pace, is indispensable to this process.

Though generations of exodus from rural communities have embodied much of the American experience, many have *retained* a strong attachment to the rural ideal (Johnson and Beale 1998, 23). "The Rural" is an imagined place as much as a geographic category for all non-metropolitan places. It has become an object for those seeking stability within the context of an increasingly uncertain and restructuring economy (Murdoch and Day 1998). Even as people embark on quests for refuge in ways that are original and individually creative, they engage in reproducing understandings contained in a culturally informed notion of the Rural—as something good or "simple," a repository for more "authentic" ways of life (Hummon 1990, Shi 1985, 1986).

As we will learn from Alan's story of down-shifting from his high-stress corporate career, finding or believing in a place of refuge can be essential to people at crucial turning points in their lives. I have come to think of these turning points as watersheds. At these times, people's guiding belief is that they might find greater balance leading to personal harmony, happiness, and fulfillment through immersion in a new existence created in commitment to a particular lifestyle, relocation to a place of personal refuge, and a refocusing of personal goals and relationship to work.

## FIELDWORK AND SETTING

Approximately 250 miles northwest of Detroit, Michigan, the Grand Traverse region is an hour's drive from the nearest highway and two hours from Grand Rapids, the nearest city. Its rolling countryside is defined by a deep, glacial bay stretching north-south over twenty miles. Although now heavily forested, a nineteenth-century lumber boom left the area almost completely denuded. After the inevitable bust in the final years of the nineteenth century and more than fifty years of relative economic stagnation, the area's economy relied heavily on agriculture and tourism in the second half of the twentieth century. Today, most of the area that is not regenerated forest is either active or idle farmland. In the past twenty years, tourism has had an increasingly large role in the local economy. Endowed with miles of sandy Lake Michigan shoreline and towering dunes, the Grand Traverse region attracts vacationers seeking recuperative rest. Nearly 70 percent of my 128 project participants vacationed here before choosing to make it home. Like many rural places once only attractive for seasonal, short-term stays, the area where I conducted research finds itself a destination today for lifestyle migrants and others who seek a more enduring, year-round retreat (see Bonner 1997, Jobes 2000, Murdoch and Day 1998, Pindell 1995).

Lifestyle migration is the most recent expression of over thirty years of urban-to-rural migration in the United States. In some rural counties where once-dominant agriculture and natural resource extraction have declined, this migration is reversing a twentieth-century trend of population loss (Boyle and Halfacree 1998, Jobes, Stinner, and Wardwell 1992, Pandit and Withers 1999). In the last thirty years of growth, U.S. Census figures show that population increase in some study area counties approached 40 percent over ten years, with in-migration contributing four times the amount attributed to natural increase. In a recent article addressing urban-to-rural migration's contribution to this "rural rebound," sociologist Kenneth Johnson (1999) features Grand Traverse County. Calling it a "Jewel of the Great Lakes," he notes that between 1970 and 1990 its population grew 64 percent, from 39,175 to 64,273.

I conducted fieldwork from early 2000 to early 2002 in the adjoining counties of Grand Traverse, Leelanau, Antrim, and Benzie that together incorporate an area extending roughly twenty-five miles from Traverse City. I gathered the data for this chapter through in-depth, open-ended, ethnographic interviews with 128 in-migrants to these counties. These interviews emphasized personal background, reasons for leaving a job and relocating, the process of relocation decision-making, and negotiating individual identity after the move. Free-form conversations allowed migrants to present detailed narratives, often in extended monologues with minimal interruption. The large number of stories gathered in interview format allowed me to consider a wide range of personal backgrounds and relocation experiences. Some of these interviews led me to follow-up conversations and participant observation in everyday work and family life, spending time with a core group of four individuals and eight families who relocated within the previous five years. They roughly represent the full study sample of lifestyle migrants.

Reflecting basic demographics of all in-migrants to the area, lifestyle migrants in the study are overwhelmingly white and middle class. Most had professional backgrounds including having worked as managers, accountants, lawyers, social workers, and others in health care-related fields (cf. Jobes 2000, 1992, Judson, Reynolds-Scanlon, and Popoff 1999, Stinner et al. 1992). After their move, however, almost half were working in a field they considered a *significant* departure from their prior employment or field of study. Nearly 60 percent had a drop in income, with the smallest drop being 5 and the largest 40 percent of pre-relocation levels. Given a shared interest of lifestyle migrants to gain a greater sense of *control* in their lives, I was not surprised to find that nearly 40 percent started their own businesses. These ranged from home-based consultancies to retail shops with several employees. Most, however, found salaried or hourly wage work in the local government, school system, community college, hospital, or other local businesses. Nearly 20 percent worked two part-time jobs in order to meet income goals. Of a total of 128 participants, roughly even amounts were in their thirties, forties, and fifties, respectively, with slightly more than half female. Nearly 30 percent were married with grown children who no longer lived at home full-time. Among the remainder, there was a roughly even split between those married with young children, married with school-aged children, married with no children, and single. Like Alan, approximately 60 percent of participants relocated from southeastern Michigan, while the rest were evenly split between other parts of Michigan, the Midwest, and the rest of the United States.

## MORAL NARRATIVES OF SELF—TAKING BACK ONE'S LIFE, REDEFINING THE GOOD

Shortly after meeting Alan, we got together for a chat on another snowy day in early January. Alan arrived at my apartment in a beat-up pick-up with a jutting yellow snowplow. Dusting icy flakes from his jacket, he strode through the front door, thrusting his generous hand forward to deliver a confident shake. Our conversation began with the weather, a central concern in this area during the winter months. He hoped to get out and do some plowing before the snow became too deep. I hoped to join him. By this time, I had learned something of Alan's past work as a "hired gun," brought in by companies to cut costs. They did this in a number of ways, including the union busting that had occupied much of Alan's former work life.

> The objective was to keep the unions out, keep the morale up, and reduce the workforce. Kind of hard to do all that at once but that was the deal. The guy who was running the Midwest division [of a large processed foods company] said, "I want a guy like you. I don't want a team player. I've got this problem . . ." They said, "We don't care if you fire everybody because in nine months we're going to close the plant . . . but we'll keep you if we like you."

Going from that sort of work to a jack-of-all-trades fix-it man and manager tending to two out-of-date rental properties was a big shift. Alan's former work as a corporate hit man is iconic of the post-industrial economy. In whatever small way, he helped give shape to this emerging landscape of work.

> [The executives] said "Raise hell with the unions." We had three walk-outs and every time I had the factory running again in fifteen minutes because I just went into the offices and said "Come on, we're going to run this thing." I would have the [machines] making noise and stuff . . . and it got the union scared that we were going to run the thing without them. I would bring in tem-

porary labor services. I was doing everything. It took them two years to clean up all the arbitrations I started. That's what I was hired to do.

Alan spoke about a life-changing decision to break from his well-established professional career and source of social identity by relocating to the northern reach of the Great Lakes region. Residents of the Great Lakes states call this area "Up North" as a way to signify both geography and, more emphatically, a state of being. The phrase both locates one spatially and orients one ideologically. The term distinguishes the northern part of Michigan from the heavily urban and suburbanized "Down State" south of an imagined "line" that appears, in the perception of many residents, to divide the state into two distinct regions (cf. Clark and Officer 1962).

As I poured coffee, Alan described what he was learning about himself toward the end of his time living and working Down State. It became a question of personal character. It was about identifying values that he could no longer violate:

> There were things building up to the dramatic decision to make the move. I had a psychologist friend who pointed out that I was taking it all too seriously and that working in corporate America was [only] a game. What [began to bother] me about the game was how people are treated. I can give you example after example of how decisions were made. One day [an upper plant manager] told me, "You know you have to fire that guy." I asked why. "His wife has got a serious illness and the insurance is costing us a fortune." There is nothing wrong with the guy. "Well, you'll have to find something." It was an inhumane decision. Another time, this one guy got prostate cancer and the president of the company said, "Well, he's a goner. We don't have to worry about him anymore." That's corporate America. Relocating and leaving all that behind was about taking control of my life and getting my self back.

This notion of turning away from an inauthentic or somehow severely compromised or violated self in order to come "back" to a true self is a common refrain in the narratives of lifestyle migrants. In a different context, a professional couple in their late thirties told me how they left well-paying jobs and what most Americans would consider successful days spent in the suburbs of Detroit to move to Northern Michigan, "take back their lives," and reconnect with "core values." Katherine and John described how they felt increasingly "dispossessed" of the locations where they lived and worked. Although their explicit intent was to express a lack of any meaningful connection, their choice of the word "dispossession" to describe their feelings suggests being deprived of a sense of security and home. Given the desire of lifestyle migrants to feel meaningful connections to particular geographic places as a kind of personal refuge, living where this connection seems impossible or impractical can lead some people to feel "disoriented" or "adrift."

Many lifestyle migrants felt that their former jobs asked them to make decisions that over time violated their inward sense of right and wrong, finally going beyond their ability to cope. At that point, everyday life, as Alan told me, can begin "tearing you down" in ways that the occasional vacation simply cannot build back up or put back together. His decision to relocate was about being able to define himself according to his own *moral narrative*, in a new physical place that helps create a personal space where he can design a new relationship to work and family. Between swigs of hot coffee, he explained:

> I knew there was something wrong with me. My job was affecting my personality and adversely affecting me as a human being. I saw it manifesting as behavior that I knew was wrong. I was drinking too much and I was chasing around. I yelled a lot [because] that's what people reacted to. Is this the right way to treat a human being? No. But that's how you got things done. That becomes your whole life. Soon you're screaming at your wife and you're screaming at your kids. Looking back, I was trading away my value system for the job and in support of the company. You are brought up with certain morals, ethics, and values and then you may find yourself in a system that is not allowing you to live your life properly. This is on your mind, whether conscious or [not]. Looking back, it is easy for me to analyze it. I was tearing myself down.

As we talked and finished the coffee pot, Alan glanced out the window from time to time. Cold Artic air continued to push over Lake Michigan, picking up moisture from the relatively warm water. Snow was piling up deep. Alan suggested we go for a ride. Maybe do some plowing. Bracing against the wind, I followed him between drifts in the parking lot to his battered blue truck. Climbing in among scattered tools on the passenger seat and floor, I cleared myself a place to sit. After waiting a few moments for a degree of heat and relative visibility, we set off into white. It was good to be out with Alan. The drafty cab of his truck was a considerable change from the comfortable living room of my apartment and no doubt a reminder to him of how far he had come from a company-provided Lincoln Towncar. As we wound our way through mostly deserted streets, I asked Alan about what it meant for him to be taking his "second chance" at life. What did it mean for him to have made a break from a life that he felt had been slowly "tearing him down?" Alan kept his focus on the road ahead with a serious expression as he navigated through the storm. A grin spread slowly over his face and he began to speak. He described how he now acted in ways incompatible with what would have been expected from him before. As a landlord, Alan still "manages" in some manner, but now he can make decisions based on what feels right and does not violate his sense of an inner, authentic self.

> Now I can make decisions, analytical decisions, based on income or I can make decisions based on people. I'm people-oriented now. There is this handicapped guy living in one of my units. He's got his little thirteen-inch TV. He doesn't

have much of life outside that TV. I went over to [the store] and picked up a big twenty-five inch for a hundred bucks. I went over, gave it to him, and told him that somebody left it in one of the units. He could have it. There's decisions that you do based on your faith. Some of those decisions are about what's the right thing to do. A lot of that is a people-related process. But in the corporate world, it is black and white—it's numbers.

Although his current work as business owner required him to closely watch the numbers of his own bottom line, Alan looked for ways to be more "people-oriented," such as through his gift of a TV to one of his tenants, in sharp contrast to his former role as "people-hater."

## THE LARGER CONTEXT:
## A POST-INDUSTRIAL, "NEW ECONOMY"

The narrative accounts of relocation and starting over told by lifestyle migrants like Alan are part of a larger moral story of what constitutes the good life in America at a time when the basic social categories and cultural meanings of family, work, community, and self are changing. My research analyzes social and structural transition by exploring the meaning of *non-economic* migration by middle-class Americans away from metropolitan and suburban areas to growing rural communities.[2] The varied journeys of lifestyle migrants are not simply idiosyncratic expressions but part of a shared cultural process of change in the historical context of economic restructuring. The prevailing model for achieving the good life, born out of the corporate largesse of post-World War II boom times, is being reworked. This model is premised on a separation of work and family into domains where work is associated with competitive individualism and home is defined in opposition as a place of caring refuge. Its widespread adoption as a worldview and a definition of the good life has depended on the availability of long-term, well-paying jobs that offered a ladder for advancement and rewarded worker loyalty. This arrangement helped sustain a commitment to expanding material consumption as an expression of success as well as a way to achieve personal comfort and well-being. According to this notion of the American Dream, the pursuit of personal goals of career advancement and consumption should be seen as working for oneself, and also for the good of the company. This contribution is a source of meaning in one's life.

Alan's story provides an intimate view into a restructuring economy, its impact on the everyday life of working families, and an ongoing redefinition of the post-War boom model for work, family, and community life. Alan himself played a part in the trend toward downsizing and the shift from paternalistic companies who reward worker loyalty to employers who do virtually anything to improve the bottom line and keep shareholders happy. In this context, it is revealing that one of the country's largest private employers is not one of the industry giants, either of the old order based on resource extraction and materials refinement, or the new order of high technology and information systems. It is in the business of selling specified, limited packets of human labor for companies increasingly interested in pursuing the "on-demand" or "just-in-time" model of business: By the early 1990s, Manpower Inc., with well over a half-million workers, had become a huge corporation and the world's largest temporary employment agency. It has flourished and its personnel swelled as traditional corporate giants such as General Motors continued to cut positions. In this context, the United States seems on the road to becoming a nation of part-timers, freelancers, temporary workers, and independent contractors, all of whom are part of a new, *contingent* workforce. Originally restricted in its use to describe a management technique of employing workers when there was an immediate need for specific work to be done, the term "contingent work" has come to refer as well to part-time work, contracted or outsourced workers, home-based work, and even self-employment.[3]

Envisioning the future status quo for work in America, a former General Motors executive who left to start his own consultancy business said that "We are going to be moving from job to job in the same way that migrant workers used to move from crop to crop" (quoted in Castro 1993, 44). Lifestyle migrants recognize the impermanence of today's world of work. One of the reasons Alan felt insecure in his former life was due to his role as a hit man, a hired gun. Not only did he see the brutality of downsizing firsthand, he knew that his own job was only a temporary assignment. It was not a "real job" in the usual (if outdated) sense of an enduring position. Rather, he had become a kind of contractor with skills that applied to certain, transient situations. Alan became an ideal worker of this emerging economy.

> I was always brought in for an assignment. And when [it's] over, what do you do? I guess that's why I was getting more and more frustrated. There was just nothing there anymore. I've been gone five years now [from my last position] and during that time they've been through three or four guys . . . my replacements. They just keep burning through them. That's the way a lot of corporate America is these days, they just hire you for an assignment. There's no pension. You just keep job-hopping. I was watching the news the other day, and that's what people are doing. They're job-hopping. Kind of like the migrant workers who come here to pick fruit.

In today's economy, success appears to depend on individuals thinking of themselves as entrepreneurs or even as products offered in the marketplace, regardless of the kind of work they do (see Murray 2000, 155–56). Business consultant Tom Peters argues that people need "to take a lesson from the big brands" in order to become "CEOs of our own companies" and head marketers of what he calls "Me, Inc." Peters insists that one's career should be viewed as a "portfolio of projects that teach you new skills, gain you new expertise, develop new capabilities, grow you a colleague set, and constantly reinvent you as a brand" (quoted in Murray 2000, 156). The take-home message to today's workers: You are now in business for yourself.

In this new working world, "workers increasingly feel like free agents, having to chart their own career paths" (Moen 2001, 6). Whether through downsizing or down-shifting, increasing numbers of U.S. workers are becoming free agents. In the world of sports, a free agent is a player whose contract with a particular team has come to an end and who is now free to sign with another team. In the world of work, the term free agent is used increasingly to characterize a growing number of Americans who are in some manner self-employed. In contrast to William Whyte's (1956) "Organization Man" of two generations ago, this free agent is largely an independent worker, whether small-business owner, temporary, or contract worker. Whyte explained that devoted post-World War II employees not only worked for their companies, in conformity to the old model, they willingly "belonged" to them as well. Whyte's Organization Man was white, middle-class, and suburban, with values, aspirations, and lifestyles that helped to define the second half of the twentieth century. They gave us the stubbornly persistent vision of the American Dream portrayed in the 1950s TV show *Ozzie and Harriet* with a breadwinner father, a homemaker mother, and two kids in school.

In contrast to the predictability and sameness of the Organization Man, today we have a shift toward unpredictability and diversity in work, family, and community arrangements in growing numbers of free-agent workers. The impact of economic shifts already discussed, together with a number of social changes, encourage workers to redefine their work and family roles and identities. The recent experience of women entering a male-dominated workplace, for example, provides today's free-agent New Worker with inventive models (both successful and not) of how to self-consciously negotiate obligations of work, family, and self.

The paths taken by today's free agents are manifold, but their decisions begin at a common point of experience and understanding. Like Mark and Diane in the following example, lifestyle migrants have become more pragmatic and proactive in their approach to work as they feel the trust or faith they might have had in finding and keeping a meaningful job with a single company erode. This erosion progresses as the old contract between employer and employee comes to an end. This old contract is what Moen (2001) labels an often-informal trade-off where workers with seniority in a company were awarded security by their employer in return for ongoing loyalty. In today's economic climate, companies shed "excess" long-time employees from their payrolls in order to hire younger, often part-time and thus less expensive, staff, instead of rewarding loyalty. These younger workers enter the field at an already insecure state with virtually no guarantee and little expectation of stability in their career. While many free agents may feel there is little choice but to accept their uncertain status and adhere to a pattern of temporary, dependent work, others reject this relative passivity and struggle to employ their free-agency in a deliberately self-fulfilling and creative way. One way to do this is to go into business for yourself.

## CHARTING HIS OWN COURSE: THE "PIE GUY" AS FREE AGENT

Nearly 40 percent of lifestyle migrants in this project went into business for themselves. Some started home-based businesses, such as information technology or environmental engineering consulting, while others started brick-and-mortar stores in the local communities specializing in everything from alternative health care services to gourmet pies. The story of how Mark and Diane went into business for themselves is iconic of the corporate-refugee-turned-small-business-owner. Mark told me their story in conversations we shared while spending early mornings in his prosperous pie shop, drinking coffee, and preparing vast quantities of dough for his shop's signature fruit pies. Mark grew up in Lansing, Michigan, in the 1960s and '70s when nearly everyone he knew worked in the venerable Oldsmobile plant. Whole families worked on the line through generations. Mark graduated from the state university there in the early 1980s, at a time when the auto industry had already been through several years of profound contraction. He was determined not to end up in a dead-end job. After going to California to find excitement and interesting work, Mark eventually landed a job there with a major defense contractor, flush with federal contracts spawned by Cold War fears (cf. Didion 2003).

Moving up into middle-management, Mark made a good salary with full benefits and stock options. By most American standards, he had achieved success. But in the face of sweeping changes in his workplace as the largesse of military budgets faded with the fall of the Soviet Union, Mark started wondering whether this was the life he wanted to live. He questioned a working life where he invested himself so fully in projects that started being routinely "axed" by his employer as government contracts were cancelled and funding dried up. In his account, I hear how he realized that this was now a world where the division he worked for was moved around in an elaborate game of corporate chess, only to be sold off according to an economic calculus unaffected by the concerns of working families. Reflecting the experience of many project participants, Mark's story tracks the transition from workplace as a kind of extended family to the radical dismemberment of this arrangement and the feeling that people like him had become little more than commodities or ignored costs in market discourse (see Lane 1991, Martin 1994). He spoke to me about what it meant to be a part of a tightly knit team in early projects as coworkers struggled together to solve great engineering and design problems on the scale of super-colliders and super-conducting magnets, only to have those projects and teams torn apart by powerful economic forces well outside their control.

> There was a great deal of pride. We were doing a great job. We had a really tight group . . . it was a real team effort. And to watch that team fragment when [a project] was canceled . . . it affects you to see that. [It] all started [when our division] was acquired [first by one company] and then by [another]. But back when [our company] started in San Diego we had a company campground up in the mountains. We had a park right adjacent to our plant. So if you're on a program, it was beer and pizza out in the recreational park. They had little merry-go-rounds and mini-trains. So you had a relationship with co-workers beyond your project. It was like a real family situation for thirty years since the War and up until the late '80s. [Then] to see that go away . . . the plant was sold, the park was closed and the campground sold . . . just watching this crumble. It was hard. Now it's the forces of business. It went from being really comfortable, "I can make a career here and build good projects and meet good people" to being like . . . *you feel adrift.* Things that you depended on being there . . . weren't. So do you allow yourself to be at the whim of whatever forces [are] at play . . . or do you go do something about it?

Although Mark continued to be well-compensated for his labor, what remained in the way of loyalty to the corporation quickly dissolved. It was becoming all too clear that there was no guarantee of reward for being faithful to a company looking out for its own interests and fully prepared to sacrifice workers in order to fulfill the demands of its shareholders. It became a question of *timing* for Mark. It was about staying "in the game" only so long as it made sense in that he was getting something useful out of it for the next step. Reacting to feelings of increasing anxiety as seismic shifts in corporate America set the ground in motion beneath his feet, Mark became savvier, shrewder, and more pragmatic in his thoughts about work. He would not allow himself to remain disoriented or "adrift" for long. Mark began to think of his corporate job as training for something else down the road where he could claim greater personal control. What remained in the way of loyalty to the corporation was scattered. Mark explains, "So, in the process I'm getting good training. This is like grad school to me now. I'm not loyal to the company, I'll do what they ask, but I'll work through the process and learn business."

At this point, he saw himself gaining important skills at the company's expense. He knew that they believed they owed him nothing. He acted with what amounts to enlightened self-interest. All the while, he was rethinking where he was and where he might be going. He was taking stock and looking for a way out that made sense to him and was likely to be best for his young family:

> So there are several things happening. I don't want to do this for the rest of my life. So that's another factor—you kind of assess. I think everybody does at a certain age. Is this a livelihood? You know? I want to get into something more simple that I can get my hands around and I want to get something where I can control my own destiny instead of just sort of floating with this company.

Like every other lifestyle migrant, Mark stressed how important it was to feel this control.

During his final year with the defense contractor, Mark began to think of his skill set and of being a free agent—getting what he needed in order to move on. At the same time, he and Diane designed a business plan that would allow them to take back control. Since opening their pie shop in Traverse City in 1997, they have successfully franchised the business plan, concept, and trademark, thereby allowing others to follow their example. The Grand Traverse Pie Company now can be found in three states. Others who have come to Mark for advice on how to start over as self-employed "free-agents" have used his business plan and concept well beyond the Midwest.

As in so many other cases, owning a small business afforded the control necessary to integrate work and family life in a balanced and rewarding manner. In some respects, Mark employed his free-agency to recreate elements of an older pre-War arrangement of work and family by creating a family business and intending to leave a legacy for his children. Mark explained that this was essential to building "self-worth or self-confidence, of providing value to my family, and building a base or a foundation that will endure." Integrating work and family life meant that he and Diane could have their children working side-by-side with them.

> My son is eleven. He can help customers and run the cash register. He makes dough with me on Sundays. My daughter is sixteen and she can do any job here [and] understands the value of good work and responsibility. Those things affect the whole family. It's a real family group. Up until my mother passed away, she was my bookkeeper. My mom had failing health over the last few years. She wasn't financially independent [enough] to retire so we provided [a job for her here]. I got to see my mom, in addition to my kids, involved in the business. It was all integrated into the lifestyle. The business became part of the lifestyle versus somewhere to go for eight hours a day to make a living.

## NEW AMERICAN DREAMING—ACTIVE FREE AGENCY

Alan continued to drive through the nearly blinding snow. We were now on a mission. He wanted to show me the place where he was driving a few years earlier when he decided to quit the work that seemed to be killing him and relocate in order to start a new life. Like the glacial ridge the road traverses, this place is a watershed in Alan's life story, a metaphorical point even as it is the physical location of the moment of his self-proclaimed epiphany. Thinking about how much the working world had changed during his lifetime, Alan told me in a manner a man might speak to a son, reaching out to touch my shoulder, "Brian, nowadays you got to put together your own life." In this simple statement, Alan suggests that today people need to figure out as individuals what the good life is. We might be told what it is through ubiquitous messages in popular culture, but that does not mean we should embrace these interpretations as our own.

> The old American Dream was to buy a house . . . or is it a dream of having a job, a career, and all of the things you receive because of that? If the definition of the American Dream is having a career, a job, a future . . . I didn't have a whole lot of career focus or direction growing up. I stumbled into a lot of stuff that I did. That's the reason why I have a two-year degree in criminal justice, and that four-year degree in social science, and then my MBA. You start on a path and then you realize maybe this is a good path, maybe this is the dream . . . a good job . . . a house in the suburbs and all those trappings. Then that became the Dream. This was all coming from outside of me. Because of the circumstances I fell into, it became this is the direction you should go. It was the logic of where I was.

Alan came to see that he was paying a very high price to maintain that vision of self particular to dominant and convincing interpretations of an American Dream. By not being true to an emerging sense of an authentic, inner self, he felt that he was losing his soul to a dream that was, in fact, never really his. He explained how even the dream itself is something someone might find themselves claiming over time as they stumble through different career decisions and related life choices. Alan came to see his old life as one that traded away his value system, violating his sense of his true self for the job. How important had that job been to Alan's identity? What does having left that life mean to him now? Being a corporate refugee, leaving behind a high-stress career, and relocating Up North is about being able to define himself according to his own moral narrative.

> I would say that working in corporate America was extremely important to my identity at that time. It really defined me. It really defined me for my daughter, for my family. A job title is a definition of a person. Now I view myself as a

more rounded person. I can accept the title "Dad." I can accept the title that "I am a husband." Those are important parts of me now. Before, those were all pushed to the side. I was Director of Operations. I was *also* a Dad or also a husband. Now I am a Dad, a husband, *and* a property owner. Now those other things are elevated in importance. I can actually put time against them. They're important enough that this can wait. I can go be Dad for a while and this can wait. Before, I had to put in my calendar to be Dad. It's a lot different now. What is the definition of success? Living life the way *you* want to.

For Alan, as with other lifestyle migrants, "success" is about living life on your own terms without having to sacrifice yourself to a dream that may not really be your own.

When Alan and I thought through it, making rough calculations on the back of a newspaper at his kitchen table, we figured that he put in much more time doing things related to his present work than he generally accounted. In particular, he spent much of his time in what he calls "running around talking to people" and other more informal responsibilities that come with managing apartments. He doesn't feel a need to account for this time as work. This unconcern is common among many of the lifestyle migrant small business owners I spoke with. "Running around" feels more like engaging in everyday social interaction, especially when one of the things that most characterizes small-town life is that people know each other and take time to stop, chat, and show that they care about one another. Making time for that kind of interaction is important to Alan and helps support and define his lifestyle choice.

> That's one of my *commitments to my lifestyle*. Thinking about that, you know [Laughs] . . . we laugh because growing up my daughter watched me wearing suits and driving a company car and my [much younger] son is now growing up watching me driving an old pick-up truck and plowing snow, wearing Carhartts. Man, those kids are going to have stories to share. "No, Dad was this . . . !" and "No, Dad was this . . . !"

Like other lifestyle migrants who left behind well-established careers, both voluntarily and involuntarily, Alan often used the term "retired" to describe his current social status. But this did not mean that he no longer worked. Alan is trying to make a statement about having left behind a part of his life defined by a career and the lifestyle to which that work contributed. He left this career, gave up that path, and therefore we would tend to say that he has retired, but he has by no means stopped working. He has simply chosen to define himself in opposition to that past. But like the ambiguity his youngest and oldest child might one day have about what kind of person Dad actually was while they were growing up (was Dad a suit or a Carhartt man?), Alan is not always sure himself where he is when it comes to typical categories. "To this day I don't know how to define myself. Beth has finally acquiesced to my preferred definition [or] my preferred word, 'retired.' I prefer to say that [Laughs]. I guess I'm not . . . I'm not retired, but I find it easier to define myself that way."

## PERSONAL WATERSHEDS

Still traveling with Alan in his pick-up, we round a corner and head eastward on the tree-lined Supply Road where it follows a long ridge above the Bay. Alan gazes at the countryside now visible through a brief break in the storm. After a few moments, he returns to an earlier description of how he felt stuck in his former corporate life. He explains how after a number of years of self-doubt about his life's direction, he was ready for something new. He had become entrenched through routine and the fear of uncertainty that comes with thinking of a dramatic change. As with so many lifestyle migrants, the choice came down to a single moment. Everything shifted on the very stretch of road we now traveled. He brought me here to share his story.

Nearly everyone can point to one or more junctures or divides in their lives where a certain critical event, or a series of events, may act as a catalyst that inspires a person to make far-reaching decisions about the course of their life. Typically, dramatic personal shifts are precipitated through more negative life events. These include such episodes as a death in the family, personal near-death experience or serious injury, a divorce, or being laid off from work. They also come in the form of such positive experiences as the birth of a child or a job promotion. In all of these watershed situations, people reach a point where they feel that they are out of the flow of time in the course of "normal" events. They pause to reflect on the meaning and direction of their lives.

In Alan's account, I can feel how the weight of meaningful possibilities tipped an inner scale, pushing him to embrace change, take a risk, and make a commitment to change his life. His crisis reached a breaking point. Work continued to grate on him, "tear him down," and violate his sense of right and wrong. At the same time, a personal history of a failed first marriage weighed in on his second, now threatened by many of the same patterns of behavior. Driving down this road a few years earlier, thinking about the direction his life was heading, Alan experienced a moment of clarity and insight that led to a self-transforming conversion.

I was coming up [to Traverse City] on weekends. I'd come up here and wouldn't have anything to do. I came up here many times alone. And I said, "Gee, this is different up here. There's something different that I can't quite put my fingers on." I was not able to identify it but you can look back, reflect, and figure it out. I remember driving down Supply Road . . . and I was making a decision. My wife and I were having problems. She was going to move Up

North [permanently]. I wasn't so sure. I started looking around, looking at the trees. They were starting to change colors in September. I thought to myself, why would I leave all this for what I got down there? Maybe I should leave all that for what's up here. I remember that day as clear as a bell. I was driving down the road looking out the window and I realize that I'm fucked up. I need to keep all this. I apparently have to give up something to keep all this. So you finally say, I'm forty-five, am I gonna make it to sixty-five? Am I gonna make it to fifty-five? Am I gonna die from an ulcer or a heart attack? I was going to the doctor on a regular basis. You just finally got to make the decision.

## CONCLUSION—MORAL GEOGRAPHIES

Lifestyle migrants tell travel stories of personal transformation much like conversion narratives. In stories like Alan's, watershed experiences may separate one life, or at least one lifestyle, from another. What is now seen as an inauthentic, often violated self, is left behind. Lifestyle migrants instead seek a more authentic self, one which may have been held as a distant ideal in the form of a potential self. As for other lifestyle migrants, in Alan's case, this transformation is literally the claiming of a kind of redemptive, second chance at life. Lifestyle migrants attempt to redefine their own personal relation to the good life by finding ways to harmonize the material domain in the form of pursuing a livelihood, with a moral sphere of family and social relations. It is about getting *reoriented*. Refugees from a way of life characterized by the corporate "rat race," the narrative accounts of relocation and starting over given by lifestyle migrants describe how they "got control" and "took back their lives." In so doing they reject feelings of disorientation, dispossession, and being adrift. Taking back one's life entails being able to define one's self and personal identity according to one's own moral narrative of self.

Identity is defined in part by the commitments and identifications that people make which provide the frame or horizon within which they can try "to determine from case to case what is good, or valuable, or what ought to be done, or what [they] endorse or oppose" (Taylor 1989). To lack a personally meaningful moral narrative of self is to be without a frame in which things take on stable significance and in which a person is able to weigh possibilities as good or bad, meaningful or superfluous. An essential part of self-identity is that a person is positioned in both physical and moral space. This orientation is not only a part of how people find their bearings and locate themselves in a particular social and physical landscape, it is also how they situate themselves within a culturally informed space of questions about what is worth doing and not worth doing in their quest to find the good life. To speak of *orientation* is thus more than mere metaphor. Speaking of whether he could have enacted the fundamental personal changes that he has realized by moving Up North had he stayed in the Detroit area, Alan explains "I'm not sure I could have. I'm not sure I could do it. When I go back there, the people act differently. For me to get my personality to where I trusted people and I liked people, I had to get away from the environment where I didn't trust people."

Relocation to new places, especially rural and small-town places, is essential for lifestyle migrants. In these places, they feel a meaningful connection that they envision will support their commitment to a new lifestyle. The choice of where to live is also one about how to live. It is not only about physical, geographic relocation, it also entails a moral reorientation. It is thus both a question of practical or economic concerns as well as of moral matters about what makes a life worth living. At a time when social and economic conditions that helped sustain an older vision of the dream are eroding, the relocation behavior of lifestyle migrants is a part of what may be a new kind of American Dreaming, one that draws on enduring values of good work and commitment to family, as it takes advantage of new opportunities and copes with new challenges.

## AFTERWORD

Since veering from a more "traditional" anthropological career trajectory where one is expected to work outside their own society and culture, my status as a participant observer has never been so acute. Although the romanticized trials of foreign fieldwork are often avoided by doing work "at home," there are other, unique challenges. For instance, it can be easy to take much for granted. Born and raised in middle-class, white America, my fieldwork in northern Michigan became an ongoing exercise in making the familiar unfamiliar. Very simply, personal background and choice of fieldwork sites influence my ethnographic work. While growing up, my father worked for IBM. Our family moved frequently as IBM grew and opened new facilities. Memories of my father's experiences working for a post-war corporate giant and my own struggles with adjusting to new places combined in an enduring interest in family, work, and issues of personal identity tied to relocation.

Within anthropology over the past twenty years, interest has grown for considering the close relationship between personal history, motivation, and the particulars of ethnographic fieldwork. Specifically, how do these factors have bearing on the construction of theory and conduct of a scholarly life? Personal and professional experiences, together with historical context, lead individual researchers to their own particular methodological and theoretical approaches. Anthropological fieldwork is shaped by personal and professional identities just as these identities are inevitably shaped by individual experiences while in the field. Unfortunately, the autobiographical dimension of ethnographic research has been downplayed historically, if not discounted altogether. This is mostly understandable given a perceived threat to the objectivity expected of legitimate science, reliability of data, and integrity of our methodology, if we appear to permit subjectivity to intervene by allowing the ethnographer's encumbered persona to appear instead of adhering to the prescribed role of dispassionate observer.

Most anthropologists today point to Bronislaw Malinowski, author of such landmark ethnographies as *Argonauts of the Western Pacific* (1922), as a kind of founding father to ethnographic fieldwork, and the practice of "participant observation." Malinowski's early-twentieth-century ethnographies were written in a voice removed and utterly unrevealing about the nature of the ethnographer and his relationship to the people studied. Since Malinowski's time, the personal account of fieldwork has been hidden away in notes and diaries. These "off-the-record" writings document the tacit impressions and emotional experiences without which we cannot, as ethnographers, fully appreciate and understand the project of our research itself. Malinowski's diaries were published after his death in a revealing autobiographical account of his inner life while in the field (1967). We learn in them that, among other details, Malinowski longed to write great novels even as his scientific writing effectively defined the practice of cultural anthropology for much of the twentieth century.

Of many important lessons for anthropologists, Malinowski's diaries hold two especially relevant ones here. First of these is that, at its heart, ethnographic writing is a means of expressing a shared interest among cultural anthropologists for telling stories—stories about what it means to be human. The other is that the explicit professional project of observing, imagining, and describing other people need not be incompatible with the implicit personal project of learning about the self. It is the honest truth of fieldwork that these two projects are always implicated in each other. Good ethnography recognizes the transformative nature of fieldwork where, as we search for answers to questions about people, we may find ourselves in the stories of others. Ethnography should be acknowledged as a mutual product born of the intertwining of the lives of the ethnographer and his or her subjects.

Just as personal background no doubt influences all aspects of ethnographic work, previous fieldwork experience informs my understanding of current research even though outwardly these projects appear quite different. In keeping with anthropological traditions of foreign-based research, as a doctoral student my interest in family, work, and relocation led me to rural Indonesia for a year of Fulbright research in 1998. I examined community-building in several migrant villages that had been established from the ground up, through the relocation of hundreds of families in a rural development program. My research revealed the means through which migrants dealt with profound dislocations of resettlement in order to establish socially, economically, and ecologically sustainable communities. Unexpectedly, fieldwork with migrants in Sulawesi, Indonesia offered insight into how I might interpret the experiences of relocating professionals in Northern Michigan. Specifically, many resettled villagers spoke of how they used relocation to selectively "edit out" or enhance certain personal and cultural elements on an individual and group level. I revealed a similar process of editing among lifestyle migrants who relocated in order to bring about what they felt was a necessary break from established personal rituals, family routines, and practices within corporate America.

## NOTES

1. See Lewis Rambo's (1993) approach to conversion as not strictly an inner event or singular moment in a person's life, but as a complex process involving varied dimensions from the social to the psychological and spiritual. Similarly, Daroll Bryant and Christopher Lamb (1999) suggest that the conversion experience can be understood as a non-religious phenomenon.

2. Research on an emergent urban-to-rural migration phenomenon in the late 1960s to 1970s challenged predominant migration models, which had relied on economic explanations: relocation behavior was thought to be driven by a desire to maximize individual earning potential (cf. Jobes, Stinner, Wardwell 1992). The term non-economic emerged as a way to describe a migration trend in which a significant number of Americans in their productive working years chose relocation to rural areas well outside centers of business and recognized forms of economic opportunity. As a term, non-economic migration was meant to distinguish the behavior of these migrants from the expected pattern of voluntary population movement where presumed rational actors were motivated by economic opportunity (cf. Williams and Sofranko 1979, Berry 1976).

3. The Bureau of Labor Statistics developed the following simple conceptual definition in 1989: "Contingent work is any job in which an individual does not have an explicit or implicit contract for long-term employment" (in Polivka and Nardone 1989). For some the term "contingent work" applies to nearly any arrangement that deviates from the standard model of a full-time wage and salaried job.

## REFERENCES

Berry, Brian J. L. 1976. *Urbanization and counterurbanization.* Beverly Hills, CA: Sage Publications.

Bonner, Kieran Martin. 1997. *A great place to raise kids: Interpretation, science and the urban-rural debate.* Montreal: McGill-Queen's University Press.

Boyle, Paul, and Keith Halfacree, eds. 1998. *Migration into rural areas: Theories and issues.* New York: Wiley.

Bryant, M. Darrol, and Christopher Lamb. 1999. "Conversion: Contours of controversy and commitment in a plural world." In *Religious conversion: Contemporary practices and controversies,* ed. Christopher Lamb and M. Darrol Bryant, 1–22. New York: Cassell.

Castro, Janice. 1993. "Disposable workers." *Time,* March 29, 43–7.

Clark, Andrew H., and E. Roy Officer. 1962. "Land use pattern." *Symposium on the great lakes basin: A symposium presented at the Chicago meeting of the American Association for the Advancement of Science, 29–30 December, 1959,* ed. Howard J. Pincus. Baltimore: Horn-Shafer Company.

de Certeau, Michel. 1984. *The practice of everyday life.* Berkeley: University of California Press.

Didion, Joan. 2003. *Where I was from.* New York: Alfred A. Knopf.

Hochschild, Arlie Russell. 1997. *The time bind: When work becomes home and home becomes work.* New York: Metropolitan Books.

Hoey, Brian A. 2005. "From Pi to pie: Moral narratives of noneconomic migration and starting over in the postindustrial midwest." *Journal of Contemporary Ethnography* 34 (5): 586–624.

Hummon, David Mark. 1990. *Commonplaces: Community ideology and identity in American culture.* SUNY Series in the Sociology of Culture. Albany, NY: State University of New York Press.

Jobes, Patrick C. 1992. "Economic and quality of life decisions in migration to a high natural amenity area." In *Community, society, and migration: Noneconomic migration in America,* ed. Patrick C. Jobes, William F. Stinner, and John M. Wardwell, 335–62. Lanham, MD: University Press of America.

——. 2000. *Moving nearer to heaven: The illusions and disillusions of migrants to scenic rural places.* Westport, CT: Praeger.

Jobes, Patrick C., William F. Stinner, and John M. Wardwell, eds. 1992. *Community, society, and migration: Noneconomic migration in America.* Lanham, MD: University Press of America.

Johnson, Kenneth. 1999. "The rural rebound." *PRB reports on America* 1 (3). Population Reference Bureau, Washington, DC.

Johnson, Kenneth M., and Calvin L. Beale. 1998. "The rural rebound." *Wilson Quarterly* 22 (2): 16–27.

Judson, Dean H., Sue Reynolds-Scanlon, and Carole L. Popoff. 1999. "Migrants to Oregon in the 1990's: Working age, near-retirees, and retirees make different destination choices." *Rural development perspectives* 14 (2): 24–31.

Lane, Robert. 1991. *The market experience.* New York: Cambridge University Press.

Luban, Ruth. 2001. *Are you a corporate refugee?: A survival guide for downsized, disillusioned, and displaced workers.* New York: Penguin Book.

MacCannell, Dean. 1999. *The tourist: A new theory of the leisure class.* Berkeley: University of California Press.

MacIntyre, Alasdair C. 1984. *After virtue: A study in moral theory.* 2nd ed. Notre Dame, IN: University of Notre Dame Press.

Malinowski, Bronislaw. 1922. *Argonauts of the western Pacific.* London: Routledge & Sons.

——. 1967. *A diary in the strict sense of the term.* London: Routledge & Kegan Paul.

Martin, Emily. 1994. *Flexible bodies: Tracking immunity in American culture from the days of polio to the age of AIDS.* Boston: Beacon Press.

Moen, Phyllis. 2001. "The career quandary." *PRB reports on America* 2 (1). Population Reference Bureau, Washington, DC.

Murdoch, Jonathon, and Graham Day. 1998. "Middle class mobility, rural communities and the politics of exclusion." In *Migration into rural areas: Theories and issues,* ed. Paul Boyle and Keith Halfacree, 186–99. New York: Wiley.

Murray, Alan. 2000. *The wealth of choices: How the new economy puts power in your hands and money in your pocket.* New York: Crown.

Pandit, Kavita, and Suzanne Davies Withers. 1999. *Migration and restructuring in the United States: A geographic perspective.* Lanham, MD: Rowman & Littlefield.

Pindell, Terry. 1995. *A good place to live: America's last migration.* New York: Holt.

Polivka, Anne E., and Thomas Nardone. 1989. "On the definition of 'content work.'" *Monthly Labor Review* December: 9–16.

Putnam, Robert D. 2000. *Bowling alone: The collapse and revival of American community.* New York: Simon & Schuster.

Rambo, Lewis R. 1993. *Understanding religious conversion.* New Haven, CT: Yale University.

Shi, David E. 1986. *In search of the simple life: American voices, past and present.* Salt Lake City: Peregrine Smith Books.

———. 1985. *The simple life: Plain living and high thinking in American culture.* New York: Oxford University Press.

Stinner, William. F., Nithet Tinnakul, S. Kan, and Michael B. Toney. 1992. "Community attachment and migration decision making in nonmetropolitan settings." In *Community, society, and migration: Noneconomic migration in America,* ed. William F. Stinner, Patrick C. Jobes, and John M. Wardwell, 47–84. Lanham, MD: University Press of America.

Taylor, Charles. 1997. "Leading a life." In *Incommensurability, incomparability, and practical reasoning,* ed. Ruth Chang. Cambridge, MA: Harvard University Press.

———. 1989. *Sources of the self: The making of the modern identity.* Cambridge, MA: Harvard University Press.

Weiss, Michael J. 1999. "Parallel universe." *American Demographics* 21 (10): 58–63.

Whyte, William Hollingsworth. 1956. *The organization man.* New York: Simon and Schuster.

Williams, James D., and Andrew J. Sofranko. 1979. "Motivations for the inmigration component of population turnaround in nonmetropolitan areas." *Demography* 14 (2): 239–55.

Zukin, Sharon. 1991. *Landscapes of power: From Detroit to Disney World.* Berkeley: University California Press.

**Figure 7.1.   Downtown Dexter's picturesque shopping district.**
Photo by Brian A. Hoey

# 7

## Patrolling the Boundaries of Childhood in Middle-Class "Ruburbia"

*Lara Descartes and Conrad P. Kottak*

"Did you wash your hands with soap when you got home from school?" This was Noreen Carroll's question of Vic, her young son, when he arrived back at their house.[1] A few minutes later, she asked him again, and then a third time. It was a lovely and sunny May afternoon. Noreen and I (the first author) had just finished walking back to Noreen's home from the local elementary school, where we had picked Vic up. He is an articulate little boy, sturdily built, sporting a closely trimmed hair cut. For part of the walk Vic held Noreen's hand and she questioned him about his school day. The twice daily ritual of bringing Vic to and from school is important to Noreen. She sticks to it adamantly, no matter the weather.

Noreen, her husband, Cy, and Vic live in a pleasant home in a residential area in the village of Dexter, Michigan. Dexter is a picturesque spot. Its Main Street is lined with brightly painted buildings housing an array of service-oriented businesses: Bakeries, gift shops, and restaurants are to be found alongside a bank, grocery store, gasoline station, and hardware store. Recent additions to the landscape include cheerful flower beds and brick-lined sidewalks. Shoppers can relax and enjoy the views from wooden and iron-work benches placed in front of the various buildings. The village's residential streets are well-maintained. Large clapboard homes with open front porches present an inviting picture of small-town family life. Outside the village proper lies the township. Here, most homes are newer, and most are built in developments labeled with a variety of pastoral names, such as Fox Ridge. These subdivisions are filled primarily with large, bi-level homes surrounded by expansive lawns. The houses uniformly are neatly kept and landscaped. Driving from the village center out to the subdivisions, one is reminded of Dexter's agricultural heritage by businesses such as a feed store and cider mill, as well as the remaining farmland.

Although many families with young children have moved to Dexter to partake in its rural ambience, there are not many other children in Noreen's neighborhood. Vic has nobody to play with. Noreen, a stay-home mother, reports that her son doesn't miss having other children around, as he spends nearly every minute of his free time with her. Vic's grandmother lives nearby, but he rarely spends time even with her. During the time I spent with Noreen, her ability to monitor Vic and his environment emerged as a very significant theme in her life, shaping her daily parenting style, as well as her work and family decisions.

We spent time with Noreen as part of a study we were conducting in southeastern Michigan on how parents think about their work and family decisions, and how they use media to gather information on those topics. As part of this research we interviewed thirty-six parents (eight men and twenty-eight women), conducted eight focus groups with a total of forty-six people (fourteen men and thirty-two women), and spent time in twelve families' homes, conducting ethnographic observation. As we did so, the themes that emerged in our discussions with parents and our observations piqued our interest in a slightly different topic: how parents conceptualize appropriate boundaries between their home and the external world. We became intrigued with how parents' values influence their decisions on where to live, how to earn a living, and how to best care for their children.

Noreen patrols the borders of her child's world and expresses resentment when there is intrusion. When she and I picked Vic up at school, she asked him how the day had gone. He told her his class had played a word game. "I don't know why they do that," Noreen said to me, in front of Vic. Noreen doesn't like Vic's teacher this year. The teacher doesn't encourage parental involvement in the classroom, and that seems to fuel Noreen's disregard. While I was with them, Noreen met every comment that Vic made about his teacher and the work she had assigned with a dismissive remark. Noreen is thinking of home schooling Vic since the public schools "are basically day care." Ironically, part of the reason Noreen and Cy moved to Dexter was the high quality of its school system.

Noreen's mistrust of the schools and her concern with separating Vic's school world from his home world is demonstrated symbolically by two ritualized practices (see Han, this volume, for a discussion of ritual). One is the formality with which Vic must dress for the school day. Noreen insists he wear tailored clothing to school. What Noreen calls "ragged" clothing is to be worn only at home. Comfort and informality are reserved for the domestic sphere. The second ritualized practice is the hand washing with soap. This is done whether or not Vic is going to eat something when he gets home: The point seems to be to mark Vic's exit from the (polluted) outside world back into the (pure) home world. These two practices clearly separate the world of school from the world of home. By controlling them, Noreen exerts some power over keeping the outside, where she has less influence over Vic's development, separate from the home, where she is in complete control.

Noreen is wary not only of her son's teacher and her influence on Vic, but of other children as well. She does not want Vic to ride the school bus, where he'd be mixing with older children. She places a great deal of emphasis on maintaining childhood innocence, and feels that such an environment would corrupt him. In our time together, she spoke more than once about her anxieties regarding Vic's maturation process. Soon he will be in a school where he will be exposed to children in grades above him, and Noreen worries about their impact upon him. She particularly fears what will happen when teenagers might start to have an influence on Vic. Noreen spoke of her special dread of the day Vic himself becomes a teenager. What seems to evoke these apprehensions is the potential for behaviors and thoughts affected by people other than her.

Vic has been sheltered as well from adult men. He doesn't spend much time with his own father. According to Noreen, they don't share the same bond as Vic and Noreen. Nor does Vic spend much time with either grandfather. Noreen reports that Vic is shy around adult men. If her husband's male work friends visit, Vic barely addresses them. Noreen realizes this has a lot to do with how she and Cy have socialized Vic. Their frequent admonitions against speaking to strangers can't help but have an effect.

Noreen's parenting style is shaped strongly by her view of the outside world and her wish to be the primary, if not sole, influence on her son's development. These concerns also affected her decision to be a stay-home mother. Once she had Vic she abandoned work outside the home. She said a person can't both work for pay and raise a child and do either one well: "There's people that think they're going to work and raising their kids, and doing a great job in both areas. And they are not." She can offer many examples to support this statement. About the children of working mothers, Noreen says: "When you go to school, and you go on field trips, you can almost pick the kids that are home with their mom all the time, and the ones that are maybe part time with their mom, and the ones that basically grew up in day care . . . the kids are just, they're different." Noreen's depiction of working mothers is that they come home and are too tired to do anything but plop their children in front of a Barney video. She connects these impressions of life in a dual-income family to disturbing events she's seen on the news:

When the Columbine incident happened . . . those were kids from working parents that were building bombs in their garage. You know what, my son's never going to build a bomb in my garage and me not know about it. I'm home every day, I go in and out of there—you know. Just like you hear about kids on the Internet and stuff. And sure enough, they come home from school, they go to their room, their parents come home at six o'clock or whatever time. I just know that kind of stuff's not going to happen in our house because it's going to be really hard for him to get around Mom, she's, like, always going to just be there.

Noreen added, "If you look at some of the big crime figures, the Jeffrey Dahmers, and this, that, and the other, they're not from a home where a mom was there every day when they got off the bus, and raised them and nurtured them."

Noreen's husband's income is sufficient to support the family, but his job keeps him away from home for long hours. Cy's commute to work is thirty to forty minutes each way, his work day is the standard eight hours, and he has to do extra traveling for his job. The division of labor in their household is very strict. Noreen does all the work associated with the home and child, and Cy earns the money to make it all possible: "We have a real set division of labor in our house. And when he's done with his division of labor, he's done." In other words, Cy does not "help out" with housework when he is at home.

Noreen's concern with keeping her home life controlled and separate from the outside world extends to screening her telephone calls with her answering machine. When I was there, she sat and listened as a relative left a message. She told me she likes to hear who is phoning and why before she speaks with someone. Noreen also is very cautious concerning the incursion of the outside world into her son's life via television and the Internet; she keeps a close eye on all media he might encounter. Noreen watches television only after Vic is in bed. She talks of children who watch television as if they were neglected. This was seen in the previous example in which Noreen criticized working mothers, saying they must be too tired to do anything but plop their children in front of videos at the end of the day. Indeed, Noreen spends a fair amount of time expressing her disapproval of other ways of parenting that put less emphasis on isolating children from the outside world. Noreen seems to measure the morality of mothering in terms of how exclusionary the home environment is.

Noreen stands at one end of a continuum among mothers we worked with in Dexter. Many were highly invested in nurturing a very specific vision of childhood and maintaining well-defined barriers between their children and various elements of the outside world. Living in Dexter itself, a semi-rural, 98 percent white (U.S. Census Bureau 2000a, 2000b), middle-class community, enabled many to live out this ideal, raising their children in the type of environment they preferred, which might be characterized as sheltered and homogenous in terms of race, family form, religion, and class. A side effect, however, as we will see, tended to be a fairly rigid household division of labor and a large parental burden of transportation.

Julie Blanding, another mother in our study, radiates an intense energy that at times crosses over into obvious irritation. The Blandings live with their two children in a large home in one of Dexter's older subdivisions. Julie's son is in first grade, and her daughter is in third. Julie has professional training, as does her husband, Bill. She works two days a week, having cut steadily back on her work time during the course of her child rearing. Of this she says: "I cut my hours back every year. As they get older, it's [balancing work and family] harder!" Even her reduced work schedule leaves her visibly frustrated and frazzled; she works mainly to maintain her credentials. Describing the days when she goes to her job, Julie peppers the word "crazy" throughout. Both of her children are involved in several extracurricular activities, including sports and church groups. Julie doesn't foresee going back to work full time until her children are in college, saying "I don't want to leave them! I don't want to miss all the practices and games and come home exhausted with no meals on the table."

Julie was clearly frustrated with her husband's participation in the home. When asked whether Bill had made any changes in his work patterns due to family Julie replied:

> No, he just keeps going! No, I worry about it, he does not. I'm the one that's always changing. . . . No, he's never even considered changing his work schedule. And I'm trying to get him into work earlier, so he can get home earlier, and we can't even do that. Because he's not an early person, he's not an early riser, and he has hours where he could do that.

She continues, "I do the juggling. He's oblivious to it. It's like, he gets up, he goes to work." Julie expresses impatience with the amount and quality of Bill's participation in the labor of caring for their children and home. If she leaves the children with him while she goes to her job, she avoids having to worry about child care, but says she faces a large mess to clean up when she gets home. If she has him put the children to bed, she says they aren't in bed at the proper time because he doesn't watch the clock. Julie reports that she does all the house cleaning, although Bill will help her with something if she asks him. She does admit that he is a loving father to the children, although this accolade comes with a small sting, as she says that what he likes to do is sit and watch videos with the children. She'd rather he spend time helping with the less entertaining aspects of their daily care. Bill's career and daily commute are demanding, however. He is gone five days a week, nine to ten hours a day. Julie's part-time position is closer to home; her commuting and working time is far less than Bill's.

When Julie's children were younger she had them in the child care facility provided by her employer; she mentions she felt they were safe there.

She initially stated that she had no negative experiences using the facility and says that it helped her children get ready for school. As Julie continued, however, she began to describe what she disliked about child care, and a theme of boundary control emerged. After talking about the day care in both positive and neutral ways, she suddenly labeled her attitude toward it as "hate." She mentioned that she didn't like it that her children were napping on cots. I never did determine why the cots were so objectionable, but it may have been because they were communal: other kids may have slept on the same cots as Julie's children. That Julie had very strong feelings about other people's capacity to affect her children's behavior and environment became apparent during the time I spent with her and her family.

I spent an afternoon with Julie in February. It was a typically busy day, as she planned to pick up her children after school and then run several errands. Upon arriving at the school and seeing her daughter, Ruth, waiting in line, Julie encouraged Ruth to disobey the teacher's rules and break formation so that we could leave. Ruth seemed hesitant, but did as Julie directed. Once Julie's children were with her, the day was full of admonitions about safety. One of the first things Julie asked her son, Bobby, to do when he came home was to throw out a piece of bubble gum his teacher had given him. She did not like that the teacher did such things, and wondered acerbically if the teacher meant also to pay her son's dental bills. Julie worries a great deal about Bobby, saying quite specifically that she does so because he is social and gregarious. She discussed her dismay when, at one of his sporting events, she saw little girls chasing him around.

Julie's concern over her children's environment and its boundaries and her wish to be the primary arbiter of their physical and moral world is further evinced by stories she related. Bobby recently asked her what "gay" meant, and she avoided answering. He persisted over a span of some weeks, however, and she finally told him it meant "happy." Bobby replied that children on the playground had said it really meant boys falling in love with other boys. Julie says she stuck to her guns, however, telling him it meant "happy." Bobby also recently asked his father, Bill, apparently for the first time, about how babies are created. His father then explained the mechanics of pregnancy. Julie was furious when she found out, and told Bill never to have discussions like that without speaking to her first.

As carefully as Julie patrols the boundaries of her family's world, it is unsurprising that, like Noreen, she is similarly watchful about both her and her children's media consumption. Julie only allows the Disney and Nickelodeon television channels for the children. When asked about her own media intake, Julie disparages the idea of a regular and unmonitored connection to outside culture, saying she doesn't watch any television shows. She reports that she hasn't seen the news in eight years because she doesn't want her children exposed to it. Julie's vision, like Noreen's, of families with full-time working mothers is that at the end of the day children are put in front of the television or the computer because the parents need to get things done. And like Noreen, Julie contrasts her own children favorably with others. Julie says children who have been in day care more than hers don't know how to play in an unstructured way, and notes that her daughter had to teach one such girl "how to play babies."

Both Noreen and Julie seem suspicious of the parts of the world they cannot control, especially in terms of how their children are influenced by them. Both do their best to mediate external influences on their children and both express disdain for parents who do not do likewise or to the same degree. Both have made these concerns central in how they parent, and in their work and family decisions. Each, for example, chose to eliminate or decrease their work hours in order to be the predominating presence in their children's lives. In all these ways, Noreen and Julie are characteristic of a number of other mothers who participated in our study. Many echoed Noreen and Julie's wishes to be the sole providers of their child's care and education. Their concerns revolved around values, specifically to whose values their children might be exposed. Many women say they want to be at home full time because only then do they know that their beliefs are being transmitted to their children. One mother, Greta, put it this way: "What you think is right and wrong is different from what somebody else thinks is right or wrong . . . and I think that it is important the moms are there, [they're] your child. That's one of the reasons we're staying home, is that then they understand what we think is important." Amity, another stay-home mother, expresses similar concerns. Her son had just begun his formal education:

> [My son and I are] both having a hard time with the concept of a full-day kindergarten. Because I viewed his education as my sole responsibility. With an assistant, my husband. But it was my responsibility to make sure that it was rounded. . . . And now I have to give that up to a certain degree. I still feel like his primary educator, think of that as my role as a parent. But I had to give it up to some degree to the school, because we chose to put him in school rather than home schooling, which was an option.

Noreen and Julie thus exemplify a trend among the stay-home and part-time-working mothers in our study, although they were stronger than most in expressing suspicions of the outside world. Seeking a refuge from this world, parents in our study chose Dexter as a haven in which to raise their families. Many are residents of the new subdivisions that are sprinkled throughout the former countryside of Dexter Township. Dexter used to be made up of a small village surrounded by a rural township. The primary land use in the township was agricultural. Not many people lived in Dexter, and most of them were not middle class. However, Dexter eventually

became part of a national trend of "white flight": white, middle-class exodus from neighborhoods that start to become racially or ethnically diverse.
A vicious cycle plays out in which minority families move into a neighborhood, property values decline, the tax base devolves, the school systems de-
teriorate, and property values decline even further (Sides 2004). Thernstrom and Thernstrom (1999) observe that this white flight may not be
racially motivated, but class motivated. Unfortunately, since minorities are
less likely to have access to the same class status as whites, the end result is
the same. Minorities move in and whites move out. In the earlier part of the
twentieth century, this white flight was from city centers into what are now
called inner-ring suburbs. These are the suburbs built directly around cities.
This pattern of urban emigration was encouraged particularly by post-
World War II single-family home loans through the Federal Housing Administration and Veterans Administration and vigorous new highway construction that enabled easier access to the new suburbs (Duany,
Plater-Zyberk, and Speck 2000). Over time, some of those left behind in the
city centers, racial minorities and immigrants, also gained the resources to
move to the suburbs. They, like the whites preceding them, were looking for
better schools and less congested areas in which to raise their families.
There followed another wave of white flight, from the inner-ring suburbs
into newer developments further from city centers: the outer-ring suburbs.
In the past several decades, however, those suburbs also have aged and become more racially diverse. There was a corresponding push ever outward,
into what can be labeled "ruburbia" (Marx 1991). These are places like Dexter, formerly agricultural areas that are now peppered with large housing developments that recreate suburban living conditions in rural surroundings.

   The rise of the suburban lifestyle corresponded to a change in middle-
class parenting. The twentieth century saw increasing cultural attention paid
to the notion of the "vulnerable child," in need of constant parental vigilance, lest he or she fall prey to any one of a number of bad outcomes such
as physical or mental illness, abduction, or juvenile delinquency (Stearns
2003). The move to the suburbs was driven in part by this idea, which saw
the urban environment as unsafe and unwholesome for raising children.
Adult roles also underwent significant transformation. After a spurt of
World War II employment, for example, women were encouraged to leave
the workforce and concentrate their energies on their homes and families
(Baritz 1989, Kessler-Harris 1982). A new movement gathered steam, one
that Hays (1996) labels "intensive mothering." The central tenets of this
philosophy are that a mother must act as a child's primary caregiver, and
that care giving should be, among other things, both *"emotionally absorbing"*
and *"labor intensive"* (1996, 8, italics original). One of the ways in which
middle-class mothers perform intensive mothering is through "concerted
cultivation" (Lareau 2003). This is the notion that parents prepare children

for middle-class lives through manipulation of their environment: by providing them with directed learning experiences and organized activities, as well as via intervening with schools and other institutions to obtain individually desirable situations for their children. A child's outcome thus is a product of the parent's success at controlling the circumstances of the child's life.

When a family moves to a Dexter subdivision, the parents gain access to a kind of lifestyle that allows them to have a great deal of control over their children's environments. The houses in the developments are big, and some of them are very big. Each has its own plot of land, usually also quite sizeable. Many have large, expensive playsets in the backyard and sports equipment in the driveways. These provide contained places for children's activities, where they easily can be observed by a parent. Most of the houses we saw were filled with an array of modern amenities: Big-screen televisions, DVD players and VCRs, stereos, and computers. It was rare for us to work with a family that had children sharing a bedroom. Most children had their own private rooms, frequently with a television and computer of their own. One mother who lived in one such house, also equipped with a pool, mentioned that her children sometimes preferred spending time at home to doing extracurricular activities because there was so much to do at home.

Large lots provide privacy and separation from neighbors. Neighbors, however, are very similar. They all have the incomes to purchase these large new homes, which means they are solidly middle class. Many are professionals. Virtually all are white. As their children also are white and middle class, the neighborhood peer group is homogenous. Parents can count on the fact that their children's friends are much like their children, and their children's friends' parents are much like themselves. Comparatively few parents are even divorced: Single parents usually cannot afford to purchase homes in these subdivisions. A number of mothers in our study said they liked the fact that there were few single-parent families in Dexter.

As the subdivisions multiplied, the population explosion in Dexter exceeded the capacity of the old schools. All-new schools were built, which raised property taxes, further limiting the capacity of non-middle-class families to purchase single-family homes there. The new schools are modern, spacious, and well-equipped. Their quality has a local reputation such that many families choose to move to Dexter largely because of the school system. Yet, the schools actually are one of the few places where kids from the subdivisions can meet children with dissimilar backgrounds. The central village of Dexter has a fairly new apartment complex, where single-parent and lower-income families reside. This complex was a source of concern for a number of the parents we interviewed. Some mentioned that they worried that the children of divorced parents presented behavior problems that would take up disproportionate teacher time in the classroom, and that might affect their own children's behavior. Perhaps relatedly, a number of women told us they like to volunteer in the schools, not only to maintain an active presence in their children's daily lives and to get to know the teachers, but to know with whom their children were friends. Amity, a mother of one, put it this way:

> If I couldn't be involved in his school, to know exactly what kinds of things that they're teaching him, what kinds of interaction he's having with the children, how do they handle discipline on a daily basis, and I could[n't] pop in there and just be there to observe it . . . I don't know if I could do it [have him in public school].

Many of the men living in the new subdivisions have incomes that allow their wives to work part time or stay at home full time. A number of women in our study said they liked Dexter specifically because there were so many stay-home mothers there: They felt a strong sense of community and support. As one stay-home mother said, "We tend to hang out with people who have similar lifestyles. . . . I hang around with people who have other kids. Other moms who are home also, we get together. It seems like that's how things are." The village center had a few bakeries that some stay-home mothers talked about fondly. They welcomed the chance to drive in to the town center from their subdivisions, get a cup of coffee, and share some time with other mothers. Indeed, in our time spent in the subdivisions, we found the experience rather alienating and lonely. There might have been other stay-home mothers around, but during the day most of the women seemed fairly isolated, unless they left the subdivision and either went to the town center to run errands or to the schools to volunteer.

Dexter also is a religiously observant community, another element that many spoke of approvingly. The majority of the families participating in our study attended services regularly and their children were involved in religious activities. Nearly all the families were Catholic or Protestant.

The overall picture of life in Dexter, then, particularly in the subdivisions surrounding the central village, is one of homogeneity in class, race, religion, and family structure. When parents choose to move to a house in one of these developments, they obtain a very specific, controlled type of environment in which to raise their children. Many parents find this very reassuring. They describe their developments as safe places for their sons and daughters to grow up in.

A side effect of living in these far-flung subdivisions is that children are completely dependent on their parents for transportation. This increases even further parents' abilities to monitor their children and to know exactly what they are up to, with whom, and when. The central village of Dexter is a good half-hour from some of the more remote developments, some of which are on dirt roads. The only regular public transportation servicing the subdivisions are the school buses, and many parents do not want their children riding those. It was common in our sample for parents to drive their children to school and to pick them up. Sometimes this was because parents felt the bus ride was too long; sometimes it was because their children didn't like the bus experience, and sometimes it was necessary just in terms of timing: Most children were involved in many extracurricular activities, and most of those were not on school property. If a child had dance class or religious instruction after school, for example, it usually was only possible to make it on time if a parent picked the child up as soon as school let out.

An effect of living in ruburbia is that parents end up spending a great deal of time driving their children to and from school and activities (see Descartes, Kottak, and Kelly 2007). Usually that parent is the mother. And, since the move to Dexter frequently means leaving extended family behind, the burden truly is on the mother, and sometimes the father, to make sure all transportation needs are met. Most do this gladly, with only minor complaining, for they value what they gain by their expenditure of time and gasoline: the ability to keep a careful eye on their children and their children's environments. Few parents of younger children even take advantage of carpooling with neighborhood parents, although this seems more common for children who are older. Life in Dexter thus necessitates a great deal of child transportation, taking up a great deal of a parent's time.

Life in Dexter also means there are few local professional jobs available. This rural area with suburban housing developments has no real economic base aside from agriculture and services. It doesn't offer the kinds of jobs for which many of the parents in our study are trained: engineering, medicine, law, and so on. Parents who work in such fields must commute to their jobs. They—usually the fathers—undertake long daily drives in order to finance their families' Dexter homes. Many parents only drove thirty to forty minutes to their workplaces, as Noreen and Julie's husbands did. But others drove much longer distances, up to two and a half hours one way. This male time away from home reinforces a gendered division of labor. If men are not at home for much of the week, then it is their wives, more likely to be employed part time or not at all, who take up the slack, caring for children and home.

In the United States this is the usual pattern: Women still are the primary caretakers of children and performers of housework. This pattern endures even if wives as well as husbands are working full time for pay outside the home (see, for example, Bartley, Blanton, and Gilliard 2005, and Hochschild 1989). We suggest that life in ruburban areas, however, particularly encourages this pattern. Someone must earn the money to pay for the large, new home on its large lot. Men still out-earn women (O'Neill 2003), and women still are associated more with home and children. Dexter's men are more likely than its women to work at professional jobs with a lengthy commute. But someone must be home to take care of the children, their transportation, and home upkeep. Almost universally in our sample, that person was female. The occasional exception was due to male disability or unemployment. With the men absent for so much of the day, and the women shouldering most of the home and childcare labor, the patterns remain entrenched. The women tend to work part time or to stay at home full time, regardless of their professional credentials. This in turn can have long-term ramifications for their work lives: It can be difficult to re-enter the workforce once the traditional career path has been interrupted. As one stay-home mother who had been in the health sciences said of her permanent exit from that field: "How difficult is it going back to the lab field? . . . [Impossible. So staying home] took care of that." Some, like Julie, find a solution by working part time to maintain their professional credentials. This, however, can bear its own penalty, as witnessed by Julie's feelings of frenzy as she balances the demands of work and home. In turn, the men can seem oddly outside their own families' lives. Fathers, deprived of time with their children, may not be able to bond with them as the mothers do.

Life in Dexter involves trade-offs. When they move there, parents get the controlled environment they wish for their children. It's fairly easy to keep children protected from the outside world in Dexter, to monitor them and their environment, and to keep that environment uniform. Partly for these purposes, many of the women in our study preferred to stay at home full time or to work part time. This ensured that someone was available to take care of the home and the children, and to provide the transportation parents felt was necessary. One result of these decisions about where and how to live and work is that the ideologies of women as nurturers and men as breadwinners are reified by the community in which these families choose to live. When women are the only parents present, they shoulder the entire burden of family and home care. When men are gone for extended periods of time, they lose out on opportunities to participate in family life. Further, the children of such families are growing up in very homogenous surroundings. Their parents' decision on where and how to live means that they gain little exposure to children who are not like themselves and families that are not like their own.

The mothers in our study thus carefully patrol the boundaries between their children and outside influences. In this way they live out the ideologies of both intensive mothering and concerted cultivation. In these families, middle-class children are being groomed for middle-class lives, enabled by their parents' class-based ability to control many factors of their children's environment. This itself is symbolized by the mothers' ability to stay home full time or part time, and the location of the home, in middle-class ruburbia.

## AFTERWORD

When I began this fieldwork, I was a doctoral student in the University of Michigan's Department of Anthropology. Conrad Kottak was my major advisor. In the summer of 1999 I was in Los Angeles finishing up my dissertation research when he wrote to tell me about the project and to ask if I could come back to Ann Arbor to work on it. I was thrilled to comply, realizing what a great opportunity this was, both to get more fieldwork experience and to work with Conrad.

This project involved a great deal more intimate contact with families than any research I'd done before. It was both exhilarating to become part of families' lives and exhausting. After an afternoon or a day spent with a family, I'd come home, still on the "high" that comes with that kind of intense immersion into someone else's world, knowing I'd gotten good data, but barely having the energy to write up my field notes. The intimacy of the experience also meant that I developed deep rapport with some individuals, and was really moved at being included into their and their children's daily lives. This warmth paradoxically created its own tension, as my relationship with the people with whom I worked was by its nature finite: We all knew that I was there for a relatively short time and would not remain a part of their lives. I felt guilty about how this might impact some of the children in the study; one little girl in particular loved to have me come over and would get excited when she heard my voice on her family's answering machine, requesting another visit. Years after the study's completion, I still feel ambivalent about this aspect of fieldwork; the researcher arrives, gets the data he or she needs, and then leaves.

I also felt ambivalent during the research as to how much of myself to reveal to the participants. They revealed a great deal of themselves to me, by letting me come into their homes and spend time with them. In an ordinary relationship, such openness would be met with reciprocation. However, the research relationship is different. When an informant spoke to me of her thoughts on a topic, it was not my role to express my own opinions, as I would have done with a friend. It was instead my role to listen, remember, and elicit more information. Yet sometimes this one-sidedness could feel forced or even exploitative. I also felt some guilt over not revealing aspects of myself to my informants. They knew elements of my identity; that I was a woman in my early thirties, single, non-Latino white, with no children. They didn't know, however, that my politics, beliefs, and even sexual identity were quite different from many of theirs, and if they had known, they might have censored themselves accordingly. This also would have meant that I would have gathered less quality data, so I chose to remain silent. Since these were indeed research relationships, I feel I made the correct choice, but I am left wishing somehow that I could've met my informants' openness with more of my own.

Lara Descartes

As a cultural anthropologist, I have done ethnographic field work in Brazil (since 1962), Madagascar (since 1966), and the United States. I can trace my interest in how media influence life in small towns back to the 1980s, when my associates and I blended ethnography and survey research in studying "Television's Behavioral Effects in Brazil." That research is the basis of my book *Prime-Time Society: An Anthropological Analysis of Television and Culture* (Wadsworth 1990)—a comparative study of the nature and impact of television in Brazil and the United States. Since 1999 I have been an active member of the University of Michigan's Center for the Ethnography of Everyday Life, supported by the Alfred P. Sloan Foundation. In that capacity, for a research project titled "Media, Family, and Work in a Middle-Class Midwestern Town" (which provided the data on which this paper is based), Lara Descartes and I investigated how middle-class families use various media in planning, managing, and evaluating their choices and solutions involving the competing demands of work and family.

I initially proposed, and then worked with Lara to plan and implement, this research project. As Lara did the bulk of the fieldwork in Dexter, I monitored media messages about work and family (mainly on TV and radio), and explored them in a class I teach called "Television, Society, and Culture." Also, I participated in several of the focus groups we held in Dexter. One of my main conclusions was that a focus group discussing a key variable, such as a mother's work outside or inside the home, should be composed of people who are similar with respect to that variable. Our focus groups were much more productive when their members either all worked or all did not work outside the home. When groups were mixed, members were less likely to speak freely about the other group. In moderating a focus group, it's sometimes difficult to know when to intervene (to probe or redirect), and when to let the group go with its own flow. Because any focus group has a list of matters to be addressed, it's sometimes necessary to stop productive conversations so that all relevant questions can be asked in the allotted time. This project enabled me to extend my previous research on media in Brazil to a local setting in the United States, where parents and children are exposed regularly to images of family and work that may complement or clash with their own.

Conrad P. Kottak

## NOTES

We would like to thank the University of Michigan Center for the Ethnography of Everyday Life, an Alfred P. Sloan Center for the Study of Working Families, and its director, Thomas Fricke, for the opportunity to conduct this research. We also would like to thank Elizabeth Rudd for her insightful editing guidance as we prepared this chapter, and the participants in our study for their kindness in letting us become part of their lives for a while.

1. All personal names used in this chapter are aliases.

## REFERENCES

Baritz, Loren. 1989. *The good life: The meaning of success for the American middle class.* New York: Alfred A. Knopf.

Bartley, Sharon J., Priscilla W. Blanton, and Jennifer L. Gilliard. 2005. "Husbands and wives in dual-earner marriages: Decision-making, gender role attitudes, division of household labor, and equity." *Marriage and Family Review* 37 (4): 69–74.

Descartes, Lara, Conrad P. Kottak, and Autumn Kelly. 2007. "Chauffeuring and commuting: A story of work, family, class, and community." *Community, Work, and Family* 10 (2): 161–78.

Duany, Andres, Elizabeth Plater-Zyberk, and Jeff Speck. 2000. *Suburban nation: The rise of sprawl and the decline of the American dream.* New York: North Point Press.

Hays, Sharon. 1996. *The cultural contradictions of motherhood.* New Haven, CT: Yale University Press.

Hochschild, Arlie, with Anne Machung. 1989. *The second shift.* New York: Avon Books.

Kessler-Harris, Alice. 1982. *Out to work: A history of wage-earning women in the United States.* New York: Oxford University Press.

Lareau, Annette. 2003. *Unequal childhoods: Class, race, and family life.* Berkeley, CA: University of California Press.

Marx, Leo. 1991. "The American ideology of space." In *Denatured visions: Landscape and culture in the twentieth century,* ed. Stuart Wrede and William H. Adams, 62–78. Museum of Modern Art. New York: H. N. Abrams.

O'Neill, June. 2003. "The gender gap in wages, circa 2000." *American Economic Review* 93 (2): 309–14.

Sides, Josh. 2004. "Straight into Compton: American dreams, urban nightmares, and the metamorphosis of a black suburb." *American Quarterly* 56 (3): 583–605.

Stearns, Peter. 2003. *Anxious parents: A history of modern childrearing in America.* New York: New York University Press.

Thernstrom, Stephan, and Abigail Thernstrom. 1999. *America in black and white: One nation, indivisible.* New York: Simon and Schuster.

U.S. Census Bureau. 2000a. "Profile of General Demographic Characteristics: Dexter township, Michigan." htttp://factfinder.census.gov/servlet/SAFFFacts?_event=Search&geo_id=01000US&_geoContext=&_street=&_county=&_cityTown=dexter+township&_state=04000US26&_zip=&_lang=en&_sse=on.

U.S. Census Bureau. 2000b. "Profile of general demographic characteristics: Dexter village, Michigan." http://factfinder.census.gov/servlet/SAFFFacts?_event=Search&geo_id=06000US2616122180&_geoContext=01000US%7C04000US26%7C05000US26161%7C06000US2616122180&_street=&_county=&_cityTown=dexter+village&_state=04000US26&_zip=&_lang=en&_sse=on.

# II

## THE (NOT SO) STANDARD
## NORTH AMERICAN FAMILY

# 8

## Gay Family Values

### Gay Co-Father Families in Straight Communities

*Diana M. Pash*

> The lesbians and gay men in town were strangers who were not all that strange: they tended to have families, respectable work; they shared many, if not most of their values, and even looked and acted very much like them . . . .
>
> —Arlene Stein, *The Stranger Next Door* (2001, 217)

It's six-thirty a.m. and the Albert-Calihan family is getting ready for their day. Rich Albert, forty-two, has already left for work and daughter, Amy, ten, is still sleeping. Son, Andrew, seven, is in his pajamas and has just come downstairs to the kitchen where he joins his father, Fred Calihan, forty-two. "Hey, Andrew? You know what? You did *all* the valentines for your class last night but you know who we haven't done a valentine for?" asks Fred. Andrew shakes his head and thinks. "Mm . . . I don't know." Fred provides a hint. "Someone that lives here." Andrew makes a guess. "You?" "I don't know if you've done one for me or not. Who else?" Fred asks. "Daddy," says Andrew. "Daddy," says Fred. "Should we do one for Daddy this morning?" Andrew exclaims with excitement, "Whoop!" and slams his hand down on the countertop. "Okay let me finish this and we'll get some stuff. Okay?" says Fred. "Why don't you grab some markers or something and I'll grab some paper for you." After getting the materials from a storage cabinet, Fred helps Andrew write and decorate the card for his father and then goes upstairs to shower and dress for work.

This weekday morning scene could have taken place in almost any American home today. A father helping a child create a Valentine's Day card before taking on the day is not an unusual activity. What is different is that the card is for the child's other father. This household is headed by two fathers, but the fact that Rich and Fred are gay is incidental to this scene and countless others that reflect their routine lives as a family. The Albert-Calihan family—and many other gay families like them—present a paradox. On one hand, they represent a radical break with mainstream society. On the other hand, they diverge from traditional notions of kinship in the American gay community, which has historically emphasized unconventional family configurations. Such configurations generally have not included children, and friends and friendship networks have taken on familial importance.

In recent years, after having established domestic partnerships and households together, an increasing number of gay male couples have chosen to become parents.[1,2] According to Barret and Robinson (2000), the decade of the 1990s will be remembered as a period in which gays and lesbians became a part of the mainstream of America. In the past, gay men usually became fathers within heterosexual unions before coming out as gay. Today more gay men are becoming parents within the context of a relatively established gay identity (Patterson 1994, 1995, Patterson and Chan 1997), years after coming out to parents, family, friends, and others.[3] In Los Angeles and in other cities throughout the United States, gay men are starting families through a variety of means, including adoption, foster care, surrogacy, and in some cases, through co-parenting arrangements with lesbian women. While the study of gay men dates to the 1960s, the study of their lives as fathers and heads of families among a larger, predominantly heterosexual society covers new ground. Little is known about how these new kinds of gay families are integrating into mainstream communities, or the degrees to which they will expand the culturally dominant notion of family or of what it means to be a gay man in America today.

This chapter explores the ordinary lives of a small group of gay co-father families in the Los Angeles area in order to better understand their integration into mainstream American life. It begins by asking questions about the families' social relations in everyday life: How do gay co-father families perceive their reception as a family? What are some of the key difficulties that they face? What are their experiences with children's schools and day care providers? What is the nature and quality of the relationships they are establishing with straight parents and neighbors? It concludes by asking whether the participation of gay co-father families in predominantly heterosexual, mainstream communities is changing dominant views and definitions of family.

## STUDYING GAY CO-FATHER FAMILIES:
## AT HOME IN A COMMUNITY

The term *community* has been generally understood to mean either a locality, which refers to a geographic or territorial notion (such as a neighborhood, city, or town), or a relational quality, which refers to one's social ties and the aspects of human interaction that bring people into contact with one another (Heller 1989). Group members who have a common history of experience and who develop emotional closeness with one another share a relational notion of community (McMillan and Chavis 1986).[4] Group membership also is characterized by a common identity (Heller 1989). This sense of community is not bounded by location but rather can extend beyond physical boundaries, and people connected in a relational community can communicate in numerous ways and across vast distances. When families locate to a particular neighborhood or town, they become part of a local community, bound together by geographic interests that are brought to bear on them. Likewise, they are undoubtedly members of various other *relational communities*, held together by common values, goals, and histories. Such relational communities include those bound by sexual orientation, religion, ethnicity, recreational interests, or type of employment, for example.

Seeking to fill a gap in research literature that overlooked the role of community relationships and institutions in working families' lives, Bookman's (2004) ethnography examines the meaning of community among forty middle-class, dual-earner families in the biotechnology industry by listening to people's stories, and by observing how they are building community relations right from "their own backyards," a place where being integrated within a community is particularly important for families. She suggests that individuals define community in various ways and that they may be members of a number of different communities that are important to family life. By understanding "how diverse forms of community actually operate in people's lives" (2004, 24) and by looking closely at the relationships that working families develop within these various communities, Bookman suggests we can better understand how such involvement may spur volunteerism and civic engagement for the betterment of the larger society. She uses the term "community care work" to refer to the informal relationships that family members nurture with childcare providers, teachers, clergy and other parents. The people who make up such communities are part of a person's social support network and "community care work offers families the sense that they are not alone" (2004, 5).

## Why Community Is an Important Concept for Studying the Emerging Phenomenon of Gay Co-father Families

For gay men and lesbians in the United States in the 1960s and 1970s, the concept of "community" arose from identity politics. Through collective political action, many gay men and lesbians, previously silenced by fear, found a voice, began to identify with one another, and stood together in opposition to a disapproving mainstream society. At the time of the gay liberation movement in the 1970s, the notion of a gay community was the embodiment of "practical wisdom emerging from the bars, friendship networks, and a spate of new gay organizations." This practical wisdom was the knowledge that "lesbians and gay men, joining together on the basis of a sexual identity, could create enduring social ties" (Weston 1991, 122). But identification with a gay community does not necessarily mean that members constitute a unified subculture; rather, "gay community" is a category that Weston argues is "implicated in the ways lesbians and gay men have developed collective identities, organized urban space, and conceptualized their significant relationships" (1991, 124). Laird argues, "the notion of a gay or lesbian 'community' is as broad and diverse as that of gay 'family'" (1993, 292). In his study of gay men in New York City, Woolwine (2000) found that the notion of a "gay community" was understood in several different ways: as a community of friendships, a community of local groups or organizations (such as with AIDS-related institutions), as an imagined or global community, and as a divided community (such as are separated by ethnicity, race, class, or special interest).[4] The type that resonated most strongly with gay men was the community of friendship because it is "one of those places where community is experienced most directly (i.e., not through the media) and emotionally" (30–31). Despite a diversity of interpretations about the meaning of "gay community," the stigma associated with gay identity has served as a powerful bond for the millions of gay men and lesbians who make up its various communities (Garnets and D'Augelli 1994).

One segment of this diverse gay community that has been little studied to date is that of gay co-father families. Existing literature on gay co-father families is scarce and has focused largely on fathers' first-person accounts of their journeys to becoming parents, and various challenges and triumphs they have experienced along the way (Gallucio, Gallucio, and Groff 2001; Shernoff 1996; Strah and Margolis 2003; Wong 2003). Mallon's (2004) research on gay men becoming parents is one of the first comprehensive studies to examine this phenomenon. The present chapter builds upon existing research by exploring how some openly gay male couples and their children in the Los Angeles area are living ordinary lives and integrating into mainstream American family and community life.

Providing an ethnographic account of their ordinary lives as members of families and communities of families, we might understand the diversity, complexity, and richness of their lives in ways heretofore unexplored (Laird 1993). In taking a person-centered ethnographic approach, this work attempts to broaden understanding about how the quality and nature of gay co-father families' community relationships are crucial for their sustenance.[5] Working from their own "backyards," the present study starts from the idea that we can learn much about gay co-father families by observing how they actually live within neighborhoods and communities and how interactions and experiences with other parents, families, teachers, and care-givers help to nurture, inhibit, and define them as a family. Their stories re-veal the challenges and rewards they face in integrating into mainstream communities and how they endeavor to form meaningful, supportive rela-tionships within them.

### Field Sites, Methods, Participants, and Generalizability

Fieldwork for this project was conducted at the homes or workplaces of participants in Los Angeles, California, and in surrounding cities in Los An-geles and Orange counties. The city of Los Angeles is home to nearly four million people and encompasses approximately 470 square miles. How-ever, it is characterized by numerous sub-communities or districts within the city, and it is these communities or areas with which residents primarily identify. The residential communities of the gay co-father families in this study range in population from approximately 3,500 to 100,000, with most falling between 40,000 and 50,000. Some families live outside Los Angeles in cities with populations ranging from 39,000 to over 150,000 (Los Ange-les Almanac, U.S. Census Bureau). Most of these communities can be char-acterized as urban or suburban, with many single-family, detached homes, condominiums or apartments, shopping and business districts, and with varied multiethnic, multilingual, and socioeconomic groups.

The families in this study are headed by gay men who have been open about their gay identities for many years and who became fathers through domestic adoption, international adoption, or foster care, either within the context of their present domestic partnership, or as single men prior to meeting their partners.[6] The subject pool from which these data are drawn includes twenty-one participants.[7] These include two gay co-father families who were initially recruited by the Alfred P. Sloan Center on Everyday Lives of Families (CELF) at UCLA as part of a larger, interdisciplinary study of thirty-two middle-class, dual-earner (opposite-sex parent) families in the greater Los Angeles area. (CELF participants also included members of the fathers' extended families, including four children, an aunt, and a single mother/friend and her son.) As part of this broader study, the two gay co-father families were videotaped at home in their everyday routines over the course of a week, for approximately twenty-five to thirty hours each (one hundred-plus hours total).[8] In addition to the two gay co-father families in the CELF study, ten additional gay co-fathers were recruited and interviewed extensively over several months in a series of hour-long interviews about their lives and personal experiences in childhood and adult life, relation-ships with partners, children, parents, siblings, extended kin, educational and professional lives, friendships, childrearing values and practices, and community relationships. (These data represent approximately 144 hours.)

All of the above participants were recruited through distribution of flyers at various gay community events including gay fathers' group meetings, workshops, gay and lesbian pride festivals, recreational events for gay and lesbian families, and through online gay fathers' group listservs. For their convenience, some interviews were conducted at participants' workplaces. In addition, I conducted participant observation at community events such as gay pride festivals and gay parenting meetings and workshops, and attended social gatherings at participants' homes.

Given the extremely small subject pool for this study, the experiences of these families cannot be generalized as typical of gay co-father families throughout the United States. However, the fact that some gay co-father families are integrating into mainstream communities signals changes in the cultural understanding of masculinity, gay male identity, and family.

## MOVING BEYOND THE GAY COMMUNITY
## AND INTO THE MAINSTREAM

The gay co-father families in this study, like many American families, have sought to live in communities that they can call home. They seek communities with good schools, an active community life, and opportunities for developing supportive relationships with friends and neighbors. While some gay co-fathers may opt to locate their families within or near towns or cities that have many resources for the gay community and that reflect a strong gay community presence, the gay co-fathers in this study choose to live in areas that are predominantly heterosexual, with less access to such support systems. Key factors in deciding where to live include the academic and progressive quality of schools, the sociopolitical climate of the area, distance to and from workplaces, affordability of housing, and whether there are other families and children living in the neighborhood. For some, this means moving away from more gay-friendly, urban communities, which historically have provided more resources for single gay men and childless gay couples, and into predominantly heterosexual, family-oriented communities, where maintaining connections to gay cultural life is more of a challenge. Becoming a parent can mean cutting off some ties with single gay friends or childless gay couples because the obligations of raising children usually restrict the types and frequency of social activities that gay co-fathers can have. With children in tow, gay couples may no longer feel that the conventional gay community reflects their needs. Rather, it is the community of other families with children that provide the context for some common values. Thus, moving into more mainstream communities provides gay co-father families with a preferable environment for raising children. But because their families are unconventional, gay co-fathers and their children are never sure of finding acceptance in straight communities. When they are in public with their children but without their partners, they are often assumed to be heterosexual, and questions from strangers about non-existent mothers are quite common. Their public presentation as a two-father family, however, is unusual and they challenge traditional definitions of family in both the gay and straight communities.

For the gay co-father families in this study, becoming part of the mainstream community is part of what it means to be a family. The presence of children provides common links with other families and parents, where child-related responsibilities and activities become a key point around which both gay and straight parents can relate. The focus on children's needs and interests brings gay co-fathers into regular contact with a range of people in different social situations, from the neighbor around the corner, to the day care provider, to the checker at the grocery store. In order to establish as supportive and as nurturing an environment as possible for their children, these fathers view openness about their gay identities as necessary for their families' well-being. They seek to be understood on their own terms and for the most part, they and their families are finding acceptance within their local communities. But being open about gay identity is something that gay fathers and their children must regularly gauge and negotiate, and it always brings the risk of rejection. Fathers are less concerned about being rejected themselves, for they have faced it often in their lives. Rather, they are more concerned about their children being rejected simply for having gay parents.

Becoming part of a community and establishing relationships with others are crucial to the everyday lives of gay co-father families. Gay fathers' relationships with straight neighbors can lead to mutual assistance with parenting and childcare responsibilities and friendships with straight parents can result in surprisingly strong alliances that cut across differences in sexual orientation, political stance, and socioeconomic status. While gay co-fathers want their children to attend schools with good academic records, they also want to be acknowledged by the school as a gay family and be secure in the feeling that their children are being protected. They want their children to have friends and to feel comfortable participating in peer activities. But there are times when gay fathers and their children have lost friends solely because the fathers are gay. Thus, the nature of some relationships and friendships can be tenuous. Because stigma against gay families is real, gay parents and children must always be prepared for rejection. But for most gay co-father families, the possibilities of developing long-lasting friendships and bonds with people in the local community far outweigh these risks.

## Being Accepted as a Gay Family in Their Communities

Being part of a community means being open about gay identity and participating in social occasions with other adults, parents, and children. Grant, forty-seven, and Brian, forty-seven, have been together for ten years. They have a son, Connor, six, and a daughter, Emily, four, whom they adopted. Grant has made a point of being open about his family and he and his partner have reached out by hosting gatherings and children's parties at their home.

> Grant: I think I do it [disclose gay identity] fairly publicly. It's about normalizing our family to them rather than withdrawing and becoming insular. It's a way of publicly inviting others into our lives and I think it's in part kind of a demystifying of our family to other people.

For Grant, inviting other parents, neighbors, his children's schoolmates, and teachers into his family's home serves a dual purpose. On one hand, he is actively participating in a typical social activity, a home gathering; on the other hand, he is inviting others to see his family in an ordinary, more three-dimensional light, as they really live, and less as a stereotype. For Grant, this means being open about gay identity.

As with Grant and his family, Stewart and Lance have also reached out to other families where they live. Stewart, forty-four, and Lance, forty-six, have been partners for eight years and have one adopted child, Yosef, who is two-and a half years old. Stewart reports general acceptance of the family, though he acknowledges that those who disapprove tend to keep their distance.

> Stew: We have been fairly lucky, though Lance is the one that pointed out if people don't like what we're doing and don't approve of us, they tend not to want to do things with us. And it becomes obvious if you invite someone a couple of times and they're always turning you down, for whatever reason they're not interested, you don't deal with them. So everyone that we socialize with in the straight community is supportive and accepting, otherwise they wouldn't be doing things with us.

Though Stewart and Lance cannot know for certain why some straight families choose not to accept their invitations, they presume families who repeatedly turn them down do so because they are gay. Parents who do accept their invitations show a willingness to regularly engage in social activities, and this is strong validation for them as a family.

Stan and Daniel have been partners for seventeen years, and have three sons ranging in age from ten to thirteen. They enjoy living in their neighborhood in a small city on the eastern edge of Los Angeles County. They are fairly open about their identities as gay parents, but they don't necessarily advertise it. Like Stewart and Lance, they have experienced subtle disapproval from other families. Often gay families have to read between the lines to discern non-acceptance, as Stan's story about a neighborhood family demonstrates.

> Stan: There's a family who lives three houses up on the other side of the street. I think once they found out we were gay, they don't associate any more with us. Our boys used to go over there and their boy came down once. But then when they found out we were gay, he doesn't come over and play any more. And the boys don't go and play with him. I think the boys just assume that he's busy and has lots of things to do. Actually I think that's the excuse the parents gave when our boys went up there: "Oh, they have violin practice" or "Oh, they have church school for three hours." So the boys finally stopped going up. I finally stopped sending them up. I can take a hint.

Stan's story illustrates the sometimes tenuous nature of ties to other families in their community. It also further illustrates the ambiguity of parents' responses to invitations. Because adults are not likely to reject the gay family outright, Stan cannot know for certain whether the parents' explanations are truthful or not. But like Stewart, Stan can conclude some parents maintain their distance for similar reasons. He must "take a hint" and assume that the friendship has broken off because he and Daniel are gay parents. Another consequence of this distancing is that the children's friendship suffers. Such instances show that despite the gay family's best attempts at openness and friendliness, their relationships with other parents and children can be short-lived.

Fred, forty-two, and his partner Rich, forty-two, have been together for fifteen years and have a son, Andrew, seven, and a daughter, Amy, ten, whom they adopted as foster children. Fred and Rich lived in a gay-friendly neighborhood of Los Angeles for three years. They felt comfortable being out and accepted as a gay family, and they even knew some other gay parents in the area. While they were happy with the private school their children had attended, they wanted their children to attend public school because it would provide them with a more diverse student body experience. But the public schools in their area were, in their view, sub-standard. Therefore, they moved to their current neighborhood, in a small city east of Los Angeles, primarily on the strength of its public schools. They value the "small-town, Mayberry" atmosphere of the area and they enjoy the fact that their house is but a stone's throw from their children's elementary school. Even though they are relative newcomers, Fred and Rich are happy to live where they do. They place a high value on the accessibility of activities in which their family can participate, making for an enriched community experience.

> Fred: We felt great about the community. I was thinking just tonight about how the kids were across the street playing for a while and while they were over

there, there was a call from Andrew's friend who lives next door for him to come over. I think it's great that there's all kinds of activity. Andrew's in gymnastics and Amy was in swimming and they have baseball and soccer, which is easily accessible. The majority of Amy's softball games are within walking distance to the park. There're the bike trails that are accessible from here and we don't have to go on very many streets to get to a trail that's off street. There's a miniature golf course down there that the kids love. All that stuff is right here—and it's great.

Fred feels that the abundance of children in the area reflects the type of neighborhood atmosphere that his partner Rich wanted to recreate for their family.

Fred: I mean, we've only been here since July, so we've only lived here for eight months. But we chose this community specifically for the schools and then all this came along with it. But we wanted to be in a neighborhood that had lots of kids so that that their childhood and after school activities could more mirror the way that Rich grew up.

Rich: Growing up, we lived in a neighborhood where you didn't come home from school and lock yourself in and watch television. You stayed out and played in the neighborhood and you went down to the local school and played football and you were out 'til the sun went down. As a kid, it was easier for me to play than I think it is for kids today to play. My parents spent a lot of time with family and family was of prime importance, just teaching and being there for the kids.

They are also pleased that their kids are making friends with other children nearby and that there are ample and convenient opportunities to do outdoor activities together as a family. But underneath Fred's feelings of contentment in his community are feelings of vulnerability about being a family headed by gay fathers.

Fred: I certainly feel vulnerable about being a two-dad family. I didn't feel that way before but I've felt that way since the move because we felt so unanimously accepted where we were. Here we're kind of coming in and we're the outsiders. I've felt myself kind of just standing back a little bit. But now when we push it we haven't encountered anything negative whatsoever. But I'm sort of feeling that it's bound to happen, and I feel vulnerable for the kids for that.

Fred's comments reveal that even though he and his family have integrated seemingly well into the neighborhood, he still feels like an "outsider." They haven't lived there very long, and despite overall feelings of acceptance, he senses that negative treatment toward his children is inevitable. His partner, Rich, comments on how being gay fathers makes their connection to a predominantly heterosexual community a fragile one.

Rich: Especially as gay men, the tenuous situation that you can have with the community and your support out there is that you're supported as a parent if you just appear to be doing everything within reasonable bounds like other parents. But if some parent, some religious right-wing parent, just doesn't like our family and wants to say something happened between me and their kid— that could be it.

Implicit in Rich's statement is a fear that, as gay fathers, they could be instantly assigned the status of sexual predators. Such a stereotype makes it extremely difficult for gay men like Fred and Rich to be accepted as parents. Like his partner, Rich feels vulnerable about being a gay family. Support is conditional—as long as Rich and Fred appear to be parenting in a "reasonable" manner, they stand a good chance of finding such support. Even so, they feel powerless to stave off a "religious right wing" parent who might want to make trouble for them. Their ties to the community are, as Rich states, "tenuous" because they are dependent upon whether his family's actions and moral values seem to match those of other parents and families.

## Children's and Parents' Experiences with Schools and Care Providers

Having young children draws gay co-fathers into the world of caregivers, schoolteachers, and other key school personnel. Like most middle-class American parents, gay co-fathers look for care providers and schools with high professional standards and academic integrity. Many gay co-father families in the Los Angeles area—particularly those of mixed ethnicity— seek out schools with ethnically diverse student bodies and schools whose curricula reflect progressive ideals. Perhaps most of all, they seek a safe environment for their children to learn without the fear of harassment or harm, and where they feel understood and accepted by school personnel and other parents and children.

Tim, forty-six, and Chad, forty-four, have been partners for over twenty years and have two pre-adolescent children, Elizabeth, twelve, and Edward, twelve. Elizabeth attends a girls' Catholic school close to home and Edward attends a private school some distance away. Chad notes the care that he and Tim have taken to protect them from anti-gay ideology in school.

Chad: When they were younger we very carefully placed them in environments where they were not going to find much kind of homophobia. At least they're in school environments where, if there were parents who had negative feelings about gay people, they knew that it wouldn't be acceptable for them to express them. A lot of people bent over backwards to be inclusive and welcoming.

Because the children's schools engender support for gay families, they are less likely to experience anti-gay harassment by other students or homophobic ideology from other parents. Being open about their family with prospective schools was important; however, Chad admits to having had initial reservations about Elizabeth's school, despite its progressive reputation.

> Chad: We were somewhat apprehensive about the idea of sending Elizabeth to a Catholic girls' school. But it's a school that has a tradition of being progressive. But it's too early for us to tell exactly about the teachers. We're only a couple of months into it, but we certainly haven't experienced anything negative.

Despite having an incomplete picture about the teachers, they had little reason to expect anything but support. Tim reflects on their meeting with the principal.

> Tim: Once we applied there we met with the principal and we liked her. She knew we were a gay family and it didn't faze her. We talked about Elizabeth's learning issues and it didn't seem to faze her. And so we settled on it pretty early and once she got in we were very happy.

Chad recalls the principal's direct endorsement, and her promise to them.

> Chad: At Elizabeth's school parents weren't usually granted one-on-one interviews. But after we sent in our application, the principal called us in for an interview. And the message that she clearly was sending us was "We'd like to have you as a family" and, you know, "We'll support you and support Elizabeth." And she's been terrific.

Experience with Edward's school also has proved to be positive and supportive.

> Chad: With Edward, we applied to many different schools and we kind of figured we'd wait and see where we got in. We did basically come out as a gay family in all of them. We know that they bend over backwards to try and create an environment where Eddie can feel comfortable about his family.

They received similar support at Edward's school, where the principal made a speech about acknowledging different kinds of families.

> Chad: At the first parent meeting the principal gave a little speech to the parents about not letting their kids come in with preconceptions about anything. They shouldn't think about what other kids are going to be like. They shouldn't have conceptions about what other families are going to be like. There are going to be all sorts of families in this school, and parents need to talk to their kids about that, and talk to them beforehand about the fact that there are going to be other kids in this school who have same-sex parents. You need to help sensitize them to that before they get here. And, you know, they were trying to do the right thing. So far it has worked out.

The principal's speech is a powerful validation of family diversity. It sets the tone from the top, and it sends the message that everyone—children and parents alike—need to check their preconceptions at the schoolhouse door before entering.

Elizabeth and Edward, both twelve, have been able to develop close friends at their schools, even maintaining friendships with children from their previous schools. Most of their friends see having two dads as cool or no big deal. But deciding whether to disclose it (and to whom) is something they must continue to negotiate. Sometimes coming out to a friend doesn't result in a positive response, as Elizabeth notes.

Liz: Well, like most of them are from the Valley [a large, northern section of Los Angeles] and they're like "Oh, cool" . . . but some like—um, some of them at my new school I haven't told yet because I've had a bad experience with that and it is not fun. So I don't wanna tell anybody.

I probe further, asking Elizabeth if she would share with me her bad experience, how it made her feel, and her reasons for being cautious. She continues:

Liz: We went on vacation and I met this girl and she was really nice, and I told her I have two dads and stuff like that 'cause she was like "Where's your mom?" I'm like, "I don't have a mom" and I explained to her and she's like "Oh, that sucks." And she went on and on and I was like "Okay," so I dunno. It was just really quick so I was like "Oh, okay" and I just left her. It makes me feel really bad but like when she said that, I didn't really understand it 'cause I was little.

The disclosure of having two dads put an end to the budding friendship. This upset her father and left Elizabeth feeling confused.

Liz: So I told my Daddy and my Daddy got really upset. When I was little and I went to my old school, I would just tell people and everybody'd be like "Oh that's fine, whatever." But now I'm just like, I don't know . . .

Initial feelings of openness and trust can turn to uncertainty when children are faced with the reality of rejection of their families. A seemingly innocent inquiry about her "mother" requires Elizabeth to explain her family circumstances, whether or not she was ready or willing to do so at that moment. Just as gay parents have faced decisions about where and when to come out during their lives, their children must calculate the risks of telling other children.

Sometimes inadvertent disclosure happens in the course of other events and it can be surprisingly positive, as Rich and Fred's daughter, Amy, found out one day when she got sick at school.

> Amy: Once when I didn't feel good and, um, my dad had said "Just call home 'cause me or Poppy will be home" and I said [to the school nurse] "Just call home 'cause my dad said that he or my Poppy will be home." And so the nurse called. She said, "Both of your parents are home and one of 'em's gonna come and get you" and, um, this girl [said] "You have two dads at home! How lucky are you!"

In this instance, the child of gay parents is seen as one who is worthy and fortunate; having two fathers is something to value rather than to condemn. Like Elizabeth and other children of gay parents, Amy must anticipate and field predictable questions about the nature of her family. She has developed her own way of dealing or not dealing with them.

> Amy: Some people think one of 'em is my step-dad and that my mother is like on a business trip or something (chuckles). And I tell 'em "No, I'm adopted" and like (imitates child's voice) "I didn't know you were adopted!" (Laughs) At my old school people were really curious and I'd get the same question by the same person every day like, "You have two dads? Are you adopted? I didn't know that." And then the same thing over and over again so I just finally stopped answering the questions 'cause it was getting annoying.

The fascination that others have with Amy's family configuration is evident. The absence of a mother is so noticeable that it requires a rationalization. Similarly, the presence of two fathers can be so beyond comprehension that one of them gets assigned to a more traditional, stepfamily association.

Grant and Brian's son, Connor, six, is enrolled in a university-based, elementary school in west Los Angeles. The school values innovative teaching, respect for difference, and a safe environment for all students. Its sensitivity toward gay families is policy. Grant explains:

> Grant: In my son's school they have kids with two same-sex parents in every class or they make sure that there's never one kid with same-sex parents who's alone. That's the school's policy so that kids never feel like they're the only one. And people get to know you and they're fine. Schools can't not talk about it now. If you've got two dads in a class with kindergartners, they have to talk about it because kids start asking questions, in Los Angeles at least.

In putting more than one child with gay or lesbian parents in the same classroom, the school shows that it values their family form, allows them to identify with families like their own, and reduces the chances that they will become a curiosity. Because "kids start asking questions," as Grant states, it behooves schools to create and implement policy guidelines for children of gay families. Fortunately for Grant and his family, Connor's school stands as a model for other public and private elementary schools.

While most experiences with school personnel have been positive, at times gay co-fathers must deal with problematic situations. Grant recalled one such encounter with a day care provider.

> Grant: Our first care provider was this Persian woman that we totally loved. She was an at-home daycare person and one time she was like, "Maybe you should tell your son to say that he's different," you know, try to deny that there were two dads in the family. And we told her "No, that's not possible." But she thought about it and we both realized she was protecting the kid from getting teased. And in part we were the first gay family at her daycare center and in part our experience was so good that we talked her up and I think that something like 40 percent of her kids now are from same-sex households. She got a reputation as being someone you could bring your kids to. And now she's got the hugest queer family contingent in her school.

Grant hears the day care provider's suggestion that Connor say he is "different" as equivalent to denying the fathers are gay. Grant rejects this explanation since it veils the truth of their family structure. This example highlights the difficult decisions gay families regularly face about openness of gay identity on one hand, and protecting their children from harm and harassment on the other. Sometimes blazing the trail is fraught with a few bumps in the road, though, in the end, it can lead to a positive outcome. By suggesting that Connor deny that he has two fathers, the day care provider thought she was doing the right thing. Her concern clearly was in protecting Connor from harassment; however, from Grant's point of view, it was like asking Connor and his family to go back into the closet.

Inevitably, children of gay families are faced with questions and taunts from other children. Sometimes other children query them about being gay. Grant recalls:

> Grant: Well what happened was—and I can't remember what I was doing with Connor—but he looked over and said "Are you gay?" and I said, "Yeah I'm gay, and so is Daddy. Why do you ask?" And he said there was a kid at school that was teasing him about having gay dads. And it was a little unclear about what he was teasing about but it definitely had "gay" associated with it. I was like, oh God, you know, kindergarten! I thought we were going to have a couple of years before we had to deal with it, particularly because we're in this progressive school. But he was around a bunch of older kids who had started teasing him for being gay.

What is perhaps most surprising about Grant's story is not that Connor was teased—this is to be expected, albeit earlier than Grant had hoped—but that Connor asked his father if he was gay. One might assume that a child of gay parents should already know that his fathers are gay. Young children often are unsure about what being gay really means. When the term is used as an epithet on the playground, it takes on new meaning. Grant explained how the school responded, and what led to the teasing initially.

> Grant: But I thought the school handled it pretty well. We went to the school and talked to them and they were pretty responsive. They kind of jumped on it. They have a program called "Safe Schools" so they brought the two kids in to the Safe Schools facilitator and she talked to them about it. But as it unfolded it turned out that earlier—they have "circle time" every morning [in Connor's class]—and something about marriage came up and people said that only boys and girls could get married. And Connor said, "That's not true. Two boys can get married or two girls can get married. That's what my parents— that's what my dads always tell us. You can marry whoever you want."

By boldly expressing what he knew to be true about marriage, Connor unwittingly set in motion the actions of the older boys. Fortunately the school was ready to address the situation and already had a program in place to deal with it. But the matter didn't end there for Connor, who asked his father to appeal directly to the offending boy's father.

> Grant: So he'd [Connor] asked me to talk to the kid's father and ask him to stop it. We talked to the dad, who was horrified at what had happened. He went into this whole thing with Brian. He was like "Oh my God, our best friend is gay, he comes over for dinner all the time." And one of their aunts is a lesbian. He was like, "Oh my kid is so busted." You know it turned into this whole big thing but it was kind of interesting.

What initially began as a negative and hurtful experience for Connor resulted in positive outcomes on the part of the school and the offending boy's parent. The value of gay identity is both affirmed and personalized by the boy's father, who assures Grant and his partner that his son should know better.

Sometimes defending same-sex marriage rights in the school classroom can have profound effects, as Rich's story illustrates.

> Rich: My nephew Joey did this incredible thing. He was in his fifth-grade class and they were talking about current events and they were talking about who to vote for and they were talking about Bush and the war and then gay marriage. And you know the teacher asked, "How do you all feel about gay marriage?" And apparently twenty of the twenty-five kids were against gay marriage until Joey stood up and cried, telling people how he has a gay uncle, and that he loves him very much and that he's very important in his life and that he has two gay uncles and that they should be married. And they have two wonderful kids who are adopted and they were the two luckiest kids because they're the two greatest dads in the world. The whole class turned. Ten of the kids also spoke up about having gay uncles. And one girl spoke up about having a gay dad. And so I guess at the end, it turned around. Twenty kids were now in fa-

vor after Joey did that. And the teacher was very touched because she said she didn't know very many gay or lesbian people and after hearing all the kids talk, she was really blown away and moved. So, you know, it's the Joeys in my life that are doing the influencing. So that's why even the young folk out there, the very young folk, are not going to let this [proposed federal constitutional amendment to protect marriage] happen.

Rich's story is a poignant example of how, in the face of opposition, a child can affect, even change, public opinion right in his own classroom. Like Connor, Joey speaks from his own personal experience and expresses what he believes to be right. By speaking out, Joey opens the door for other children to do the same. In sharing his personal experience about his gay uncles, Joey acts as a change agent in the classroom, and perhaps beyond. He also acts as an educator, not only for the students but for his teacher as well. It is this kind of advocacy that Rich sees as having the greatest positive effect on the future of equal rights for gay people.

### Gay Co-fathers and Straight Parents Build Friendships of Support and Understanding

For gay co-father families, becoming part of a community means developing meaningful friendships with their straight neighbors and with straight parents that they meet through school and day care. Close friendships between gay and straight families arise out of concerns and needs that families share in managing the obligations and responsibilities of everyday family life.

Stewart and Lance have become close friends with a straight couple and their two young children. The families have similar interests and their children enjoy playing together. The families have enjoyed taking trips to Disneyland and plan to take a trip to New York together later in the year. Stewart describes their friendship with the couple:

Stew: They're very good friends of ours. Typical American family. Mom and dad, daughter that is four months older than Yosef and now a son who is about three months old. We were struggling where to put Yosef for preschool and they were struggling with where to put their child into preschool. They have been really, really supportive to the point that we have no hesitation leaving our child with them for a couple days if we had to run out of town for an emergency. It just helps that we all can talk. They're just comfortable people and we all get along. Occasionally we'll talk politics like, you know, same-sex marriage, which is now on the forefront for everybody, or issues of family problems.

For Stewart and Lance, support from the couple goes beyond acceptance. For these friends, support means a willingness to be relied upon, should Stewart and Lance ever need them. Being good friends means feeling comfortable enough with one another to communicate freely about a range of issues—from the most practical family concerns to the most potentially contentious political topics. Perhaps most salient of all is the way that Stewart and Lance are treated and understood by the couple's children.

> Stew: Generally speaking, it's the ideal situation. They treat us like we're just like everybody else except that Yosef has two dads. And nobody makes an issue of that. I will hold onto Meg, their daughter, or walk her across the street and she knows me and she trusts me. And she calls—and I don't know where she got this from—but she calls Lance "Mr. L" and she calls me "Mr. S" and that's it. That's how she distinguishes between us because she can't say "Daddy" and we don't use last names. So it wouldn't make sense because it's two "Mr. M's" so she just uses first names and that's fine. We don't have any problems; it's not an issue for her and not an issue for her family.

For Meg, the fact that Yosef has two dads is a non-issue. Meg understands Stewart and Lance to be trusted adults and she has figured out her own terms of address to distinguish them. Because Meg's parents see and treat Stewart, Lance, and their son, Yosef, as a family, so too does Meg.

Grant and Brian have established close friendships with straight families as well. Interestingly, Grant identifies more with straight families than gay families.

> Grant: We have straight friends with kids. A lot of time we have more in common with straight people than we do with gay people now. It's just that I gravitate more toward other parents than I do necessarily to other gay people on some levels . . . And to assume I'm going to like a family because they're also gay seems kind of silly to me. I think we're definitely closer to some heterosexual families than we are to same-sex families because it's a more organic personality click than necessarily, "Oh you're a gay family so we have to be close to you."

As parents, childrearing and family-centered concerns are an organizing focus in Grant and Brian's lives. Thus, they tend to identify more with couples who have children, regardless of the couple's sexual orientation. Shared gay identity with another family is not a sufficient enough basis for establishing a close friendship. Grant prefers that friendships with other parents and families be grown from "organic" roots, that is, arising naturally from a combination of mutual interests, shared values, or personality preferences. In Grant and Brian's case, their political preconceptions about what it means to be Republican obscured their ability to view a family as potential friends.

> Grant: Our son's two best friends in his class are from a two-mom family and the other kid is from a Republican family, probably the only Republican fam-

ily in the class. Or probably the only "out" Republican family in the class! You know the election was last fall and we talk about politics at home. Now the horrible thing is I would disown a friend if I thought he was a Republican (Laughs). It'd be hard for me to tolerate a friendship with somebody that's so politically opposite to me. I felt so bad because Connor was afraid he wasn't going to be allowed to play with William because William's family voted for Bush. And meanwhile we all went on a field trip together and here's William, the kid with the Republican parents, whose two best friends are from the two-dad family and the two-mom family. So there we are—the two moms, the two dads, and this Republican family—just kind of finding out we all kind of like each other. And actually I was all prepared to really dislike the Republican parents. But my kids neutralized it for me in a funny way.

Grant realized his and Brian's anti-Republican feelings were translating in a hurtful way for Connor. Ironically, it was Connor and William's friendship that served as a catalyst, drawing the families together, and helping Grant and Brian re-examine their own negative preconceptions. I wanted to probe Grant's assumptions further and so I asked him why he was prepared to dislike the family. Who did he think they were and what apprehensions did he have, I wondered. It was about judgment. Grant realized he was prematurely judging the family as one-dimensional while not wanting to be judged himself.

Grant: I think I feel concern about being judged by people like that. And actually I don't particularly want to be put in a position to be judged. And of course that was what I was doing—I was judging them. So you kind of have to acknowledge the irony of that. As I've gotten to know the family more I've learned that they're Republican for financial reasons rather than for social reasons. But to my discredit, I tend to paint everybody with the same brush, which is not accurate.

Because Grant assumed that Republicanism equated with social conservatism, he initially ruled out any potential for getting to know William's family. However, taking the opportunity to spend time together on the field trip gave Grant greater clarity into the family's social values that, as it turned out, were not as radical as he had originally believed.

Sometimes friendships with straight parents can take on familial-like qualities, evolving into mutually supportive relationships where parents rely on one another for much more than companionship and coverage in a pinch. After moving into their suburban neighborhood, Rich and Fred developed a close friendship with Kate, a single mother with three sons, one of whom, Jason, seven, lives with her. Though the families have only known each other for a few months, they have become quite close. Andrew and Jason are best friends, and Kate has asked Rich and Fred to be godparents and father figures to Jason, to which they readily accepted. Even with such unequivocal support, Rich is sometimes uncomfortable with the extraordinary level of Kate's advocacy within the straight-family community.

> Rich: It's almost too much. She lets everyone know how wonderful we are (Laughs). She named us as godparents for her kids and we had a godparent naming ceremony to announce we were the godparents. It felt like she invited the whole town, in order to stand up and say that she goes out of town a lot and it's hard being a single parent mom and these guys, meaning us, have been wonderful and they take care of Jason and they've also agreed to be godparents to my two older kids. I think to some extent she was saying to the community, "Look at all you out there. You're all parents"—'cause it was a bunch of parents and kids—"you know all of them as my friends. But I chose THESE two guys as the godparents and THESE two guys to take care of MY children and they're the only ones that I would trust to do this." And it was a little—and if I were one of her other friends I would have gone, "Oh this is a little awkward" you know? But it was out of the sincerity of her heart. I wonder if it's driven subconsciously or by a conscious effort to prove we are equal sort of, to prove our cause.

Rich is clearly touched by Kate's gesture yet he wonders whether she advocates a bit too much. Rich worries that Kate's high praise sets him and Fred up as too-perfect, super-human parents, thus leaving them little room for making mistakes.

Kate's position as advocate uniquely places her as a bridge between two relational communities—one gay and one straight. From a geographic standpoint, she is located in the same community as Rich, Fred, Amy, and Andrew. As a straight mother, she can relate to other straight parents; as Rich and Fred's close friend and ally, she provides a firsthand perspective into what the lives of gay families are really like. At the same time, Kate is also privy to discriminatory comments from within the straight community, viewpoints that Rich and Fred rarely hear directly.

> Rich: She's such an advocate for us and she talks about us everywhere. She sees all sides of it. She had no idea the depth of prejudice from otherwise liberal, free-thinking people.

Kate has defended Rich and Fred against straight parents who have questioned her about the safety of leaving her child in their care. Rich recalls:

> Rich: Kate's reaction was like "What? What's to discuss?" you know, "Two men love each other, they create a home, they create a family." She said to this one father, "Why would it be any different than any relationship you have? I mean, look at them. If you just change the sex, they're raising kids, they're sending them to school, they're doing their homework, they're you know putting them to bed at night. It's simple." It's not so simple I guess for a lot of people.

By focusing on some of the common concerns of raising children, Kate challenges other parents' moral prejudices. She compels wary parents—those who maintain stereotypes of gay men as sexual predators—to see Rich and Fred as they are, with many of the same values as other families.

Beyond her role as advocate, Kate is also an active and involved female figure in Rich and Fred's family. She is someone who Rich and Fred can speak to honestly and openly about very personal, family matters. In the following excerpt, Kate, Rich, Fred, Amy, Andrew, and Kate's son Jason are walking home from having dinner at a nearby neighborhood restaurant one Sunday evening. Out of earshot of the children, Rich, Fred and Kate are talking about menstruation. Rich shares with Kate how he and Fred have already prepared for the day that Amy's period will come.

> Rich: 'Cause we had a really good talk with my older sister about when the period comes and she showed us all the equipment and how to attach it (Laughs).
> Kate: You guys are hysterical. Okay.
> Rich: And she explained the anatomy again to us. It's been years since I, uh, had my anatomy class so that was good. And actually we went out and purchased it [feminine hygiene items] because she has a twelve-year-old daughter and she had showered with Amy and she thought that Amy was closer to the time (Laughs) than Vickie was.
> Kate: She may be. Do you know—you don't know the age of Amy's mother obviously because that's the best . . .
> Rich: No.
> Kate: You have no idea.
> Rich: I have no idea. But she does have her older sister.
> Fred: Which we could find out.
> Rich: Which would also be an easy way.

Rich and Fred know that they can share these personal and intimate family matters with Kate. They are not hesitant to reveal their lack of familiarity with female physiology and they are even proud to display to Kate their forethought and preparedness. This exchange provides insight into the nature of the close friendship between Kate, Rich, and Fred. It reveals Kate's willingness to see Rich and Fred's family as a viable unit, and it shows that she can play an important and supportive role in the family.

## CONCLUSION

This research shows how some gay co-father families are integrating into mainstream, predominantly heterosexual communities, how they are being received as families by friends, neighbors, schools, and caregivers, and how fathers are able to develop meaningful relationships with straight parents. By exploring the intersections between gay co-father families and the larger communities of which they are a part, we obtain an enriched view of the ways in which they are living in mainstream America today. As Bookman points out, "community care work" is relationship building that takes place outside the family in an effort to help support families on various practical, financial, and emotional levels. It is required "to knit families and communities together in long-term sustainable relationships. These ties create a sense of community and social support that makes work-life and family-life possible. Without them, families suffer on both practical and emotional levels" (2004, 60). As the gay co-father families in this study settle into everyday routines of work, school, and family life, their relationships with straight friends, neighbors and others become important on a day-to-day basis, and fathers are committed to cultivating and maintaining them for the benefit of their families' lives. These ties to the local community are important for fostering support for their children who, like them, have faced homophobia, misunderstanding, and disapproval from members of mainstream society. Despite all the ways that these gay co-fathers demonstrate their commitment to parenting and family life, some can never be completely sure of how they and their children are being accepted. This uncertainty remains despite having established seemingly good relationships with other families and people in their communities. Like other families, they come to depend on the everyday, interpersonal relationships that living in a community can foster. Even so, the potential for losing connections with other parents and children is real. For the sake of their children, however, gay co-fathers try to strike a balance between being visible and open, yet remaining sensitive to the needs of their children, who are frequently faced with having to defend and explain their family configuration.

For some of these families, friendships are potentially tenuous. Straight parents generally do not express their disapproval to gay fathers themselves; rather, they withdraw or disassociate. Children in gay co-father families are vulnerable to anti-gay harassment, although open communications between parents, schools, and families help build safe environments for children to learn and to develop healthy peer relationships. But even in the face of tenuous ties and disapproval, these gay co-father families persevere; this is a testament both to the web of support that gay co-fathers strive to provide their children and to the level of openness and honesty with which they approach the parenting challenge.

The extent to which other gay co-father families in the United States are accepted depends largely on the willingness of straight community members to look beyond their assumptions about what a family can be, and to embrace these families and welcome their participation in everyday community and family life. Routine, everyday encounters provide opportunity spaces for gay and straight families to get to know one another on more than a superficial level; rather, they experience relevant opportunities to know one another on a personal level and to understand what they have in common as families. Benkov states, "families headed by lesbians and gay men certainly highlight how deeply embedded in society families really are, how much a matter of socially created meaning each family unit is. But they also show us the converse, that is, how individuals, in creating new ways of being together, influence the larger society" (1995, 62). Indeed, by creating families and integrating into larger societal constellations, gay co-fathers and their children expand existing notions of the family unit. Through engagement in everyday activities and interactions with various members of their communities, they demonstrate to others—and to themselves—how they are a family and what family means to them. They show that they value many of the same things other families do—good schools, neighborhoods with lots of children, and active engagement in community activities.

When gay families are accepted by straight neighbors and friends in their local communities, strong ties can develop. These relationships become an essential part of the family's well-being and can provide them with both practical and emotional support. Common bonds of childrearing and child-centered concerns between gay and straight parents overshadow seeming cultural differences based solely on sexual orientation. While political, legal, and moral debates over same-sex marriage and adoption rights for gays and lesbians rage on, gay co-father families continue to go about their everyday lives raising children and working to create supportive environments for their families. Despite the achievement of many important social and legal gains in gay rights over the past few decades, much remains to be done if gay families are to achieve equality with their heterosexual counterparts. A first step toward greater acceptance and understanding begins at the local level, where interpersonal communication and interaction brings members of both gay and straight family communities together amid shared values and common goals.

As we have seen, some of the gay co-father families in this study are beginning to change hearts and minds. Grant and Brian have made friends with straight Republican parents, surprising themselves in the process. Rich and Fred have become close friends with Kate, a single mother who named them as godparents to her son. Rich's nephew spoke up and defended his uncle's right to marry in his classroom, affecting the attitudes of schoolchildren and teacher alike. Their friendships with straight parents have become essential to their lives. Parents like Kate provide both practical and emotional support to both fathers and children. They act as advocates by building bridges between the gay father community and the larger heterosexual community. They work to inform straight parents and others of the realities of the gay family and to reduce ignorance and discrimination. They find common ground with gay co-fathers through their mutual concern for the well-being of children. And as a single parent, Kate also looks to Rich and Fred as father figures to her son, Jason.

By closely examining the nature and quality of the relationships gay co-father families share with others, we may learn something about how they value family and community. The participation of these gay co-father families within straight communities reveals that they share many of the same values held by their straight counterparts. They seek to live in areas where schools have high academic standards, where other families and children are present, and where they can be on friendly terms with neighbors, children, parents, and school personnel. Like straight families, gay co-father families seek to live in communities where they can feel safe. But unlike straight families, gay co-father families contend with societal disapproval because their families are headed by same-gender parents and because much of society views gay identity and sexuality as immoral.

This chapter has endeavored to demonstrate that when it comes to family values, families headed by gay co-fathers are not that different from many other middle-class families. Gay co-father families are but one variation on an existing familial theme. Accepting them into the cultural notion of "father" and "family" would greatly expand present conceptions of what makes a father, and what makes a gay man. Gay co-father families challenge deeply held assumptions about family, sexuality, and morality. When they locate to more mainstream, predominantly heterosexual communities, gay co-father families become more visible and thus challenge conventional beliefs about what it means to be a family. Whatever common family values may actually exist between families headed by same-sex parents and those headed by opposite-sex parents, they are often obscured by a focus on sexual and moral difference. But when gay co-fathers open their homes for a child's birthday party, share a quick chat with the next-door neighbor over the hedge, or a friendly wave on the way to work, opportunities exist for straight community members to meet them on common ground. At the same time, this requires members of the straight community to re-evaluate their own moral values and revise their existing views of gay people. In seeking some of the same things that many American families value—safe places to raise children, good schools, affordable housing, friendly and supportive community relations—gay co-father families challenge prevailing notions of what a family can be. They raise questions about the presumption of heterosexuality as a prerequisite for fatherhood, or that men are not suited for primary parenting. In choosing parenthood and creating family units with partners and children, gay co-fathers expand definitions of the gay community and the gay man.

As evidenced in this study, some members of straight-family communities can see that so-called "gay family values" are, in large part, similar to their own. When a gay family moves in next door or across the street, they become part of a particular local community. Close proximity, common goals, and shared values bring gay and straight communities together in ways neither group has experienced before. Thus, contact with gay families at the local level can potentially provide an organic environment for greater acceptance. Understanding is built from the ground up, within the context of social interaction, one step at a time. But it is up to members of both communities to reach out to one another, and to set aside previously held beliefs about the other. As we have seen, children of gay co-fathers—as well as those who would be their friends—are potential agents of social change. As generations of children experience the stigma of having gay parents, they—like Rich's nephew—may become more vocal or defensive about the normative and positive qualities of their families. By living their ordinary, everyday lives, these gay co-father families are beginning to be accepted in routine ways in mainstream communities. In so doing, they may begin to change public opinion and hasten greater acceptance of gay families generally. While such community encounters surely will not change every heart and mind, there may be a positive, cumulative effect over time as future generations question or reconsider the values and beliefs that many hold today about families who, by culture or structure, differ from their own.

## AFTERWORD

For as long as I can remember, I have been an advocate for social justice and social change. At every step of my academic career, I have sought to gain greater knowledge about the lives of gay and lesbian people, and to illuminate their lives in new and revealing ways. I have had a long-standing interest in the lives of gay men—particularly adolescents and fathers—because both of these groups share the struggles for moral approval from society yet possess very different life-stage priorities. My research is informed by my identity and socialization as a gay person in a predominantly heterosexual society, and I share this cultural perspective with my participants. As a woman, however, I cannot understand completely the experience of being a gay man or father and this difference allows me to approach my fieldwork both from the *emic* and *etic* perspectives. The men I have studied are at once familiar to me yet strange. And so I have approached the ethnographic process working back and forth between these two places—one with a foothold in a familiar world as a gay minority, and the other in the lesser known world of gay fathers and the gay family community. I have endeavored to take up this insider-outsider re-positioning throughout the stages of research design, fieldwork, and data analysis. Doing so is a way to guard against taking anything about my participants' lives for granted while at the same using my own understanding about being a gay person as a tool for unearthing new knowledge about the gay experience.

## NOTES

The research on which this chapter is based was made possible by the Alfred P. Sloan Foundation and the UCLA Center On Everyday Lives of Families (CELF).

1. Following Patterson and Chan (1997), I use the term "gay" to refer to those fathers who self-identify this way and who are in domestic partnerships with other men.

2. For the most current information on U.S. households headed by same-sex couples and parents see the U.S. Bureau of the Census special report, "Married-Couple and Unmarried Partner Households: 2000" (Simmons and O'Connell 2003). See also Gates and Ost (2004).

3. For previous research on homosexuality, gay men, and gay fathers see Bieber et al. (1962), Bieber (1969), Brown (1976), Clark (1977), Mager (1975), Shilts (1975), Miller (1979a, 1979b), Bozett (1979, 1980, 1981, 1984, 1985, 1987, 1988, 1993), Robinson and Skeen (1982), Skeen and Robinson (1984, 1985), Bigner and Bozett (1990), Sbordone (1993), and McPherson (1993).

4. This is a term originated by Benedict Anderson in *Imagined communities: Reflections on the origin and spread of nationalism* (1991).

5. "Person-centered ethnography" refers to "anthropological attempts to develop experience-near ways of describing and analyzing human behavior, subjective experience, and psychological processes" (Hollan 2001). Its emphasis is on understanding the salient experiences of the inhabitants of a community. See also Levy and Hollan (1998) and LeVine (1982).

6. None of the gay co-fathers in this study became parents through surrogacy. While gay male couples are increasingly able to choose this route, it is considerably more expensive than adoption or foster care.

7. Pseudonyms are used throughout this chapter in order to maintain the confidentiality of participants.

8. The CELF study also included a number of additional instruments, including education interviews, social networks surveys, health interviews, children's interviews, daily routines questionnaires, and psychological questionnaires and measurements.

## REFERENCES

Anderson, Benedict. 1991. *Imagined communities: Reflections on the origin and spread of nationalism.* London and New York: Verso.

Barret, Robert L., and Bryan E. Robinson. 2000. *Gay fathers: Encouraging the hearts of gay dads and their families.* San Francisco: Jossey-Bass, Inc.

Benkov, Laura. 1995. "Lesbian and gay parents: From margin to center." In *Cultural resistance: Challenging beliefs about men, women and therapy,* ed. Kathy Weingarten, 49–64. New York and London: The Haworth Press.

Bieber, Irving, Toby B. Bieber, Harvey J. Dain, Paul R. Dince, Marvin G. Drellich, Henry G. Grand, Ralph H. Gundlach, Malvina W. Kremer, Alfred H. Rilkin, and Cornelia B. Wilbur. 1962. *Homosexuality: A psycho-analytic study.* New York: Basic Books.

Bieber, Irving. 1969. The married homosexual male. *Medical Aspects of Human Sexuality,* 3: 76–84.

Bigner, Jerry J., and Frederick W. Bozett. 1990. "Parenting by gay fathers." In *Homosexuality and family relations.* 155–75. New York and London: The Haworth Press.

Bookman, Ann. 2004. *Starting in our own backyards: How working families can build community and survive the new economy.* New York and London: Routledge.

Bozett, Frederick. W. 1979. "Gay fathers: The convergence of a dichotomized identity through integrative sanctioning." PhD diss., University of California.

———. 1980. "Gay fathers: How and why they disclose their homosexuality to their children." *Family Relations* 29: 173–79.

———. 1981. "Gay fathers: Evolution of the gay-father identity." *American Journal of Orthopsychiatry* 51: 552–68.

———. 1984. "Parenting concerns of gay fathers." *Topics in Clinical Nursing* 6: 60–71.

———. 1985. "Gay men as fathers." In *Dimensions of fatherhood,* ed. Shirley M. H. Hanson and Frederick W. Bozett, 327–52. Beverly Hills, CA: Sage Publications.

———. 1987. "Gay fathers." In *Gay and lesbian parents,* ed. Frederick W. Bozett, 3–22. New York: Praeger Publishers.

———. 1988. "Gay fatherhood." In *Fatherhood today: Men's changing role in the family,* ed. Phyllis Bronstein and Carolyn P. Cowan, 214–35. New York: John Wiley & Sons.

———. 1993. "Gay fathers: A review of the literature." In *Psychological perspectives on lesbian and gay male experiences,* ed. Linda D. Garnets and Douglas C. Kimmel, 437–57. New York: Columbia University Press.

Brown, Howard. 1976. "Married homosexuals." In *Familiar faces, hidden lives: The story of homosexual men in America today,* ed. Howard Brown, 108–30. New York: Harcourt Brace Jovanovich.

Clark, Donald. 1977. *Loving someone gay.* Millbrae, CA: Celestial Arts.

Gallucio, John, Michael Gallucio, and David Groff. 2001. *An American family.* New York: St. Martin's Press.

Garnets, Linda D., and Anthony R. D'Augelli. 1994. "Empowering lesbian and gay communities: A call for collaboration with community psychology." *American Journal of Community Psychology* 22: 447–70.

Gates, Gary, and Jason Ost. 2004. *The gay and lesbian atlas.* Washington, DC: The Urban Institute Press.

Heller, Kenneth. 1989. "The return to community." *American Journal of Community Psychology* 17:1–15.

Hollan, Douglas. 2001. "Developments in person-centered ethnography." In *The psychology of cultural experience*, ed. Holly F. Mathews and Carmella C. Moore, 48–67. New York: Cambridge University Press.

Laird, Joan. 1993. Lesbian and gay families. In *Normal family processes*, 2nd ed. Froma Walsh, 282–328. New York: Guilford Press.

LeVine, Robert A. 1982. *Culture, behavior, and personality: An introduction to the comparative study of psycho-social adaptation*. New York: Aldine.

Levy, Robert I., and Douglas Hollan. 1998. "Person-centered interviewing and observation in anthropology." In *Handbook of research methods in anthropology*, ed. H. Russell Bernard, 333–64. Walnut Creek, CA: Altamira Press.

*Los Angeles Almanac*. http://www.laalmanac.com/cities/ci93.htm.

Mager, D. 1975. "Faggot father." In *After you're out*, ed. Karla Jay and Allen Young, 128–34. New York: Links Books.

Mallon, Gerald P. 2004. *Gay men choosing parenthood*. New York: Columbia University Press.

McMillan, David W., and David M. Chavis. 1986. "Sense of community: A definition and theory." *Journal of Community Psychology* 14: 6–23.

McPherson, D. 1993. "Gay parenting couples: Parenting arrangements, arrangement satisfaction, and relationship satisfaction." PhD diss., Pacific Graduate School of Psychology.

Miller, Brian. 1979a. "Gay fathers and their children." *The Family Coordinator* 28: 544–52.

———. 1979b. "Unpromised paternity: The lifestyles of gay fathers." In *Gay men: The sociology of male homosexuality*, ed. Martin P. Levine, 239–52. New York: Harper and Row.

Patterson, Charlotte J. 1994. Lesbian and gay couples considering parenthood: An agenda for research, service, and advocacy. *Journal of Gay & Lesbian Social Services* 1: 33–55.

———. 1995. Lesbian mothers, gay fathers, and their children. In *Lesbian, gay and bisexual identities over the lifespan: Psychological perspectives*, ed. Anthony R. D'Augelli and Charlotte J. Patterson, 262–90. New York: Oxford University Press.

Patterson, Charlotte J., and Raymond W. Chan. 1997. "Gay fathers." In *The role of the father in child development*, 3rd ed., ed. Michael E. Lamb, 245–60. New York: John Wiley & Sons.

Robinson, Bryan E., and Patsy Skeen. 1982. "Sex-role orientation of gay fathers versus gay nonfathers." *Perceptual and Motor Skills* 55: 1055–59.

Sbordone, A. J. 1993. "Gay men choosing fatherhood." PhD diss., City University of New York.

Shernoff, Michael. 1996. "Gay men choosing to be fathers." *Journal of Gay & Lesbian Social Services* 4: 41–54.

Shilts, Randy. 1975. "Gay people make babies too." *The Advocate*, October 22.

Simmons, Tavia, and Martin O'Connell. 2003. *Married-couple and unmarried partner households: 2000*. Washington, DC: U.S. Department of Commerce, Economics, and Statistics Administration, U.S. Census Bureau.

Skeen, Patsy, and Bryan E. Robinson. 1984. "Family backgrounds of gay fathers: A descriptive study." *Psychological Reports* 54: 99–105.

———. 1985. Gay fathers' and gay nonfathers' relationships with their parents. *Journal of Sex Research* 21: 86–91.

Stein, Arlene. 2001. *The stranger next door*. Boston, MA: Beacon Press.

Strah, David, and Susanna Margolis. 2003. *Gay dads: A celebration of fatherhood*. New York: Jeremy P. Tarcher/Putnam.

U.S. Census Bureau. State and county quickfacts. http://quickfacts.census.gov/qfd/states/.

U.S. Census Bureau. Factfinder. http://factfinder.census.gov/home/saff/main.html?_lang=en.

Weston, Kath. 1991. *Families we choose: Lesbians, gays, kinship*. New York: Columbia University Press.

Woolwine, David. W. 2000. "Community in gay male experience and moral discourse." In *Gay community survival in the new millennium*, ed. Michael R. Botnick, 5–37. Binghamton, NY: The Haworth Press.

Wong, B. D. 2003. *Following Foo: The electronic adventures of the Chestnut Man*. New York: Harper Entertainment.

**FIGURE 9.1.  Time to feed the baby.**
Photo by Riché Jeneen Daniel Barnes

# 9

# Black Women Have Always Worked

## Is There a Work-Family Conflict Among the Black Middle Class?

*Riché Jeneen Daniel Barnes*

"I did not know any black women who stayed at home when I was growing up," Gail related, "Now I stay home . . . my mom . . . says she did not raise me to be dependent and thinks my husband will grow tired of it too." Gail is an African American, middle-class mother who left a business-management career to stay home for a while with her children. Her situation is unusual among middle-class black women and invisible in mainstream scholarship on black families and on work-family conflict. However, the existence of a growing group of middle-class black women who feel they have choices about how to balance their work and family commitments, including the option of staying home, signals a critical change in the situation of black families. It means that African American, middle-class women find themselves at a new point that has great implications for the ways in which they view motherhood, family, and work.[1]

This chapter challenges the notion of work and family conflict for African American, middle-class families and explores the ways in which African American mothers conceptualize and respond to this perceived conflict. While African American and white middle-class mothers have similar options, including part-time work, full-time work, flex-time work, and staying home, there remains a distinction between black and white middle-class families that is rooted in separate work and family histories. The African American mothers in this study found that the real conflict was in how to negotiate family and community expectations for educational and professional achievement while responding to the very real concern for the survival of black marriages and families. This analysis does not aim to discard the use of the phrase "work and family conflict" as useless, but rather it shows how the phrase operates within a different meaning system for

African American middle-class mothers, and is therefore understood and articulated differently even when the work and family practices are the same.

## BLACK WOMEN HAVE ALWAYS WORKED

Since the first African woman came to America during slavery, black women have worked. In those years men and women labored side by side and received no wages. Even after slavery ended, in the period after the Industrial Revolution, black men's wages were so low they needed their wives' earnings to support their families. At the start of the Industrial Revolution, white men were encouraged to move from an agricultural society to a manufacturing society through jobs in factories and mills. Some white women worked in factories and mills as well, but they usually worked in gender-segregated industries and stopped working outside the home after they married (Lerner 2005). The Victorian model of womanhood dictated that "respectable" women refrain from working outside the home. This model, also termed the "cult of domesticity," was espoused by the landowning ruling class and carried into less well-off communities. Poor whites, immigrants, and recently freed blacks all aspired to this ideal. It represented a higher station in life even if families could not afford it. The conditions for most industrial workers (primarily men) were very bad; they worked long hours for low wages. For African Americans, who gained their independence following the advent of the Industrial Revolution, the circumstances were even worse. Because of the color of their skin, it was difficult for them to find jobs, and they were usually the first fired. Not only did the cult of domesticity pose an economic conundrum, but it also threatened the increasing struggles for civil rights, better living conditions, and getting the entire black community to a better station in the American class/caste system.[2] Therefore, in most instances, men and women in the black household performed full-time wage labor.

The first black female doctors, lawyers, college instructors, and administrators pushed themselves to excel and exceed their meager backgrounds; their success urged all black women to achieve in their educations, careers, and community commitments, while simultaneously raising their families. Decades before the feminist movement, African American professional women were "having it all and doing it all," and encouraging others to do the same (Shaw 1996). Rather than suggesting that women stay at home with children, this model placed the educational achievements and professional employment of black women as central to "uplifting" the black race. The uplift movement was very important to the success of black communities following Reconstruction and prior to the Civil Rights Movement. Its focus was educating the masses of black people, for education was seen as the means to equality.

In addition to the tradition of viewing black women's professional work as a contribution to community uplift, another legacy of African American family history is important for middle-class African American mothers to-day—the maternally oriented structure of the black family. This structure is reflected in that most of the African American women in this study, regard-less of their parents' marital status, believed that they were trained to view their children and their careers as their first priority. The black family struc-ture has been erroneously labeled "matriarchal," but anthropologists define a matriarchal society as one in which women are the heads of the commu-nity, that is, they are the decision makers and have power over the design and implementation of social resources.[3] For African American families who live within the U.S. patriarchal structure, which also has race- and class-based systems of inequality, matriarchy is nonexistent—black women do not control the distribution of resources. However, black women do of-ten find themselves making decisions and allocating resources for their families.

## CULTURE, WORK, AND FAMILY VALUES

Since the Civil Rights Movement, Affirmative Action, and the Feminist/ Womanist Movement, opportunities have opened up for black men and for black and white women. The Civil Rights Act of 1964 outlawed discrimina-tion on the basis of race, color, religion, sex, or national origin. While change was slow for black men and for both black and white women, the federal mandates ushered in changes that affected the whole country. An unprecedented number of white middle-class women with children entered and remained in the labor force, while the changing opportunity structure for African Americans meant some black mothers were part of the middle class and could consider staying home full-time.

Now, some African American men are able to raise a family and reach middle-class status comfortably without their wives' paychecks, and some black women find that they too are entering careers that push their families into the upper-middle-class tax bracket. Studies show that African Ameri-cans are faring better economically than they have in the past. According to a study released by the Joint Center for Political and Economic Studies, the black median household income in 1997 was $25,050. That income level placed about 40 percent of black households in the middle class, compared with about 60 percent of white households. This proportion was almost double that of 1960. Between 1960 and 1997, the black middle class grew at a faster rate than the white middle class, increasing by 20 percent.

Although middle-income status today more often demands two-paycheck households within all ethnic groups, black wives are one and a half times more likely than white wives to work full-time. Nonetheless, as black male wages have risen with increasing career opportunities, black women have had more opportunity to become stay-at-home moms, or at least change their relationships to work. It is difficult to determine the true extent of stay-at-home mothers, but recent evidence suggests that "the relative number of black full-time moms is catching up with the number of white full-time moms. In 2000, 29 percent of white women and 22 percent of black women with children under 18 were full-time moms" (Fisher 2005).[4] Given these social, cultural, and economic shifts, this chapter asserts that African American, professional, middle-class families are at a critical crossroads.

African American, middle-class women confront the option of staying home, however, within a larger context of threats to African American families. Despite financial gains, African Americans continue to lag behind whites in income, net worth, college graduation, and stable first-time marriages. Several studies have found that during the days of slavery black children were more likely to grow up with both parents than they are today (Cherlin 1988, Gutman 1976). Black males ages eighteen to twenty-four are more likely to be victims of homicide and to be perpetrators of homicide than men in any other group (U.S. Bureau of Justice 2004). Black men make up 41 percent of the inmates in federal, state, and local prisons, but only 4 percent of all students in American institutions of higher education (Maxwell 2004). As a result there remains a level of cultural discord that negatively affects the whole community. These challenges that are seemingly attacking the fabric of black families and, by extension, black communities, are an important part of the context in which African American, professional, middle-class families respond to the recent debates about work and family conflict.

## BLACK FAMILIES AND STAY-AT-HOME MOTHERS

The African American family has been researched and critiqued extensively (Billingsley 1992, Gutman 1976, Stack 1974), but African American mothers have been largely under-theorized outside the mass perceptions of "matriarch," "welfare queen," and highly sexualized "jezebel" (Collins 1991). The history of black women at home is also fraught with stereotypic images. One common perception is that of a black woman, unmarried, with several children, on welfare, and even though "at-home," exhibiting minimal parenting skills. In fact, when research began for this project, a literature search on black motherhood produced an overwhelming number of references on black teenage mothers, black single mothers, black welfare mothers, and black mothers in poverty. There were a few references on black professional mothers (Landry 2000, Shaw 1996), but no references for black stay-at-home mothers (see Mack 1999 for a historical treatment). Additionally, issues of class bias the literature, as black middle-class women may self-identify as stay-at-home mothers, while single black women on public assistance may not. In fact, media representations of welfare mothers are typically depicted as black, whereas stay-at-home mothers are most often portrayed as white (West 2003).

In this chapter, I draw on a long-term ethnographic project with middle-class black mothers to explore the specific meanings of work-family conflict for middle-class black women and their families. I examine how class and race inform motherhood ideology and gender strategy and affect mothers' negotiation of career and family, and consider the implications of the findings for understanding and theorizing middle-class family life. By focusing on the particular themes and struggles articulated by women who have left professional careers to stay home with their children, I illuminate the changes in gender and family they are creating through their choices.

## ETHNOGRAPHIC METHODS AND CONTEXT

This chapter is based upon three years of anthropological research in Atlanta, Georgia, with married professional women (defined as women holding or having previously held a corporate executive or professional position and/or having an advanced degree) with at least one child under the age of five. The research included ethnographic observations of three formal support groups for women, one white American and two African American, who self-identify as "stay-at-home moms;" semi-structured life histories of twenty African American stay-at-home and full-time working mothers and their husbands; and twenty couple/family histories, including contextualized genealogy charts. Each of the women was contacted through two stay-at-home mothers' support groups and a private school in southwest Fulton County, where 90 percent of the parents are married, college graduates, and African American.

Due to Atlanta's unique racial history, a sizable black middle class has been a staple of the city since the Civil War. African American citizens have long held powerful positions in city and county government, including the first African American mayor of a major city in 1973 and, in 2001, the first African American female mayor of a major city. A relationship between the city's white business elite and black public officials kept Atlanta from following the hostile racial path of its neighbors during the Civil Rights Movement while developing seemingly voluntary racial segregation in which middle- and upper-class blacks live in upscale, expensive neighborhoods separate and apart from middle- and upper-class whites (Bayor 2000). My respondents, who live in a Zip code recorded by the census as 98 percent black, reported a median income of $151,000.

This chapter introduces five African American women—Gail, Nancy, Gia, Cara, and Marilyn—who made changes to their work and family practices based on perceived "work and family conflicts." At the beginning of my research, four of the women were members of formal stay-at-home mother support groups, which I observed for several months. Later, they stopped their memberships and either attended intermittently or formed informal groups with others. The fifth woman was a part-time (thirty-two hours per week) employee for most of her mothering years but made modifications to her schedule based on the needs of her family. Each of the women's stories illustrates common themes that I found during my fieldwork. These include: persistent images that negatively portray black men and build distrust within black male-female relationships; the contemporary socioeconomic and cultural crises within black communities (especially "ghetto culture" that pervasively represents blacks, particularly black youth, in the media); and the strong black woman model of African American motherhood that provides guidelines for mothers and children but leaves marriage a dream often deferred.

## NOT MY MOTHER'S DAUGHTER: REFRAMING THE MYTH OF THE STRONG BLACK WOMAN

Just inside "the Perimeter" (the term used by residents to denote the circular highway that goes around the city of Atlanta), as you pass one of the city's most prestigious black land-owning areas, sits a large church. The church was established in 1927, but this location just inside the Perimeter is new, and it mirrors the church's ascendance from a middle-class white congregation to an upwardly mobile, professional, middle-class black congregation. This church was home to one of the stay-at-home mom support groups observed for this study. This group claimed as its mission a biblical focus for women who were transitioning from professional careers to being stay-at-home mothers. This was uncharted territory for many of these women, who had left their expensive educations, careers, and salaries behind to be full-time caretakers of children. Many of these women's mothers had worked full-time (often as single parents), managed a family, and encouraged their daughters to excel academically, to obtain prestigious careers, and to create two-parent dual-income families so they could have a better life than their parents. But the women who met in this room once a week were among the ranks of a growing number of African American women who are choosing to stay at home with their children. They found themselves in an ambiguous position, trying daily to decipher whether they were doing the right thing, with no clear model for success.

This uncertainty was reflected in the women's discussions. At one meeting seven women were present: a doctor, a fundraising manager for a national nonprofit research center, a hotel management executive, two teachers, a small business owner, and a cosmetologist. All of the women were college graduates, married, and considered themselves stay-at-home moms. Following the opening pleasantries and an update on families and careers, the meeting began with the topic for the day. The group leader (one of the members, who had volunteered to lead) began the meeting with the topic "friendship." The biblically based workbook used to guide the class introduced the story of Nancy and Ruth and the friendship that developed between mother- and daughter-in-law. As the respondents talked about the text (Ruth 1:6–2:23) and explored all that Ruth had given up for her mother-in-law, the conversation quickly turned to a more personal discussion of the relationships the women had with their mothers-in-law, which in turn moved to the fragile relationships some of them had with their mothers. They discussed how they had been raised to think of family life in one particular way, but were working hard in their own marriages and as mothers to do something different. Nancy, a doctor with three children said:

> It's like my mom does not want me to be happy or she thinks I am an idiot. She thinks my husband is taking advantage of me or something because I try to be the type of wife God wants me to be and she does not understand that . . . to her it is about being in charge with my dad . . . for me it is about being submissive and letting my husband do what he needs to do for our family and supporting him.

Many of the women could relate to what Nancy said. They suggested that there were generational differences in how they and their mothers understood their roles as mothers and wives. Karen, a fundraising executive with one child, said:

> Our mothers did not know how to be wives. They were focused on their careers and their children, but they did not realize that not having a supportive model of marriage would negatively affect us and how we raised our families. We just have to stay prayerful.

Each of the women discussed their own predicaments as daughters of "strong black women" who expected them to be independent—able to take care of themselves and their children—first and foremost. From the slave past, to the Great Migration, to contemporary structural inequities, there has been relatively little concern over men who may or may not be present.

For black mothers, teaching their daughters to be "strong black women" was more about basic survival than gender equality. Black mothers have traditionally felt that they must maintain a delicate balance of preparing their daughters to survive in interlocking structures of race, class, and gender oppression, while rejecting and transcending those same structures.

The model of the strong black mother was what sustained many of these women through college, graduate school, or professional training, often while they faced subtle racism and sexism. However, what researchers are beginning to understand is that the "strong black woman" myth can also be detrimental to African American women and their families because it expects them to single-handedly take on all of the ills that plague their communities.

One of the respondents in the study, Gail, spoke at length about the effects this strategy for survival had had on her perception of herself and her desire for a marital relationship. Gail grew up the oldest of five children in St. Louis, Missouri. "I could not wait to get out of there," she recalled as we talked over lunch at one of her favorite restaurants. "I never thought I would be married, have kids, or even think about being at home with them." She was thirty-five, and pregnant with baby number two, a girl. The first was a boy. She had been married for three years and was a stay-at-home mother. Gail and I talked extensively over several months. I ran errands with her, went to her ultrasound appointments, and followed her around the house as she tended her two-year-old boy, folded laundry, and cleaned the bathrooms. Her husband was an accounting executive at a major corporation headquartered in Atlanta and they lived in a quiet subdivision in south Fulton County.

When I asked Gail how she decided to stay at home with her children, which she had not planned to do, she explained that she was laid off from her company just after she found out she was pregnant with her first child. She and her husband discussed her going back to work and decided that since she was pregnant they would just wait until the first child was eighteen months old and then she would return to work. When the eighteen months had passed, Gail was not ready and neither was her husband. They decided she would stay home indefinitely "as long as our finances could handle it." Since being at home, Gail had actually tried her hand at several things. She had worked on developing training to do billing for medical doctors (an at-home business). She had been the part-time property manager for her subdivision's homeowners association. She had worked on local politicians' election campaigns. And she had earned her property manager's license.

When I asked Gail how she would describe herself, she said as a part-time worker and full-time stay-at-home mom. It is a title she never thought she would have. Her perception of married life and motherhood was very negative before meeting her husband and entertaining the idea of marriage and family. She always knew she would be successful, but she was raised in a working-class family where her mother worked all the time and had very little time to interact with her children. And although Gail was raised in a two-parent home, her father was her step-father, and he and her mother had a rocky relationship at best. "There just weren't any good models of how to do marriage and family," Gail concluded. The only other married person she knew was an aunt, who, according to Gail, was a religious zealot and explained marriage as being submissive to a man. Gail said, "While I understand what it means now, as a kid I did not get it and I knew I did not want what she had." In fact, said Gail, "I was totally against being married." Once she did entertain the idea of being married, being a stay-at-home mother was not part of that equation. Gail explained:

> I was raised to be independent. I did not know who would be there for me and so it was very important for me to have my own money and my own everything. Depending on my husband now is so contrary to how I think of myself I sometimes think I need to go back to work just to make sure he knows I am making a contribution.

All the women I talked to expressed these same sentiments. They all valued being independent and being able to take care of themselves; children were often a family expectation; marriage was something families wanted but did not expect. The seeming pessimism around marriage is well-founded. As stated previously, although families produced during slavery faced the constant threat of separation, black children born then were more likely to grow up living with both parents than children are today (Ahlberg and DeVita 1992). In fact, according to recent reports, only one-third of black children have two parents living in the home (Page and Stevens 2004). Reports by the National Urban League and others suggest that once one takes into consideration incarceration, drug abuse, and unemployment, the number of marriageable black men to marriageable black women is a stark one man for every two women (Davis et al. 1997). Additionally, the divorce rate among African American couples has risen sharply: two-thirds of all black marriages end in divorce, and by the time they are sixteen, two-thirds of all black children will experience the break-up of their parents' marriage (U.S. Bureau of the Census 1991). These realities, coupled with economic policies that have focused on the advancement of women in education and career development, and social services that have historically focused on mothers and children, mean that black women are raised to assume that at some point they may have to support their families and therefore must learn to depend upon themselves.

## MAKING BLACK MARRIAGE AND FAMILY WORK

Despite all of the "baggage" that weighs down young black couples, many hope that marriage and family can work and are willing to give it a try. It is in this attempt at reformulating marriage within the confines of a matrifocal marriage and family system that women like Nancy reveal how different the work and family conflict is for African American women and their families than what is commonly depicted in contemporary treatments and understandings of family formation.

Nancy was born in Waco, Texas, to a sixteen-year-old mother and an eighteen-year-old father. Her father was on his way to college so the two parted ways, unsure of their future together, but they later married when Nancy was seven. Nancy spent most of her formative years being raised by her maternal and paternal grandmothers while her mother worked as a critical care nurse, often with very long and late hours. Although her parents married, had three more children, and continued to be married, Nancy said their marriage was terrible and she knew she did not want a marriage like theirs. But, instead of believing she would never marry, as Gail did, she hoped to be married in a much better relationship.

At the time of this research, Nancy was thirty-six, the mother of three children under the age of four, and a medical doctor, who formerly practiced internal medicine. She did not self-identify as a stay-at-home mother, although she was her children's primary caretaker. When I asked her how she identified she was not sure how to answer but she knew she did not identify with women who sat at home and ate "bon-bons." "I am too busy to be a stay-at-home mom!" Nancy exclaimed. Her husband, a former attorney, owned a home-building company, and they were living in a gentrifying Atlanta neighborhood near Turner Stadium. The home was built by Nancy's husband's company and they were in the process of building their next home in a nearby neighborhood.

When Nancy first left her position as a medical doctor, her family was very supportive. Her mother had recently become a fan of Dr. Laura Schlessinger and would often quote the popular radio personality's famous motto "I am my children's mother."[5] Nancy lived many miles away from her family, and they certainly did not want a stranger taking care of the first grandbaby. However, when one year turned into three, the women in her family decided Nancy had been home long enough: "I can remember being home for Christmas and I was taking care of the kids and it was difficult because the baby was really small. My grandmother walked by and said, "I don't know why you doing all that, they ain't gonna appreciate it." Nancy continued:

> It hurt a lot when she said that and I decided that, even though I appreciated my mother and my grandmothers and all that they had done for me, I did not

want to raise my family the way they had raised theirs and I battle with that every day.

Nancy's grandparents and her parents were married, so she did not fall into the category of having been raised by a strong black *single* mother. But she had watched both her grandmother and her mother interact with their respective husbands in ways that were often conflictual, argumentative, and stern. "There is no love," said Nancy. "I mean there is. I know my grandmother loved my grandfather and my mother loves my father but you cannot see their love in how they interact and how they treat their husbands. There is no respect. I do not want that kind of relationship with my husband." Even though Nancy critiqued her mother and grandmother, she realized that the interaction they each had with their husband was directly related to the strength they had to have to maintain their families. Nancy was taught this same strength when she saw her mother work days and nights to earn her license as a registered nurse. She saw it when she worked as a volunteer at her mother's hospital and when she saw her mother take orders from doctors while her mother did all the work. It was Nancy's mother and grandmother that provided the encouragement and finances to go to college and become a doctor, not a nurse. And Nancy knew it was that strength that they thought they had passed on to her and expected her to exhibit. That strength was not demonstrated when Nancy stayed home, seemingly forsaking all that they had given her, to help her husband manage his business and take care of their children. For African American professional women, such as Nancy, their worth as black women is deeply connected to the strength of their mothers.[6] For women who struggle with standing on their foremothers' shoulders while making new decisions for themselves and their families, a disapproving statement can be demoralizing.

Nancy articulated a purposeful position of building a "healthy marriage and family," in which the needs of her family, and particularly her husband, were foremost. She saw this as a way to break what was seemingly a multigenerational pull on her and her contemporaries that helped to elevate divorce rates and diminish marriage rates. What Nancy called for in her decision to leave her career as a medical doctor, co-manage her husband's company, and be the primary caretaker for her three small children, was a change in the black community from an emphasis on career and individual achievement to family centeredness. This perspective diverges from traditional debates about work and family conflict that focus on the issue of time pressures dual-professional families face. Instead, Nancy and the other women in this study saw the work and family conflict through the lens of the ideology of black motherhood, which teaches independence, individuality, and a focus on black women's roles as community leaders, mothers, and professionals, but less frequently as wives.

When asked if they were raised by their parents (or guardians) to be more career women, wives, or equal parts both, all of the twenty women in this study responded that they were raised to be career women, with 50 percent responding that they were raised to be equal parts career women and wives. Twenty-five percent felt they had not been prepared to be wives. The tenuous male-female relationships in the black community have created a conundrum in which black women are raised to "take care of themselves," with the understanding that children are a blessing from the Lord, but husbands often are not. While women, particularly middle-class women, continue to be encouraged to marry, these "mother-wit[7]" cultural cues do a lot to disrupt marriage by suggesting that marriage is not expected to last. One participant expressed her own exasperation when, as she was preparing for her marriage, her mother encouraged her to keep her maiden name, saying that it was difficult and expensive to change your name back once you got a divorce. From this young woman's perspective, planning for a divorce before you were married was not a good sign. The women in my study were members of couples who had made it to the altar. Now they were learning that lasting marriages were built on negotiation. This was a difficult lesson when earlier representations and personal understandings of male and female relationships had been antagonistic at best. These women had to negotiate the larger society's expectation that they would contribute to the rising divorce rate and make another female-headed household. They also had to make sense of centuries-old warnings that black men will leave, won't work, and will cheat, and they had to maintain their own independence—never depending on a man—if they wanted to be good, strong, black women and mothers.

## ENCULTURATING MIDDLE-CLASS BLACKNESS

Marilyn, raised to be an independent career woman, said she was ambiguous about marriage and family until she met her husband. "I never daydreamed about my wedding day or what my husband and kids would be like," she said in a matter-of-fact manner. But then she met her husband. "We had been dating for a couple of years, I loved him and he asked so it seemed like a good time to get married. Then a few years later it seemed like a good time to start having kids." But Marilyn and her husband separated after their seventh year of marriage. Marilyn attributed their separation to having too much "I" and "me" in their relationship.

> I was going through a point where I was redefining who I was and we hit a point where he did not connect with me at all. I felt exasperated. We learned valuable lessons during that period. We learned that we need to grow and

change but stay connected to each other. Too much "I" and "me" makes it hard on a marriage.

Marilyn was a very achievement-oriented woman. Before reducing her hours, for the second time, as an account executive for a national health insurance firm, she also managed her church bookstore, served as moderator for several women's groups, volunteered as a class parent at her children's school, and dabbled in an at-home marketing firm. Working part-time for her insurance firm eight to ten hours per week, Marilyn continued the same "extracurricular" activities. "The only difference is I get seven hours of sleep per night instead of five and we are not rushing around as much," she said. Marilyn's three children were in school, ranging from preschool to fifth grade. She kept a tight grip on their organization and time management. In previous years, Marilyn was the president of the P.T.A. During my research, she served as her three-year-old's soccer coach and her seven-year-old's team parent. Her husband was the coach.

Marilyn and the other mothers in this study were engaged in "concerted cultivation," as defined by Annette Lareau (2003). Lareau's groundbreaking study explored what she called the "unequal childhoods" of children who grow up in families from middle-class backgrounds and from poor/working-class backgrounds. She defined concerted cultivation as purposefully exposing children to many opportunities so that they are accustomed to functioning in privileged settings. While Lareau suggests these efforts are not racially motivated, the African American women in this study felt the stakes were even higher for their children. The families in this study were faced with the challenge of remaining an integral part of the black community while simultaneously mediating many of the seemingly negative influences that are currently and historically associated with blackness. With school children taunted for "acting white" when they are high-achieving students, and blackness identified as speaking in Ebonics, demonstrating little motivation in school, and following hip-hop fashion trends, black middle-class parents are at a loss.

Gia, another study participant, worried for more than a year about where her son would go to middle school. She was concerned about the environment of her neighborhood school, where delinquent behaviors instead of academic success were celebrated by students. She opted to send her son to a school almost an hour's commute on the other side of town because it was a math and science magnet school where her son could excel in the subjects he liked and receive encouragement from parents, teachers, and peers. "What their friends think is so important to these kids and I need to make sure that what his friends say lines up with what we are telling him."

Gia also struggled with what she saw as the reality of raising an African American boy into a man. "He needs to be prepared for a lot of things his white counterparts will not have to think about. He has to excel at school but he also has to know how to cope in a world that will always see him as black no matter how successful he is." Gia believed that to make sure he was well-prepared she had to be at home. She had left her career in information technology five years earlier to stay at home with her three children while her husband continued working as an advertising account manager at a major corporation. Now, even though all three of her children were in school (pre-kindergarten, kindergarten, and sixth grade), she stayed home so she could be the carpool parent for her middle-school son, the grade parent for her pre-kindergarten daughter, and the parent volunteer for her kindergarten son. When her husband was diagnosed with multiple sclerosis, her need to be at home to sustain her family was even greater. "I need to shuttle everyone to practices, and meetings, make sure my husband has a home-cooked meal every night, and help him to manage his stress."

There were costs to these mothers associated with this reformulation of African American families and their focus on sustaining their families, especially in the arena of gender equity. When asked to categorize household tasks by the person responsible for completing them, all the women in the study stated that they completed more of the tasks than their husbands. While they were dissatisfied with how much of the responsibility was their own, when asked if and what they would change, none of the women suggested their husbands do more but indicated instead that they would like to outsource more. At first glance, this position seems like a return to what has been termed neo-traditional gender roles, but a conversation with another respondent suggests other identity formulations may be materializing. Cara Sanders, a thirty-six-year-old mother of three and former school psychologist turned real estate investor, related that when people learned she worked from home, her children attended preschool, and she employed a housekeeper:

> They say "What do you do all day?" But I say why shouldn't I have a housekeeper or someone to help out around the house? White women have been doing it for years. . . . When I think of black womanhood I think struggle and I don't want to live like that. We shouldn't have to.

While Cara pushed against normative expectations of African American women, her sensibilities were a little ruffled. For African American women, hiring help is mired in social dictates that are not easily overcome. Many are daughters or granddaughters of domestic workers, nannies, or washer women, and they find hiring women to do similar tasks synonymous with hiring their own kin. They are well aware of the history of the exploitation of black women's labor and understand that women who provide productive labor for one household are typically unable to afford household services for their own families (Dill 1994, Mack 1999).

The conundrum for professional African American women in general and the women in this study in particular involves a rearticulation of race, class, and gender. In most instances they are faced with reconciling a connection to the black community which has in most instances supported them emotionally and financially, while simultaneously withdrawing from many of the parts of the culture that are deemed "black."

## CONCLUSION: BLACK AND MIDDLE-CLASS MOTHERHOOD

The cultural memory around African American, male-female relationships has long held that they are fragile and susceptible to the forces of racism, sexism, and classism, in ways that other ethnic groups are not.[8] This knowledge has motivated African Americans to bolster their families through the use of support systems such as the church, extended family, and governmental assistance. A folk culture arose that understood, articulated, and disseminated the belief that African American women could and most likely would, at some point, experience being a single mother and with that "fact" firmly set in place, African American women must be able to take care of themselves and their children.

It is within this context and this cultural memory that the women in this study found themselves juxtaposed between an educational and family of origin background that thoroughly prepared them to be professionals and mothers, often at the expense of marriage, and an upper-middle-class social location that expected and often demanded stable, two-parent homes. For Nancy and Gail it meant ignoring the advice of mothers and grandmothers who cautioned them "not to depend on a man," or otherwise exhibit "laziness." They both saw what that type of attitude did to their parents' marriages and knew they wanted different marriages, unions that were both intact and happy.

While Gail and Nancy dealt most specifically with the contradictions inherent in their desires to be good wives and mothers and their educational, professional, and family background, Marilyn and Gia grappled with enculturating middle-class values into their pre-teen children, who were often inundated with a view of African American youth culture that focused attention on violence, misogyny, hypersexuality, and hyperconsumption. They too reformulated their identities as high-achieving corporate women to nurture their families, taking a reduction in hours in Marilyn's case, and in Gia's, staying at home. But managing grade-schoolers and middle-schoolers introduced different challenges, particularly for black males, who continue to be the highest percentage of individuals in the justice system, and the lowest percentage in college.

It was Cara who provided the most telling depiction of the ambiguities inherent in these women's lives as each and every one of the respondents in the study made some reference to being a strong black woman, an independent woman, or a woman who could take care of herself and her children. The mythic view of the strong black woman has been passed down within families and communities. Its origins are in African tribal customs and in the capitalistic nature of the slave trade, which designated black men and women as perfect chattel. The title, although a badge of honor, has dictated through cultural memory that black women must be able to do it all. However, what is carried forth along with the apparent strength of the black woman is the constant sense of struggle. While these women want to be responsible to their communities, their families, and themselves, often choosing to live in racially segregated, black, middle-class neighborhoods, they also want a bit of reprieve, a "lighter" way of life, wherein they are not constantly called upon to carry the weight of the black family on their backs. The women in this study were working to build strong marriages; however, this framework often meant rejecting the good advice of mothers, grandmothers, sisters, aunts, and friends, who traditionally have been the people African American women depended on when the men were not around.[9] It was difficult to turn away from the cultural models they had always known and that they identified with and built their futures on. But these women recognized that the framework in which African American women were taught to expect to be alone, while praying not to be, was bad for their well-being. While it was not an easy statement to make, and may have felt like betrayal, Cara and the other women in this study were beginning to assert, "I don't want to live like that. We shouldn't have to."

In academic and popular press publications, placing husbands and children before personal career and professional goals has been termed neo-traditional (Gerson 1985, Hochschild 1989, Moen 2005). However, for African American, middle-class women, although taking care of family has always been a priority, it was not at the expense of a professional role, but in tandem with it. These African American women experienced a conflict between career and family that results in them reducing their employment hours, changing their professions, and becoming stay-at-home moms. However, these choices are not a result of the reasons the scholarship suggests. The literature, concerned mostly with white couples, talks about the demands and inequities of the workplace, and the inequalities inherent in the gendered division of labor. The women in this study, however, were reformulating their identities as they turned away from the icon of the "strong black woman" and built up one of the "strong black family."

## AFTERWORD

When I began this work I was a fourth-year graduate student, married, with a newborn baby. Like much of the literature suggests, as an African American woman, I had planned to continue working after I had my daughter. Two things sparked my interest in mothers' work and family decisionmaking and constructions of class identity. First, shortly after the birth of my daughter, I began to see and hear about African American professional women who were opting out of the workforce to care for small children. I was surprised to say the least, as I had never heard of black women who were "stay-at-home moms" or housewives. Second, as I began to look for literature that would explain these "options" I found very little on the relationship between African American professional married women and their careers and families. There was a good deal of literature on white women's entrance into the workforce and the conflicts and negotiations they experienced. Likewise there was plentiful literature on black women and other women of color who were in low-wage, low-skill jobs, and managing work and family with inadequate resources and fewer options. However, neither of these perspectives resonated for me and as I began to discuss these things with other African American professional women, I found that they did not really resonate for them either.

What was different about my particular situation was work and family had never seemed at odds, they had never needed to be negotiated because in my African American, middle-class, southern upbringing, black women had always worked. In fact, until I became pregnant with my own child, I had not known one black woman nor heard of a single black woman who had been a "stay-at-home" mom, or even a housewife, as earlier epochs had dubbed women whose primary responsibility was hearth and home. The closest I had heard of was African American women of the Jim Crow South who had worked from home as washer women, domestics, and in any other "unskilled" labor wherein they could earn some money while simultaneously tending hearth and home. In fact I had been raised, and every other African American woman I knew had been raised, to acquire as much education as possible, become a professional middle-class woman, get married, have children, and continue professional employment, homemaking, and community service simultaneously. We were taught that it was our responsibility to stand on the shoulders of our foremothers and have it all, manage it all, and then help other women achieve even higher markers of success (Shaw 1996).

Once I began the research, I encountered a number of professional, middle-class, married, African American women who were stay-at-home moms, at least for a time, or had negotiated another unconventional relationship with work. I immediately became intrigued by the idea that African American women were opting out of careers that many (and their families) had worked so hard to achieve. I was mired in personal contradictions and I wanted to locate a way to explore this unacknowledged, invisible conundrum while maintaining scholarly distance. To do so, I drew upon the tradition of work by women of color in anthropology who have been engaged in native anthropology and its sister, autoethnography, for decades. Black female anthropologist Irma McClaurin (2001) outlines the importance of this type of research while denoting the challenges involved when conducting research with respondents and in communities that resemble one's own.

The interactions with the women in my study were more like talking with friends than with research participants. We had experienced many of the same things and they often asked me what I thought of particular things they said or did. While I worked to maintain a good deal of distance between the participants and myself, I must say we engaged in a journey together, somewhat following the model of participatory research, of trying to make sense out of lives that had no representative model or analysis.

## NOTES

I am eternally grateful for and to the women who participated in this study who let me poke, probe, and prod them and their families much more than they probably thought when they volunteered. I have been tremendously blessed to have made each one of their acquaintances. I am also thankful to Dr. Bradd Shore, Dr. Peggy Barlett, Dr. Karyn Lacy, and Dr. Johnnetta Betsch Cole, who have read portions of this chapter in its various incarnations and found it and the questions that drive it intriguing and necessary. I am thankful to the editors, Elizabeth Rudd and Lara Descartes, who saw a diamond in the rough and chipped away at it until it shone a little more clearly. I must thank the Ford Foundation, Vice Provost of Spelman College, Myra Burnett, and the NSF-sponsored Spelman College and University of Wisconsin Science and Social Transformation Collaboration Grant, and the Emory University Sloan Center for Myth and Ritual in American Life for funding the project through its completion. I thank my mom and dad, my friends and family, my othermothers, sisterfriends, and their husbands. And finally I thank God for blessing me with my wonderful husband and partner, Darnel, and our three beautiful children who inspire me, sustain me, and support me every step and move I make.

1. In both the Weberian and Marxian traditions, the upper class is defined as the propertied class. They control ownership of income-producing property. The middle class includes those having white-collar and professional occupations, and those with blue-collar, manual jobs are considered working-class.

2. Class and caste are often used interchangeably in the U.S. context due to the history of a racially based class designation during slavery and in the Jim Crow South.

3. Daniel Patrick Moynihan introduced the term "matriarchal" to describe African American families in 1965, and blamed this family structure for problems in the black community that actually stem from racial and economic inequality (Billingsley 1992, Gutman 1976) (see also Moynihan 1965).

4. Luchina Fisher's article appeared in the online publication *Women's E News*, February 2005. Corresponding data were reported in the National Women's Law Center Report, July 2003, and by Kelly Starling Lyons of *The New Observer* online publication, June 2006. This information is hard to tease out since the Census just started analyzing stay-at-home parents in 2004. Most of the data are collected through private surveys. In addition, several reports have disputed the Census findings, citing the fact that many women move in and out of the workforce over the course of their and their children's lives and in many instances women "at home" are there because of a weak labor market (U.S. Congressional Report 2007, Moen 2005).

5. Dr. Laura is a national radio talk show host who advocates men and women putting all of their focus on what is best for their children. When listeners call with a dilemma about work or family or extended family, her response is usually "Be your children's parents." Listeners often call in and begin their question by saying "I am my child's mother/father."

6. "Strength of their mothers" refers to the book penned by Niara Sudarkasa (1997), *Strength of Our Mothers*, in which she discusses the strength African American women have had to demonstrate from slavery to the present to preserve their families.

7. According to Joy Bennett Kinnon, "mother wit" is referred to in the dictionary as simply "common sense." In black history, the word usage began in the seventeenth century. Thus the word was born and distilled in the brutality of slavery and has survived to enter the new millennium. It was a code word then, and is still a code word for the knowledge you must have to survive. Kinnon states, "It is, as author Toni Morrison says, 'a knowing so deep' that the lesson has been instilled and distilled to its essence. Collectively these words are a gift—from your own mother, or anyone's mother. They are wise words for life's journey" (1997).

8. Cultural memory is a relatively new area of inquiry. For the purposes of this study I draw from the interpretation set forth by feminist scholars who use cultural memory to theorize gender and women's perspectives on hegemonic normative histories. Hirsch and Smith (2002) define cultural memory in their introduction to a special edition of *Signs: Journal of Women in Culture and Society*: through cultural memory "identity, whether individual or cultural, becomes a story that stretches from the past to the present and the future, that connects the individual to the group, and that is structured by gender and related identity markers . . . [it] . . . is the combined study of what has happened and how it is passed down to us" (8–9).

9. See Angela Davis's (1971) "Reflections on the black woman's role in the community of slaves" (reprinted in Beverly Guy-Sheftall's *Words of Fire* (1995)). Davis discusses the importance of the black slave woman in the maintenance of the domestic sphere, how that sphere was seen as a place of resistance, and how black women worked together to take care of the needs of children and men around them who were often not members of their immediate family.

# REFERENCES

Ahlberg, Dennis A., and Carol J. DeVita. 1992. "New realities of the American family." *Population Bulletin* 47 (2): 8.

Bayor, Ronald. 2000. *Race and the shaping of twentieth century Atlanta.* Chapel Hill, NC: University of North Carolina Press.

Billingsley, Andrew. 1992. *Climbing Jacob's ladder: The enduring legacy of African American families.* New York: Simon & Schuster.

Cherlin, Andrew. 1988. *The changing American family and public policy.* Washington, DC: Urban Institute Press.

Collins, Patricia Hill. 1991. *Black feminist thought: Knowledge, consciousness, and the politics of empowerment.* New York: Routledge.

Davis, Angela. 1995[1971]. "Reflections on the black woman's role in the community of slaves." In *Words of fire: An anthology of African American feminist thought.* ed. Beverly Guy-Sheftall, p. 200–18. New York: New Press.

Davis, Larry, Shirley Emerson, and James Herbert Williams. 1997. Black dating professionals' perceptions of equity, satisfaction power, romantic alternatives and ideals. *Journal of Black Psychology* 23: 148–64.

Dill, Bonnie Thornton. 1994. *Across the boundaries of race and class: An exploration of work and family among black female domestic servants.* New York: Garland.

Fisher, Luchina. 2005. "Mocha moms downshift careers for motherhood." *Women's E News.* February 22, 2005. www.womensenews.org/article.cfm/dyn/aid/2194/context/archive.

Gerson, Kathleen. 1985. *Hard choices: How women decide about work, career, and motherhood.* Berkeley, CA: University of California Press.

Gutman, Herbert. 1976. *The black family in slavery and freedom, 1750–1925.* New York: Pantheon Books.

Hirsch, Marianne, and Valerie Smith. 2002. "Feminism and cultural memory: An introduction." *Signs: Journal of Women in Culture and Society* 28(1): 1–19.

Hochschild, Arlie R. 1989. *The second shift: Working parents and the revolution at home.* New York: Viking.

Joint Center for Political and Economic Studies Data Bank prepared by Cassandra Cantave and Roderick Harrison. www.jointcenter.org/DB/factsheet/famincm.htm.

Kinnon, Joy Bennett. 1997. "Mother wit: Words of wisdom from black women." *Ebony Magazine* March 1997. findarticles.com/p/articles/mi_m1077/is_n5_v52/ai_19201537.

Landry, Bart. 2000. *Black working wives: Pioneers of the American family revolution.* Berkeley, CA: University of California Press.

Lareau, Annette. 2003. *Unequal childhoods: Class, race, and family life.* Berkeley, CA: University of California Press.

Lerner, Gerda. 2005. *The majority finds its past: Placing women in history.* Chapel Hill, NC: University of North Carolina Press.

Mack, V. Kibibi. 1999. *Parlor ladies and ebony drudges: African American women, class, and work in a South Carolina community.* Knoxville, TN: University of Tennessee Press.

Maxwell, Bill. 2004. "On campus, grim statistics for African American men." *St. Petersburg Times, Tampa Bay.* January 4, 2004. www.sptimes.com/2004/01/04/news_pf/Columns/On_campus__grim_stati.shtml

McClaurin, Irma. 2001. *Black feminist anthropology: Theory, politics, praxis and poetics.* New Brunswick, NJ: Rutgers University Press.

Moen, Phyllis. 2005. *The career mystique: Cracks in the American dream.* Lanham, MD: Rowman and Littlefield.

Moynihan, Daniel Patrick. 1965. "The Negro family: The case for national action." *U.S. Department of Labor.* www.dol.gov/oasam/programs/history/webid-moynihan.htm

Page, Marianne E., and Ann Huff Stevens. 2004. "The economic consequences of absent parents." *Journal of Human Resources* 39: 80–107.

Shaw, Stephanie. 1996. *What a woman ought to be and to do: Black professional women workers during the Jim Crow era.* Chicago: University of Chicago Press.

Stack, Carol. 1974. *All our kin: Strategies for survival in a black community.* New York: Harper & Row.

Sudarkasa, Niara. 1997. *Strength of our mothers: African and African American women and families.* Trenton, NJ: Africa World Press.

U.S. Bureau of the Census. 1991. *Population profile of the United States.* Current Population Reports, Special Studies, Series P–23, No. 173. Washington, DC: Government Printing Office.

U.S. Bureau of Justice. 2004. *Homicide trends in the U.S.* Office of Justice Programs. www.ojp.usdoj.gov/bjs/homicide/race.htm.

U.S. Congressional Report. House Committee on Education and Labor. 2007. *Strengthening the middle class: Ensuring equal pay for women,* by Heather Boushey. Washington, DC. April 24, 2007. http://edworkforce.house.gov/testimony/042407HeatherBousheytestimony.pdf

West, Laurel Parker. 2003. "Welfare queens, working mothers, and soccer moms: The socio-political construction of state child-care policy." PhD diss. Emory University, 2003. wwwlib.umi.com/dissertations/fullcit/3103824.

# 10

"It's Like Arming Them"

## African American Mothers' Views on Racial Socialization

*Erin N. Winkler*

Michelle laughs freely when sharing stories about her thirteen-year-old daughter, Elina, and her ten-year-old son, Carlos, often beginning, "Now, *this* is *so* funny . . ." Her pride in her children is clear as she shares details about their talents, interests, and personalities.[1] "They just tickle me sometimes," she says, smiling. However, she becomes very serious when the topic turns to her deep concerns about how racism may impact her children's lives. Although she expresses uncertainty about *when* and *how* it is best to talk to Elina and Carlos about racism, she is unequivocal about her responsibility to do so. "As a parent," she says, "it's like arming them. You *have* to let them know that it's there, because it's a way of protecting them. . . . You hate to teach it to them, but at the same time, if you're going to be able to keep them safe, they have to know."

Children in the United States are born into a powerful, albeit increasingly covert, racialized order. For African American children, this racialized order strongly influences the neighborhoods in which they are likely to live, the schools they are likely to attend, their future employment prospects, and even their longevity. African American families are faced with the difficult challenge of socializing their children in a way that equips them to address this reality and thrive in spite of it. Michelle's assertion that preparing her children for racism is one of her primary parenting responsibilities is a conviction shared by all of the African American mothers who participated in this study. These mothers consistently express the view that preparing one's children to grow and succeed in a racialized society—a process called racial socialization—is a critical aspect of good parenting in African American families.

How do children come to understand race in today's society, and what role does the family play in this process? Families have traditionally been charged with the primary responsibility of socialization (Boykin and Ellison 1995, Demo and Hughes 1990, Hill 1999, Thornton 1997). Socialization is defined as the process through which individuals acquire an understanding of their own identity, role, and position in society, as well as the roles and positions of others (Boykin and Toms 1985, Bronfenbrenner 1979, Damon 1988, Thornton et al. 1990). Racial socialization, then, is the process through which children develop identities and internalize social roles within a specific racialized context. For African American children, this often means receiving mixed messages—negative from society and positive from family—about what it means to be black in the United States. Societal institutions, such as mainstream media, schools, policy-making bodies, and the legal system, tend to explicitly and implicitly tell children that being black is negative in a number of areas, such as beauty, intelligence, culture, heritage, productive citizenship, and life chances. African American families counter these negative messages by teaching their children that being black is something of which they should be proud, and that racism is at the root of negative representations of blackness. Through familial racial socialization, African American families teach children how to function in a racially hostile and inequitable society, while still maintaining racial pride and a positive sense of self (Hale-Benson 1990). As such, racial socialization is a complex and interactive process between children, their families, and the larger society (Hughes and Johnson 2001, Scott 2003). In this process, African American children sift through all of the various and conflicting things they are taught about being black, and make conscious and unconscious decisions about what to internalize and what to reject.

African American children learn about race from several sources. Family, schools, media (especially television), neighborhoods, peers, police officers, retail store clerks, and community and religious organizations all can send young people vastly different messages about what it means to be black. Which sources and messages are the most powerful? There is considerable disagreement about this among scholars. The literature falls into two broad camps: those who believe the family is the most critical agent of socialization and those who argue that forces outside the family have more influence. Authors in the first camp claim that the family is the primary socializer because it decides "what to filter out, [and] what to promote" (Boykin and Ellison 1995, Harrison et al. 1990, Hughes 2003, Jackson et al. 1997, Spencer 1990, Thomas and Speight 1999, Thompson 1994). However, scholars in the second camp argue that racial socialization is controlled by forces outside of the family, such as schools and media (Billingsley 1992, Irvine and Irvine 1995, Stanton-Salizar 1997, Wilkinson 1995). Tatum (2003) compares negative racial socialization messages from sources outside of the family, which "affirm the assumed superiority of Whites and the assumed inferiority of people of color," to "smog in the air," arguing that such negative messages are ubiquitous and unavoidable in American culture (2003, 6). The scholars in this second camp agree, arguing that, although the family does act as an agent in racial socialization, it cannot completely overpower the pervasive negative racial socialization messages communicated by society. According to the mothers interviewed for this study, the truth lies somewhere in between these two perspectives. While they concede that some negative messages may, as one mother says, slip "straight into their [children's] subconscious," they also believe that their own racial socialization practices, as Michelle puts it, can arm their children against racism.

In this chapter, we will hear from three mothers: Audrey, Michelle, and Lena—all middle-class African American mothers raising their middle-school-aged children in Detroit, Michigan. First, to put their childrearing experiences into context, we will briefly cover the design, methods, sample, and setting of this study. Next, we will meet each of the three mothers and learn a little bit about her family and her background. Finally, through the narratives of Audrey, Michelle, and Lena, we will see how a racialized position in society shapes parenting responsibilities, and leads African American families to employ racial socialization as an integral component of childrearing and care. We will learn how racial socialization includes lessons about the importance and value of African American culture and heritage, or *procultural* racial socialization, and lessons about dealing with racism, or *responsive* racial socialization. Using these mothers' narratives, this chapter will outline how African American families struggle to protect their children from racism, prepare their children for eventual encounters with racism, and teach their children to critique racism and narrow or stereotypical definitions of blackness.

## STUDYING RACIAL SOCIALIZATION IN DETROIT

The three women whose experiences are presented in this chapter were part of a larger study that sought to examine how children learn to negotiate all of the various and conflicting messages they receive about race. This study was designed by the author of this chapter and involved forty-seven open-ended, qualitative interviews conducted in Detroit from August 2003 to January 2004. These interviews were conducted with a purposive sample of nineteen African American mothers[2] and their twenty-eight middle-school-aged children. Participants were recruited through computer literacy programs, neighborhood associations, fliers, and word of mouth. The participating families represented a wide range of incomes, employment situations, educational backgrounds, and household structures. Five of the families in this study reported household incomes that were below the city median of $29,526 (U.S. Census Bureau 2000), six families had household incomes roughly equal to the city median, and eight families reported household incomes above the city median. When asked to describe the highest level of formal education they had completed, two mothers reported some high school, nine a high school diploma, two an associate's degree, four a bachelor's degree, and two a graduate degree. While this study found that the kinds of racial socialization issues discussed here are confronted by African American families of all class backgrounds, this chapter presents the experiences of three middle-class mothers.

The nineteen families interviewed for this study all lived within Detroit city limits at the time of their interviews, and were drawn from seven different Zip codes. All of the families lived in neighborhoods that were predominantly African American, and most lived in Zip codes that were at least 95 percent African American. Of the twenty-eight children interviewed in this study, only four attended schools that had less than 95 percent African American enrollment (National Center for Education Statistics). These neighborhood and school demographics reflected the demographics of the entire city. In the year 2000, among U.S. cities with populations of at least 105,000 people, Detroit had the highest percentage black population, with 83 percent of its 951,270 residents reporting as black or African American (U.S. Census Bureau 2001).

This chapter is based mostly on interviews conducted with African American mothers in Detroit, but in order to illustrate the specificity of the Detroit environment and its influences on racial socialization, it will also include brief references to findings from interviews conducted with African American parents in the San Francisco Bay Area. The California sample was smaller than the Detroit sample, but was similar in terms of educational attainment, employment status, and marital status. In contrast to the Detroit sample, however, all of the families interviewed in California were living in predominantly white or Latino areas.

Detroit's racial context is significant and somewhat unique in the United States, both because of racial demography and because civic life is largely governed by African Americans. Since 1974, when Coleman Young became Detroit's first black mayor, all of the city's mayors have been African American. This transformation from white to African American leadership and control also was mirrored in other arenas, such as the public school system, the police department, city council, and city government as a whole (Welch et al. 2001). Hartigan (1999) argues that these factors have created a cultural context in Detroit in which "whiteness is not hegemonic" and "Blackness is locally dominant" (1999, 16). As we will see later in this chapter, the city itself acts as a co-socializer for children, and it also shapes how mothers envision their own role in the racial socialization of their children.


## "WHEN I WAS COMING UP":
## THREE MOTHERS TALK ABOUT RACIAL SOCIALIZATION

Audrey is a forty-seven-year-old attorney in Detroit's juvenile and family court system. Audrey's husband, Dumay, is a physician. Together they have three sons: eleven-year-old Toussaint, six-year-old Talib, and Kwesi, who is almost two. Audrey and Dumay have the highest degrees and arguably the most prestigious occupations of any of the adults in this study, but they do not have the highest household income, partially because they are committed to serving in the public sector. They also live in one of the most impoverished areas represented in this study, in a Zip code that had a median household income of $21,044 in 2000, about 29 percent lower than the city-wide median of $29,526, and about 50 percent lower than the national median of $41,994 (U.S. Census Bureau 2000). In Audrey and Dumay's Zip code, 37 percent of individuals were defined by the United States Census Bureau as living below poverty level in 2000, a percentage almost three times the national average of 12 percent in 2000 (U.S. Census Bureau 2000). Audrey and Dumay live in a two-story, wood-frame house on a block of similarly structured and well-maintained two-story homes, some of which are single-family dwellings and others of which are two-family flats. The houses are set closely together with very small front yards, but behind the houses on Audrey's side of the street is a large, open field where people garden and children play. Many of the houses on Audrey's block are owned by the same landlord, who also has lived on that same block for decades. Audrey describes their block as "a jewel," characterized by "ethnic diversity" and "urban environmentalism," noting that her neighbors keep "ducks and pigs and chickens . . . not to mention the goats. And the kids have a great time." Several children on the block play outside together, and brightly colored, hand-painted street signs warn drivers to proceed slowly and watch for children at play. While the architecture is similar, Audrey and Dumay's block is visibly different in many ways from the surrounding blocks. Proceeding down the narrow, one-way street just one block in either direction, one passes vacant lots, abandoned houses, and burned-out buildings that have become ad hoc dumping grounds for mounds of garbage and, according to Audrey, spaces for criminal activity. Audrey shares that Dumay "just didn't want to move over here [to this neighborhood]. He just figured it'd be too much crime. And, you know, he didn't want his kids getting up and looking at a burned-out building every day." However, Audrey says that she "finally convinced him," because she wanted the experience of this "dynamic community." She laughs as she shares that the neighbor "has even gotten Dumay to commit to go milk the goats. It is the funniest thing watching him down there, pulling it, with the goat stepping in the bucket!" However, she adds, "it's been a struggle to keep my husband here . . . [because of] all the blight in the area. We could go one block in any direction, and it's just, it's devastating to look at that everyday. It's depressing." The couple is planning to relocate to Dumay's hometown in the Caribbean in a matter of months, but decided to keep their children in Detroit until their move because of the importance they place on living in a predominantly black community. Audrey is clear that she and her husband want their sons to be surrounded by examples of strong, successful, and proud black people. For this reason among others, they also have enrolled their elder sons in one of Detroit's African-centered schools, a school in which African and African American history, culture, and worldview are central to pedagogy and curriculum.

Audrey herself was born and raised in southwest Detroit. She describes her parents as "working class," and credits them with "exposing us to a lot of things." Audrey believes that her parents' support and encouragement allowed her to become the first in her family to graduate from college, despite what she calls "the deficits of my public school education" in Detroit. However, Audrey is clear that her parents did not adequately prepare her to deal with racism. In fact, she says, they did not tell her anything at all about racism. She says that she is not sure if they thought "they were shielding me, or if they were living in a world that they *wished* it was like, what everybody said it was *going* to be like." Either way, Audrey concludes, "I had no idea of racism. I was clueless." She says that "it was hurtful" when she left home for college and began to experience racism, because she was forced to figure out how to deal with it on her own. As a result, Audrey states, she was always clear that when she had children, she would be certain to prepare them for racism, so that they would not be blindsided by racism in the way that she was as a young person.

Michelle is the mother of a thirteen-year-old daughter, Elina, and a ten-year-old son, Carlos. She is a graduate of one of Michigan's public universities, and reports that she comfortably supports her family through her job as a computer repair technician in a wealthy Detroit suburb. Michelle, who is in her mid-thirties, is divorced from Elina and Carlos's father, who now lives in a different state. Michelle describes her former husband as being "black Puerto Rican," but adds that "most people cannot recognize that [he] is Hispanic. Their assumption is that he's black." Nevertheless, Michelle says that her children are sometimes questioned about their racial or ethnic identity because of their hair texture or skin tone. Regarding her children's reactions to such inquiries, Michelle says, "Sometimes they'll just tell you, 'I'm black.' And sometimes they'll do the whole thing . . . 'I'm black and my dad's Puerto Rican . . . I'm an African American Puerto Rican.'" However, Michelle adds, "Their main identity really is black, and I think it's really environment, because everybody around them is black."

Born and raised on the west side of Detroit, in a neighborhood that she says exemplified the philosophy "It takes a village to raise a child," Michelle describes her family of origin as "nuclear" and "fun." As the youngest of three children, Michelle says that she had "a lot of freedom, a lot of autonomy" growing up. When Michelle attended middle school in the early 1980s, she was bused to a predominantly white school, which she said was her "first introduction to white people outside of just, like, at the store or on TV." Unlike Audrey, however, Michelle says, "I got taught . . . that racism exists." In fact, she says that her parents clearly told her, "Because of my color, people are going to treat me different. There are some things I'm not going to get. There might be a job I don't get, or I might walk into a store [and be followed by security]." Michelle explains that this preparation was important in helping her understand her experiences with a group of white friends she met during her high school years through her biracial cousin, who lived in a predominantly white neighborhood with her white mother. "When I [was] hanging with her friends," Michelle says, "I [was] like the only black face for miles. I mean there was one black girl and all these white kids." Unlike her black friends in her own neighborhood, her white friends were into shoplifting and drugs. Early on, she says that her white friends realized that the security guards at the mall racially profiled Michelle, viewing her as likely to steal because she was black:

> So, I became bait once [my white friends] found that out. They would send me into a store, make me divert security and clerks, and five-finger-discount the place. [Laughs]. It was interesting being in their world because, my God, their world was so different from mine.

Michelle found that her white friends were not criminalized and punished by the police in the same way that her black peers were. She relates that, when her white friends were caught shoplifting, "all the security did was they busted them and put them out, and just made them leave the mall. Didn't arrest them. No questioning. I was like, 'Wow, this is *different!*'"

Michelle says that her parents taught her explicitly that she would receive negative treatment based on her race, but also modeled meaningful interracial friendships and relationships within their own family and circle of friends. She is now teaching her own children about race in a similar way: She wants them to be prepared for racism, but also to treat people as individuals. "I think I'm doing a pretty good job," she says, "because I think they're open [and] they don't judge much, they don't have a problem with white people. They're not fazed if they're in a place where there's all white kids—out they go to play. They know it [racism] might come, but it's not going to restrict them. So, for me, I think that's the best I can do."

Lena is the mother of thirteen-year-old Tanika and ten-year-old Lanáe, whom she is raising with her husband, Michael. Lena works as a travel agent, and, unlike Audrey and Michelle, she was not raised in Detroit. Lena spent much of her childhood in Colorado, but also in Texas, Hawaii, Oklahoma, and the Philippines. She describes life growing up with her mother, whom she says was "a hippie" and "very Afrocentric," as full of "a lot of different kinds of people—white, black, African, what have you." When Lena was young, her mother was a college student "majoring in African Studies [and] African American Studies," and Lena says that her mother "always tried to let us know [about] African American history." Lena's father lived in the San Francisco Bay Area, and worked as an early child development professional. "Being an educator," she says, "he always showed us how to—any situation that we came across—how to evaluate the situation." Lena says that both of her parents taught her to think critically about race and racism. She gives an example from one summer when she worked at a daycare center, and a white child "always rubbed my skin . . . [trying to] kind of rub it off, and then finally she asked me why I was that brown." Lena continues:

> I think, had my parents not educated me on [race and racism], then I guess I could have had a harsher response. But I understood that she just wanted to know and she didn't understand. So, they must have taught me well. I guess I should tell them that every now and then. [Laughs]

She adds, "I think they were great for me in that regard. I think I was always pretty proud, more or less, to be black."

As an adult, Lena joined the military and also "married a military man." They lived in Maryland before moving to her husband's hometown of Detroit when their daughters were very young. Lena describes herself as "a military brat" and says that, because of this, she can live anywhere. However, she finds Detroit to be "a very strange city in regards to race." Having spent most of her childhood in areas where African Americans made up a small minority of the population, Lena appreciates the sense of community Detroit provides for her children. However, she worries that "everything is so separate" racially, and wishes that "there was more of a mix." She expresses concern that her daughters might pick up what she sees as Detroit's "close-minded" approach to race, in which "people tend to stay to themselves and look at other things as being foreign." Although Lena is raising her daughters in a different context than that in which she was raised, she feels that they still need the same racial socialization lessons that her parents taught her as a child: to know that racism exists and "to be cautious," but also to "know how to coexist" and "to be willing to communicate with people from different backgrounds."

## RACIAL SOCIALIZATION:
## PROCULTURAL AND RESPONSIVE

Racial socialization is a dynamic process in which children struggle to reconcile the conflicting things they are taught about race from various sources. The mothers in this study clearly see much of their role in this process as "damage control" in response to the negative racial socialization messages their children receive, or will potentially receive, from sources outside of the family. They are deeply invested in helping their children sort through the conflicting things they hear about race, steering them toward rejecting the negative things they are told about blackness, and embracing the positive. As we will hear in their narratives, these women consider the positive racial socialization of their children to be an imperative aspect of good mothering.

The mothers interviewed in this study displayed two broad categories of racial socialization, which I call *procultural* and *responsive*.[3] Procultural racial socialization messages focus on the value of African and African American heritage in and of itself (and are not in response to external racism), and responsive racial socialization messages are those messages that respond to negative messages about blackness communicated to children through sources outside of the family.

## "EVERYBODY AROUND THEM IS BLACK":
## PROCULTURAL RACIAL SOCIALIZATION

While a few mothers in this study indicate sending explicit procultural racial socialization messages—or talking to their children about the value of black culture and a black identity in and of itself—a majority of the mothers say that the racial environment of Detroit does this for them. In other words, the city in which they are raising their children acts as a co-socializer, sending procultural messages about black history, leadership, creative expression, beauty, and so on. As discussed earlier in this chapter, because of its unique racial history and demographics, Detroit provides a cultural context in which, unlike much of the United States, African American culture is "locally dominant" (Hartigan 1999). Audrey even refers to the city of Detroit as "Blacktown." As Michelle points out, the city's collective racial identity influences her children's identities. In Detroit, Michelle says, the "main identity really is black. I think it's really the environment, because everybody around them is black." These mothers feel that, because black culture is omnipresent and implicit within everyday life in Detroit, its value is not something that needs to be explicitly emphasized, as would be the case in most other cities and towns in the United States. In contrast, the African American parents interviewed in the San Francisco Bay Area for this project live in predominantly white or Latino areas and feel that they have to frequently and explicitly discuss black culture with their children. The parents interviewed in California all say that they purposely seek out predominantly black settings to which they can take their children to show them positive examples of black culture, leadership, and the diversity of experiences among African Americans. Even if they are not practicing Christians, for example, the parents in the California study consistently emphasize the importance of the black church as a space for the affirmation of black cultural heritage and shared history. In contrast, mothers in the Detroit study refer to the church as a very important religious and social institution, but do not perceive it as a space they must seek out to show their children positive representations of African American people and culture.

Detroit's status as "Blacktown" and its influence on racial socialization stems from more than simple racial demographics—virtually every position of civic leadership in the city is held by an African American. The city has had African American mayors, police chiefs, school superintendents, and other civic leaders since before the children in this study were born. The public school system also has included three African-centered schools since before these children were born, and in June 2006, the school board approved the planning of a broader "African-Centered Education Curriculum Program." Such educational programs are designed to encourage African American student achievement through the creation of relevant and supportive learning environments and a teaching philosophy focused on African core cultural values (Detroit Public Schools 2006). Several mothers argue that these are just a few of the aspects of everyday life in Detroit that implicitly teach their children to value African American culture, history, leadership, and achievements. Their children, as one mother puts it, do not feel pressure to "act like what they're not" or to devalue African American culture in favor of white culture. "Detroit is such a black city," one mother explains, "[that] I probably don't emphasize being black so much [with my children]. They grew up in Detroit—very black." In this context, the mothers in this study entrust much of the procultural socialization of their children to the environment of the city itself.

## "JUST TO KEEP THEM SAFE": RESPONSIVE RACIAL SOCIALIZATION

The mothers describe responsive racial socialization as a set of active strategies used to combat the effects of racial discrimination on their children.

These strategies fall into four groups: *protective*, in which mothers attempt to shield children from encounters with racism; *preparatory*, in which mothers explicitly educate children regarding the existence of racism and provide them with coping/adaptive mechanisms to deal with life in a racist society; *critical*, in which mothers help children engage in critiques of racism so that they will neither internalize nor accept racism; and an *inclusive definition of blackness*, in which mothers dispute unidimensional understandings and portrayals of African Americans.

## "We Keep Them Insulated": Protective Racial Socialization

The mothers in this study all express the desire to protect or shield their children from racism as long as they can. However, they conceptualize and go about this protective racial socialization in different ways. For Audrey, attempting to delay her three sons' encounters with racism means placing her children in predominantly black settings and controlling the media to which they are exposed. Audrey feels that being in predominantly black settings shields her children from racism. First, the city of Detroit itself, by its sheer demographics, often keeps them from encounters with racist whites, and prevents them from feeling out of place or having to explain themselves or their culture. This is one reason why she and her husband have chosen Detroit and the Caribbean as their homes.

> [Detroit's predominantly black environment] is one of the reasons why I haven't moved out . . . Because, you know, essentially, Detroit is Blacktown. I want to be here, in Detroit, for my children. We shop in Detroit. I want my kids to look at their people moving around and doing it for themselves.

Audrey and Dumay's desire to shield their sons from racist ideas also led them to place their children in a school where the curriculum and materials were centered on black history, realities, and issues:

> [W]e chose an African-centered school, because unlike when I went to school, no one in the books that I read—See Susie run, where is Spot? Spot jump?— Nobody in the book looked like me . . . I wanted to put them in an environment that I knew it was going to be loving and embracing of them and their blackness and their energy and their melanin.

Audrey explains that the African-centered school her children attend not only reflects their own reality in the course materials, but also actively rejects the common stereotype that African American boys are "bad," "dangerous," or misbehaved simply because of "their energy level."

> [At our school,] it won't be anybody making them sit down or stand in the hallway . . . [just] because of their energy level . . . And even if there is discipline—and they do focus on self-control and self-discipline—it won't be

because they just don't want to deal with this little black kid. You know? Or, "He's bad!" Or whatever else it is. And having boys, you want to continue to develop that in them, that they are strong and they have a purpose and they're not second-class citizens.

Audrey notes that, as much as they try, she and her husband are not able to shield their children entirely from racism. She shares an example, still fresh in her mind, that occurred eight years before our interview.

I just remember being at an ATM and my son Touissant might have been three-and-a-half. And there was a white woman in front of me, and he was kind of moving close to her. And I'm like, I could see she was nervous, so I was bringing him back. And I said, "You know, he's only three-and-a-half, he can't steal your PIN number." And she's like, "Well, you don't know how early they can start."

Audrey admits that this and similar incidents, such as receiving poor service at white-owned businesses, have exposed her son to racism and prompted him to ask, "Well, what's wrong with *us*?" However, she still believes she has succeeded in keeping them "pretty much insulated from all of that."

All of the mothers in this study realize that they do not have control over all of the racial socialization messages that their children receive during their daily lives, but many work to filter the sources over which they do have control. The most often-cited source mentioned in this regard is television. For example, Audrey tries to shield her sons from negative messages about black people on television, but acknowledges that some of these messages may nevertheless get through to them. She worries about the general aesthetic put forth in the media that encourages a racial hierarchy with white people at the top and black people at the bottom.

I try to focus on and tape programs that have black people on so I can put it on the television. "Gulla Gulla Island," or some of those earlier shows from those early years. But [the general aesthetic on television], it's like in the same book that I'm describing to you where they call black people the "Ethiopian" or "Negroid race.". . . I bought it at an antique shop and it was from the 1800s. But it's like when they're talking about the Caucasoid race, it says, "In no other race is the mark of beauty so high and so noble a bearing." And that's what comes across [in the media]. And then it's like, about the African people it says, "In no other human—the ties to humanity are slim and tenuous at best." You know? I think that that still comes across through the media.

Here, Audrey argues that the contemporary mainstream media reinforce the same ideas about racial superiority and inferiority that were prominent in the antebellum period. Because she finds this to be overwhelmingly the case, she makes it a point to videotape the few shows she feels portray black people accurately, positively, and holistically. Audrey adds that she thinks that, despite her best efforts to direct her children toward safe/nonracist television shows, some racist messages may still slip through and "go straight to their subconscious." Audrey, like many of the other mothers, recognizes the subtle power of television in influencing young people's ideas about race.

### "You Have to Let Them Know It's There": Preparatory Racial Socialization

While mothers do try to shield their children from encounters with racism for as long as possible, preparation for racism is really the top racial socialization priority among mothers in this study. They believe that their children will inevitably encounter racism, and they want to be sure that their children are not caught unaware when these situations arise. Most of the mothers interviewed report that their children know about the history of black people's struggles in the United States, but many worry that their children do not understand the nuances and manifestations of present-day racism and racialized inequality.[4] The mothers say that it is important that their children know that racism may have changed over time, but that it still exists. Lena argues that, not only does racism still exist, but it is unlikely to ever be eliminated because it is inherent within our social structure. She cites as an example Jane Elliott's famous 1968 "Eye of the Storm" experiment (Elliott 1970). Elliott, a third-grade teacher, temporarily awarded superiority and privilege to her blue-eyed students and inferiority and disadvantage to her brown-eyed students, creating instant social inequality in her all-white classroom.

> Unfortunately it's the ruling class that makes the rules, and you have to assimilate regardless of who the ruling class is. There's always going to be some form of racism or prejudice. I don't think we'll ever be away from that. And what that one study proved—you know the blue eyes against the brown eyes—shows that no matter what, there's always going to be some kind of distinction to pit people against each other, unfortunately. So, you know, racism is not going to just go away—and I try to show the girls [that].

Lena says that she worries that the racial homogeny of Detroit, while it may protect her children from early encounters with racism, will have the longer term effect of leaving her children naïve and unprepared for eventual, inevitable encounters with racism when they leave Detroit. For this reason, she thinks it is especially important to explicitly tell her children that racism exists and that they need to be alert. She adds that she was startled, upon moving to Detroit, to learn that a high-ranking Klu Klux Klan leader lived and held rallies in Howell, Michigan, about sixty miles northwest of Detroit. "This is something that I have told the girls," she says, "that you still do have to be cautious . . . I don't want to teach the girls to think, 'Oh, no, here comes the white people, let's hide, close the door, or whatever.' But at the same time, you never know who is who and you have to be cautious."

Michelle agrees that preparing her children for racism is important not only to protect them from being emotionally scarred, but also to protect them from physical harm. It is her duty, Michelle argues, to educate her children about racism because, under certain circumstances, it can put them in physical danger.

> As a parent, it's like arming them. You have to let them know that it's there, because it's a way of protecting them. And you need to have them cognizant that things—bad or good—will happen to them because of it. So, you hate to teach it to them, but at the same time, if you're able to keep them safe, they have to know. They have to know that if you go a certain place, it might be physically endangering to you. You have to let them know that sometimes really unfair things are going to happen to them, not because they've done something wrong, it's just how somebody perceives them. And you have to let them know that some of the things they want they can't have just because of who they are. So, you maybe teach it to them because it's something you have to, because it's just part, it's just as much a part as teaching kids not to put their hand in the fire because it will burn you. You know, I think, as a black parent, it's something you teach, you know, just to keep them safe.

As is clear from Michelle's fire analogy, these mothers understand preparatory racial socialization to be an integral part of protecting their children from harm.

All of the mothers interviewed incorporated explicit verbal messages regarding the existence of racism as part of their preparatory racial socialization. Although some were worried about burdening their children with the knowledge of racism, all felt that it was more important to prepare their children for it so that they would not be caught unaware and be hurt emotionally or physically.

Having ensured that their children understand that racism is alive and well in contemporary times, these mothers then work to provide their children with a repertoire of adaptive behaviors to help them cope with it. When asked, "What do you teach your child(ren) about racism?" a majority of the mothers cite the ability for their children to function successfully in both white and black cultural realms as the most important coping tool they could give to their children. In this kind of racial socialization, sometimes called *dual consciousness* or *biculturalism*, African American families encourage their children to embrace and orient themselves toward their own culture, but to be able to participate in that of whites in order to advance in society, or "have success within mainstream institutions." (Boykin and Ellison 1995). Stanton-Salazar (1997) articulates the goal of racial socialization for African American families as enabling their children to "cross borders" between "different sociocultural worlds." Hale-Benson (1990) argues that African American children need to learn "the information and skills necessary for upward mobility, career achievement, and financial independence in the American mainstream," while still "feel[ing] pride in their own ethnic culture."

For a majority of the mothers interviewed, a large part of the ability to "cross borders" is dependent upon language. The mothers in this study assert that their children need to be able to, as Michelle says, "speak the vernacular" but also know when to "adopt the white voice." What Michelle calls "the vernacular" is perhaps more accurately described as African American Language (AAL), but is also sometimes referred to as "Black English, Black Language, African American Vernacular English, Ebonics, and African American English" (Smitherman and Baugh 2002). Smitherman (2001) notes that African American Language is *"not* 'broken English,' nor is it sloppy speech." Rather, she continues, it is a "systematic, rule-governed, and predictable" language (29). Indeed, "a massive body of research" exists showing that African American Language is "a communication system with its own morphology, syntax, phonology, and rhetorical and semantic strategies" (28–30).

In his Memorandum and Opinion regarding the 1979 Michigan court case *Martin Luther King Junior Elementary School Children, et al., v. Ann Arbor School District Board,* Judge Charles Joiner wrote: "It is clear that black children who succeed, and many do, learn to be bilingual. They retain fluency in "black English" to maintain status in the community and they become fluent in standard English to succeed in the general society" (quoted in Smitherman 2001, 33). Smitherman (1997) gives the term "switching codes" to this practice of changing language repertoires based on environment, and argues that it is critical to African American achievement in mainstream American institutions. Lena agrees that her daughters will need to learn how to "switch codes" in order to succeed in most colleges and professions.

> If they can't speak properly, if they can't construct a sentence without using our little idioms, then you're already going to—I mean, not saying that you won't still succeed, but it's going to be harder depending on where you plan to go in life. If you're going to be a movie star, then you do whatever you want. But if you want to be an engineer or [laughs] you know, a business executive, then they're going to expect—And it's sad that you should have to change, but unfortunately we do.

Lena strongly emphasizes language in her preparatory racial socialization messages, and thinks that this is particularly necessary because she and her husband are raising her girls in a predominantly black environment. Although she does see Detroit's demographics as a shield against racism in some ways, she also sees them as "a hindrance against" her daughters because she thinks this environment makes it more difficult for her girls to learn how to effectively switch back and forth between black and white cultural realms.

> And a lot of people [who live in Detroit] think that everything in the world is the same as it is here in Detroit. And I think it is important for them to know that you're going to have to—I mean, if you plan to or hope to succeed—then you're going to have to expand your horizons beyond Detroit, which means you need to learn how to speak correctly—and so much of the speech pattern within the inner city is not correct, but because it's not emphasized because that's the way everybody speaks, then it's not something that anybody really addressed.

Referring to a systematic semantic strategy used in AAL, in which the word "they" is used where standard English speakers use "their," Lena continues, "So when you go out, later on in life, or when you go to write a paper, and you're so used to saying 'they' instead of 'their,' you're going to write 'they' instead of 'their' almost subconsciously." Although she values AAL, she worries that if her daughters do not learn to "switch codes," their speech and writing will be erroneously interpreted by a non-AAL speaker as "sloppy."

Lena finds it unfortunate that her children should have to adjust their language based on environment. "I am pro-Ebonics," she says, "I feel it is a valid language." However, she adds, "unfortunately, if you don't speak a certain way, then you are going to be perceived a certain way . . . and maybe be passed up for an interview or maybe thought of as being illiterate." As such, Lena says she is "on the fence" because, while she finds racist assumptions based on language to be offensive, she also does not want her children to have any strikes against them if they move beyond Detroit. In the end, Lena tries to strike a balance by encouraging her children to value AAL, but to be aware of how to "switch codes" depending on the setting in which they find themselves.

Michelle also believes that being able to move seamlessly between black and white cultural realms is a necessary skill for her children to succeed in a racialized society. She tells her children that "people identify what you are . . . what your qualifications are" based upon speech. Therefore, she encourages her children to adjust their language, or "flip the script," depending upon their environment. "[I tell my kids,] 'Flip the script. You know, if you're in there [with white people], talk just like them.' I was like, 'Adopt the white voice.' And [my kids] learn. They know. Depending on where you are, change your tone. Change how you speak."

Michelle tells her children that they can use language to counteract racist expectations and to make their interactions with white people proceed more smoothly. She emphasizes that this practice does not preclude them from embracing and valuing AAL.

> You know, it's like, if anybody questions you, show your intelligence. Yeah, okay, fine, we can be home and you can drop the "–ing" from every word you know! It can be "goin'," "fixin'," "we fixin' to go," "my mama and thems," "we be clubbin'," [laughs], okay? Look, be Ebonically how you feel. And then, when you're in a social situation, [*snaps her fingers*] flip the script. Clean up the language. You know, make it light on yourself.

Michelle encourages her children to use code switching to make interracial interactions easier, or "light on themselves." She says she imparts to her children the lesson that "language is a weapon, and it's also a shield." Michelle and Lena are in agreement that they want to teach their children to value black culture, including AAL, but also to be able to "switch codes" and prosper within the "mainstream realm."

The mothers in this study also reveal that their children's gender and skin tone play a role in their racial socialization practices. The majority of mothers in this sample are very clear that they believe that all African American children need to be prepared for racism, but that boys need to be especially well prepared. When asked if their child's gender affects how they teach their child about racial identity or racism, the clear consensus was that, as one mother puts it, "the boy, he's going to be knocked down because they always going to quote-unquote destroy the black man."

Audrey, Michelle, and even Lena (who has no sons of her own) all share the belief that black boys are more hindered by racial stereotypes than are black girls. The mothers say that this affects the boys in terms of access to opportunities and even physical survival. Audrey, the mother of three young sons, says that it is a fact of the racist power structure in the United States that black women have more mobility than black men and that black men face more overt racism in everyday life. She argues that black men are portrayed as more threatening than black women, and that this results in white people being more comfortable with black women than black men. As such, Audrey feels that the most powerful way to prepare her sons for the gendered racism they will confront is for them to see their father interacting with white people and successfully confronting racism. Audrey worries that, if her sons see only their mother handling interactions with white people, this might teach them that they should accept or give into misconceptions about black men, or that they should avoid confronting racism when they encounter it.

> Because of the—just the dynamics of the black man in America [and] black women in America, I know that women get more mobility than men . . . because we live in a racist society. I think that [my sons] need to have some different tools in addition to—I mean, they need to have some different tools than black women specifically because of the mobility and the doors that open. . . . One example, and there are multitudes of them, is for me to be quiet when we're out, like yesterday, at the bowling alley, and to make the white male deal with [my husband] instead of me making it easier [by] talking to him [the white male]. Make him [the white male] deal with it. They don't want to deal with that brother; let them deal with the brother. Sit back and be quiet. Make them deal with it.

Audrey frequently and actively teaches her sons about confronting racism. However, she feels strongly that it is important for them to also see their father confronting racism. For this reason, she says that it is sometimes important for her to refrain from intervening in difficult racial situations, even though her intervention might "make it easier" to resolve that situation. Audrey wants her sons to see their father successfully dealing with gendered racism.

Likewise, Michelle thinks that it is especially important to prepare her son for racism. Like Audrey, Michelle believes that her son is "going to deal with [racism] more just because he's a male and white people are more threatened by black men than black women. They just are. They just are." However, Michelle believes that skin tone can positively or negatively impact the effects of this gendered racism. While she does think that her son will have to deal with more racism than her daughter, she also believes that his skin tone may lessen some of the gendered racism he will face.

> I think that he's going to deal with [racism] more [than his sister] just because he's a male. . . . For Carlos, what I'm going to teach him is really, really based on how he looks in the years to come. Because, if he grows up like his [black Puerto Rican] father, to look more like him, which he does—the older he gets, the more pronounced I think his ethnicity will become. And, interesting enough, it will be to his advantage because color plays a part, even when you're dealing, interesting enough, even dealing with white people, the lighter you are, the more comfortable they are.

How Michelle will socialize her son to respond to racism, then, will be impacted by both his gender and his skin tone.

## "Think It Through": Critical Racial Socialization

In addition to protecting their children from and preparing their children for encounters with racism, African American families also communicate a critique of racism as an aspect of racial socialization. The mothers in this study encourage their children to resist the internalization of racist ideas and to always treat others fairly, even when they are not treated fairly.

Some of the most common messages the mothers in this study report sending are those that discourage their children from internalizing racist stereotypes. Indeed, Harrison et al. (1990) argue that African American families work to discredit the "negative portrayals of [their] ethnic group" through racial socialization (1990, 354). Audrey, Michelle, and Lena feel they must work especially diligently to combat the notion that whiteness is better than blackness, or that it would be better to be white than to be black. Audrey admits that her friends have teased her about her children's apparent fondness for white people. She hypothesizes that this gravitation towards white people might come from her own light skin, from television, or might just be "the beginning of the oppression cycle."

> I think that [the idea that white people are better or more beautiful than black people] still comes across through the media . . . . Because of television and societal pressures, [my children] have said to me, "I wish I was white." And you know, we, we just have to work through it. And eventually they come through it. But they have to go through that. [We] just tell them that—we give them an idea of their history and where they came from.

Audrey argues that she and her husband continually work to counter the insidious idea that being white is better than being black, by placing their children in African-centered schools, teaching them African and African American history, helping them to process racist messages in the media, and modeling pride, ambition, and success.

Michelle, too, worries about her children internalizing the idea that whiteness is better, especially her oldest child, Elina, who recently proclaimed her intention to only date white men because they are "cuter."

> Elina. . .is starting to become—she's at some scary point that's actually been kind of disturbing to me, because she has hit a "white is better" mode in her life. She has verbally decided that she is going to have a white boyfriend, and she's going to marry white, and she just naturally thinks that white men are cuter to like. She just put it out there like that.

Michelle responded to Elina's assertion by encouraging her to question her assumptions about race and attractiveness. Michelle continues:

> So I'm like, "Okay, why do you think this [that white men are cuter]?" She's like, "Well, because, they are!" She said, "Like, look at TV!" [Laughs] And we had to have this discussion. She's like, "Because the guys on TV are always like cute." And . . . I said, "But, Elina, you know, TV is not real. Everybody does not look like those guys. That's why those guys are on TV, because they're pretty like that. They're cute like that."

When Elina remains skeptical of her mother's argument, Michelle guides her through a critical thinking process, asking her to draw upon her own life experiences instead of relying on media portrayals.

> So I actually had to make her say this and think it through. I said, "Well, think about it. When you're at the mall, when we're walking through the mall and you see all those white people, do all the white guys look really, really cute to you?" She's like, "Well, no, not all of them. Some of them look good." I was like, "Well, right, because that's regular people." I said, "Regular people are all shapes and kinds, baby, so every white guy is just not cute because he's white." She was like, "Hmmm. Well, yeah."

According to Michelle, Elina still was not entirely convinced that simply being white did not make someone more attractive, so Michelle encouraged Elina to think about all of the attractive black men she knew: "So I was like, I started naming black guys, and she was like, 'Well, he's cute. He's cute.' So I had to get her to concede, that, okay, black guys are cute."

Even so, Michelle says, Elina still believes that it would be better to have a white boyfriend than a black boyfriend, and Michelle is deeply concerned that this might be indicative of Elina's underlying ideas about race.

> So, but still, she was like, "Okay, well, but I still think I want a white boyfriend." So, okay. So somewhere in her head, white has become an ideal thing. I'm not going to stop her from being attracted to white kids, but somewhere in her, it's gotten incorporated that white's better, which is a little disturbing to me.

Michelle considers Elina's determination to date a white man to be evidence of the internalization of the racist stereotype that "white is better." In this case, the racial demographics of Detroit combine with media images to create the conditions in which Elina began to believe that white men are more attractive than black men. Because Elina does not come across many white boys or men in her everyday life, she began to believe that all white boys and men look like those portrayed on television. Thus, Michelle had to take her daughter to a shopping mall in the suburbs in order to help her to understand that there are "regular" white people, too.

The mothers also mention that they try to keep their children from adopting racist ideas by teaching them to be critical of the language they use. They believe that the words their children hear and use can affect their worldview. Part of critiquing racist ideas, then, involves critiquing racialized language. Audrey says that she and her husband talk about African and African American history with their sons, but that they make important linguistic distinctions. "We give them an idea of their history and where they came from," Audrey says. "We give them an idea of enslavement. We don't call it slavery. It's enslavement. It's like, no, you weren't a slave, you were *en-slaved*. And the distinction between that." Teaching their children to think critically about language, Audrey and her husband believe, helps to keep their sons from internalizing racist ideas.

Another part of critical racial socialization is a focus on messages about universal values, such as individual character and fairness. Demo and Hughes (1990) found that "individualistic and/or universalistic" messages are an important part of racial socialization, and Thornton et al. (1990) note that African American families emphasize "human values" in addition to more specific racial values. Indeed, three-quarters of the mothers in this study cite universalistic messages when asked what, if anything, they teach their children about racial identity and racism. While the mothers in this study are clear that they need to prepare their children for racism, they also want their children to recognize people as individuals. This serves as a critique of racism, proving to their children that it is neither logical nor humane to generalize too broadly about people based on race. Michelle articulates how she balances preparing her children for the inevitability of racism with emphasizing that her children ought to approach people as individuals. "I guess with my kids," she says, "I'm trying to teach them that, you know, you're going to have to grow up and be a little alert, but, you know, don't lose your humanity about it. Don't just assume that all of them are like that." Lena concurs, stating that she tells her children "to accept everybody, more or less, as who they are." She continues:

> And we just happen to be black, and in some cases people don't like that, for whatever reason, but, you know, you still have to—you can't assume that everyone is going to treat you differently because of the color of your skin. But because of that, you also need to be cognizant not to treat other people a certain way because of the color of their skin, because then you're just perpetuating the same thing.

This kind of message, while acknowledging the existence of racism, critiques its logic, and instead emphasizes the idea of human equality. The mothers admit that it can be, as one mother puts it, "very confusing" for children that they "are supposed to treat people equally even though people don't always treat [them] equally." This echoes Peters's (1985) pioneering work on racial socialization, in which she found that African American families "encourage honesty and fair play" even though, because of their children's racial status, it will not always be returned.

## "It's Okay to Be Who You Are": Inclusive Definition of Blackness

The final component of parents' responsive racial socialization is the encouragement of a broad and inclusive understanding of what it means to be black. In addition to stressing the value of a strong African American identity in and of itself, these mothers also emphasize an inclusive and broadly defined black identity as a coping strategy for confronting racialized challenges from both inside and outside of the African American community.

Lena, Audrey, and Michelle all lament the fact that blackness is often defined too narrowly. Lena explains that she models a definition of blackness "out of the box" for her two daughters. She tells them that they do not need to be partial to particular types of music, or dress in a certain way, or play specific sports in order to be authentically black. "I try to let them know that it's okay to be who they are" she says. Lena adds that, growing up in a smaller city in the southwestern United States, she learned to love Latin and country western music. She finds that her racial identity is sometimes challenged by others because her musical tastes do not conform to narrow definitions of "what black folks like." She says, "[Because I'm] not from an urban environment, so often you hear people say, 'You're not black. Black folks don't listen to that kind of music. Black folks don't do this, black folks don't do that.'"

Lena worries that this kind of narrow definition of what it means to be black might cause her children to buy into the idea that they have to conform to particular norms in order to be "authentically" black. She continues:

> It's a message that—I don't know where we get it from—where we'll tell our kids, "Oh honey, you can grow up and you can be whatever you want to be! The sky is the limit!" But if they're talking about skiing, "Black folks don't ski!" So how can you give your child a message that they can do whatever they want, and then the first time they do something, play hockey or something, then you tell them that they can't do it?

To counter this message, Lena says that she models a broad and inclusive definition of blackness, showing her daughters that listening to Latin or country music does not make her any less black. She encourages her children not to be ashamed of their tastes, whatever they may be, and to always "be true to themselves."

> So, in regards to music, I listen to all kinds of music and I try to tell them that it's okay. If you enjoy it, it doesn't matter what, you know, Tom, Dick, or Harry thinks, you have to be true to yourself and you have to do what makes you happy, regardless of what other people say. So I make it a point to, whatever kind of music I'm in the mood to listen to at that time, playing it regardless of where I am. So, I like Latin music, I like country music, I like all kinds of music. And I'll play it. And they look at me a little funny. "Oh, there's Mom playing that strange music again." But, to me, I'm hoping that they'll see that it's okay to be who you are regardless of where you are. You shouldn't have to hide certain things because it's not quote-unquote the black thing to do.

Lena encourages a definition of blackness that is wide in scope. She wants her children to have strong black identities that can withstand challenges, both internal and external. By modeling a secure, dynamic black identity, Lena hopes to provide her children with a powerful example of the heterogeneity of African American life.

Another issue that the mothers raise is skin tone. Audrey laments the higher value placed on lighter skin "even within our community," and Michelle points out that it is not considered favorable "to be really dark dark. You never want to be a Hershey chocolate dark." On the other hand, the mothers also noted that light skin also can be a disadvantage within the black community. Audrey shares that, "people [have been] challenging me and my blackness all my life" because of her lighter skin tone. However, the mothers in this study are universally disapproving of both the notion that "lighter is better" and the idea that one has to be a certain shade of brown before one can be considered "authentically black."

Michelle's thirteen-year-old daughter Elina is often on the receiving end of comments like those Audrey mentions. Michelle has had to reassure Elina that, regardless of what her peers within the community might say, her lighter complexion does not make her any less black.

> Elina was like, "Well, am I white? Because so-and-so says I'm white because I'm light-skinned." This was when she was probably, like, seven. You know? And I'm like, "No, you're black." And then she was like, "Well, then, if I'm black, then how come I'm light?" [Laughs] And I was like, I said, "Well, one, because your father is black Puerto Rican and he's light, so your color kind of comes from both." I was like, "But you know, essentially, you're black." [Laughs]. . . . So, she was like, "Hmm." I said, "So, look, you are black. Don't worry about it."

Michelle's messages are intended to build a positive black identity in Elina strong enough to withstand challenges based on skin tone and to reassure her that her racial identity is not reliant upon skin color.

The mothers also emphasize solidarity and a strong, positive black identity as a means to dismiss the idea that lighter skin is better, particularly in relation to beauty and attractiveness. Lena shares that some of her daughters' peers refuse to go outside in the summer because they do not want their skin to get any darker. She says that the idea that lighter skin and more "Anglofied features" are more beautiful is reinforced in the media, adding that "Michael Jackson didn't help it any." For her part, Lena tries to model the opposite value for her children, telling them that skin tone is irrelevant to beauty, and that they should come out and enjoy the sunshine.

> Unfortunately [skin tone impacts how my children learn about race], yes. But more so, not from the Caucasian to black standpoint, but from the black to

black standpoint. Because regardless of what anybody says, people are still color-struck. I mean, there are more and more African Americans that are darker that are getting prominence, whether it be TV—well, I'm talking specifically, I guess, about the show biz industry. But for the most part, it's still, even if it is a darker-skinned person, a lot of times they still had more Anglofied features: a narrower nose, or different color eyes, or something. So, it still plays a major role. When Alek Wek—I think that's her name, the Sudanese model—a lot of people cannot find anything, a lot of black people especially, can't find anything pretty about her at all, because she's just so dark. So, I mean, it's still an issue. I coach a softball team in the summertime, with my oldest girl. I tried to get my neighbor on the team. She's darker. She didn't want to play because she didn't want to get any darker. She didn't want to be in the sunshine. Which, you know, was the last thing on my mind. Obviously, I mean, it's still, unfortunately, an issue.

Lena says that she actively tries to counteract the idea that lighter skin is better, but she is worried it is something that her daughters are going to "internalize anyway," the same way that she did when she was younger.

I think they're going to internalize it anyway. So, I can say whatever I'm going to say, without drilling it into their head, and hope that some time, at some point, it will trigger a response. You know, our parents tell us all kinds of things and we don't necessarily listen to it at the time. But hopefully, somewhere down the line, it will ring a bell. I know I had a problem with [my own skin] color growing up, partially because I didn't grow up in an all-black area. Also, my mother and my brothers were lighter than me. And people would make comments, and you know, I remember those comments.

However, Lena says, as she got older she came to understand that lighter is not better. She hopes that modeling her own lack of concern with skin tone will help her daughters eventually recognize the beauty and value of all skin tones. She concludes:

Now it's to the point where I like to get darker. Summertime, I'm out there in the sun. And my kids look at me and they think I'm a little crazy or whatever else, and maybe that's my own way of combating [the idea that lighter is better], with the fact that they know that in the summertime I'm looking to get a tan versus hiding from the sun.

Lena is not confident that she can compete with social forces enough to fully prevent her daughters from internalizing the idea that lighter skin is better, but she actively verbalizes and models the idea that all skin tones are beautiful, and hopes that "at some point, it will trigger a response."

Encouraging a strong racial identity based on an inclusive definition of blackness, then, is a responsive racial socialization message that the mothers use to help their children confront racialized challenges both external and internal to the African American community. The mothers send messages that encourage solidarity and community, including the messages that skin tone does not determine racial identity or "authenticity," that lighter is not better, and that blackness cannot be narrowly defined by music, clothes, speech, and popular trends.

## RACIAL SOCIALIZATION AS GOOD PARENTING

Audrey, Michelle, and Lena, the three middle-class African American mothers introduced in this chapter, see racial socialization as an imperative component of parenting—part of what it means to be a good mother. They describe engaging in forms of *procultural* racial socialization in which they teach their children the value of African and African American heritage, and *responsive* racial socialization in which they give their children tools for confronting the racism they encounter in everyday life. While they see the racial environment of Detroit as doing much of the work of procultural socialization for them, they feel that they must directly and consciously engage in responsive socialization. Strategies of responsive racial socialization articulated by the mothers in this study include shielding children from direct experiences with racism, preparing children with knowledge of racism, teaching children to critically assess negative messages about blackness, and promoting an inclusive definition of blackness.

The socialization of children is one of the primary responsibilities of any family. Through socialization, parents prepare their children for anticipated life challenges and equip them with the tools needed to succeed in society. For African American children, many of the challenges they will face will be racialized, and their success in society may to some extent depend on their ability to straddle the two realms of white and black culture. In order to prepare their children for these realities, African American families engage in racial socialization. The mothers interviewed for this project differed in their ideas about precisely when and how it is best to communicate messages about racial identity and racism to their children, and what the exact content of these messages should be, but all of these mothers articulate the conviction that racial socialization is an essential part of raising black children. Regardless of income, household structure, marital status, education, or geographic location, all of the African American mothers in this study see racism as an inevitable reality for which they must prepare their children.

Even the most optimistic of the mothers are in agreement with Lena that "racism is not going to just go away." In fact, they concede that racism is so ingrained in American culture and society that, despite their best efforts, their children may, as Lena says, "internalize it anyway." Indeed, racial socialization itself cannot eradicate racism or even enable African American children to overcome all of the structural barriers that racism places in their paths. What racial socialization can and does do, however, is create a critical point of intervention, in which parents are empowered to help their children negotiate the racialized structures of the larger society.


## AFTERWORD

Having talked about Detroit's unique racial context, I think it is important to talk about the research process in the context of race. How does my own whiteness enter into this study, and how can I expect to conduct interviews in Detroit about race and come away with reliable and valid results? The answer to this question is complex and could fill an entire book, but I will speak to it very briefly here.

It would be inaccurate to presume that the cross-racial context of these interviews would have no effect on their outcome and interpretation. As Silverman (1993) argues, the results of an interview cannot be assumed to be "basic truths" (1993, 90). Instead, Young (1993) contends that the interviewer is actually the "co-author" of the narratives produced through interviewing (1993, 72), noting that race, gender, and class dynamics between the interviewer and the interviewee can affect the content of these narratives (1993, 56). The lack of shared experience between researchers and participants of different racial groups can lead to both reluctance in sharing information and misunderstanding of the information that is shared (Duneier 2000, Edwards 1993). In part due to the historical misrepresentation and exploitation of black study participants by white researchers, there exists a legitimate apprehension on the part of black participants as to any white researcher's intended use of the information that they are providing (Duneier 2000, Morton-Williams 1993, Sieber 1993). This study was methodologically designed to address, as much as possible, these racialized issues. Of course, as with most studies, researcher effect cannot be entirely controlled, but there were several steps taken in order to try to acknowledge and reduce or mitigate this effect in particular ways.

First, in terms of methods: I chose open-ended, qualitative interviewing because it allows the interviewees to guide the discussion. Unlike with close-ended interviewing or surveys, participants are not forced to select their answers from a set of predetermined responses. It follows, then, that I am also not forced to presuppose that I already know all of the possible answers or even all of the possible questions. Instead, open-ended interviews create a conversational atmosphere in which the participants have the space to discuss the topics that they think are the most important. This kind of interaction "implies talk between two subjects, not the speech of subject and object. It is a humanizing speech, one that challenges and resists domination" (hooks 1989, 131, as cited in Collins 1990, 212). Open-ended, qualitative interviews shift the interviewees' position from that of passive object to active subject (Silverman 1993, 94), empowering the interviewee through her ability to "talk back" (Rubin and Rubin 1995, 36).

Second, in terms of recruitment and the interviewing process: The first few months I spent in Detroit, I really just put in time on porches and in living rooms, getting to know people, discussing politics, family, sports, and current events, attending block parties, and working with an after-school program. Over time, I received the trust and endorsement of a core group of people who were respected in the community (one community elder in particular) and this group helped me with recruitment. Interviewees were therefore recruited through third parties whom they knew personally and who vouched for my credibility and intent. Having the blessing of respected people within local neighborhoods did build confidence and trust and rapport in a particular way. And the mothers in this study seemed to be very frank in their discussions of race and racism. The cross-racial context of the interview was discussed openly prior to the interviews, and several of the mothers asked questions regarding my qualifications and intent, and how this study would benefit the African American community. After thorough discussions of their concerns regarding theoretical and methodological issues, all of the mothers said that they accepted my research approach and agreed to participate in the interviews.

Third, in terms of setting: These interviews took place in homes in Detroit—either in the home of the participant, in the home of a neighbor or friend, or in the home of a local community leader. The participants were not driving out to the suburbs or being interviewed in some institution or unfamiliar place. I was meeting and talking with the women on their terms, inside the city of Detroit.

Finally, although I no longer permanently lived in Michigan at the time of this study, I am originally from Ann Arbor, Michigan, which is about forty miles west of Detroit. People from both Ann Arbor and from Detroit will be quick to point out that Ann Arbor and Detroit are very different cities. Ann Arbor is a college town of about 115,000 residents, about 9 percent of whom were black and 75 percent of whom were white in 2000 (U.S. Census Bureau 2000). Detroit, as you have read, is a large city of about 950,000 residents, 83 percent of whom were black and 12 percent of whom were white in 2000, and is surrounded by a ring of largely white suburbs (U.S. Census Bureau 2001). Ann Arbor is not considered a suburb of Detroit—it is outside of the suburban ring—but growing up in Ann Arbor, I heard about Detroit politics and events from the television and radio and major newspapers, all of which came from the city of Detroit. Much of what I heard from those sources was both highly racialized and highly negative— Detroit as "Murder Capital of the World" and the annual arson of abandoned buildings on "Devil's Night" were among the headlines favored by the local news as I came of age. Luckily, my parents were critical of such sensationalized reporting and taught me to be as well. When I was a teenager, I began to research Detroit's history and explore the city for myself. Growing up in the area and studying Detroit in high school, college, and graduate school contributed to the development of a considerable knowledge of the city's history, as well as a familiarity with contemporary Detroit politics, local personalities and celebrities, parks, street names, restaurants and bars, local nicknames for things and places, and the physical geography of the city. All of this translated into both my deep personal investment in the city of Detroit (which some of the participants said was important to them), and a bit of cultural currency, which allowed me to engage meaningfully in conversations about the city with study participants.

Having said all of this, let me be clear that I still believe that the cross-racial context of these interviews inevitably impacts their outcome and interpretation; the deeply racialized nature of American society guarantees as much. Methods, research design, recruitment practices, personal experiences, cultural currency, demeanor, and other factors can mitigate, but not eliminate, researcher effect. The most important thing, I believe, is for researchers to always interrogate how our own identities impact our work, from design, to implementation, to data analysis, and beyond.

## NOTES

This research was made possible through the generous support of the Berkeley Center for Working Families, The American Association of University Women, the Berkeley Center for the Development of Peace and Well-being, and the Northwestern University Postdoctoral Fellowship in African American Studies.

1. "Michelle," like the names of all study participants cited in this chapter, is a pseudonym.
2. Although the recruitment information for this study made a non-gender-specific request for middle-school-aged children and their parents or primary caregivers, all of the adults who agreed to be interviewed were mothers of the interviewed children.
3. These broad categories of racial socialization overlap with Stevenson's (1995) discussion of "creative" and "reactive" racial socialization, Boykin and Ellison's (1995) discussion of "tricultural socialization," and Hughes' (2003) discussion of "Cultural Socialization" and "Preparation for Bias."
4. As a part of this study, interviews also were conducted with the middle-school-aged children of the adult participants. These interviews revealed that the children do generally think that racism is dissipating, but only two out of the twenty-eight children said that they think that racism no longer exists.

# REFERENCES

Billingsley, Andrew. 1992. *Climbing Jacob's ladder.* New York: Simon and Schuster.

Boykin, A. Wade, and Constance M. Ellison. 1995. "The multiple ecologies of black youth socialization: An Afrographic analysis." In *African-American youth: Their social and economic status in the United States,* ed. Ronald L. Taylor, 93–128. Westport, CT: Praeger.

Boykin, A. Wade, and F. Toms. 1985. "Black child socialization: A conceptual framework." In *Black children: Social, educational, and parental environments,* ed. Harriette Pipes McAdoo and John Lewis McAdoo, 33–51. Beverly Hills, CA: Sage Publications.

Bronfenbrenner, Urie. 1979. *The ecology of human development: Experiments by nature and design.* Cambridge, MA: Harvard University Press.

Collins, Patricia Hill. 1990. *Black feminist thought: Knowledge, consciousness, and the politics of empowerment.* New York: Routledge.

Damon, William. 1988. "Socialization and individuation." In *Childhood socialization,* ed. Gerald Handel, 3–10. New York: Aldine De Gruyter.

Demo, David H., and Michael Hughes. 1990. "Socialization and racial identity among black Americans." *Social Psychology Quarterly* 53: 364–74.

Detroit Public Schools. 2006. "African-centered education at the Detroit Public Schools." http://africancentered.detroitk12.org/.

Duneier, Mitchell. 2000. "Race and peeing on Sixth Avenue." In *Racing research, researching race: Methodological dilemmas in critical race studies,* ed. France Winddance Twine and Jonathan W. Warren, 215–26. New York: New York University Press.

Edwards, Rosalinda. 1993. "An education in interviewing: Placing the researcher and the research." In *Researching sensitive topics,* ed. Claire M. Renzetti and Raymond M. Lee, 181–96. Newbury Park, CA: Sage Publications.

Elliott, Jane. 1970. *The eye of the storm.* VHS. New York: ABC News; released by ABC Media Concepts.

Hale-Benson, Janice. 1990. "Visions for children: Educating black children in the context of their culture." In *Going to school: The African-American experience,* ed. Kofi Lomotey, 209–22. Albany, NY: State University of New York Press.

Harrison, Algea O., Melvin N. Wilson, Charles J. Pine, Samuel Q. Chan, and Raymond Buriel. 1990. "Family ecologies of ethnic minority children." *Child Development* 61: 347–62.

Hartigan, John Jr. 1999. *Racial situations: Class predicaments of whiteness in Detroit.* Princeton, NJ: Princeton University Press.

Hill, Shirley A. 1999. *African American children: Socialization and development in families.* Thousand Oaks, CA: Sage Publications.

Hughes, Diane. 2003. "Correlates of African American and Latino parents' messages to children about ethnicity and race: A comparative study of racial socialization." *American Journal of Community Psychology* 31 (1-2): 15–33.

Hughes, Diane, and Deborah Johnson. 2001. "Correlates in children's experiences of parents' racial socialization behaviors." *Journal of Marriage and Family* 63: 981–95.

Irvine, Jacqueline Jordan, and Russell W. Irvine. 1995. "Black youth in school: Individual achievement and institutional/cultural perspectives." In *African-American youth: Their social and economic status in the United States*, ed. Ronald L. Taylor, 129–42. Westport, CT: Praeger.

Jackson, James S., Wayne R. McCullough, and Gerald Gurin. 1997. "Family, socialization environment, and identity development in black Americans." In *Black families*, ed. Harriette Pipes McAdoo, 251v66. Thousand Oaks, CA: Sage Publications.

Morton-Williams, Jean. 1993. *Interviewer approaches*. Brookfield, VT: Dartmouth Publishing Company.

National Center for Education Statistics. http://nces.ed.gov/globallocator/index.asp?search=1&State=MI&city=Detroit&zipcode=&miles=&itemname=&sortby=name&School=1&CS=CD559B3C.

Peters, Marie Ferguson. 1985. "Racial socialization of young black children." In *Black children: Social, educational, and parental environments*, ed. Harriette Pipes McAdoo and John Lewis McAdoo, 159–73. Beverly Hills, CA: Sage Publications.

Rubin, Herbert J., and Irene S. Rubin. 1995. *Qualitative interviewing: The art of hearing data*. Thousand Oaks, CA: Sage Publications.

Scott, Lionel D. Jr. 2003. "The relation of racial identity and racial socialization to coping with discrimination among African American adolescents." *Journal of Black Studies* 33 (4): 520–38.

Sieber, Joan E. 1993. "The ethics and politics of sensitive research." In *Researching sensitive topics*, ed. Claire M. Renzetti and Raymond M. Lee, 14–26. Newbury Park, CA: Sage Publications.

Silverman, David. 1993. *Interpreting qualitative data: Methods for analyzing talk, text, and interaction*. London: Sage Publications.

Smitherman, Geneva. 1997. "'The chain remain the same': Communicative practices in the hip-hop nation." *Journal of Black Studies* 29 (1): 3–25.

———. 2001. "Black language and the education of black children: One mo once." *The Black Scholar* 27 (1): 28–35.

Smitherman, Geneva, and John Baugh. 2002. "The shot heard from Ann Arbor: Language research and public policy in African America." *The Howard Journal of Communications* 13: 5–24.

Spencer, Margaret Beale. 1990. "Parental values transmission: Implications for the development of African American children." In *Black families: Interdisciplinary perspectives*, ed. Harold E. Cheatham and James B. Stewart, 111–130. New Brunswick, NJ: Transaction Publishers.

Stanton-Salazar, Ricardo D. 1997. "A social capital framework for understanding the socialization of racial minority children and youths." *Harvard Educational Review* 67 (1): 1–40.

Stevenson, Howard C., Jr. 1995. "Relationship of adolescent perceptions of racial socialization to racial identity." *Journal of Black Psychology* 21: 49–70.

Tatum, Beverly Daniel. 2003. *"Why are all the black kids sitting together in the cafeteria?" And other conversations about race*. New York: Basic Books.

Thomas, Anita Jones, and Suzette L. Speight. 1999. "Racial identity and racial socialization attitudes of African American parents." *Journal of Black Psychology* 25 (2): 152–70.

Thompson, Vetta L. Sanders. 1994. "Socialization to race and its relationship to racial identification among African Americans." *Journal of Black Psychology* 20:175–88.

Thornton, Michael C. 1997. "Strategies of racial socialization among black parents: Mainstream, minority, and cultural Messages." In *Family life in black America*, ed. Robert Joseph Taylor, James S. Jackson, and Linda M. Chatters, 201–15. Thousand Oaks, CA: Sage Publications.

Thornton, Michael C., Linda M. Chatters, Robert Joseph Taylor, and Walter R. Allen. 1990. "Sociodemographic and environmental correlates of racial socialization by black parents." *Child Development* 61: 401–409.

U.S. Census Bureau. 2000. Fact sheet: Detroit city, Michigan, Census 2000 demographic profile highlights. http://factfinder.census.gov/servlet/SAFFFacts?_event=&geo_id=16000US2622000&_geoContext=01000US%7C04000US26%7C16000US2622000&_street=&_county=Detroit&_cityTown=Detroit&_state=04000US26&_zip=&_lang=en&_sse=on&ActiveGeoDiv=&_useEV=&pctxt=fph&pgsl=160&_submenuId=factsheet_1&ds_name=ACS_2005_SAFF&_ci_nbr=null&qr_name=null&reg=null%3Anull&_keyword=&_industry=.

U.S. Census Bureau. 2001. "Majority of African Americans live in 10 states; New York City and Chicago are cities with largest black populations." Press Release, August 13, 2001. www.census.gov/Press-Release/www/2001/cb01cn176.html.

Welch, Susan, Lee Sigelman, Timothy Bledsoe, and Michael Combs. 2001. *Race and place: Race relations in an American city.* New York: Cambridge University Press.

Wilkinson, Doris Y. 1995. "Disparities in employment status between black and white youth: Explaining the continuing differential." In *African-American youth: Their social and economic status in the United States*, ed. Ronald L. Taylor, 143–54. Westport, CT: Praeger.

Young, Melvina Johnson. 1993. "Exploring the WPA narratives: Finding the voices of black women and men." In *Theorizing black feminisms: The visionary pragmatism of black women*, ed. Stanlie M. James and Abena P.A. Busia, 55–74. New York: Routledge.

# 11

## Seeing the Baby in the Belly

### Family and Kinship at the Ultrasound Scan

*Sallie Han*

In this chapter, I describe and discuss the ways in which a routine practice of medical care during pregnancy—the ultrasound scan, or sonogram—is meaningful as a ritual practice of American middle-class family and kinship. For cultural anthropologists, ritual long has been a topic of interest for apparently paradoxical reasons. On the one hand, rituals are formulaic and even repetitious, so that the preparations one makes regularly at bedtime (which itself is another kind of transition) can be called one's nighttime ritual. On the other hand, ritual commonly is described as a ceremony that marks a special event, usually associated with a transition, such as the rites of passage of weddings or funerals. In fact, the regularity of a ritual also seems to make it distinctive as an occasion. Its meaning is shared and recognized within a community. Rituals are important and meaningful cultural practices in the lives of individual persons, families, and other social groups.

Examining the sonogram as a ritual practice emphasizes its significance as a cultural and social practice. As Descartes and Rudd and others in this volume suggest, a diversity of cultural practices, including rituals, are involved in the making and re-making of American families. They call attention to the wide range of activities that must be considered "cultural" in the first place. For example, although work and class have been considered matters of economics, apart from culture, the ethnographic accounts in this volume demonstrate how economic activities are meaningful practices of belonging in a community, being a body, constructing a gender, and constituting a person. In short, they are matters of what anthropologists conveniently call "culture." Similarly, my discussion of fetal ultrasound imaging illustrates why science, medicine, and technology also must be considered cultural practices of American middle-class family and kinship.

This chapter is an ethnographic account of fetal ultrasound imaging. In it, I consider the ultrasound scan as a ritual, both in the sense that it is a transitional event and that the event itself is formulaic and regular. I describe and discuss the perspectives both of the expectant parents who see the scans, and of the sonographers who perform them. In the United States today, fetal ultrasound imaging is one of the more widely used prenatal diagnostic technologies. As I discuss here, many American middle-class parents embrace the ultrasound scan less for its medical value than for its "family value," as it represents, for them, an opportunity to see the baby in the belly. In addition, although sonographers perform sonograms for their medical value, they recognize the technology's significance in terms of family and kinship. Indeed, the sonographer's work both shapes and is shaped by the family value attached to fetal ultrasound imaging.

This discussion of the ultrasound scan draws from a larger project that examines contemporary American middle-class pregnancy practice in anthropological perspective. It is based on anthropological research that I conducted with pregnant women in and around Ann Arbor, Michigan, from June to August 2000 and from October 2002 to January 2004. In my fieldwork, I used a variety of methods to collect and analyze data that revealed various aspects of women's childbearing experiences. I conducted formal and informal interviews with pregnant women, their partners, and other family members, as well as with sonographers, doctors, midwives, and other birth professionals. I also engaged in participant observation in a variety of settings, including prenatal visits, baby showers, and childbirth education classes, as well as ultrasound scans.

These settings seem unlikely places for an anthropologist to be at work. However, I found that because doctors and midwives regarded the training of new practitioners as an important and meaningful aspect of their work, they were generous in their support for my study as a graduate student in anthropology. The doctors with whom I observed prenatal visits regularly trained medical students and interns. Similarly, the sonographers also were accustomed to explaining their work to observers. As a result, there seemed to be no difficulty incorporating me into their routines. Expectant parents themselves also seemed to appreciate the importance of teaching and allowed me to observe at their visits without comment.

At ultrasound scans, I usually stood to the side of the room, distancing myself from the sonographer as well as from the pregnant woman. Primarily, I positioned myself so that I could observe the sonographer at work as well as the pregnant woman and her partner or other family members or friends who might have accompanied her into the exam room. However, as I reflect now, I believe that I also was acting with more hesitation than the interns and residents whom I have seen in seeking my own medical care—for example, I always paused near the door, poised to leave, as either the sonographer or the doctor or I asked permission from the pregnant woman to observe the appointment.

Seeing sonograms performed as well as talking about them with pregnant women, sonographers, doctors, and midwives clarified for me the meanings attached to them. While I observed doctors and midwives performing ultrasound scans during regular prenatal visits, the focus of this chapter is on the sonograms performed by sonographers at a specialized clinic for perinatal care—that is, maternal and fetal care before birth. Most of the pregnant women who were seen at the clinic had been referred there because their pregnancies were considered "high risk" for a range of reasons, including personal and family histories of complications during pregnancy and childbirth, miscarriages, and birth defects. Pregnant women above the age of thirty-five were referred to the clinic because of what doctors called "advanced maternal age," which increased their "risk," or the statistical chance of having a child with a chromosomal anomaly such as Down syndrome. Interestingly, as I describe in this chapter, even these "high risk" women, who seemed to have the most reason to regard their sonograms in terms of their medical value, treated them as rituals of family and kinship.

My discussion of fetal ultrasound imaging is organized around two stories, one of a sonographer, Joan, and the other of a pregnant woman, Josie.[1] First, I tell and consider each story separately to contrast their divergent expectations of the ultrasound scan. I emphasize the significance of the scan for Joan as a medical practice, and for Josie as a family practice. Then, I discuss the stories together to compare their common interests in seeing the baby in the belly. In that expectant parents look to ultrasound scans for signs of the health and well being of their expected children, they also value the technology for its medical significance. In that sonographers see their work as providing information about expected children to their expectant parents, they acknowledge its family significance and even incorporate this perspective into the performance of their work. For example, as a sonographer, Joan is not obligated by her job description to offer such "extras" as "cute" pictures for expectant parents to take home. That she does this routinely calls attention to the work of family that she as a sonographer also performs. I conclude with a consideration of the special significance of science, medicine, and technology as cultural practices of family and kinship in the United States today.

## GETTING "GOOD VIEWS": JOAN

The blinds are kept drawn and the lights dimmed in the room where Joan performs ultrasound scans. She whisks closed the ceiling-to-floor curtains, which separate the exam space from the anteroom, where the day's schedule for all three sonographers is kept, facedown (as a privacy measure), on the counter near the sink. The clinic staff slips in and out of the anteroom, checking the schedule and washing their hands with fruit-scented antibacterial soap before and after scans. Meanwhile, behind the curtain, Joan prepares for another scan, exchanging pleasantries with the expectant couple as she ushers the pregnant woman to a large, leather-like chair, which lowers and flattens into a bed. The woman's husband seats himself in the chair wedged into the narrow space between the head of the bed and the wall. Joan has wheeled in another chair for "Grandma" as the woman's mother has accompanied the couple on this appointment.

She asks the pregnant woman to pull up her shirt bottom and to roll down the waist of her pants so that her belly is exposed from the bottom of her ribs to the top of her pubic bone. Joan tucks paper towels into the woman's clothes to prevent their staining from the blue silicon gel that she removes from a bottle warmer, which keeps it heated, and squeezes onto the woman's belly. The warmed gel was an unusual nicety upon which many pregnant women commented appreciatively. The gel itself enables Joan to glide the plastic transducer—the scanning device that produces sonar waves—over the skin. Even the chattiest patient falls silent, watching as Joan skates the transducer across the belly. The room now stands hushed, with all eyes upon the black-and-white images darting and pulsing across the monitor mounted to the wall, angled so that the pregnant woman, lying on the exam table, can see.

Joan barely lifts her eyes from her own monitor as she maneuvers the transducer across the woman's belly with one hand. With the other hand, she hits keys on her keyboard to "freeze" the flickering images that provide views of the vital organs and types labels on the views—for example, noting "4CH," or four chambers of the heart. Joan enjoys chatting with patients before and after the scan, but during the scan itself, she works quickly and quietly, breaking the silence to apologize for the discomfort as she presses the transducer against the woman's abdomen. When making their appointments, patients are reminded to come to the clinic with a full bladder as the fluid provides a medium for the ultrasound waves that produce the images. During the scan, Joan usually "gives tours," pointing out the baby's arms and legs, hands and feet, and face, though she tends not to say much else. To the expectant parents' questions regarding the baby's condition, Joan is guarded about what she says. "Does everything look normal?" the parents ask. "From what I can see," Joan answers, "but the doctor will take a look at the pictures."

Only after she is satisfied that she got some "good views" for the obstetricians does she then turn to taking "cute pictures" for the expectant parents to take home. A sonographer with almost twenty years of experience,

Joan has performed hundreds, probably thousands, of scans, but seeing a baby yawn or suck its thumb still can cause her to smile and chuckle. With the measurements and views all taken, Joan allows herself to relax and enjoy the "show" that she puts on for the expectant parents, who ooh and ahh over each movement.

The patient on the bed now is being scanned for a routine fetal survey at twenty weeks. Joan casually asks the woman if she is sure of her "dates," that is, her LMP, or last menstrual period, which is used to estimate the due date. Later, during a brief consultation with the obstetrician who is examining the "pictures," I learned that Joan was concerned because the measurements she took seemed small for a fetus that is supposed to be around eighteen weeks in gestational age. This was why, at the end of the scan, when Joan had asked the couple if they were interested in knowing the sex of their expected child, there had been a slight edge to her voice. Before the pregnant woman herself could speak, the grandmother-to-be quickly replied, "That's the whole point of this." Though in a light and joking manner, Joan rejoined, "Not about making sure the baby is okay."

## FROM A MEDICAL PERSPECTIVE

Although Joan makes efforts to accommodate the expectations of parents-(and grandparents)-to-be—giving "tours," putting on "shows," and taking "baby pictures" that she prints for them to take home—she takes most seriously that ultrasound scans are performed for medical reasons. In this section, I describe these reasons, which shape the way that Joan experiences the scans.

Aside from the home pregnancy test, fetal ultrasound imaging is one of the more widely used prenatal diagnostic technologies in the United States today. According to the National Center for Health Statistics, at least 67 percent of women who had live births received ultrasound scans in 2000, and the use of fetal ultrasound imaging appears to be growing. There is a range of reasons for performing scans. Doctors use the images to evaluate the condition of a woman's pregnancy, including not only the fetus but also the organs that support it, such as the placenta and cervix. The ultrasound scan also is used as a screening for serious developmental problems caused by genetic anomalies, such as Down syndrome. As Joan reminds the grandmother-to-be, the "whole point" of the scan is "about making sure the baby is okay." In fact, as I mentioned earlier, Joan works at a perinatal care clinic, and most of the pregnant women whom she scans are defined as "risk" patients because of their personal or family medical history or their age. So, it is not surprising that Joan takes seriously the medical reasons for performing scans. Regardless of their risk, however, most American women have at least one scan performed during their pregnancies, typically a fetal survey at around twenty weeks to check on fetal growth and the development of vital organs. A scan might be performed as early as several weeks into the first trimester to detect a fetal heartbeat, confirming that a pregnancy is "viable." When no heartbeat can be detected, the pregnancy is considered not viable. For some women, then, the scan confirms a miscarriage, sometimes even before their bodies display any signs of it, such as menstrual-like cramping and spotting and bleeding. An early scan also can be used to measure the developing fetus and estimate its gestational age as well as calculate a due date—an especially important function for time-crunched modern Americans, including not only calendar-conscious expectant parents but also over-scheduled doctors.

As medical tests go, the ultrasound scan has a number of advantages for both doctor and patient. It generally has been regarded as non-invasive, benign, and convenient. Some prenatal diagnostic tests require drawing blood. Another test, amniocentesis, requires passing a long needle through the wall of the belly in order to draw a small sample of amniotic fluid. Although the statistical odds that the test will cause a miscarriage are minute, the fact that there is an increased risk can cause distress for the expectant mothers who consider amniocentesis, which also is considered the most accurate test for genetic anomalies such as Down syndrome. Indeed, as anthropologist Rayna Rapp (1999) observes in her book on the social impact of amniocentesis, to test or not to test is one of the dilemmas that pregnant women face today. I vividly recall an anxious conversation with Audra, another pregnant woman in my study, who commented on the cruel ironies of being pregnant, finally, at thirty-nine, with a much wanted baby, whose existence might be threatened by a test she had decided to have in order to check on his or her well-being.

In contrast, ultrasound scans do not require needle sticks. A scanning device, called a transducer, is held against the abdomen, so that the pregnant woman whose belly is being scanned need not even undress, but merely roll up her shirt to expose her middle. The transducer produces sonar waves, which in turn produce visual images of the developing fetus and its internal organs. Viewed on a monitor, the images move in real time, but they generally do not look like a "real" baby. Unlike the indiscernible, unreadable X-rays that the images actually resemble, the scans are not associated with any known risks to the pregnancy. Short scans, such as to check on the baby's position in the womb, can be performed quickly during a regular prenatal check-up with a doctor or midwife, although the twenty-week fetal survey, typically performed by a sonographer at a specialty clinic, usually lasts about one hour. However, questions have been raised recently about the possible effects of repeated and prolonged exposure to sonar waves. Indeed, concern about possible cellular damage was one reason why Faith and Radha, two independent midwives whose prenatal visits I also observed, did not use, prescribe, or recommend ultrasound scans for their clients, who were planning births at home. Another reason was that Faith and Radha felt that reliance on these technologies usually were substitutes for what they considered their most valuable diagnostic tools—palpating or feeling the belly with their hands, and listening to (and trusting) the pregnant woman's own concerns.

Over the years, Joan has developed her own way of working, literally from head to toe, to check off the boxes on her mental checklist of the views that the doctors required. After completing a scan, Joan would help the pregnant woman wipe the blue gel off her belly with a few tissues, then review the images that she had taken for the obstetricians, even re-typing labels to correct typographical errors before she transferred them from the ultrasound machine to the computer network. As the patient waited, Joan walked around the corner and up the hall to a back office where she and the doctor on call together viewed the images and discussed them. "Beautiful scan," Joan might tell the doctor, meaning that the images were clear because the pregnant woman had been thin (since fat hinders the sonar waves, producing indistinct images), and the fetus itself had lain in a position that was convenient for scanning—as well as that there seemed no signs of problems to diagnose. "Beautiful" seemed to refer to how Joan herself had experienced the scan in terms of her work. Similarly, the doctor also might compliment Joan for having taken "beautiful pictures," commenting on her skills as a sonographer.

As an observer, I still recall being surprised by the way in which their conversations about problematic images seemed more engaged and, though it seems strange to say it this way, more enthusiastic than their talk about "beautiful" scans. When Joan felt that there might be a cause for concern, she alerted the doctor to it before and during their review of the images. Then, they seemed to linger longer over these images. In part, this is because problematic scans are more interesting professionally for doctors and sonographers, who are trained to detect problems. In part, this is also because problematic scans are ambiguous. There might be problems with the images themselves, making them difficult to read. More important, there generally are no clear signs of problems to diagnose, and a cause for concern might be a measurement that "seems small" (or big). Being able to see these images clearly can require such efforts as discussing them.

As a result, the reliance upon ultrasound scans to make certain kinds of diagnoses is not without controversy. A number of medical researchers and practitioners caution that there is an overuse of fetal ultrasound imaging in the United States today. As I mentioned previously, Faith and Radha, the home birth midwives, emphasized the importance of listening to the pregnant woman and trusting her ability to identify concerns regarding the pregnancy. This is to say nothing of the unanticipated uses of fetal ultrasound imaging in other societies, notably as a tool of prenatal sex selection. For example, anthropologist Barbara Miller (2004) describes an increase in sex-selective abortion in Asian societies that support son preference. Medical researchers Linn Getz and Anne Luise Kirkengen (2003), in a recent review of studies available from the national Library of Medicine, concluded that the routine use of ultrasound scans has not necessarily improved the health and well-being of mothers and newborns (maternal and infant outcomes). With the development of ever-more sophisticated technologies, there are expectations that the scan can be used to detect and diagnose a wider range of conditions, but evidence suggests that these expectations are outpacing the technologies themselves.

Even as medical research casts doubt on this particular medical practice, the medical reasons for performing ultrasound scans still are regarded as the "legitimate" or "real" meaning of the scan. Notably, fetal ultrasound imaging is available generally to American middle-class women because health insurance companies will cover the expense of what is considered a necessary medical test. However, as Josie's story (in the next section) vividly illustrates, the "non-medical" meanings are equally real and legitimate in the everyday lives of the women and men who experience the scans as expectant parents.

## CARRYING "BABY PICTURES": JOSIE

At four months into her pregnancy, Josie already was carrying "baby pictures" and showing them to family members, friends, co-workers at the real estate office where she worked, and an anthropologist who happened to ask. "I wouldn't be a good mommy if I didn't," she exclaimed as she pulled out from her wallet a pair of grainy, white-on-black images, which already were showing a little wear.

Josie had told me excitedly that she had some "cute" pictures to show me. However, when she handed me the thin, curling slips of paper, what I saw were black-and-white blurs that bore no resemblance to a baby. Cuteness, I thought, lies in the eye of the beholder. Josie explained that they had been taken a few weeks earlier at a ten-week ultrasound scan, which her obstetrician had performed as a "quick look" for the heartbeat to confirm that she was pregnant. She eagerly interpreted the pictures for me. "So, the baby was only about two inches. So, you can see. There's the probe here, and then there's the profile. There's the eye and the little nose. There's the big head, obviously, and the little body, and then his little legs fluttering out there," she explained. "I just say 'his,'" she added, because at the time, Josie did not know if she were expecting a boy or a girl. Turning to the next image, she continued: "Then this is actually looking straight down. There's his little bud arms, and then looking at his or her face." As she narrated for me, a large, bulbous head and spindly, little arms and legs took shape. Here was Josie's baby. The mommy-to-be beamed.

As she carefully replaced the images in her wallet, next to photographs of family and friends, Josie told me that she and her husband now were looking forward to a "major" scan at twenty weeks. This would be when the couple could learn the baby's sex, though they preferred rather to "keep it a surprise." Josie planned to bring her parents and her grandmother—the great-grandmother-to-be—to the screening as it presented an opportunity for the whole family to see the baby on the way.

Later, she likened the experience to that of watching a movie together. "Amazing," she gushed. "It was like family bonding." Josie also had a new set of baby pictures to show and tell. They had been clipped from a longer series of images and then stapled into a card, the cover of which featured an illustration of a baby carriage with a balloon and the words, "Fetal Imaging." Printed on the inside of the card, beneath the pictures, were the words, "My Baby." As happy as she had been with both the screening and the still images that she now held in her hand, Josie still had some minor complaints. "I do not know why they chose these," she groused, "because they're not the cutest. There were other ones that were cuter."

## SEEING LIKE A FAMILY

So routine is its use as a medical practice of prenatal care that fetal ultrasound imaging has come to symbolize pregnancy and parenthood in the United States today. In popular culture, it has become a symbol of the goods desired and needed for the "good life"—that is, the idea and ideal of American middle-class family life. For example, dramatizations of ultrasound scans are depicted in television commercials for Honda minivans, and still images from the scans are featured, in place of more traditional baby pictures, in magazine advertisements for Huggies diapers.

In fact, anthropologist Janelle Taylor (2000) observes that the ultrasound scan itself has become a consumer good. Up to now, fetal ultrasound imaging has been available primarily only at hospitals and medical offices, and health insurance companies have covered (and continue to cover) most of the cost of the scans as a standard practice of prenatal care. However, in 2005, it was reported widely that actor Tom Cruise had purchased an ultrasound machine to use at home with his partner, actress Katie Holmes, who was pregnant with their child. Some women and men also seem to be willing to pay a few hundred dollars out of their own pockets for scans at "ultrasound boutiques" that recently have been opening for business in cities and even suburban malls across the United States. In an article on ultrasound keepsakes that appeared in *The New York Times* on May 17, 2004, Marc Santora reported on the opening of an ultrasound boutique in New York City called A Peek in the Pod, where pregnant women can receive prints, a CD-ROM, and a DVD of an ultrasound scan for $295. In their advertisements, ultrasound boutiques make no claims regarding fetal ultrasound imaging as medical technology. Instead, they offer entertainment and, more important, promise memorable experiences and keepsakes.

As Josie's story illustrates, many expectant parents, women and men alike, express their enjoyment of the experience as an opportunity to see and "bond" with the baby, learn if they will be welcoming a girl or boy, as well as take home a "picture" or video of the expected child. Women in my study wrote about their scans in their journals and baby books, displayed their "pictures" in frames and photograph albums, and even featured the images as illustrations on their Christmas cards. One expectant couple posted their "pictures" on their Web site. Another father later included them in the introduction to the digital "slideshow" that he had created from photographs taken before and after his child's birth.

My own encounters with fetal ultrasound imaging as a pregnant woman also echo the experiences of Josie and other women and men in my study. About two months after I started my research, I discovered that I was pregnant. During an ultrasound scan at my first prenatal visit at twelve weeks, I learned to my grief that the pregnancy was not viable. There was no fetal heartbeat. Three days later, I experienced menstrual-like cramping and bleeding. My first pregnancy had ended. Six months later, I discovered that I was pregnant again. Figure 11.1 is the "picture" that was taken during my prenatal visit to confirm the viability of my second pregnancy. The "bean," as I called it, had a heart that beat and small limbs that fluttered on the monitor. The doctor who performed the scan estimated that it was about ten weeks old. I kept (and still keep) this image in a small photograph album, which also displays the "baby pictures" taken at my twenty-week sonogram. Figure 11.2 depicts the profile of the expected child in utero. Figure 11.3 depicts its face and its arm "waving" from the screen. Although the twenty-week scan involved examination of the internal organs and various parts of the body, the "pictures" that I took home clearly have no medical value.

In short, the ultrasound scan can be experienced less as a medical test and more as a family event. Megan showed the video of her twenty-week scan during a family potluck, which her mother organized specifically for the purpose of announcing if the expected child were a girl or a boy. Siblings, cousins, aunts and uncles, and close friends from both sides of Megan's family settled around the television after the dinner, joking, laughing, and

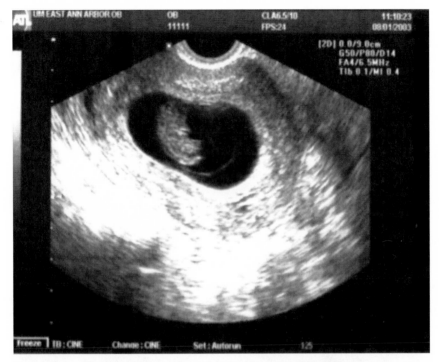

Figure 11.1.　Ultrasound "baby picture" of the "bean" at ten weeks.

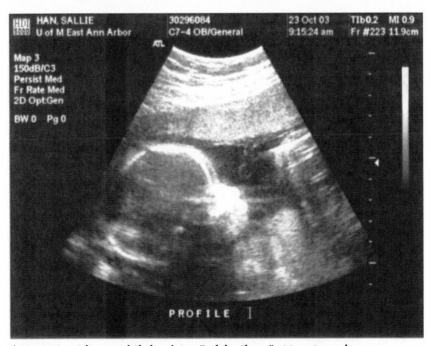

Figure 11.2.　Ultrasound "baby picture" of the "bean" at twenty weeks.

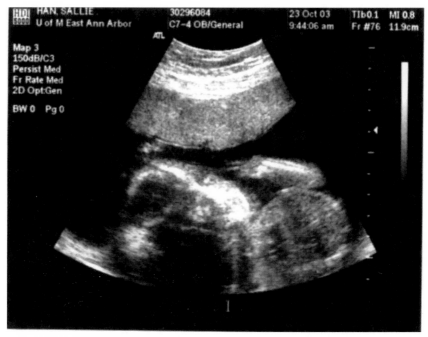

**Figure 11.3.    Ultrasound image of face and arm "waving" at twenty weeks.**

applauding the news—"It's a boy!" The gathering became hushed as the screening began, though it should be noted that no sound accompanies the scan.

It is difficult to imagine blood draws or amniocentesis inspiring the same kinds of sentiments. Only the home pregnancy test compares with fetal ultrasound imaging in terms of its significance as a symbol of pregnancy and parenthood. However, not even the home pregnancy test has captured public and private imagination as a ritual and symbol of middle-class family life in contemporary America in quite the same ways that the ultrasound scan has. In large part, this is because the ultrasound scan replaces imagining with imaging. It has been noted that one of the features of so-called Western cultures is a hierarchy of the human bodily senses in which sight or vision is privileged. However, the "senses" themselves are cultural and historical constructions. Anthropologist Constance Classen (1993) notes that although Americans commonly describe five senses—seeing, hearing, touching, tasting, and smelling—people in other places and other times have identified fewer or more senses. Americans themselves recognize the connection between tasting and smelling food. Classen also notes that although Western societies now emphasize the importance of seeing, early

Europeans especially emphasized smell, describing how the rose historically had been bred for its odor and only recently for its looks.

In the case of the baby in the belly, if seeing is believing, then being seen is seen as being. Or as Josie explained to me when she first showed me the images from her ultrasound scan: "It was like reality. It wasn't really real until we saw it." Indeed, feminist scholars have called attention to the importance of fetal ultrasound imaging in the social construction of fetuses as "babies" and as persons. Writing in the 1980s, Rosalind Pollack Petchesky (1987) warned of the consequences for women's reproductive rights, especially access to legal and safe abortion. For Americans, the more the fetus resembles a "baby," the more "real" it appears to be, and the more its status as a person becomes taken for granted. However, historians have documented different ideas about American personhood in the past. For example, infants were not always given names at birth, as they are today in the United States. Anthropologists, in their studies with people in various cultures and societies, have demonstrated that like a name, status as a person is conferred. Personhood is not a "natural" attribute, but one that is cultural and social. As anthropologist Lynn Morgan (1990) observes, questions about what defines a person are central to ideas and practices in all societies and cultures, and the answers are, in fact, various. Although Americans today typically understand personhood as defined by science and medicine— and revealed through technology such as fetal ultrasound imaging—such an understanding has not always been true historically, and it is not shared universally. The importance placed upon science, medicine, and technology in determining what is a person is a historical and cultural idea and practice.

Where Josie saw a "cute" picture of a baby—in fact, her baby—I saw black-and-white blurs. This illustrates two points about seeing itself as a cultural practice that seem especially relevant in this discussion of fetal ultrasound imaging. One, seeing is not passively perceiving what already is there to be seen but actively apprehending it. Josie and I were looking at exactly the same black-and-white blurs, but to her eye, they took shape as the face of her expected child. Two, seeing occurs in a context that can shape who, what, when, where, how, and why one can see. As I briefly discussed earlier, doctors and sonographers are invested professionally in detecting and diagnosing problems. They cast what might be described as a "medical" eye on the baby in the belly.

In contrast, expectant parents maintain interests that are close to home. Certainly, they recognize the ultrasound scan as a type of medical test that they hope to "pass" without worry—in other words, that there are no problems to detect. For example, when I asked about their scans, some women in my study noted that they had "looked normal." However, when women and men in my study described their scans, it was in such terms of family and kinship that the inventors of fetal ultrasound imaging never could have imagined. Sociologist Ann Oakley (1984) notes that the ultrasound scan is derived from sonar imaging, which had been developed during World War I as a military device to detect submarine activity. Later, in the 1950s, Scottish physician, Ian Donald, attempted to use it to detect cancerous tumors without much success. However, he observed that the nurses with whom he worked were using the device on pregnant women to determine the position of the fetus in the uterus—head "down" in the pelvis, or feet or bottom down in a breech position. This led to the development of fetal ultrasound imaging as a technology to diagnose or detect problems with the pregnancy or with the expected child.

Expectant parents experienced fetal ultrasound imaging in ways that are both "familial" and familiar. The scans were experienced as baby pictures, home movies, and videos. Although often taken for granted as trivial matters, such things perform important cultural work in the making of families. A practice such as carrying pictures in one's wallet is recognized socially as appropriate and not unusual behavior for mothers. By carrying "baby pictures" in her wallet, Josie has become a card-carrying member of what she calls the "good mommy" club—even months before her due date. The fact that the images were taken as part of the medical care Josie has sought to manage and monitor her pregnancy serves as further demonstration of her standing as a "good mommy."

What she does with the pictures is significant, but so also are the pictures themselves. Josie's "baby pictures" offer proof of the existence of an anticipated family member who can be imaged and not only imagined. Her "baby pictures" make concrete her expectations of a particular child and the new kinds of kin ties that will be formed with and around him or her, such as between Josie and her husband, now not only partners, but parents. "Pictures" are important and meaningful as material objects that can be touched, held, and shared among family and kin. As "pictures" that could be displayed in frames and photograph albums, the scans were important and meaningful items of material culture. Indeed, anthropologists long have observed the significance of material culture in the making of family and kinship, and of social relations in general. Ties become established between individual persons and social groups through the giving and receiving of gifts. These might include everyday items of food as well as prized possessions of jewelry and even houses, which might be bequeathed as inheritances or legacies. In my study, "baby pictures" were considered precious items to be preserved in baby books or otherwise held as keepsakes, possibly to pass along to the child.

In addition to being items of material culture, baby pictures, home movies, and videos are also forms of visual media, which both shape and are shaped by the experience of family and kinship. Participating in the creation of photographic images marks one as family or kin. Family photographs do not merely "preserve" family memories. Apparently inconsequential decisions such as inclusion in the family photograph album or exclusion from a wedding-day portrait define and demonstrate who is a family. Indeed, visual anthropologist Mary Bouquet (2000) describes family as a "photographic condition."

To this point, I have considered two stories, one from the perspective of a sonographer, Joan, and the other from the perspective of a pregnant woman, Josie. I have emphasized the ways in which their expectations and experiences of the ultrasound scan diverge. However, as I discuss in the next section, their stories also illustrate the intersections of their interests. It is not only expectant parents like Josie who see the scans in terms of family and kinship. Although Joan's primary concern is with providing images for the doctor to make a prenatal diagnosis, she also recognizes the "family value" of fetal ultrasound imaging. In the next section, I describe how American middle-class family values shape, daily, the work that Joan performs as a sonographer. Also, participation in the viewing of pictures, home movies, and videos can mark family and kin, and incorporate friends and neighbors into the family experience as well.

## THE WORK OF FAMILY

When I spoke with Megan before her twenty-week ultrasound scan, she expressed little anxiety about it as a medical test. Instead, she listed her priorities as learning the expected child's sex, getting "pictures" for her scrapbook, and making a video to screen for her family. In fact, these kinds of expectations are encouraged and supported in the medical setting. When I observed at routine prenatal visits, I sometimes heard the doctor or midwife mention to the pregnant woman that the scan provided an opportunity to "get a picture." They sometimes also suggested that the woman might take a blank tape in order to have a video made. In addition, pregnant women also were told that they could bring their partners or other family members with them to the screening.

While the doctors and nurse-midwives in my study were concerned most with the information that the scans could provide them, I was struck by these small, subtle ways in which they also helped to shape fetal ultrasound imaging as a family experience. Sometimes, their engagement in such work of family was more calculated. For example, one doctor told me that she had felt frustrated in her previous experience working in a large urban hospital with Medicaid patients, who generally sought prenatal care late in their pregnancies and frequently missed their appointments. To these patients, she carefully but consciously had described scans as opportunities to "see the baby" in order to encourage women to continue their prenatal care and to take better care of themselves in general. In contrast, she said that some of the educated, professional, middle-class pregnant women whom she now saw could be overanxious about their pregnancies. Talking about "pictures" to these women might have been an attempt to address and assuage their anxieties.

Most of the scans that I observed in my study were performed not by doctors or midwives but by sonographers, who seemed more likely to participate in the scans as family experiences, for reasons that I discuss further later. Almost as a matter of course, Joan printed "pictures" of the expected child's face, profile, and even boy or girl "parts" (labeled as such) for the expectant parents to take home. Occasionally, she also printed "doubles" for expectant grandparents who attended the screenings with a pregnant woman. Joan would record videos when they were requested, even when doing so tacked on extra time to a scan that had run long or was running behind schedule. The videos were recorded after the hour-long survey. They were not recordings of the entire scans themselves. Typically, the videos ran no more than one or two minutes, and included the same kinds of images as the "pictures," plus some footage of the baby's movements.

The promise of a "picture" or video seemed to be offered as an incentive for patients. During an appointment with a nurse-midwife, one pregnant woman wondered aloud if it were necessary to perform the scan, given that she was young and healthy, and that the pregnancy also seemed normal. After a brief discussion about the medical reasons for performing scans, the woman herself decided: "I can get a picture." Across town, at a community health clinic that provided services for poor women, another nurse-midwife reminded her patients that they could "get a picture" at the ultrasound scan. In both instances, a "picture" motivated pregnant women to have a medical test that the care provider recommended. Sometimes, it was at great inconvenience for the woman, who might have to take off additional time from work for another appointment at another location. However, I observed that most women arrived at their appointments early or on time. They also followed instructions to drink water beforehand and arrived with bladders already full. I was told that a full bladder aids the sonographers in their work, but such instructions also varied—for example, depending on how far along a woman was in her pregnancy or the kind of ultrasound machine in use. In any case, a full bladder causes not inconsiderable discomfort for a woman who is five months pregnant, so it is significant that Joan only occasionally had to wait while a patient "filled up."

In short, sonographers, doctors, and midwives have a hand in constructing the ultrasound scan as a family event, describing it as an opportunity for a "picture" or video, and an occasion to invite partners or other family members. Casting the scan in terms of its "family value" even appears to enable their work. Patients regard the ultrasound scan as an enjoyable event, and tolerate the inconvenience and discomfort that it might pose to them. It also enhanced the sonographer's enjoyment of the scan, and her satisfaction with the work in general. All of the sonographers whom I met were women. In fact, women account for almost 85 percent of registered sonographers working in obstetrics today in the United States (Taylor 2004, 192). Many of the women I met were also mothers. They could chat with patients about what they had picked in terms of name, and colors for their nurseries.

In a 2004 article about the work of sonographers, anthropologist Janelle Taylor describes the significance of sonography as a new form of "women's work" in the health and medical professions. Notably, it is a position that is considered "subordinate," as sonographers are regarded as technicians performing repetitive work. As with other occupations such as secretarial work and nursing, women have been seen as well suited to sonography because of certain skills and traits associated with femaleness and femininity in the United States, such as manual dexterity and orientation toward detail work, which would contribute to the technical work of performing sonograms. However, most important is the skilled caring that is required of women working as sonographers. Anthropologist Lisa Mitchell, in her 2001 book about fetal ultrasound imaging in Canada, notes that doctors in her study hired sonographers to work in their offices "not just for their technical skills, but also because they were 'friendly and know how to talk to patients'" (Mitchell 2001, 119). Skilled caring is evident in the "tours" and "shows" that Joan gives, as well as the "pictures" that she prints for expectant parents to take home. Caring also is evident in the other "little things" that Joan does for patients and their partners or other family members who accompany them. As I noted above, not only does she tuck paper towels into a woman's clothes to prevent their staining from the blue silicon gel that she spreads on the pregnant belly, but she also keeps the "blue goo" in a bottle warmer, so that it is not unpleasantly cold on contact with the skin. Joan also acts as a hostess for visitors in the exam room, wheeling in chairs and chatting pleasantly with them. These "little things" that Joan does in the exam room are not superfluous "extras." Rather, they contribute to the pregnant woman's experience, whose comfort and cooperation during the sonogram contributes also to Joan's own experience and enjoyment of her work. In fact, skilled caring marks Joan as a professional woman.

Sonographers themselves sometimes felt their caring and professionalism tested by what they perceived as displays of parental and especially maternal uncaring. Their complaints regarding their work often arose from interactions with pregnant women whom they felt had behaved less than satisfactorily as patients and as parents. For example, what seemed to strike Joan and other sonographers at her clinic as thoughtless demands for "pictures" and videos discomfited them, since there were medical reasons for performing the scans. Another situation that disturbed them arose when expectant parents seemed overly concerned with the sex or "gender" of the expected child, especially if one parent expressed a strong preference. (As the sonographers themselves noted, the preference usually was for a boy.) On these occasions, I heard comments such as "all they care about is the pictures" or "they just want a video" or "they just want to know boy or girl." Such comments usually were heard when a particular pregnant woman was perceived as especially demanding—"gimmee, gimmee, gimmee" as I heard one sonographer remark to another during their break.

On other occasions, a pregnant woman might not have exhibited enough interest in seeing the "baby." Lana, another sonographer at Joan's clinic, had performed a scan on a pregnant woman who was especially tense and quiet. The woman had accepted a "picture" to take home without comment, or even thanks. Later, Lana questioned aloud the woman's future fitness as a mother. To her eye, the woman had seemed "unhappy" and "not even excited" about being pregnant. She recalled that the woman had not even smiled when she saw her expected child on the ultrasound monitor. Joan herself suggested that the woman might have felt anxious about the medical reasons for performing the scan—that is, detecting and diagnosing possible problems. However, from Lana's perspective, the woman failed to participate in the proper sentiment regarding her "baby."

Taken together, these complaints revealed expectations of how women should act and feel as patients and as parents. To place too much importance on "pictures" and videos—or to place not enough importance on them—was to fall short of expectations of "good" behavior as a patient and as a parent. For pregnant women in the United States today, being a "good" patient is linked closely with being a "good" parent. In the next section, I consider the association between being a patient and being a parent. Starting with the construction of pregnant women as patients, family and kinship increasingly have become drawn into the domain of science, medicine, and technology.

## THE MEDICALIZED FAMILY

The story of a pregnancy in the United States today typically begins with the purchase of a home pregnancy test, then an appointment with a doctor. When the test revealed to Josie that she was pregnant, she immediately scheduled a prenatal visit with a doctor, who performed the first ultrasound scan, and then prescribed a second scan. Seeking medical care during pregnancy seems a matter of course for contemporary Americans. However, it should be recognized as a historical and cultural practice.

In an earlier period of American history, childbearing and childbirth were matters left in the hands of women, who tended to each other in their homes and relied on their own previous experiences to guide them (Wertz and Wertz 1989). When mothers and infants died, family members and friends mourned their losses, but also regarded such deaths as part of the natural course of life. Not until the early twentieth century did pregnancy and parturition become regarded as medical problems with medical solutions. This historical shift in ideas and practices has been called the "medicalization" of childbearing and childbirth. The involvement of doctors who bore credentials from medical schools, and the removal of birth from home to hospital often became described in terms of the "progress" of science, medicine, and technology. However, medical anthropologist Brigitte Jordan (1992), in her pioneering study that examined childbirth practices cross-culturally, demonstrated the complications and complexities of medicalization. In particular, pregnancy has come to be treated as a health problem or kind of sickness, and pregnant women become regarded as "patients" at the hospital, despite the fact that they are in good health. Contributing to the medicalization of childbearing and childbirth in the United States were significant changes in the ways that Americans lived their lives. Industries expanded, the assembly line was invented, and women found manufacturing jobs outside their homes. In sum, anthropologist Emily Martin (1987) suggests that the medicalization of childbearing and childbirth—which applied ideas and practices of science and technology to what previously had been regarded as "natural" processes—mirrored the mechanization of other aspects of American life.

Observers of everyday life in the United States have suggested that science, medicine, and technology strongly influence culture and society. For example, anthropologists of reproduction have discussed the social impacts of various reproductive technologies, including assisted conception techniques such as in vitro fertilization, and prenatal diagnostic tests such as fetal ultrasound imaging. Such scholarship assumes that science, medicine, and technology exert a one-way influence on cultural ideas and practices. However, the lesson to draw from even this brief history of medicalization is that ideas and practices of science, medicine, and technology themselves are historical, cultural, and social.

Similarly, my discussion of fetal ultrasound imaging suggests the significance of science, medicine, and technology as cultural practices. In this chapter, I have considered the importance and meaning of the ultrasound scan as a ritual practice of American middle-class family and kinship. However, my examination of fetal ultrasound imaging suggests that there is a two-way influence between science, medicine, and technology and other cultural ideas and practices, such as those concerning material culture ("baby pictures" in frames and photograph albums) and visual media (home movies and videos). In particular, I described and discussed the ways in which the "family value" of sonograms shapes the experiences of both sonographers at work and expectant parents.

Drawing from the close observations and continual conversations that ethnographic fieldwork allows, I was able to piece together a picture of the ultrasound scan in all its ordinariness for sonographers and pregnant women. It is in the everyday experiences of sharing "baby pictures," receiving compliments on "beautiful" scans, and complaining about "unhappy" mothers that one can appreciate the extent to which science, medicine, and technology are involved in the making of families. In its un-remarkableness, fetal ultrasound imaging is remarkable as a cultural practice of family and kinship.

## AFTERWORD

The anthropology of reproduction, in which I locate my work, emerges from the experiences of the anthropologists themselves. Rayna Rapp and Faye Ginsburg (2001) describe the scholarly interest that they have taken in issues of disability, which builds upon both their previous work on reproduction and social activism, and especially their interests and involvements as parents of children with disabilities. Gay Becker (2000), reflecting on her experience as an anthropologist engaged in a study of infertility and as a woman making sense of her own infertility, writes:

> I realized that this study was helping me to work my way through the personal issues infertility had raised for me. Sometimes I was a few steps ahead of the people I interviewed, simply because I was finished with medical treatment, but sometimes they were ahead of me. I learned from the women and men I interviewed, and in the process I regained my inner sense of balance and refocused my life (Becker 2000, 3).

The work of anthropologists like Rapp and Ginsburg and Becker suggest that it is important to consider the bodies and persons of anthropologists themselves as important sites in the production of knowledge.

"Seeing the Baby in the Belly" is based on research that I conducted for my doctoral dissertation. During my fieldwork, I experienced a pregnancy and a miscarriage, then another pregnancy. My daughter was born two months after I completed my fieldwork. As a result, I see my own experiences as connected intimately with the experiences of the women in my study. However, this is not only because they were experiences in common or because they occurred concurrently. Taking seriously the notion that learning and knowing are activities of the body as well as of the mind, I am convinced today that the pregnancy with my daughter and her birth were the embodiment of the learning and wisdom that were shared with me during fieldwork.

## NOTES

My deepest gratitude belongs to the women and men who shared their experiences of expectancy with me. I offer my special thanks to the women whom I call Joan and Josie in these pages.

I am grateful for the guidance of the editors of this volume. I received funding for this research from the Alfred P. Sloan Foundation through the Center for the Ethnography of Everyday Life at the University of Michigan, and the Rackham School of Graduate Studies and the Department of Anthropology at the University of Michigan.

1. All names were changed in order to protect the identity and respect the privacy of the expectant parents and birth professionals involved in my study.

## REFERENCES

Becker, Gay. 2000. *The elusive embryo: How women and men approach the new reproductive technologies.* Berkeley: University of California Press.

Bouquet, Mary. 2000. "The family photographic condition." *Visual Anthropology Review* 16 (1): 2–19.

Classen, Constance. 1993. *Worlds of sense: Exploring the senses in history and across cultures.* New York: Routledge.

Descartes, Lara, and Elizabeth Rudd. This volume. "Changing landscapes of work and family."

Getz, Linn, and Anne Luise Kirkengen. 2003. "Ultrasound screening in pregnancy: Advancing technology, soft markers for fetal chromosomal aberrations, and unacknowledged ethical dilemmas." *Social Science and Medicine* 56 (10): 2045–57.

Jordan, Brigitte. 1992 [1978]. *Birth in four cultures: A cross-cultural investigation of childbirth in Yucatan, Holland, Sweden, and the United States.* Prospect Heights, IL: Waveland.

Martin, Emily. 1987. *The woman in the body: A cultural analysis of reproduction.* Boston: Beacon Press.

Miller, Barbara. 2001. "Female-selective abortion in Asia: Patterns, policies, and debates." *American Anthropologist* 103 (4): 1083–95.

Mitchell, Lisa. 2001. *Baby's first picture: Ultrasound and the politics of fetal subjects.* Toronto: University of Toronto Press.

Morgan, Lynn. 1990. "When does life begin? A cross-cultural perspective on the personhood of fetuses and young children." In *Abortion rights and fetal "personhood,"* ed. Edd Doerr and James W. Prescott, 97–114. Long Beach, CA: Centerline Press and Americans for Religious Liberty.

Oakley, Ann. 1984. *The captured womb: A history of the medical care of pregnant women.* New York: Basil Blackwell.

Petchesky, Rosalind Pollack. 1987. "Fetal images: The power of visual culture in the politics of reproduction." *Feminist Studies* 13 (2): 263–92.

Rapp, Rayna. 1999. *Testing women, testing the fetus: The social impact of amniocentesis in America.* New York: Routledge.

Rapp, Rayna and Fay Ginsburg. 2001. "Enabling disability: Rewriting kinship, reimagining citizenship." *Public Culture* 13 (3): 533–56.

Santora, Marc. 2004. "Fetal Photos: Keepsake or Health Risk?" *The New York Times,* May 17.

Taylor, Janelle. 2000. "Of sonograms and baby prams: Prenatal diagnosis, pregnancy, and consumption." *Feminist Studies* 26 (2): 391–418.

———. 2004. "A fetish is born: Sonographers and the making of the public fetus." In *Consuming motherhood,* ed. Janelle Taylor, Linda L. Layne, and Danielle F. Wozniak, 187-210. New Brunswick, NJ: Rutgers University Press.

Wertz, Richard W., and Dorothy C. Wertz. 1989. *Lying-in: A history of childbirth in America.* New Haven, CT: Yale University Press.

# 12

## Stabilizing Influence

### Cultural Expectations of Fatherhood

*Todd L. Goodsell*

In September of 2001 the St. Louis County Fair and Air Show was held at the Spirit of St. Louis Airfield, a second-tier airport in the western suburbs of St. Louis. With the good weather the area enjoyed that weekend (around eighty degrees and relatively low humidity), attendance was expected to reach 200,000. I observed a great deal of activity that day—not only in terms of official venues but also informal interactions that caught my eye as a family scholar interested in fatherhood.

One such episode was a man and woman arguing as they walked through the crowded fair. The man was pulling a plastic wagon in which were two children, perhaps four or five years old. The man had his hand on the wagon handle and pulled it a bit while he and the woman spoke harshly to each other. The children had to have heard it. The two adults went on arguing with each other, their backs to the children. The children said nothing and did not interact with each other. They just sat in the wagon looking down.

A few feet away was a gymnastics setup. It featured an inclined plane on which a coach helped children do forward tumbles; a low balance beam; a small, round trampoline; and a large, rectangular double pad. Everything was well-padded and monitored by attendants. One little boy, around two years old, jumped up and down on the large pad. A man (perhaps his father) stood off to the side, watching and smiling. He didn't overtly encourage the little boy, but he stayed and watched. The boy's frequent glances at the man suggested that he appreciated the audience. The boy would jump several times and then fall (for show, apparently, since he did not teeter as one losing his balance and he always fell in the same form) and roll over four times. Once or twice the man pointed out other things to do and the boy did try some, but he kept going back to that big pad on which he could jump and roll. The man did not criticize the boy's choice of activity. He just watched over him—smile on his face—and occasionally pointed out other options.

These vignettes illustrate how the social world around each of us is constantly sending us messages of what does and does not constitute appropriate components of a given role, in this case, a fatherly role. While most of us do not typically give our attention to these messages as advertisements or lessons, they help us to construct our expectations for and evaluations of our own role performances. When a man is about to become a father, he can draw upon a lifetime of such observations and experiences that contribute to his construction of the role he is about to assume.

## FATHERHOOD AND EXPECTATIONS

The recent rise of scholarly interest in men's roles in families (e.g., Bengtson et al. 2005, Blankenhorn 1995, Marsiglio 1995, Parke 1996, Popenoe 1996) is in part a response to the popular and scholarly assumption that "parenting" usually means "mothering." Women have typically been defined as being primarily responsible for managing relationships in the home and with family members. One author did argue that fathers should play a more prominent role in the home, and even listed "nurturing" as one of the attributes of a "good family man," but found that "even as these men [good fathers] describe the sharing of household duties, and even as they affirm the importance of close-in, emotionally bonded fatherhood, they clearly recognize that they are, at best, 'junior partners'" to their wives in this area (Blankenhorn 1995, 216). It long has been assumed that women express emotional leadership within the family (Parsons and Bales 1955). Indeed, research on men and on fatherhood has suggested that feelings are problematic for men (Hochschild 1983, 2003, Townsend 2002). Our culture regards men's emotional closeness to their family members as vital, but their normative breadwinning responsibilities pull them away from environments and relationships in which familial emotional ties can best be fostered (Townsend 2002).

People are expected to monitor themselves to make sure that they are acting appropriately within their particular context. For example, Hochschild (1983) explained that we often recognize that we are supposed to feel a certain way, and then act in ways to create that feeling. The expectations can vary according to "sex, age, religion, ethnicity, occupation, social class, and geographic locale" (Hochschild 1983, 252). Cultural expectations, then, can vary in several ways, and it is important to investigate the various sets of expectations that follow from various social positions. Family life and the roles within families are key sites of cultural expectations.

One of my goals here is to investigate and explain some of the cultural expectations that guide fatherly activity. I do this by investigating the stories parents-to-be tell about what it means to be a good father. The people I spoke with reflected upon role models they knew over the years, and described those memories to me in an effort to clarify what being a "good" father meant to them. Emotions were often central to those narratives. With Lupton and Barclay (1997, 24), I argue that discourse—what people say about their experiences—is a good way to access a person's "feelings and emotional states," which in turn cue us into how people make their evaluations (Cooley 1983). By examining stories that are emotional for the storyteller, I can begin to consider men's feelings about their own positions in their families in a way that emphasizes that becoming a father is a unique experience in its own right, constructed and defined as part of a continuous process of adult development (Hawkins and Dollahite 1997).

## RESEARCH SITE AND SAMPLE

Health statistics obtained from the State of Missouri indicate that in 2001 in the St. Louis area (St. Louis City, St. Louis County, St. Charles County, and Jefferson County) 27,972 babies were born.[1] More than 99 percent of those births occurred in hospitals, and 40 percent were first births. Data on the fathers of these babies are not available, but some information on their mothers is. The average age of all women who gave birth in the St. Louis area during 2001 was 27.7, while the average age of women giving birth for the first time was 25.4. Seventy-two percent of the women giving birth were white, as were 73 percent of the women giving birth to their first child.

Most of the research participants in this study (and all of those whom I discuss in this chapter) were obtained through the cooperation of a large medical facility located in the suburbs of St. Louis, which I call Midwest Medical Center.[2] The medical center was of particular interest to this research because of its local reputation: It is nicknamed "the baby factory" because so many births happen there—more than in any other medical center in the state. While there are fifteen hospitals and medical centers in the St. Louis area, Midwest Medical Center hosted more than 22 percent of the area's births in 2001, along with 23 percent of first births. Midwest Medical was known for having a full range of obstetrical support staff and facilities, and its convenient location helped make it the medical facility of choice for thousands of expectant parents each year.

## Prenatal Education Classes

Midwest Medical Center allowed me to visit its prenatal education classes to describe this project and ask for volunteers—men who were expecting to be a father for the first time and their partners—to participate. Those who volunteered were interviewed at a place and time convenient for them. Usually this meant at their homes; sometimes we found another location such as a spare room at the medical center before one of their weekly classes. I explained that I was interested in their sense of what it means to be a "good father," and I asked them to tell me stories that have influenced their ideas about being a good father.

I also attended several of the prenatal education classes (also by permission of the medical center). Each was taught in a classroom on-site by a nurse who specialized in labor and delivery. Class members usually came in pairs: the mother-to-be and the individual who would be her "coach" during delivery (usually the father-to-be, but sometimes the grandmother-to-be or the lesbian partner). Various classes were offered—some focused on questions and answers about medical interventions during labor and delivery, some on Lamaze techniques, and one was especially for expectant fathers. I attended a range of the classes to get a sense of the questions participants asked and the messages they received both from the class itself and from other class members.

In some respects, these classes were an indication of just how much new parents stood to learn about what they were getting into. In one class, two of the "coaches" were the mothers of the pregnant women, while the rest of the "coaches" were the pregnant women's male partners. During one session, the nurse-instructor invited all the "coaches" to a table where there were several dolls that "needed" a diaper change. She announced that they would have a race to see which "coach" could change the diaper the fastest and that the two fastest diaper-changers would receive a prize: one of two diaper bags. The two grandmothers-to-be finished the diaper changing well ahead of any of the men.

Some men in these prenatal education classes expressed doubts about the necessity of their presence. They saw most of the course material as relevant to their partners but not themselves. During introductions in one class, however, one man took a novel approach. Class members were asked to mention, after introducing themselves, what they hoped to gain from the class. Many men were not sure what they were to gain, but came because their partner or the advertisement for the class said they should. But one man said he was there to find out what he could do to make his wife more comfortable. That comment won several approving chuckles.

In this context, the invitation to meet with a researcher and tell stories about fatherhood was welcomed by many. This was an opportunity for men's experiences to become central. In these interviews men and women who chose to participate could reflect upon what fatherhood meant to them and on the roles that men have played in their lives and their families' lives.

## Sample

In all, I interviewed seventy-nine men and women in the St. Louis metropolitan area during 2001 and 2002. This number consisted of forty-two men, and for thirty-seven of those men, their partners also. At the time they were invited to participate in the project, the couples were pregnant with their first child. Thus, they had little or no experience actually doing parental things at the time of interview. The average age of men who participated in the study was twenty-eight, and the average age of women who participated in the study was twenty-six. All were married except for two couples who were cohabiting. Eighty-five percent of them were white, although a few of that number were partially of mixed heritage. They discussed their partially minority ancestry (Native American, Filipino) in their interviews even though they initially identified themselves as "white." This was, on the whole, a well-educated group. Of the seventy-nine, thirty-one had at least some education beyond a bachelor's degree. Twenty-four had only a bachelor's degree; sixteen had some college but not a bachelor's degree, and eight had at most a high school diploma.

In designing the research, I planned to obtain religious diversity. Nearly all of the men and women recruited through the medical center were Catholic or some other branch of Christianity. I also attended weekly worship services at three minority religious congregations in St. Louis: a Jewish synagogue, a Muslim mosque, and a ward of The Church of Jesus Christ of Latter-day Saints (Mormon, sometimes abbreviated "LDS"). Through my involvement in these congregations a number of additional participants joined the study. It turned out that the particular LDS ward that year had a baby boom of couples having their first child. Of the seventy-nine men and women I interviewed, seventeen were Catholic, twenty-seven were Protestant or non-denominational Christian, nineteen were LDS, three were Muslim, five were Jewish, two were Hindu, one was Baha'i, and five claimed no religious affiliation.

## FATHERS-TO-BE

I focus my analysis here on the life stories of three men who were soon to become fathers at the time of the interviews. Each presented different family experiences and each had trajectories different from the others, but together their stories converged on common patterns of what constitutes ideas of good fatherhood. My purpose is to explore who each of these men became through their life experiences. Then I will address themes that cut across their histories. I argue that they saw good fathers as stable and patient. Periodic emotional outbursts were acknowledged and permitted, however, within certain boundaries.

## Thomas

Thomas, a thirty-year-old public relations specialist, described his Italian American family as "large, close-knit" and "loving, caring." Indeed, the positive emotions that dominated his memories of his family initially eclipsed his narratives of actual events, as he kept repeating words like "love," "emotion," and "compassion" when describing his family of origin, and "genuine," "honest," and "sincere" when describing his father.

Thomas switched over to memories of concrete events when he began to talk about how his father encouraged his involvement in sports and was "a very stabilizing influence" on Thomas when he would get "frustrated at different things." Thomas's father was a manager, and with two sons who were heavily involved in various extracurricular activities it was hard for him to keep up with everything, but Thomas recalled that his father kept everything in balance and "organized so nothing got too chaotic or too out of hand."

Thomas discussed how going away to college was quite a significant moment, since he was the first in his immediate family to do so. His father had attended a junior college before and after a tour of duty in Vietnam. To move away from home and attend a residential, four-year college was something his father had never experienced. Thomas recounted how, on the day he moved in, he and his father walked around the campus. His father stopped, looked around, and said to Thomas, "I want you to enjoy your time here, because this is something I wish I would have had. I want you to really enjoy it and savor every moment and make the most of it." The connection Thomas then felt with his father made it "a poignant type of moment" to him.

Indeed, Thomas was so consistent in characterizing his father as being patient and stable that I asked him directly whether this man had any shortcomings—a question that elicited laughter from both Thomas and his wife. He first told me that his father "was a very good guy. Like anyone else," he said, "he had a temper." Thomas' father did lose control on occasion, but Thomas was quick to assert that it was not evidence of any character flaw. After all, he explained, having two teenaged sons "would make anybody go crazy after a while." No, Thomas concluded, "He's a wonderful guy and I look at him as a great role model for me to emulate."

## Kyle

Kyle, a thirty-three-year-old intern and bartender, began by saying that he had had a happy childhood. His father started a private school that taught broadcasting technology, and Kyle would sometimes go with him to the school. He saw that his father was popular and easy to approach, and students liked to hang out there. Other times, Kyle and his father would go boating together on the river.

As Kyle got older, he started getting to know better his half-brother, Ben, his father's child from a previous marriage. Ben began doing some things with Kyle that Kyle thought in retrospect his father should have done with him. Ben taught Kyle how to go hunting and how to use firearms. The two "had fun together" and talked a lot.

It was about the time Kyle graduated from high school that Ben "set [him] down" to tell him that the family was going to go through a lot of changes. Their father was in trouble with the IRS, and as a result Kyle's parents would lose their home and the school. They soon moved to a different part of the country, but Kyle stayed in St. Louis, hoping to maintain a little bit of stability in a world that suddenly became very unstable. He missed all he had lost, but his world continued to slide.

Kyle had seen that something was wrong with his father, but it wasn't until his parents had settled into their new home that his father was diagnosed with Alzheimer's disease. He called it "surreal" to watch his father become progressively more disabled, finally dying when Kyle was only twenty-five years old. After his father passed away, Kyle's mother confided in him that his father "wasn't always very nice to her. He wasn't faithful to her, but she stuck by him because she felt that to have a family you have to be together."

Kyle's narrative began with tales of a happy family, but step by step the story became more complex. As he reflected back upon his life, he explained how he gained new appreciation for some people, like his mother, whom he felt he had not fully valued while he was growing up. At the same time, Kyle came to see people as more whole individuals, with both positive and negative qualities. Yes, those happy memories he had with his father really happened. His father could be the person in those memories while also being a man with "some flaws in his life and some insecurities . . . [someone who] didn't really know how to do some things or talk with us."

## Gabriel

In contrast to Thomas's and Kyle's life history narratives, Gabriel, a twenty-nine-year-old automobile technician, characterized his family of origin as "fragmented, not super-close." His parents had problems both individually and in their relationship with each other, which left "a strain and a gap" that he and his older brother had to deal with.

Gabriel's parents divorced when he was seven. His father was, in his words, "a cheater, a womanizer." Still, Gabriel's memory of living with his father is that his father was "a nice guy." He explained, "Again, that's a relative term, because he didn't smack me around, so the guy was nice." That was in decided contrast to the series of boyfriends his mother had after she divorced. He said that his mother was "so lonely, desperate, or whatever. She was craving for love after my dad ditched us," and so she ended up in several abusive relationships. "Pretty rough" was how Gabriel described his mother's boyfriends. Beginning at age seven, Gabriel found himself physically defending his mother.

Gabriel's father apparently had difficulty settling into a career, and so returned to the Navy before Gabriel was old enough to remember anything different. His father's work meant that the family had to move a lot: "there wasn't any real deep roots," Gabriel said—not with any particular place, and not with any extended family. His parents' divorce meant that he and his mother stopped moving around so much, but his life was hardly more stable. In addition to the abusive boyfriends, his father's periodic visits made him "a jittering mess" in anticipation of his coming and "crying [his] eyes out" when it was time for his father to leave.

When Gabriel was about sixteen, his older brother got married and had a son. He was really excited to see this—"a family can be normal," he said. Then his mother started having some health problems that culminated in her death about a year later. At about the same time Gabriel's sister-in-law died in an automobile accident. Gabriel and his brother both struggled with the loneliness and the bitterness they felt, especially toward their father, whose act of abandonment they saw as beginning the long years of pain.

Gabriel's brother eventually remarried, and then Gabriel married too, which gave him a sense of moving on to a different life. Gabriel's wife proudly asserted that there has never been a divorce in her family. Clearly she did not intend to be the first. Gabriel's father-in-law showed him a different model of manhood from the men he saw growing up: "very gentle, very patient, very funny."

## FATHERHOOD

There are several ways that men are expected to manage their emotions to display appropriately fatherly feelings. In this analysis, I focus on four imperatives that fatherhood expectations place upon men: exercising self-discipline, controlling anger, communicating with children, and being attuned to the child and the environment. According to the expectations that govern fatherhood, a man should do each of these things—each of which requires managing his emotions, whether to feel something he should feel or to not feel something he should not feel. We can infer the existence of these expectations from how men like Thomas, Kyle, and Gabriel assessed the behaviors of men they knew. The central concept in their stories is that fathers are culturally expected to show patience and stability—a calm, dependable state. This is not the same as having no emotion, since a man with no emotion is not sympathetic or understanding toward those around him. Fathers play important, emotional roles in families, and in fact these roles are central to the definition of good fatherhood.

## Exercising Self-discipline

Self-discipline is vital to being a good father. Again and again fathers-to-be spoke of patience and stability as key components of their stories about father role models. Both patience and stability appear to refer to the same concept, because each is counterposed against frustration. The men valued the example of a man who had self-discipline—who showed patience under pressure, who offered stability in the face of change. These are qualities that make him reliable. He may not always be present, but when he is, his level-headedness makes him invaluable.

Though impatience is a common characteristic of fathers, it is not appreciated nor framed as something to emulate. Gabriel related how he still struggles to think of anything in particular that his father taught him. Once, his father told Gabriel how his own father taught him to do some electrical work. It was an awkward moment, as Gabriel felt his father expected him to give an example of something he had taught Gabriel. Gabriel could only think of one thing: "A lack of patience is what I learned from him." He went on to describe another event that underscored his appreciation for patience as a fatherly characteristic:

> I'm not much on the plumbing end of things. I re-did the bathroom, and I had a weekend and this house, nothing was square with the plumbing in this house. Trying to align this house and not knowing what to buy; buying several different things and trying to get it right. [My father-in-law] comes over and says, "All right, sport. Let me come over." He got over [to my home] bright and early. He spent twelve hours working on this leak and made about twelve trips to the store about a mile away. Probably spent a hundred dollars on a one-foot section of pipe. And my dad happened to be in town [from out-of-state] that weekend. He comes over, and he's wanting to say something to me. So my dad says [trying to pull Gabriel away from the project he is working on with his father-in-law], "Hey, you know. Can you come in here for a minute?" I feel like I'm skipping out in my own home. And he gets kind of impatient with me. I'm

just like, [my father-in-law] spends twelve hours and is patient and is nice and smiles . . . and I know his knees are killing him and he's tired. And my dad's here an hour-and-a-half or two hours and he's already impatient with me. I'm like, "Go back to your state and call me on the weekend sometime."

Men who could be patient and controlled were greatly admired. For Thomas, it was his father who exercised a "stabilizing influence" on him. "Even when I was frustrated," he explained, "and I vented that frustration even at him sometimes, he was always very good at knowing when to leave me alone and knowing when I need a little kick in the rear end and helping me get some sort of guidance on what I was doing." A memory that illustrated that for Thomas was how his father would "make the time for [him] to practice" driving, and be "patient" when Thomas would weave in and out of the traffic or struggle to parallel park. And in Kyle's case, it was his half-brother who was "stable and close by" as his parents' lives started to fall apart. Over and over these men expressed their appreciation for the men in their lives who showed self-discipline even in the face of pressure and change.

### Controlling Anger

Still, these men acknowledged that anger is part of the emotional life of fathers. This does not contradict their admiration for patience and stability in father figures. Respect comes out of understanding the reason for the anger and the ways that the fathers recognize and respond to it. Kyle's father, for example, lost his temper in a memorable incident:

I stole the car one time and my mom told him. I had a friend over and it was Saturday morning and he kicked open my bedroom door. I could just tell that he knew. I felt like I let him down. I felt bad I was caught, of course. He was just really angry at me. I didn't get my license when I was sixteen right away. I had to wait. I [was] going to go to Sears Driving School.

Kyle felt that his father's anger was justified, and that the punishment was in keeping with the misdeed, and was intended to teach him to respect the privilege of driving.

Gabriel related a similarly emotionally charged incident between his father-in-law and himself:

We had one fight. The whole time we worked together we had one argument, and that was just because I lost my temper and threw something. We rectified it. You could just feel the tension between us for a couple days. We were both brokenhearted but both too stubborn to say anything. And finally one day we were having a party or something. Maybe it was [my wife's] birthday. We went out to Walgreen's for something and in the middle of the store we were like,

"Oh, I'm sorry!" We looked like a couple of fruits in the aisle. It's been good for him to be in my life.

Thus, anger is acknowledged as part of the emotional life of fatherhood, but it does not dominate the terrain. Instead, anger is constructed as something that is situation-specific, controlled, and ultimately resolved.

## Communicating with Children

Self-control extends to a man's interaction with children. Kyle, Thomas, and Gabriel drew lessons on what kind of father they wanted to be from how they saw other men speak with children. Interestingly, there is continuity here in how they saw men talk with children regardless of their age. The expectations of emotional control seem to be consistent: Stay calm. Get to their level. Find out what their problems are. Be candid.

Kyle reported how much he was affected by watching a certain man who taught elementary school interact with the children in his class. Kyle's work as a teacher's assistant gave him the opportunity to see many small interactions that cumulatively taught him about how he wanted to speak to children. He said of the teacher,

He'd have a very calm voice, very quiet voice. Kind of talking with them. The kids at school, they were two-and-a-half to like six years old, so they were smaller. Getting down with them, talking with them, really working out what their problems were. Just the stuff that he had with them, I felt like that was the right thing to do, like that's how you should talk with somebody. That's how you should talk with your kids.

Kyle felt that these kinds of interactions led to positive outcomes, ones that he wanted to define his relationship with his own children.

Thomas similarly appreciated the ability to "sit down and talk" with his father, no matter their respective ages. Thomas explained:

[My wife and I] got married when we were twenty-three and I remember very distinctly right before we got married, my dad and I sat down and we were talking. And he looks at me and he goes, "You're twenty-three, right?" I said, "Yeah." And he goes, "You know, when I was twenty-three, I had a wife, a kid, a house, a car, a job, and had fought in a war." And I kind of laughed and I looked at him and I said, "Well, I got a car. And I'm about to have a wife." But it was very interesting that we are twenty-three years apart, because that's how old he was when I was born. The generational gap of how much different his life was at that time versus my life!

At this stage in these men's lives, they were coming to appreciate the value of oral communication in building and maintaining emotionally close relationships. They saw that talking with children—whether those children are preschool-aged or adults—helps to create common understandings, and those common understandings build positive feelings in the relationships.

### Being Attuned to the Child and the Environment

Gabriel, Thomas, and Kyle valued a man who is emotionally aware. He can sense someone else's emotions and gauge his own emotional response to the situation—especially as it pertains to the feelings of a child. Kyle put it directly when he observed that a father needs to know "what [his children are] thinking and feeling." What he was saying is that being a good father requires an awareness of what is happening with other people and in the situation to be able to respond appropriately. Kyle explained how a friend of his was good at continually adjusting the amount of freedom he gave his children according to how trustworthily they acted. In order to do that the friend had to be constantly aware of his children, sensing their intentions and psychological states.

There are, of course, some situations where men fail to exercise emotional awareness. They get caught up with their own emotions and fail to align themselves with those around them or respond appropriately to the circumstances. Narrators told me of this several times. I take just one memory, from Thomas, as an example:

Sports is a big thing because sports are so very competitive . . . I think a lot of times you see a lot of dads live vicariously through their kids when they're on the field. And so their competitive juices are going and I'd be playing in a big, league championship soccer game or something like that. And you'd see some of these dads who are drunk or red-faced. They're screaming at the refs. They're screaming at their kids. They're screaming at the coaches. They're screaming at other parents in the stands. And you always felt so bad for the kid whose father was doing all this. It was sort of like, not only are you embarrassing yourself and hurting yourself in some way, but what are you doing to your child? And I don't care if the child's six or sixteen. You hope that you know there's an emotional threshold that you really shouldn't break.

An event like this breaks all of the normative expectations the narrators were constructing. The fathers Thomas saw at the soccer games were not stabilizing influences. They overreacted to the situation and did not resolve their anger, did not speak calmly, and were not attuned to their children or others around them.

## CONCLUSION

I started with two short accounts of images of fathers at the St. Louis County Fair and Air Show. In one, two adults argued with each other in the presence of two children. In the other, a man encouraged a small child in his gymnastics play. These and many, many other examples of fatherly behaviors surround us all the time. By the time a man is to become a father himself, he has obtained a large stock of memories of things he saw and heard, things he approved of, and things he did not. From them he defines what kind of father he hopes to be himself.

Each of the three men whose lives I highlighted, Thomas, Kyle, and Gabriel, had unique biographical journeys that led to a common understanding of the meaning of fatherhood. One of the insights of sociology is that the unique is connected to the general. Everyone's life is different. Each individual has unique experiences in his or her family, at work, or in the community. Still, when different people belong to the same society, they make decisions within an environment that encourages them to see things in similar ways. Every society carries sets of cultural expectations, and these expectations frame what individual people do and how they think. Thus, when someone knows that it is wrong (within one's culture) for a man to lose control of himself, he is likely to evaluate negatively a man whose explosive anger is out of proportion to the behaviors of those around him. In this way every life can be different, but those differences exist in an environment of shared cultural standards.

The men I interviewed sensed that there are normative expectations that govern the role of a father. Fathers are expected to be a "stabilizing influence" on those around them, and there are several ways in which they can do that. Those ways include (1) self-discipline: being patient and understanding, even under pressure and when others are becoming frustrated; (2) controlled anger: if anger is expressed, it should be responsive to the situation and resolved in a timely manner; (3) communication: speaking calmly and directly to the child as an equal, and listening so you can come to understand the other's perspective; and (4) alignment to the child and to the environment: staying emotionally aware of others and the situation, and acting appropriately within that context. The men in this study developed a deep sense of respect for a father (or other fatherly figure) who observed these expectations in his everyday life.

## AFTERWORD

I started off my college career in human geography (I like maps), and when I switched to sociology for graduate school, community studies was an interdisciplinary research area that put me comfortably in between the two fields. While I was working on my master's degree at Brigham Young University, I got interested in how people develop and maintain a cooperative spirit. At the suggestion of a professor, I looked into the Mormon Village.

That's a name given to a set of classic community studies that were done back in the 1920s. The studies were replicated in 1950, but no one had studied the villages since. I decided to do a replication of one of them. Being at BYU was a help, since BYU is *relatively* close to the villages so I could spend some time in them (but remember that states in the West are really big), and BYU has archives with original documents from those first studies.

After doing field work in Ephraim, Utah, I argued that community doesn't have to fall apart, that community members can find ways to maintain place-based solidarity. My master's experience left me with an affinity for research that drops you in a particular place and in the flow of everyday life of a community in an effort to figure out what the world is like from the perspective of ordinary people in that place. It also started my interest in stories. I still love the story about two neighbors in Ephraim who have a race each garbage day to see who can take *each other's* trash out first!

I went to the University of Michigan for my Ph.D., and I studied fatherhood narratives in St. Louis. Going to St. Louis meant that I got to miss at least one Michigan winter (the field period was twelve months), plus I had a big metropolitan area with lots of social life and social problems to sink my teeth into. I narrowed down the research to focus on fatherhood narratives—and that's the material you read in this chapter. Lots of people guessed that I have lots of fatherhood experiences of my own to talk about but, to their surprise, I am not a father myself yet. I thought the people's stories were great, though.

After my Michigan years and a stop in Indiana, I returned to my alma mater as a faculty member in sociology. Somehow I wanted to integrate my previous research into fatherhood and community. That's how I ended up studying housing (the interface between family and community). Lately I've been spending time touring construction sites and gathering people's home improvement stories, both here in the West and back in the Midwest.

What am I finding? You know, people can tell stories about almost anything. To know something is to be able to tell a story about it. Substantively, well, you need to look for the forthcoming articles!

## NOTES

Funding for this research came from grants from the Center for the Ethnography of Everyday Life at the University of Michigan, an Alfred P. Sloan Center for the Study of Working Families, the Department of Sociology at the University of Michigan, and the Rackham School of Graduate Studies at the University of Michigan. Address correspondence to the author at 2008 JFSB, Brigham Young University, Provo, UT 84606.

1. Statistical data were obtained from the Missouri State Vital Records Office.

2. The name "Midwest Medical Center" and all personal names I use here are pseudonyms.

## REFERENCES

Bengtson, Vern L., Alan C. Acock, Katherine R. Allen, Peggye Dilworth-Anderson, and David M. Klein, eds. 2005. *Sourcebook of family theory and research.* Thousand Oaks, CA: Sage Publications.

Blankenhorn, David. 1995. *Fatherless America: Confronting our most urgent social problem.* New York: Harper Perennial.

Cooley, Charles Horton. 1983. *Human nature and the social order.* New Brunswick, NJ: Transaction.

Hawkins, Alan J., and David C. Dollahite, eds. 1997. *Generative fathering: Beyond deficit perspectives.* Current Issues in the Family, vol. 3. Thousand Oaks, CA: Sage.

Hochschild, Arlie Russell. 1983. *The managed heart: Commercialization of human feeling.* Berkeley, CA: University of California Press.

———. 2003. *The Second shift.* With Anne Machung. New York: Penguin.

Lupton, Deborah, and Lesley Barclay. 1997. *Constructing fatherhood: Discourses and experiences.* London: Sage.

Marsiglio, William, ed. 1995. *Fatherhood: Contemporary theory, research, and social policy.* Thousand Oaks, CA: Sage Publications.

Parke, Ross D. 1996. *Fatherhood.* Cambridge, MA: Harvard University Press.

Parsons, Talcott, and Robert F. Bales. 1955. *Family, socialization and interaction process.* Glencoe, IL: The Free Press.

Popenoe, David. 1996. *Life without father: Compelling new evidence that fatherhood and marriage are indispensable for the good of children and society.* Cambridge, MA: Harvard University Press.

Townsend, Nicholas W. 2002. *The package deal: Marriage, work, and fatherhood in men's lives.* Philadelphia, PA: Temple University Press.

# 13

## Focused on the Chinese American Family

### Chinese Immigrant Churches and Childrearing

*Carolyn Chen*

Describing her frustrations with raising children in the United States, Mrs. Kau, a Taiwanese immigrant in her mid-forties, proclaims, "We just can't use our OBC (Overseas-Born Chinese) ways on our ABC (American-Born Chinese) children!"[1] Children in the United States, she claims, have too much freedom and consequently are uncontrollable, disobedient, and disrespectful. Her Taiwanese practices of parenting, based on Confucian notions of filial obligation, are no longer effective on her Taiwanese American children. To solve her parenting problems in the United States, she turns to religion—specifically, evangelical Christianity. Evangelical Christianity has become immensely popular among many Chinese immigrants, including Taiwanese (Chen forthcoming, Dart 1997, Ly 2003, Yang 1999a).[2] When Mrs. Kau came to the United States, she, like most Taiwanese immigrants, was nominally Buddhist and non-practicing. But like many Taiwanese immigrants, Mrs. Kau converted to Christianity and became actively involved in a local Chinese evangelical church after moving to the United States. She claims that the main reason she and her family became involved in a Chinese church was for the family: "We wanted to make sure that the kids were on the right track—so we took them to church." It is commonly known within the Taiwanese community that children will not go astray if they attend church.

Mrs. Kau is not alone in turning to religion to solve the intergenerational tensions in immigrant families. The growing body of scholarship on religion and immigrant adaptation addresses the importance of religion to parenting, particularly in reproducing traditional values and culture in the second generation (e.g., Ebaugh and Chafetz 2000, Warner and Wittner 1998, Zhou and Bankston 1998). This is the case even among groups who are largely converts to Christianity, like Koreans (Min 1998, 2003) and Chinese (Yang 1999a, 1999b). Like Mrs. Kau, other immigrants find that religion protects the second generation from the "immoral" influences of American culture (Ebaugh and Chafetz 2000, Waters 1999, Yang 1999a, 1999b, Zhou and Bankston 1998).

But Mrs. Kau's statement implies that ethnic religion does something more than reproduce traditional, or "OBC," ways when it comes to parenting. In fact, traditional ways don't work on second-generation children, and making sure that kids are "on the right track," as she puts it, requires something different than just reinforcing traditional ethnic values.

Based on my ethnographic fieldwork in Grace Church, a Chinese immigrant church in Southern California, and in-depth interviews with Taiwanese Christians, I suggest that Chinese churches offer new models of parenting and family life to Taiwanese immigrants in the United States Churches occupy prominent positions in immigrant communities and shape how immigrant families adapt to and transform in American society. In particular, through these Chinese Christian churches and networks, Chinese immigrants are influenced by mainstream American evangelical Christian models of the family. Where immigrant parents struggle to apply Confucian principles of parenting to their American children, evangelical Christianity offers an attractive new moral model of the family. In this essay I first discuss some of the problems that Taiwanese immigrant parents face in raising children in the United States and why they turn to religion for parenting solutions. Second, I discuss how religious conversion to Christianity shifts the moral vocabulary of the family from one of filial duty to religious discipleship. Third, I consider how Christianity can restructure the family by democratizing relationships between parents and children and consecrating the individuality and autonomy of the children. While the church may provide new models and strategies of parenting, I argue that these have tendencies to both reproduce and transform Taiwanese traditions in the United States.

My findings are based on a larger ethnographic study of Taiwanese immigrant Christians and Buddhists in Southern California. To maintain the anonymity of this institution and the persons involved, I give it the pseudonym "Grace Evangelical Church." At Grace Church, I participated in Sunday services, Sunday School, Friday Night Fellowship meetings, church visitations, church social events, youth group activities, and children's Vacation Bible School. Although I concentrated most of my fieldwork at Grace Evangelical Church, I also observed the services and meetings of other local Chinese churches and para-church Chinese Christian organizations.

In addition to participant observation, I conducted twenty-five in-depth interviews with Taiwanese immigrants who converted to Christianity. The respondents, recruited through snowball sampling, were members of different Chinese churches in Southern California, including Grace Church. They varied in age between the mid-thirties to mid-fifties. One person was divorced, and the rest of the respondents were married. All but one had children. The age of their children varied from two to twenty-three. The majority had children between the ages of twelve and eighteen. I also interviewed religious leaders, both lay and clergy, at Grace Church and at other local Chinese religious congregations. Taiwanese and English were used in the interviews.

## THE PERILS OF RAISING CHILDREN IN THE UNITED STATES: SEX, DRUGS, AND NURSING HOMES

Commenting on the perils of raising children in the United States, Dr. Lin, a father of two junior high school children, proclaims, "Freedom built this country and freedom will destroy it." He embarks on a litany of the downfalls of American freedom—school shootings, teenage pregnancies, rampant drug use, and last but not least, nursing homes. Although Dr. Lin is fairly Americanized—he received his doctorate in engineering from a prestigious American university twelve years ago and speaks flawless English— he echoes a common sentiment among Taiwanese immigrants about raising children in a land of excessive freedom. Lacking an adequate sense of limits and boundaries, children in the United States are "wild," "unmannered," "disobedient," and "disrespectful." Parents remark that children in the United States have too much individual choice. In this environment, Taiwanese parents fear that their children might succumb to the vices of American freedoms, and among these vices, sending parents to nursing homes tops the list.

Most American parents can identify with immigrants' fears of school violence, drug abuse, and teenage pregnancies, but placing nursing homes in this list of social ills seems odd. However, to Taiwanese and other immigrants from a Confucian heritage, nursing homes, along with the social problems that plague American youth, are all consequences of the same root cause—lack of filial piety, the sense of duty and indebtedness to one's parents. That is, children become involved in shameful activities ranging from violence to parental neglect because they do not respect the parents who made great sacrifices in raising them.

To immigrants from Confucian traditions, filial piety is a central moral principle that guides human behavior. The principle of filial piety is based on a conception of the self and the family that is quite different from that of most Americans. In Confucian tradition the individual self is inseparable from a set of hierarchical relationships and obligations within the family, not an autonomous self as it is regarded in the West. The family is based on a clear hierarchy of members of the family, where the young are deferential to the elderly. For the sake of harmony, the individual will is subordinated to the will of the family, and, more specifically, to the will of the parents.

Central to filiality is the concept of obligation and indebtedness to one's parents. This sense of duty and gratefulness toward one's parents weaves an iron web of material, emotional, and spiritual interdependence between members of the family. Studies of Chinese immigrant families show that this critically shapes children's behaviors (Ng 1998). For example, if the child fails or shows deviant behavior, the whole family loses face. Similarly, if the child is very successful, the whole family shares in this achievement. This awesome responsibility is a powerful form of constraint on children's behaviors, and is also a source of intergenerational tension among immigrant families from Confucian tradition (Zhou and Bankston 1998).

The tension between Chinese traditions of collectivism and American traditions of individualism are a constant theme in dialogues about the family in the Chinese church. According to American moral traditions children must be given a certain allowance of freedom to develop their moral selves (Bellah et al. 1985). The goal of parenting is to raise children who eventually can become independent and self-sufficient (Tobin, Wu, and Davidson 1989). Strong middle-class families are measured by healthy relationships among individual members where the mutual exchange of respect, communication, and affection do not cultivate codependency and loss of self.

But Taiwanese perceive the individual freedom that Americans celebrate as a threat to family harmony. American individualism leads Taiwanese parents to warn their children as one respondent does, "When we get old and sick, you must take care of us. I don't want the American way where you don't take care of mom and dad!" Many immigrants claim that Americans face so many family problems, such as high rates of divorce, marital affairs, and runaway children, because they are too individualistic. Without a moral tradition that sets collective obligations before the individual, the stability of the family falls victim to the vicissitudes of the individual wills of its members.

## REPRODUCING CONFUCIAN TRADITIONS
## IN THE UNITED STATES?

While Taiwanese parents bemoan the fact that their children are not so obedient and pliable in the United States, they also know that reproducing traditional Taiwanese children is neither practically feasible nor desirable, particularly among middle-class immigrants like the Taiwanese. Many of the respondents work in American companies and recognize that inculcating Confucian virtues such as obedience and deference may create a harmonious home, but will not lead their children to success outside of the home. When I ask respondents what qualities lead to success in the United States, they reply independence, aggressiveness, and courage. To succeed in Taiwan, they say one must be studious, hard working, and obedient.

Respondents agree that to succeed in the United States, their children need to be aggressive and independent. In many ways, the qualities that immigrants inculcate in their children are ones that stem from an *immigrant* experience, that is, the experience of being a foreigner and a minority in the United States. Immigrants realize that because they lack the networks and cultural capital to further their children's upward mobility, their children not only need to be aggressive and competitive with other Americans, but they need to be *more* aggressive and *more* competitive than the typical American. Taiwanese immigrants, many of whom are professionals, are especially cognizant of this fact. They have learned through their own experiences in the professional workplace that, despite having comparable if not superior credentials than their American coworkers do, their job mobility is limited by the glass ceiling. The combination of lacking connections, American cultural sensibilities, and being Asian works against immigrants' upward mobility.

Having experienced the same barriers that will limit their own children's success, immigrant parents now encourage their children to be independent and aggressive—not to conform to one's particular station or status in life, but to jockey for more. For example, Dr. Su, an engineer who works in a large American company, claims that, because of his own experience of racism in the workplace, he encourages his sons to develop qualities of leadership and independence. He comments:

> In America I encourage my children to be more outgoing and social and develop leadership skills. If you're shy you'll never be a leader. In Taiwan you have more relatives and protection. Here you're by yourself. Alone. Especially for us immigrants who don't have white skin. I feel like I know something about American society, so I want them to be leaders in order to survive. Based on my experience, you have to be this way or you'll fall behind.

As Zhou and Bankston (1998) note in their study of Vietnamese American children, concerns for social mobility and cultural preservation may often work at cross purposes. Sometimes parents are forced to choose between cultural reproduction and upward mobility. They know that the traditional Taiwanese child is not going to succeed in a white American society and yet, the child who is too "American," meaning too independent and individualistic, can threaten family harmony and solidarity.

Taiwanese immigrant parents find themselves in a dilemma regarding the family. Surrounded by the mainstream culture of American individualism, some Confucian traditions have lost their moral legitimacy within the family. Pressured by the demands of surviving and thriving in American society, Taiwanese immigrants realize that it is neither feasible nor desirable to preserve traditional family practices. Yet what immigrants perceive as a morally bankrupt mainstream America does not offer more attractive models for the family.

Where then do Taiwanese immigrants turn for models and traditions of family and parenting in the United States? How do families establish a common moral language that both generations can regard as legitimate? Where some traditions of Taiwan have lost their relevance, and the traditions of mainstream America offer no desirable alternatives, Taiwanese parents turn to the solutions offered to the immigrant public. The immigrant church is one of the most vocal institutions in this arena.

## THE CHINESE CHURCH AND FAMILY IDEOLOGIES

On Sunday mornings at Grace Church, about three hundred Taiwanese immigrants and their families gather for worship. The Mediterranean-style church is located in a pleasant middle-class suburb of Southern California. Parents come eager to reconnect with other Taiwanese who share the same language and culture. The youth attend the service, and then socialize and play sports with their friends. The church is a busy social scene where young and old gather. On one particular Sunday in late spring, the senior pastor preached about spiritual maturity in his sermon. He took the opportunity to admonish Chinese parents for only being concerned about their children's academic achievement while neglecting their spiritual development. Playing on his Chinese congregation's fears of nursing homes, the pastor asked, "So what if your child becomes famous and successful but neglects you in your old age?" His message was loud and clear: Raising a spiritually mature child was equally as—if not more—important than raising a successful child. Later in the service, the presider made several announcements about upcoming events—a presentation on Friday night titled "Communicating with your children," a youth retreat in two weeks, and a family picnic at the end of the month.

Chinese American churches' emphases on the family are strongly informed by the larger mainstream evangelical tradition to which they belong. Chinese evangelical leaders are influenced by concerns about the dissolution of the traditional family that have preoccupied conservative Christianity since the 1970s (Hunter 1987, Smith 1998, Wilcox 2004). Many Chinese pastors have been trained in American evangelical seminaries. Chinese churches like Grace Church use Bible study guides and Sunday School materials from evangelical religious education sources. For example, in one Chinese church I visited, the congregation was collectively reading the popular evangelical best seller, *The Purpose Driven Life*. Chinese Christian publishing houses translate and distribute mainstream evangelical literature on the family to Chinese immigrants. The well-known evangelical Christian organization Focus on the Family is a familiar and respected name in the homes of many of my respondents. It should be no surprise that immigrants might be attracted to evangelical Christian ideologies of the family, for both reject and feel threatened by trends in the American family. Where Taiwanese immigrants are searching for a solution to the problems of creating a family in the United States, the evangelical Christians have a ready answer in hand.

Like other immigrant groups (Min 1998, Yang 1999a), non-Christian Taiwanese start attending an ethnic Christian church in the United States out of a concern for their children's moral upbringing. For example, Mrs. Lee, a mother of two girls in high school, claims, "When I came to the United States, people told me that the children wouldn't go the wrong way if I brought them to church. At the time I myself had no desire to attend church but I wanted my children to go to church." Another respondent, Mr. Wong, says that after his twelve-year-old daughter started coming home from school and copying the language and behavior of "American" kids, he and his wife decided to bring their children to Grace Church. One man, Mr. Liu, used to belong to a Chinese Buddhist temple, but claims that he switched to Grace Church because the temple lacked a children's moral education program for his two teenage children.

Promoting strong families is a ministerial priority to Grace Church and other Chinese evangelical churches. For example, the cover of the Grace Church bulletin depicts a church as a hospital healing families and individuals. Knowing that immigrants struggle with intergenerational and bicultural tensions in the family, pastors are particularly mindful of addressing these problems in their ministry to maintain membership and attract new members. The pastor frequently addresses family issues in his Sunday sermons.

Many of the programs at Grace Church and other Chinese churches are devoted to the family. In addition to a summer and winter retreat, Grace Church sponsors a special "family retreat" that concentrates specifically on issues of parenting and marriage, and attracts many who do not belong to the church. Chinese churches frequently invite family professionals, such as therapists, psychologists, and pediatricians, to speak on family issues during their weekly fellowship meetings. At Grace Church, children and parents gather together to study the Bible, pray, and socialize during their weekly Family Bible Studies. Frequently the discussions revolve around how to incorporate biblical teachings into their family lives.

Chinese churches introduce Chinese immigrants to evangelical Christian literature and resources on the family. Grace Church's publishing house translates and distributes many mainstream American evangelical books about the family that are sold in Chinese Christian bookstores. For example, three of the five new titles that one Grace Church newsletter introduced were related to parenting: *What My Parents Did Right, Different Children, Different Needs,* and *Parents' Guide to Sex Education.* One Chinese church has its own library, and another church has a small bookstore, where both English and Chinese-translated books, many of them family-related, are available.

Chinese churches distribute the literature of and publicize events for not only Christian organizations, such as Focus on the Family but also national Chinese Christian family-centered organizations, like Focus on the Chinese Family and Chinese Family for Christ. These para-church organizations publish newsletters, hold workshops and retreats, such as for marriage enrichment, and family vacation camps. For immigrants who are involved in these tight-knit church communities, evangelical Christian ideologies and models of the family are easily accessible and widely known.

The church also serves as a network where immigrants informally share information on family life. During social hours at Grace Church, parents exchange tips on such topics as college applications, music lessons, teenage dating, and baggy pants. Parents with older children give advice to younger parents. And more established immigrant families serve as role models for others. Parents will frequently seek the advice of the youth pastor in dealing with a variety of issues, and not only spiritual problems. The youth pastor at Grace Church told me that parents often approach him for advice on how to motivate their children to study, or how to steer their children away from "bad" friends. For example, when one respondent's daughter ran away from home, the youth pastor counseled her family regularly. Now, the mother says, things have returned to normal in her home.

The church offers a supportive environment to the immigrants' children, who also struggle with family issues. The youth group is a venue for children to voice their concerns and needs to their parents. For example, at Grace Church the youth group sponsors an annual "Family Night," a banquet to express their gratitude to their parents. At one Family Night, an American-trained Chinese psychologist delivered a talk describing the struggles that Chinese immigrant parents and their children face in the United States. He discussed how Chinese American children are overwhelmed by parental pressures to achieve academically and feel emotionally neglected by their parents' "Chinese" lack of expressiveness. These concerns have legitimacy and authority when delivered at the church and by a credentialed professional.

Although most Taiwanese come from a Buddhist heritage, they do not look to Buddhist temples for family guidance. From my fieldwork at one Chinese Buddhist temple and observations at other Chinese temples, I noticed that monastics and laypeople would occasionally discuss family issues during meetings; however, the temple offered no explicit programs, talks, or literature devoted to the family. Most immigrant Buddhist temples struggle to offer even modest children's religious education programs because they lack English-language materials (Suh 2005). As mentioned, part of the Chinese Christian preoccupation with the family stems from the influence of the mainstream evangelical Christian culture. Chinese Christian churches are a part of a larger culture where models of and resources to support "the Christian family" exist.

## RAISING GOOD TAIWANESE KIDS: FROM FAMILY DUTY TO CHRISTIAN DISCIPLESHIP

In this section I discuss how the immigrant church shifts the moral foundation of Taiwanese immigrant families from filial piety to religious piety while simultaneously reinforcing what are perceived as traditional Taiwanese values. Rather than the Confucian language of indebtedness and obligation, immigrant parents use the new moral language of Christian discipleship to achieve traditionally Confucian ends.

A plaque that reads "Christ is the Lord of this House" adorns the homes of many Taiwanese Christians. Symbolically, it replaces the ancestral altar in the traditional Taiwanese home, where family members ritually offer fruit, food, and incense to their ancestors, who in turn protect their living descendents. The plaque symbolizes that Christ, rather than their ancestors, is the source of their protection, and whom they owe their obedience.

The symbolism of the plaque replacing the ancestral shrine vividly illustrates how evangelical Christianity shifts the moral foundation of Taiwanese immigrant families from filial to religious piety. Whereas the Confucian family is based on a sense of duty and indebtedness to one's parents, the Christian family is based first and foremost on discipleship to Christ. As a Christian, one is an obedient daughter, a nurturing mother, or a loving father because this is what Christ commands. Taiwanese parents in my sample used evangelical Christianity to reproduce some traditional Taiwanese values by morally reframing these as acts of Christian discipleship rather than using the Confucian vocabulary of family duty.

Some Taiwanese parents who fear the decline of their authority in the United States invoke the authority of Christ to discipline their children. Many Taiwanese immigrants claim that Christian teachings are very similar to traditional Taiwanese values and morals, such as respecting elders, shunning drugs and alcohol, and prohibiting divorce and premarital sex. Parents use Christian teachings to reproduce traditional Taiwanese values. For example, in this quote, Dr. Wu discusses how God's authority replaces his own loss of control over his two middle-school-aged children in the United States:

> Because of too much liberty in the United States, they allow some behaviors here that they don't allow in Taiwan. So parents start to worry about kids going in the wrong direction. Like if they get addicted to drugs or become a punk or become sexually active. What can you do? I've already talked to a lot of parents, and some who have children who are older than mine. They say you just cannot control your child because of all the liberties and human rights here. You can make suggestions, but beyond that what else can you do? For example, if they get sexually involved with someone, what can you do? Well, in Taiwan we didn't know about sex at so young an age. Believe me, it's true. But in the United States, getting sex education is very important for kids these days. But if you are a Christian you have some way to guide them in the right direction. If you have sexual relations before marriage, that's not allowed in the religion. You've already crossed the boundaries before God!

As Dr. Wu's response suggests, Christianity replaces the moral authority that parents have over their children in a traditional Confucian society. His comment, "But if you are a Christian, you have some way to guide them in the right direction," is particularly elucidating. Both parents and children now have an objective and common source of moral reference—the Bible. Immigrant parents claim that their American children often talk back to them. When children ask "why," immigrant parents realize that the traditional answer, "because I say so," holds little ground. With Christianity, parents now have an answer. They find legitimacy through the Bible, a source of authority that is recognized by both children and parents. Immigrant parents are able to reclaim their authority by referring to the biblical teaching to honor one's parents. In so doing immigrant parents legitimate their authority over their children as God-given.

An example from a Family Bible study meeting illustrates how parents use the Bible to legitimate their authority. On a monthly basis, church members and their families meet at each others' homes, share a potluck meal, and study the Bible together. At this particular meeting children and parents read a passage from the gospel of John, where at the request of his mother Mary, Christ turns water into wine, despite his own reluctance. Parents and children offered varying interpretations of how this passage applied to their daily lives. One child teasingly suggested that the passage advocated children drinking alcohol, to which parents responded by pointing to other biblical passages where drunkenness is condemned. After much discussion, parents and children concluded that children ought to obey their parents, for Christ obeyed his mother, despite his own disinclination.

## AFFIRMING MORAL AGENCY

Both traditional Taiwanese and Christian approaches to parenting advocate the same end—children's obedience to parents—but the *means*, that is, the moral concepts by which these behaviors are framed, are very different. Parents realize that it is no longer effective to use the language of familial duty and indebtedness to their American children to discipline them. As one respondent told me, "in the end they will do what they want." Christianity, however, frames these issues as personal choices. From the earliest ages the church teaches children that Christianity is a personal choice that one makes to commit one's life to Christ. For example, in Sunday School, teachers ask third graders whether they would like to make a "personal decision" to "ask Jesus into your heart." In true discipleship one must have the moral freedom to choose to do right. By framing things in the language of moral agency—the choice to follow Christ—rather than the traditional language of moral obligation to the family—indebtedness to parents—parents affirm children's personal freedom and simultaneously discipline them. This is not to say that children are always obedient, but at least now children and parents speak the same moral language.

The church's youth education program plays a crucial part in instilling this sense of Christian discipleship in the children. Grace Church provides youth programs on Friday nights and Sundays where it is hip and cool to be Christian. Instead of traditional hymns, services always open with contemporary Christian rock music. Trendy Chinese American youth with dyed hair and baggy jeans lead the band, drawing connections between the latest in teen pop culture and God. The youth support each other in their "walk with Christ" through a panorama of evangelical Christian youth media and technology.

Youth programs at Grace Church affirm the language of moral agency. In a high school Sunday school class, for example, Charlie, the instructor, an Asian American student at a local evangelical seminary, challenges students to keep track of what they do in their free time. "Are you using this time to honor God?" he asks. Charlie goes on to discuss how mainstream American culture has become increasingly immoral. He points to the language and pornographic references in television, radio, and movies, as well as the teaching of evolution as a scientific fact in public schools. "It's almost come to a point where we cannot live in this world and be Christian," he concludes. The solution is a challenge to these middle-class suburban students ensconced in our media-frenzied consumer culture: "We have to step away from the values of this culture." Consider how Charlie frames "honoring God" in one's free time:

Your free time is that one area where you have freedom to exert your independence and develop your identity. It's in those small details of life that it's hard to be uncompromising. You're not just impulsive kids anymore. You're given a certain amount of freedom to align your life with God's will.

Here Charlie suggests that doing the right thing, such as watching wholesome movies, not engaging in premarital sex, and obeying one's parents, is an act of individuality and independence from our fallen culture. Doing the moral thing is not about suppressing one's individuality and meeting social expectations, but having the freedom to resist an oppressive secular culture and do what is right, or "align your life with God's will." Christianity thus frames morality as a personal choice, an interpretation that is far more palatable to American children.

On another occasion in a Bible study, the students examined why particular sins, such as premarital sex and drugs, were wrong. They referred to different biblical passages to substantiate their claims. They then came up with concrete strategies to resist these temptations and sins in their daily lives. The church instills the parents' own traditional moral values, but uses the language of Christian moral agency. By training them to be good Christians, parents in turn raise them to be good Taiwanese children.

## SOFTENING HIERARCHIES: BECOMING FRIENDS WITH YOUR CHILDREN

Immigrant churches do more than simply reproduce Taiwanese values by repackaging them in Christian trappings. My findings suggest that the church offers a new model of parent-child relations that challenges Confucian hierarchical styles of parenting. In comparison to traditional Taiwanese parent-child relationships, evangelical Christian teachings sacralize more egalitarian relationships. When asked if and how they have changed after converting, respondents frequently said they had changed as parents and softened from more authoritarian styles of parenting. For example, Dr. Wu, an engineer in his mid-forties who is the father of two teenage children, recalls that in Taiwan his father was the "king" of his family. His father's word was the sole authority and indisputable.

> My father followed the traditional way. He was like a king. The son must follow. He cannot say anything. He cannot fight back. If he says, "you must study now," as a son you cannot argue. You just go. That's the way it was in my family. If you don't follow then there will be all kinds of punishment.

In his own family in the United States, Dr. Wu continued this pattern of being "king" over his wife and two children until he and his wife converted to Christianity in 1997. He claims that when he and his wife converted, they confessed their sins before God and asked God to remove the sinful patterns that had burdened their lives. One of these sinful patterns that God removed was something that he inherited from his father—the manner of relating to his children as a king.

Through the church Dr. Wu and other Taiwanese immigrants learn that being an authoritarian parent is "wrong" and un-Christian. On this point Dr. Wu reflects:

> In the Bible God represents two things—love and justice. I am too much justice and I don't show enough love to my kids. I just want them to be good, but I don't give them enough love. *I've done it the wrong way. The old me who just showed justice but no love is wrong and I must change.*

Dr. Wu's account illustrates how evangelical Christianity can alter immigrant styles of parenting. The emphasis on love Dr. Wu refers to reflects the expressive and therapeutic turn in evangelical Christianity in the 1970s (Hunter 1987, Wilcox 1998). Studies show that relative to white Americans, Chinese parents tend to be more controlling (Lin and Fu 1990). Asian American evangelicals, who have been influenced by therapeutic evangelicalism, now recognize the "dysfunctions" of their own Confucian upbringings and seek "healing" from what they perceive as the psychological damage of their emotionally distant and controlling fathers (Jeung 2004).

In place of the traditional hierarchical relationship between parent and child, the church promulgates a new relationship that is based on a friendship between two near-equals. For example, at a Chinese Christian event, Dr. Hsu, a Western-educated Chinese psychologist, encouraged parents to shed their authoritative demeanor. "To be a good parent you need to be on the same level with your kids. You need to become friends."

Although the idea of becoming friends with one's children is admittedly foreign to most Taiwanese immigrants, accepting this proposal is far more palatable under the aegis of a Chinese Christian church than an American secular institution. Chinese Christians look to Western psychology for advice in the arena of the family. Like Dr. Hsu, many of the experts are Chinese who are trained in Western psychology. Through religion, Western models of parenting are filtered to Taiwanese immigrant parents through the visage of a familiar Taiwanese face.

## FRIENDSHIP STRATEGIES: RESPECTING INDIVIDUALITY AND COMMUNICATION

To become friends with their children, parents must recognize that children are separate and autonomous individuals who belong to God. At a Grace Church fellowship meeting, Dr. Lin, a child psychologist, spoke at length about the unhealthy tendency for Chinese parents to want perfect children and therefore make excessive demands on them. To solve this problem, he offered two principles of parenting:

> 1. Remember that your children are gifts from God. As parents you are managers of God's gifts for eighteen years of their lives. Learning how to be a good manager means learning not be a control freak.
> 2. Remember that kids are their own person—God's person. Learn to respect them.

Here Dr. Lin offers a new model of the self and family. Instead of prioritizing the collectivity over the individual, as the traditional family does, Dr. Lin suggests that in the Christian family, the collectivity exists for the development of the individual. Christianity consecrates, and does not repress, the individuality of each child by referring to her as "God's person." The role of Christian parents is not to lord their will over that of the child but to respectfully develop the particular calling that God has given their child. Parents must help their children become the unique selves that God created them to be. No matter how well intentioned, parents, as managers, need to be wary that their own self-will does not interfere with God's plan for their children. As Dr. Lin warns, "Don't try to make a Mozart out of a Michael Jordan."

Immigrant parents also learn that the key to becoming friends with their children is communication. Friendship is perhaps a trickier type of relationship to negotiate than the hierarchical relationship that characterized traditional parental interactions. Whereas in traditional parent-child relations communication is unidirectional from the parent to the child, a friendship assumes a mutual relationship between two equals. A friendship requires both parties to give and take, speak, and listen. Taiwanese children are well trained to listen to parents, but parents don't know the language of their children. In a family retreat at Grace Church, another American-educated Chinese psychologist told the audience of immigrant parents ranging from their thirties to fifties, "You have to speak to kids in their own language. Learn the trendy words like "cool" and "phat." Learn the names of popular rock stars like the Backstreet Boys and Britney Spears."

Immigrants articulate this very same emphasis on communication in their own families. "Communication skills are the key to a strong family," Mrs. Su, a mother of three, tells me. She claims, "We can't order our kids any more, we have to communicate with them. It's not the way it used to be in Taiwan, where you can just say 'no.'"

Respondents shared how they now try to listen to their children. Consider the experience of Mrs. Chang:

> Before, if my kids did something wrong I would yell, "Why do you do this and why do you do that?" I didn't know what they were feeling. Now I look back

and think that they must have been very scared. Now I've changed my behavior because I know that I acted wrong. I discuss things with my kids and I encourage them to tell me how they really are feeling. I changed. I seldom yell now.

Parents are more likely to designate special "family times" on a daily or weekly basis. For example, respondents told me that they incorporate daily or weekly family Bible studies where family members gather to sing, read the Bible, share their experiences, and pray together. By cultivating their children's spiritual lives, parents are simultaneously cultivating family ties.

Immigrants learn through the church that strong families are no longer built on a sense of obligation and indebtedness, the pillars of the old ways of filial piety. Instead, parents and children now cultivate lasting family ties through developing communication and affection for one another. In fact, traditional styles of parenting are more of a liability than an assurance of continuing family ties in the United States. Commenting on traditional styles of parenting, Dr. Wu said, "Once your children grow up and become teenagers, then there will be a lot of trouble if you follow the old traditional way. The gap will only grow."

Mrs. Wong, a mother of two, expressed similar fears of excessively individualistic children:

As a parent I worry. But if you don't have good communication with your child before they become mature adults then you will worry even more. They'll become teenagers and graduate and then say "bye-bye." No more parents, because I don't understand you and you don't understand me. They'll just leave you!

## THE COSTS OF FRIENDSHIP—RELINQUISHING PARENTAL CONTROL

Despite the solutions that the immigrant Christian church offers to Taiwanese parents, these benefits do not come without some costs. By making Christ the head of the family and attempting to become friends with their children, parents lose some of the authority that they might have in Confucian tradition. Just as the parents can use biblical teachings to justify their own disciplinary decisions, children can use biblical teachings to defend their will against that of their parents. For example, one respondent recounts how after scolding her son for misbehaving he responded, "Mom, you didn't listen to what the pastor said at church! You didn't listen. You should just talk to me and not yell at me!" Another respondent claims that she feels ashamed if she misses church on Sunday because her daughter will reprimand her.

Some parents complain that their children can be "too Christian" by prioritizing church over their schoolwork. One high school student even printed on his namecard, "Part-Time Southern California High School Student, Full-Time Christian," to advertise that his Christian commitments supersede his academic commitments. Planning and participating in church youth activities can occupy precious time that parents prefer to be spent on academic work. Christian parents have a very difficult time justifying to their children that schoolwork comes before church. The youth pastor, Pastor Tom, claims that several parents have come to him, hoping that as the pastor he can convince their children not be so involved at church. Given what he truly believes, that Christ comes first, he is in a difficult position.

When religious commitments compete with academics, Christian teachings do not necessarily work to further parents' interests. Indeed, Christian teaching may not always create family harmony, but can lead to new and different tensions. Taiwanese youth who feel beleaguered by excessive academic demands from their parents may strategically use Christianity to lessen their parents' expectations. These educated and professional parents who see their children as the beneficiaries of their own academic excellence may find these teachings challenging and threatening.

With Christ as the head of the household, parents can be proven wrong. Some respondents told me how they have learned to apologize to their children: Before they could not imagine doing any such thing. Parents learn that in their "friendship" with their children both parties must be willing to change and compromise. Mrs. Huang told me that her disapproval of her daughter's white boyfriend had caused a great deal of tension in their relationship. After her daughter pointed out that God created everyone equal, she reflected on this for awhile and prayed about it. She then came to the conclusion that she was wrong. She asked for her daughter's forgiveness and made the attempt to accept the young man for "who he really is."

Consider how Mrs. Lin, a deaconess who is a dentist in her mid-forties, now speaks of parenting as a collaboration between her and her two teenage sons:

> The difference between me as a mother versus my parents is that I am able to come down to their [the children's] level and tell them that I'm not perfect. These are my limits and I need you to chip in and help out. When I was a child, we were taught in school the Confucius teaching that parents are never wrong, and therefore you don't dare challenge your parents. But here, as an immigrant family, my husband and I both have to work. I'm not at home a lot, and my influence is so limited, and yet they're so open to the world online and on TV. I was very worried, especially when my sons were in that fourteen, fifteen age range. What helped us go through that was for us to bring it up and talk about it. I was fearful, and I talked about how difficult it was for me, and I told my son at the time, "I am only one mother. Only one pair of hands. I'm pulling

you on one side and the world is pulling you on the other side. Compared to the world, I'm powerless. If you chose to fall on this side, then the tug-of-war is over. And so I need your help.

## CONCLUSION

Given the dominance of the surrounding American culture, Taiwanese immigrants have little choice but to accept a loss of control over their children. But rather than viewing this as a threat, Christianity redefines what it means to be a good parent. God does not want parents lording over their children. God is the head of the household, and parents are to be good managers by helping children develop their God-given talents and callings. A good family is based on relationships of mutual respect, love, and communication rather than fear and obligation.

At the same time, Christianity helps parents maintain control over their children, however, using a very different moral mechanism than Confucianism—religious piety rather than filial piety. Through the language of religious discipleship rather than familial obligation, parents are able to effectively discipline their children and teach them traditional moral values. By framing these traditional values as Christian values and by considering moral agency rather than moral indebtedness the basis of their actions, the church melds Confucian ends with more culturally effective Christian means.

While sharing certain Confucian values, evangelical Christianity is also critical of the generational hierarchy and lack of emotion that characterize traditional Confucian parent-child relationships. Instead, evangelical Christianity sanctifies more democratic relationships between parents and children, and teaches new practices that cultivate open communication and sharing. Instead of regarding these changes as the loss of tradition or Americanization, Taiwanese American Christians welcome these transformations as a movement toward becoming a more Christian family.

## AFTERWORD

I am a second-generation Taiwanese American and stood on the receiving end of the Taiwanese-immigrant parental fears I write about. This was both an advantage and disadvantage to my research. Because I was ethnically one of them, I fit fairly seamlessly into the community I studied. The church perceived me as familiar and sympathetic, which I was. Most respondents trusted me very quickly. Many respondents thought that I was an expert on family issues and were eager to share their stories. Although I had very little constructive advice for these parents, their perception of me as a familiar expert allowed me access to their family lives. At times I was shocked, but of course deeply honored, by people's openness with me. They cried, they confessed, they confided. I truly think it was this combination of being both an insider and an outsider that allowed them to both trust me like one of them, and to freely air their dirty laundry to me like to a stranger.

Distance from those issues I struggled with as a teenager helped me to see things from the perspective of immigrant parents. I was personally moved by their stories and felt a great deal of compassion and indeed empathy for them. At the same time, my training as a sociologist taught me to view their personal stories in the larger context of impersonal social institutions and structures. Sometimes I felt torn about dissecting experiences that felt so close to me under the sociological apparatus. The stories hit close to home. Conducting ethnography on something so familiar was at first disorienting. I imagine it's like wearing bifocals for the first time. I saw the same phenomenon through two different lenses. The challenge for me as an ethnographer in this project was to learn to operate biculturally, as a sociologist and Taiwanese American, in a familiar world.

## NOTES

Portions of this chapter appeared previously in my article "From Filial Piety to Religious Piety: Evangelical Christianity Reconstructing Taiwanese Immigrant Families in the United States," published in *International Migration Review* 40 (3): 573–602.

1. I use pseudonyms to protect the identity of individuals and institutions in this paper.
2. By "Chinese," I am referring to people of Chinese ancestry rather than national identity, and thus include people from Mainland China, Taiwan, Hong Kong, and others in the Chinese diaspora. "Taiwanese" specifically refers to people from Taiwan, including post-1945 Mainlanders.

## REFERENCES

Bellah, Robert N., Richard Madsen, William M. Sullivan, Ann Swidler, and Steven M. Tipton. 1985. *Habits of the heart: Individualism and commitment in American life.* New York: Harper and Row.

Chen, Carolyn. Forthcoming. *Getting saved in America: Taiwanese immigrants converting to evangelical Christianity and Buddhism.* Princeton, NJ: Princeton University Press.

Dart, John. 1997. "Poll studies Chinese Americans." *Los Angeles Times,* July 5.

Ebaugh, Helen R., and Janet S. Chafetz. 2000. *Religion and the new immigrants: Continuities and adaptations in immigrant congregations.* Walnut Creek, CA: AltaMira.

Hunter, John D. 1987. *Evangelicalism: The coming generation.* Chicago: University of Chicago Press.

Jeung, Russell. 2004. *Faithful generations: Race and new Asian American churches.* New Brunswick, NJ: Rutgers University Press.

Lin, Chi-Yau Cindy, and Victoria R. Fu. 1990. "A comparison of child-rearing practices among Chinese, immigrant Chinese, and caucasian-American parents." *Child Development* 61 (2): 429–33

Ly, Phoung. 2003. "Immigrants help to reenergize U.S. Christianity." *The Washington Post,* February 4.

Min, Pyong Gap 1998. *Changes and conflicts: Korean immigrant families in New York.* Boston: Allyn and Bacon.

———. 2003. "Immigrants' religion and ethnicity: A comparison of Korean Christian and Indian Hindu immigrants." In *Revealing the sacred in Asian and Pacific America,* ed. Jane Naomi Iwamura and Paul Spickard, 125–42. New York: Routledge.

Ng, Franklin. 1998. *The Taiwanese Americans.* Westport, CT: Greenwood Press.

Smith, Christian. 1998. *American evangelicalism: Embattled and thriving.* Chicago and London: University of Chicago Press.

Suh, Sharon A. 2005. "Mapping the Buddist terrain in Korean American communities." Paper presented at the Association for Asian American Studies annual conference, Los Angeles, CA.

Tobin, Joseph J., David Y. H. Wu, and Dana H. Davidson. 1989. *Preschool in three cultures: Japan, China and the United States.* New Haven, CT: Yale University Press.

Warner, R. Stephen, and Judith Wittner, ed. 1998. *Gatherings in diaspora: Religious communities and the new immigration.* Philadelphia: Temple University Press.

Waters, Mary. 1999. *Black identities: West Indian immigrant dreams and American realities.* Cambridge, MA: Harvard University Press.

Wilcox, Bradford. 1998. "Conservative Protestant childrearing: Authoritarian or authoritative?" *American Sociological Review* 63:796–809.

———. 2004. *Soft patriarchs and new men: How Christianity shapes fathers and husbands.* Chicago: University of Chicago Press.

Yang, Fenggang. 1999a. *Chinese Christians in America: Conversion, assimilation, and adhesive identities.* University Park, PA: Pennsylvania State University Press.

———. 1999b. ABC and XYZ: Religious, ethnic and racial identities of new second generation Chinese in Christian churches. *Amerasia Journal* 25: 89–114.

Yang, Fenggang, and Helen Rose Ebaugh. 2001. "Transformation in new immigrant religions and their global implications." *American Sociological Review* 2: 269–88.

Zhou, Min, and Carl L. Bankston III. 1998. *Growing up American: How Vietnamese children adapt to life in the United States.* New York: Russell Sage Foundation.

# 14

## Choosing Chastity

### Redefining the Sexual Double Standard in the Language of Choice

*M. Eugenia Deerman*

Twenty-five years after Woodstock, thousands of teenagers from across the nation rallied on the National Mall. Just like at Woodstock, the talk on July 29, 1994, was all about music and sex. Only this time the music was contemporary Christian rock, and the sex was really not-sex, since these teens had gathered to champion chastity. That morning, teens belonging to True Love Waits, the first (and now the largest) chastity campaign in the nation, pushed more than 200,000 wire wickets into the acres of grass stretching from the Washington Monument to the U.S. Capitol. Each wicket bore a three-by-five-inch index card in a plastic sleeve. Each card, signed by a teenager (and sometimes by his or her parents), read:

> Believing that true love waits, I make a commitment to God, myself, my family, my friends, my future mate, and my future children to be sexually abstinent from this day until the day that I enter a biblical marriage relationship.

At the rally, Baptist youth minister Richard Ross recounted to 25,000 cheering teens the story of how the pledges came about. The year before, he said, he had been approached by teenaged girls in his youth group at the Tulip Grove Baptist Church in Nashville, Tennessee. Sure that they were the only virgins in their school, the girls felt isolated and under pressure from their peers to have sex. To help them and others facing the same situation, Ross started True Love Waits, a group that gets chaste teens to promote chastity to other teens. During the ensuing year, the Southern Baptist Convention extended organizational and financial support to True Love Waits, thereby ensuring the success of this rally on the Mall.

Holding the rally concurrently with the annual Youth for Christ conference guaranteed the presence of thousands of evangelical teens in D.C. that weekend. A teen-to-teen evangelism group founded in 1944, Youth for Christ teaches young people to "bring others to Christ" in an activist mode, much as 1960s organizations trained civil rights movement activists to recruit young people for the movement. Many evangelical Christian churches cover travel and lodging costs for teenagers wishing to participate in Youth for Christ events. Underway for two days before the True Love Waits rally, the conference already had teens revved up.

Between Ross's cheerleading and the explicitly pro-chastity lyrics of the bands that played into the rainy evening, teens got the message: Virginity is in, and chastity until marriage will keep you safe from AIDS. One band, DC Talk, covered songs from their gold album, including "I Don't Want It" and "That Kind of Girl." That this virginity campaign especially targets teenage girls can be seen not only in the latter song's title but also in the ubiquitous presence of "pledge rings." Pledge rings resemble wedding rings, and girls wear them as symbols of virginity to be presented to husbands on their wedding night.

On the same day as the rally, one hundred and fifty representatives from True Love Waits met with President Clinton to give him the important message that they were waiting for true love and marriage. Their political agenda sought more federal support for abstinence-based sex education.

## A BROADER TREND?

During the same period that found conservative evangelical teenagers pledging chastity, popular media were proclaiming virginity a chic trend among young people throughout the country. In magazines ranging from *Teen* to *U.S. News & World Report*, self-proclaimed virgins related how and why they stayed chaste. Rarely did their explanations refer to their religious convictions. A representative example from an October 1994 *Newsweek* article reads, in part:

> Back when Mom was a fledgling feminist, it was hip to declare, "It's my body and I'll sleep with as many guys as I want to." Now, even high-schoolers insist, "It's my body and I don't have to sleep with anyone if I don't want to." Of course, it's hard to lose a boyfriend—especially if it's because you didn't sleep with him—but life doesn't end. Sitting in her dorm room at tiny Rivier College in New Hampshire, Ebony Doran, a freshman and a virgin, admits that sex is a big part of life. "Yes, I think about it," says Ebony, 17. "But I know that I control my body and my mind." For many teenagers, that makes virginity even more liberating than sex.

Throughout the 1990s, popular magazines enthusiastically proclaimed that many young adults, like Ebony, were choosing chastity. Journalists presented their choice as a change of heart from the previous generations' espousal of sexual liberation; young adults of the 1990s wanting to say "no" to sex.

## THE CIRCULATION OF STORIES ABOUT FAMILY LIFE

This chapter examines an unusual type of teen sex story, a story about teenagers and young adults not having sex, or "choosing chastity" until marriage, in order to be prepared both physically and emotionally to become good marriage partners in good families. This story about young people and virginity started circulating in the early 1990s in magazines ranging from *Teen* to *Time*. The analysis of such stories presented in this chapter is based on eighty-five journalistic accounts about teenagers and young adults choosing chastity before marriage that were published between January 1, 1990, and December 31, 1999, in periodicals ranging from teen magazines (*Seventeen, Teen,* and *Sassy*) to magazines for an older female readership (*Glamour, Vogue,* and *Essence*), as well as several news and political commentary periodicals including *Time, U.S. News & World Report,* and *Harper's.* This sample contains all of the popular press stories about young adults choosing chastity that appeared in widely circulated magazines and that could be identified by searching Lexus-Nexus, using the keywords *virginity, chastity,* and *abstinence,* from 1970 to 1999. No such stories were published in the 1970s; one appeared in the 1980s, the rest in the 1990s.

Approaching these accounts of young adults choosing chastity as stories allows us to exploit the unique relationship between stories and human experience—stories are performances that mold experience, even as they comment on prior experience and events (Bruner 1986, Polkinghorne 1988). Stories can represent what is considered by the tellers to be morally desirable by modeling "good" behaviors, experiences, or events. In this sense, stories hold generative power, and we can use them to create identities, for example. Stories can also represent what is undesirable and selectively show us the predicted consequences of doing wrong. In this sense, stories are constraining and may be used to do the work of teaching what is shameful or criminal, as well as how such actions may be punished. Stories convey particular viewpoints about what we should value and how we should see our world. So, what do these stories about chastity offer us? According to their promptings, how can each of us be our best self? According to their admonitions, what kind of families should we value? In presenting a case study of stories about young adults choosing chastity, I answer these questions. I show that these stories use the language of freedom, choice, and sexual liberation, while at the same time offering normative conceptualizations of femininity, masculinity, and heterosexuality that are elements of the ideology of the SNAF, a powerful family ideal against which other family types are judged as deviant and lacking (Smith 1993).

## CHOOSING CHASTITY: PLOT, CHARACTERS, AND THEMES

The narrative below has been distilled from the eighty-plus journalistic accounts that appeared throughout the 1990s about teenagers choosing chastity. The narrative arc of "Choosing Chastity" unfolds as follows:

> Nowadays, teens aren't sexual innocents. And we teens realize that sex is dangerous. We're taking our destiny into our own hands and making a personal commitment to abstinence until marriage, or at least until we are really in love. Abstinence is especially crucial for girls, since teen girls who have sex risk being labeled sluts, while boys who have sex get to brag about it. But both boys and girls recognize that having sex too soon risks squandering our chances for true love, for example by getting an STD (sexually transmitted disease) or getting pregnant. So, by choosing chastity, we're achieving real freedom, and the freedom to say no to sex will keep us safe until we meet our true loves and live happily ever after.

This narrative is told in a first-person voice because journalists structured their accounts as if young people were telling what happened. In the narrative example of "Choosing Chastity" the causal sequence conveyed is that, having identified sex as an extremely dangerous activity, young adults are therefore launching a new sexual revolution. This second sexual revolution champions (as a choice) a mandate to remain abstinent until marriage.

"Choosing Chastity" relies heavily on one protagonist, the "sexy-but-chaste" young adult. Virgins are described in terms like the following drawn from a February 1995 *Vogue* article on the new interest in virginity:

> Witness Lakita Garth, a born-again, 26-year-old spokesperson for a Los Angeles-based group called Athletes for Abstinence. Her agenda was heavy Christian, but she was no humorless, scrubbed-faced zealot. She was a beautiful African-American entertainer who delivered her abstinence rap with impassioned ease, talking about condoms and blow jobs and sperm with relaxed candor.

This *Vogue* account suggests that virginity is no longer about sexual innocence. In place of the blushing virgin of an earlier era, the reader confronts a virgin who talks easily about sex, seems to know a lot about sex, and yet, abstains from sex. That is the virgin of the 1990s.

The magazine stories attribute great "personal resolve" to the sexy-but-chaste hero of "choosing chastity." Resolve is necessary in this story, because peer pressure and popular culture present tantalizing images of sex. Even if fully persuaded that sex is a more dangerous activity than these images admit, the teen hero faces a daunting challenge because sex outside marriage is popularly treated as the ultimate sexual freedom. According to the "Choosing Chastity" narrative, sexy-but-chaste teens realize that the sexual freedom portrayed by the media promises far less than the freedom promised by chastity. For example, the narrator of the *Newsweek* article, "Virgin Cool" (October 1994) claims, "For many teenagers control over one's body makes virginity even more liberating than sex." Similarly, the March 1994 *Mademoiselle* article on "The New Chastity" asserts, "In the 90s, young people who just say no to sex see abstinence as a way to get control of their lives and bodies." Thus, readers are encouraged to understand choosing chastity as an effort by young adults to act responsibly—to be abstinent—in the face of dangers posed by sex. According to the plotline offered by "Choosing Chastity," abstinence affords a safe haven from these dangers.

That theme, virginity-as-safety, undercuts the repeated assertions that young adults are *choosing* to abstain from sex. The narrative plainly suggests that sex poses particular dangers for unmarried, young adults by describing a setting marked by risk. For example, the May 24, 1993 *Time* article titled "Making the Case for Abstinence" opens with "Amid all the anguish, confusion and mixed signals surrounding teenage sexuality . . ." *Mademoiselle*, in March 1994, suggests that "The New Chastity" involves young women like Lisa Peluso, abstinent for two years, who is described in these terms:

> The slender brunette had enjoyed her relations with men, "[but] sex outside of marital commitment is only full of fear and anxiety." In choosing celibacy, she became part of a growing number of young people who abstain from sex for many reasons. The threat of being infected with HIV or one of many other sexually transmitted diseases now on the rise has caused many would-be sexually active people to have second thoughts about having intercourse. [Therefore] in an age when intercourse can be life-threatening, people are taking the time to decide whether or not to have sex.

Though *Mademoiselle* hints at various motivations behind the decision to abstain from sex, the narrative in fact only offers one reason: Young people are afraid to have sex because it is dangerous. In a *Seventeen* article (June 1994), the narrator says, "I spoke with a lot of virgins and every one said she was terrified of AIDS . . . abstinence is always going to be the best way to avoid STDs, AIDS, and pregnancy." Included in this article were quotes (ranging from five to twelve sentences in length) from nineteen young women. Three say that having sex is dangerous:

> A: I'm not ready to NOT be a virgin . . . there's so much pressure—pregnancy, AIDS, it can make you nervous.
> B: I came close once. But . . . something about the situation didn't feel right. . . . At this point though, I'm just worried about diseases.
> C: I enjoy hanging out with my friends and feeling comfortable, rather than worrying about what's going to happen after the movie. Knowing my luck, I would get pregnant the first time.

Not one of the young women interviewed mentions condoms or contraceptive use as a means of preventing disease and unintended pregnancy. It is as if these women see sex as irrefutably dangerous, with virginity and abstinence affording the only safe harbor. It is primarily women and girls (not men or boys) who voice this view of sex as entailing both physical and emotional dangers. For example, a young woman interviewed in the last article quoted says:

> There's no way I'm going to jeopardize my feelings [by not waiting]. If girls go to a party and end up doing it, the guys won't call the next day. Can you imagine how that makes girls feel? I'd be totally hurt! I don't want to get hurt that way.

Another says, "It's stressful trying to wait" . . . "but if he weren't willing to wait, he would get nowhere because there's no way I'm going to jeopardize my feelings." It seems clear that these young women construct virginity as a haven from the dangers of sex. And they appear to believe that, somehow, those same dangers will evaporate once they are married or in a committed relationship. While it might seem natural for this narrative to focus on the dangers facing unmarried young adults, it is not quite credible, since neither marriage nor commitment necessarily precludes all physical or emotional harm from a relationship. Nevertheless, the narrative logic of "Choosing Chastity" constructs sex within committed relationships very differently from all other kinds of sex. Marital or committed relationship sex is safe sex; that is, young adults will not face emotional or physical hurt in sexual relations with their spouses or committed partners. It is this logic that forms the foundation for the virginity-as-safety theme.

Virginity-as-safety undercuts the assertion of choice in "Choosing Chastity" in two ways. First, although the narrators of these accounts suggest young adults are choosing to abstain from sex, the young virgins themselves describe their fear of the dangers posed by sex. Instead of choosing to be chaste, they actually are seeking sanctuary. Second, the narrative assumes (by the internal logic of the narrative arc) that virginity is safe for unmarried or single young adults, while married or partnered young adults face no sexual dangers at all. This assumption will appear again in the "myth of happily ever after," which I take up later in the chapter.

## THE NEW VIRGINITY

In "Choosing Chastity," provocative language describes chastity itself. In fact, for some virgins, chastity is redefined in terms that amount to "everything but" intercourse. A few accounts claim that virginity is about "maintain[ing] deniability," as *Vogue* put it in a May 1992 story titled "Virgins with Attitude." The virgin author of a June 1997 *Glamour* article titled "The Hot, Happy Sex Life of a Virgin," as well as respondents interviewed in "Virgins with Attitude," champion "technical virginity," defined as follows:

> A technical virgin believes she does not necessarily need to be innocent, as long as she maintains deniability. Virtually any sexual activity short of penetrative intercourse is on the menu—and sometimes it's smorgasbord night . . . Bonnie explains that with each of her boyfriends, "I progressively went further. We have oral sex, both cunnilingus and fellatio; we engage in humping or dry sex, and mutual masturbation. I don't necessarily believe that all these things are scripturally ok, but one thing led to another, and I guess it's a safe compromise."

Similarly, the narrator of a July 1993 *Essence* article titled "Young, Hot, and Celibate" states:

> The new celibacy isn't the new morality. Just because you're not having intercourse doesn't make you asexual. We're engaging in sex on different levels. Those levels range from strict chastity unless one is in a "serious relationship" to "getting to know a whole lot more than a lover's first name before we go to bed."

According to this story, it's not virginity per se that is the issue, but "casual sex," that is, sex that occurs outside an ongoing relationship or with a casual acquaintance, that marks the boundary between good sex and bad sex. These stories appear purposefully to stretch traditional notions of virginity, while staying within a boundary that allows some women to continue identifying as virgins.

## TRADITIONAL VIRGINITY AND THE NEW VIRGINITY

The new virginity retains some elements of what we might call traditional virginity. These elements include defining virginity in heterosexual terms and limiting discussion of virgins almost entirely to women. In these stories virginity is explicitly a concern of (some) heterosexuals and can only be "lost" through heterosexual intercourse. This construction emerges very clearly in a *Seventeen* "Sex and Body" column. This is a regular advice column which answers questions, ostensibly from readers, about their physical bodies (menstruation is a frequent topic) and sexual activity. In September 1993 the column was exclusively about virginity. The title "VIRGIN TERRITORY" appeared in bold print in the center of the page. Three letters from readers were positioned around this title. Each letter had a bold-faced heading. The first two headings appeared almost directly across from each other and read "I lied and said I wasn't a virgin" and "I lied and said I *was* a virgin." The third heading, which appeared in the lower-right-hand corner, read "Are you still a virgin if you use tampons?" The top of the opposite page was taken up by an ad for a douche (the bolded caption is "Put Your Body in a Good Mood"!) and the bottom half had one last letter asking "Am I a Virgin or Not?"

The first two letters were from young women worried that their boyfriends (with whom they are considering having sex) will discover their "real" sexual status. The response reassures them "there's no way that a guy can tell whether or not you're a virgin," yet nevertheless advises that "you ought to tell [your boyfriend] the truth." The risk of STDs is summoned in both cases. The virgin should be "comfortable enough" to talk honestly with her boyfriend, and the non-virgin "owe[s] it to [her boyfriend] to let him know" because of the health risk involved. In both cases the sexual status of the boyfriend is not mentioned. Leaving unquestioned whether the boyfriend is a virgin or not makes his sexual status strangely irrelevant in a context where girls' sexual status is considered to have great importance. It appears that we do not ask "Is he a virgin?" or "Can sex with him put me at risk for STDs?" Instead, we ask what girls need to do, whether they are sexually inexperienced or not. The implication here is that what counts is what girls are doing sexually. And it counts because, whether the girl has had sex or not, STDs are a risk. The logic is little unclear. We can imagine that a sexually active girl might be a carrier of some STD, but the article does not clearly state that the virgin might risk contracting an STD from her boyfriend. Although the risk receives only a nebulous articulation, responsibility for averting it more obviously falls on her shoulders.

The letters asking for clarification of the boundary between virgin and non-virgin explicitly define virginity in heterosexual terms. Girls want to know "how far they can go" and still be virgins. One worries that tampons will tear her hymen; her request that the advice columnist "straighten me and my friends out" makes this question appear common to many girls. The response positions heterosexual intercourse as the dividing line between virginity and non-virginity.

> A virgin is quite simply someone who hasn't had sexual intercourse. Using tampons is obviously not the same as having had sex.

The second girl says that she and her boyfriend were "starting to have sex when we decided not to. He already put it in and tore the hymen." She appears to separate penetration from intercourse in her description of this sexual encounter. She offers a sort of sliding-scale from completed sex (which she and her boyfriend did not have) to this uncertain point of contact with retreat. The response acknowledges the ambiguity of her situation, but again, heterosexual intercourse remains the defining factor.

> Technically, if you've had sexual intercourse, you're not a virgin. I'm not sure whether what you and your boyfriend did qualifies as sexual intercourse. If you think you really didn't have sex, then you can probably think of yourself as someone who didn't really lose her virginity.

Here, normative heterosexuality defines what counts as sex and what counts as virginity. The hedges in the response (if you think . . . you can probably) dance around the declaration in the letter writer's description: "we decided not to." Such hedging may not offer a contradiction; however, it does offer at least two definitions of virginity. The first is physiological and is tied to penetrative, heterosexual sex. The second is psychological and is tied to an interpretive process of making sense of one's own experience. Both definitions assume heterosexuality, again bringing traditional notions of virginity to the fore.

At a very literal level, women carry the "Choosing Chastity" story. The main characters are female, which encourages the reader to think of virginity in terms of women. Traditional associations of virginity with "good girls" or purity as an asset possessed by women are thus made accessible as meaning-making tools for the reader. This happens immediately in titles that signal readers to expect a story about girls and young women, such as: "He's Ready, You're Not" and "Girls, Just Say Not Now." When titles are directed at young women, as if the narrator were speaking directly to a female readership, the entire story presents itself as relevant primarily to young women. The story titled "He's Ready, You're Not" offers sample phrases to use with "ready" boyfriends and advocates practicing in front of a mirror to achieve effective assertiveness. The second title unequivocally asserts that it is girls who must say no, or at least postpone sex until a later, presumably more appropriate, time.

Other story titles that let us know the protagonist is female right up front include, "What Girls Are Saying About All the Sex They're Not Having and Why" and "I've Read that Girls Can Feel Really Bad . . . After First Sex." These titles place responsibility for sexual boundaries squarely on young women. "All the sex [girls] are not having" suggests girls could choose to be very sexually active but are not doing so for some good reason that will be explained in the story. (As we saw above, boyfriends "are ready" for sex, but girls are not.) First sexual encounters appear to be portrayed as harmful to girls, at least in this venue where girls read about it, and the female reader presumably wants to know more. These stories are repeating an oft-stated expectation that unmarried young women must shoulder the entire burden of deciding the limits of sexual intimacy. Additionally, one can read these stories as saying that young men will nearly always be unable to decide in favor of less intimacy, thus leaving the limit-setting to women. Another way to think about it would be that the expectation for young men is that they are supposed to be sexual, whereas women are expected to set the limits on that sexuality. The differences here are subtle. I take these stories to say not that men are unable to make this decision, but that normatively men should not. In my view, then, it is not that men "can't help themselves," it is more that women are supposed to be responsible for setting the limits on sexual intimacy.

Virginity as primarily a matter of concern for women and girls is especially clear in first-person stories where a female protagonist tells her story. For example, in two stories titled "The Last American Virgin" and "Am I the Last Virgin?" only women talk about making decisions about virginity. These stories are only three years apart; the first appeared in *Seventeen* in August 1991 and the second in Essence in June 1994. Stories in the sample sometimes restrict discussion to women and virginity quite blatantly, as in the story from *Sassy* in December 1995 titled "Virgin Bride," for which there is no obvious "virgin groom" counterpart. Even titles without reference to a gendered subject (for example, "Virgin Cool," "Virgins with Attitude," and "Young, Hot, and Celibate") open with statements making it clear that the protagonist is female. The critical point here is that although virginity is, by definition, equally applicable to men and women, the stories about choosing chastity center virginity on women.

## RECREATING THE SEXUAL DOUBLE STANDARD IN STORIES ABOUT CHASTITY

The prior discussion showed how stories about choosing chastity focus on women and virginity. But why is virginity about women? Most people would say it is because women have something to lose, that is, sexual experience carries particular risks for women. A woman known to be sexually experienced could suffer a loss of reputation, and she runs several potential risks, for example, an unplanned pregnancy. The following passage from a 1994 article in *Newsweek* titled "Virgin Cool" explicitly states, but does not question, the continued power of the normative assumption that having sexual experience is positive for men, but negative for women.

By the time she's bought her first bra, every female child knows there's a sexual double standard—and that she's doomed to be on the losing end. . . . Girls explain how guys view them:

"Guys have a preconceived notion of what you are by what you look like," says Miesha, a 15-year-old woman-child.

"If you dress a little preppy, they think you're a virgin," adds Sweeney, shrouded safely, in work shirt and jeans.

"And on the day you put on something nice, they call you a 'ho,'" says Miesha. "They say, 'she's oversexed—she's no virgin.'"

The way this story is told, the narrator implies that a sexual double standard simply exists, with evidence provided by two protagonists, Sweeney and Miesha. First, we hear that the sexual behavior of a young woman is judged by her dress—and Sweeney, who identifies how this works, is playing it safe by dressing "in work shirt and jeans." Second, Miesha offers support for the claim by pointing out how dressing "nice" can lead to being judged as practicing undesirable sexual behavior. Neither Sweeney nor Miesha offers any challenge to the sexual double standard. It seems girls are simply obligated to protect their reputations by monitoring their behavior.

The gendered dictates of "Choosing Chastity" achieved by defining virginity in heterosexual terms and by limiting the discussion to young women's behavior become even more prescriptive when the double standard is repeatedly invoked as a reason for committing to abstinence. "Choosing Chastity" perpetuates the sexual double standard by naturalizing the social control over young women that rests upon the derogatory label "slut." Nowhere is this double standard questioned; rather, it serves to construct and constrain young women's sexual choices. For example, the September 1992 *Teen* article titled "He's Ready, You're Not!" offers this warning:

You may feel that sleeping with a guy will bring you closer together, make you an instant couple. But in fact, it can drive you further apart. Sex is no guarantee that a guy will stay with you. Turns out, guys who pressure a girl to say yes actually want a relationship with a girl that says no.

Coming from an "expert voice" in a popular teen magazine, this warning presents the double standard as both inevitable *and* something to work with: Be the girl that says no, and you will have the secure and intimate relationship you want. Because we can see the double standard so clearly deployed in these stories, we may find their failure to contest this lopsided construction of sexual behavior troubling. Instead of being contested, the double standard is simply to be integrated into young women's decisions to remain virgins.

In some cases, experts commenting on the double standard go even farther by implying that the double standard is irrevocable, making the best course of action for girls to monitor their behavior. This is clear in the following passage from an April 1992 *Psychology Today* article titled "Girls, Just Say Not Now":

> "I've asked teens, 'What would you call a guy who had sex with several different girls?'" says Cassell [author of a book on how to talk to teenagers about sex]. "The answer: 'a stud' or 'lucky.'"
>
> Cassell's advice to teens: Wait until you get out of high school, which is a small world unto itself with its own values and people who are ready to judge you.

Here, "the expert" appears to accept the double standard while also assuming that it is not part of the world outside high school. Her advice to "just wait" offers no way to view as unfair the fact that boys may gain prestige through sexual activity and girls may lose prestige through the same actions. There are two points deserving of challenge here. First, the sexual double standard (and its seemingly widespread acceptance) appears to afford young men and boys greater latitude in their personal relationships. The implicit acceptance of young men gaining sexual experience before marriage contrasts with the gendered dictates calling on women to avoid even the mere appearance of being sexually experienced, in order to escape being labeled "slut" or "ho," whereas young men have no such concerns. Evading this label might be connected to concerns about the place of women in families. It is not just that the label is pejorative; it is also that our expectations of women make sexual promiscuity (or the suggestion of sexual promiscuity) a threat to good standing, as a woman. Second, these stories implicitly threaten that men will not marry sexually experienced women, and may even not want to be in romantic relationships with them. These ideas reflect a traditional notion that men and women should have different approaches to sex: Men date sluts and marry virgins, but women should save sex for love and marriage.

## THE MYTH OF "HAPPILY EVER AFTER"

"Choosing Chastity" ultimately offers little more than a retreat to a fairytale wherein chastity promises to keep teenagers safe until they meet their true loves and live happily ever after. Consider how the virginity-as-safety theme undercuts claims of sexual agency. In these stories, sexy-but-chaste teens say they won't have sex now because of the dangers: STDs, AIDS, unintended pregnancy, and emotional injury. "Choosing Chastity" ties abstinence to the morally charged claim that sex before marriage provides only an illusory, and very dangerous, sexual freedom. The young adults in these accounts tell us that they recognize the dangers and realize that sexual freedom actually entails sexual restraint. Jenny, age seventeen, in *Seventeen's* "The No of the Nineties" (January 1991), bluntly states: "I don't have sex because I'm scared of getting AIDS." Emphasizing fear of the potential consequences of sex thus undermines the choice in "Choosing Chastity." Teenagers are not finding empowerment, they are running scared. They say that by waiting, they ensure for themselves fulfilling sex in a 'til-death-do-us-part marriage. For example, a 1994 article in *Teen* quotes three "vocal virgins" who say:

"True love will wait. If you really love someone and you share your feelings with them, you don't have sex until you get married." Jeremy Smith, 16.
  "I've chosen to give up a moment's thrill for an eternity of rewards." Michelle Donachy, 17.
  "I want to give the gift of virginity to my wife. I want it to be special, not something I do just to fit in." David Medford, 17.

When "Choosing Chastity" includes male virgins, very different terms describe their motivations and behaviors. For men, virginity involves an account of personal development and preparation on nonsexual dimensions. Interviewed by Dobie Green in *Jet* in January 1994, athlete A.C. Green, founder of "Athletes for Abstinence," states:

This is my lifestyle right now. I honestly look forward to getting married one day. I am not in my opinion, going to be a virgin all my life. . . . When God brings me a wife, a mate, then I look forward to joining with her and build [sic] that which is for us to build. So yes, I look forward to marriage very much, and I am preparing myself for her right now. And how I am doing this is by: (1) waiting, practicing abstinence, maintaining control in that area, and (2) developing all the other tools: emotional, social, financial, and of course, spiritual aspects of my life to get them in tune, in sync.

Green claims to be actively working *to achieve a marital relationship*—not running away from STDs or other dangers. Despite his statement that it is God who will "bring" a wife, Green expresses agency and is forward-looking in his actions. Although some articles that include male virgins stereotype them as inadequate men, all of the male virgins sound like Green, or assert their masculinity even more strongly. For example, in a description of a rally of virgins in D.C., Elgen Strait is quoted: "I don't want some stank ho who's going to leave me the next day!" He also described himself as waiting for a virgin bride so that he "could boldly go where no man has gone before." Presenting male virgins as proactive and perhaps hypermasculine levies no costs on men who choose abstinence. In contrast to women, who are reduced to safeguarding their virginity in order to procure a man who will marry them and make them safe from harm, male virgins gain a moral high ground from which to protect their interests (Green) and scorn sexually active women (Elgen).

"Choosing Chastity" equates virginity with safety, perpetuates a sexual double standard, and asserts that abstinence bestows true personal freedom. "Choosing Chastity" provides a prescriptive map of how one moves through teenhood and into adulthood. The plot line is that personal resolve (backed up by parental support) will carry young adults past the temptations of sex and through to happily ever after when they enter into the safety of marriage. The exhortation, "Be abstinent until marriage," is about family because it promises young adults a happily-ever-after family of their own. Marriage is the end of the story since it is clear that no one is advocating chastity for life.

## CONCLUSION

The package of ideas examined here describes these stories as being about heterosexuality; virginity presumes heterosexuality and has meaning for young men and women who envision themselves (eventually) married and forming families. Furthermore, these stories emphasize sexual restraint for girls and young women, with only cursory reflections on the virginity of boys or young men. The language of choice shapes the narrative arc, suggesting that young adults achieve some autonomy by choosing chastity, but the stories reinforce the sexual double standard. "Choosing Chastity" narrowly defines suitability for marriage (particularly for women) by reducing the desirable choices to just one: Virginity equals safety and the path to the "happily-ever-after" marriage fairytale. In this concluding section, my aim is to step back from the stories themselves to illustrate how they are also tied to ideas about the kind of women girls should want to be when they grow up, and how this, in turn, is connected to what kinds of relationships women should want to have. What makes these stories about family is that they offer prescriptions for what women *should* do and *why* if they want, in the future, to form their own families as wives and mothers.

The central, but implicit, assumption in these stories is that a family is made up of a suitable man and a suitable woman, but women's suitability for marriage depends upon standards different from those applied to men. Girls and women should remain virgins until marriage to signal that they are the right kind of woman for a traditional marriage. Young men and boys are not exactly pushed toward sexual experience, but during the pre-marriage period they clearly have different sexual options than their female counterparts.

In sum, the stories about choosing chastity analyzed in this chapter suggest that virginity implies something about the preconditions necessary for a successful and appropriate marital relationship. They suggest that by enacting proper sexual roles before marriage, these young men and women potentially demonstrate their suitability *for* marriage. It is important to note that these are not the only stories we as a society have about teenagers and sex, and certainly these are not the only stories we have about what it takes for "good families." I've presented an analysis of one kind of story that offers one set of cultural images of what makes a "good family." I want to suggest here only that these stories about teenagers choosing chastity offer a restricted set of representations of what is morally desirable (and undesirable), thus contributing to a similarly restricted understanding of what is of value about women, and of men.

## AFTERWORD

Studying these media stories about chastity involved a kind of mental shape-shifting, that is, trying to work my way toward seeing from the perspective of journalists writing for diverse audiences at a time of heightened efforts to advocate sexual abstinence for unmarried young people. As others have pointed out, abstinence is an enduring theme in American politics and culture, thus we trivialize it at the cost of losing purchase on the generative power of elements of American civil religion (our optimistic faith in the perfectibility of the individual, from bootstraps rhetoric to "just say no" campaigns). The trend I identified in the 1990s of describing abstinence as the "second sexual revolution" remains an important factor in the shaping of sex and sexuality in American culture. Beyond the True Love Waits rallies, such as the one described here, we now have "purity balls" (festive affairs where young women symbolically hand over their virginity to their father for safekeeping until marriage) and "abstinence-based" education, which lacks information on contraception and advocates abstinence until marriage. Such developments point to the continuing importance of heeding how abstinence, sex, and young people are framed in the popular media.

My sociological interest in these media stories grows out of a broader interest in how narratives figure in politics. I believe that stories not only carry meaning, they also provide the materials for the creation of new meanings. My analysis of these stories aims to show the richness of meanings around sexuality and gender offered by accounts of young people choosing chastity. Certainly, these are not the only stories circulating throughout American popular culture about young adults and sex. Other stories inform our understanding of the proper place for sex (and hence, for family) in the life course and in public life. The interplay of competing stories might be the next place to look for the origins of transformations to our public conceptions of sex and family.

## REFERENCES

Bruner, Jerome. 1986. *Actual minds, possible worlds.* Cambridge, MA: Harvard University Press.

Polkinghorne, Donald. 1988. *Narrative knowing and the human sciences.* New York: SUNY Press.

Smith, Dorothy. 1993. "The standard North American family." *Journal of Family Issues* 14: 50–65.

# AFTERWORD

# 15

## What Is a Family?

*Kathryn M. Dudley*

It has become commonplace to observe that American families aren't what they used to be. Usually we know what is meant by this: More marriages end in divorce, more mothers are in the workforce, and more children are raised in households headed by single, lesbian, or gay parents. That "the family" is changing seems undeniable, regardless of how we feel about these changes. Yet, as the ethnographic studies in this volume suggest, perhaps it is time to reexamine the received wisdom. Are families *really* changing? And what is a "family" anyway?

When ethnographers study families, they typically keep an open mind about who constitutes a family in a particular society. Rather than deciding what a family is (or isn't) before beginning their research, they allow the subjects of their study to define the contours of family life in personally meaningful terms, even if their particular conception of family is not widely shared. Thus, for example, a young man may say that he is trying to reunite his "family" after the state has acted on evidence of neglect and forcibly removed children from his home (see Young, this volume). Although this man is not the biological father of both children involved and is not married to their mother, the ethnographer does not challenge his assertion of spousal and parental responsibility. Rather, through the sensitive exploration of what "fatherhood" means to this individual and other low-income African Americans, we come to appreciate how important secure employment is, not just to the formation and maintenance of family ties but to the provision of a safe home for children.

An openness to claims of kinship that are not recognized by the society at large allows ethnographers to document the significant relationships that people create in their everyday lives. What matters most in an ethnographic portrait of the family is identifying who actually performs the work of kinship in a given culture or community: who participates in the relations of exchange—economic and otherwise—that support and maintain the family unit, however it may be defined by participants themselves. Therefore, the ethnographer interested in "gay families" will document the familial status of non-biological gay or lesbian co-parents, even if the church and state do not. Including these individuals in the social institution under investigation—i.e., in "the family"—not only acknowledges their *claim to be* family members but recognizes that they are *claimed as* kin by other members of the family. Thus, when a young boy announces in a classroom discussion of same-sex marriage that his gay uncles are valued members of his family, he personalizes the issue for his teacher and classmates by asserting his own familial identity in relationship to these men (see Pash, this volume). From this perspective, it is being enmeshed in intimate domestic relationships involving reciprocal obligations of material and emotional support—of claims and counter-claims—that makes you a member of a family.

A focus on the reciprocal obligations at the core of family life requires the ethnographer to look at how families provision themselves and how these survival strategies structure relationships within the household. What family members believe they *owe one another* is always a creative synthesis of normative expectations concerning ideal family relationships and the social realities impinging upon a particular kin group. Therefore, if we wish to investigate how the institution of the family may be changing in America today, it is especially instructive to examine the potential tension between the kind of family people aspire to have and the kind of family they are able to achieve. Framing our question this way allows us to distinguish between the cultural ideal people say they are striving for and the social opportunities or barriers they confront in their efforts to realize it. Moreover, such a distinction allows us to determine where exactly a transformation may be occurring: Is it in the cultural conception of what "the family" should be, or in the social conditions that support or undermine certain family forms? Or is it a combination of both?

Among the surprising findings of the research in this volume is the discovery that relatively few Americans seem satisfied with their work and family lives, even when they belong to social groups whose lifestyles are commonly taken to epitomize the ideal form of the family. The anxieties that bedevil the prototypical "soccer moms" of the nation's predominantly white, middle-class, suburban communities are, at first glance, hard to reconcile with evidence of their wealth and social privilege (see Descartes and Kottak, this volume). After all, these are women who, supported by a spouse's income, have the option of cutting back on or eliminating paid work outside the home in order to devote themselves intensively to the socialization and well-being of their children. Yet even in their demographically homogenous, ostensibly "safe" residential enclaves, dangers lurk in the form of unmediated exposure to the deviant ways of life thought to thrive outside the community's boundaries. Thus, despite the considerable resources these households are able to draw upon to construct their version of the family, one senses that complete control over the environmental hazards they fear will always elude them. No amount of "boundary maintenance" can ever fully banish daily threats that appear in the guise of unsolicited phone calls, untoward messages on the evening news, or unregulated contact with children from families unlike their own. Under these circumstances, we would do well to ask if the cultural ideal American families aspire to can be realized by anyone at all.

The burden of "intensive mothering" assumed by middle-class white women is remarkably similar to the maternal vigilance exercised by African-American women who elect to raise their children in a predominantly black urban environment in an effort to protect them from the ravages of racism (see Winkler, this volume). Although the neighborhoods in which middle-class black parents seek refuge tend to be more diverse economically, these families share with their white counterparts a model of parenting which places the onus of responsibility for a child's socialization on a "mother" who must mediate between a dangerous world and the presumed safety of the domestic sphere, and on a "father" who must provide the economic wherewithal to allow them to fulfill this moral obligation. Yet even in households where such a division of labor is feasible, the cultural ideal remains difficult, if not impossible, to fully realize. For, as these mothers readily admit, the task of helping children contend with a racialized society is never simply a matter of counteracting negative images or experiences with positive portraits of their own racial group. Rather, it involves a heightened alertness to the multiple cultural contexts within and between which children must learn to move, and a simultaneous commitment to avoiding the indoctrination of racist ideas themselves. It is a tall order in the best of worlds, but especially so when residential segregation is employed, by choice or necessity, as the means to this end.

To complicate matters, we must remind ourselves that cultural ideals have a social history. Different class, ethnic, and racial groups develop survival strategies to cope with historically specific conditions, and these collective experiences give rise to distinctive conceptions of normative sex and gender roles. Thus, although the parental division of labor epitomized by the "breadwinner husband" and the "stay-at-home wife" is often said to be based on "traditional" gender roles, it is imperative to ask: traditional for whom? As the historical and contemporary experience of African American families attests, powerful social forces have actively prevented some social groups from forming families that conform to this sex and gender ideal. So pervasive have such barriers been that this form of the family is regarded, within certain communities, as a risky or impractical goal (see Barnes, this volume). From this perspective, the process of actualizing a particular family form involves not only attaining the economic status required to support it but negotiating potentially conflicting cultural expectations about the desirability of that choice. For women raised in communities that value a woman's academic achievement and work outside the home, the decision to leave professional careers to devote time to their families may be met with disappointment and dismay. Our understanding of their predicament—as well as that of those who remain in the workforce—is not aided by the popular notion that staying at home with children is a "return" to traditional values. These women are forging a new social identity, one that oscillates between competing cultural ideals.

The weight of tradition is keenly felt by immigrant families who raise children in a culture that differs in significant respects from their own. Rooted in another place and time, ethnic values that once guided old world ways eventually come to feel out of step when they fail to address the needs of a younger generation growing up in a different society. Immigrant groups must therefore find ways to combine native traditions with those of their adopted land, creating syncretic cultural forms that speak to the concerns of young and old alike. Under these circumstances, the middle-class model of vesting primary responsibility for a child's socialization in the natal family—and the "mother," in particular—is not an option. Other institutions and organizations, such as schools, churches, and civic groups, must be drawn into the orbit of the domestic sphere in order to reinforce traditional values and, just as importantly, to inculcate new ones. The trade-offs involved in this intergenerational project can be painful and poignant, especially when what is at stake is the moral authority of "the family" itself (see Chen, this volume). Thus, when Taiwanese parents replace a household Confucian shrine with a Christian plaque that proclaims Christ to be "the Lord" of their home, they symbolically cede to Christ and His earthly representatives the power to compel filial obedience that once resided in the ancestral family and parents themselves. In so doing, these parents hope to acculturate their American-born children to an individualistic sense of moral agency, while also seeking to uphold a Chinese sense of obligation to family. Ironically, they must relinquish a degree of control over their children in the hope of gaining it.

The trade-offs that families make to honor cultural tradition may just as easily stem from contradictions between the values extolled in American culture as they do from a clash of values between different cultural systems. Households that cannot afford a "stay-at-home mother" or a culturally acceptable substitute, such as a nanny or an au pair, are often forced to fashion survival strategies that compromise the very values they are designed to express. Thus, women who work at an auto parts factory find themselves falling short of cultural expectations regarding the amount of time a mother should spend with her children and the type of work a respectable person should do (see Rudd and Root, this volume). Despite the scheduling flexibility that shift work permits and the relatively high wages that unionized factory work pays, these women feel they are simultaneously short-changing their "real work" as mothers in the home and sacrificing their desire to do more rewarding, but lower-paid, work in the white-collar world. Not only does the value of unpaid labor inside the home conflict with the value of paid labor outside the home, the *quality* of labor in both spheres is called into question when women who have young children attempt to perform them both. Mothers who enter the blue-collar workforce therefore confront a no-win situation when judged in terms of mainstream American values concerning family and work: they cannot claim the respect accorded to full-time homemakers, nor can they offset that stigma by claiming the prestige that accrues to white-collar work.

When work and family values conflict, class and gender hierarchies are thrown into bold relief. Households that require two income earners to achieve a middle-class standard of living are hard-pressed to realize in full the male breadwinner/female homemaker model of the family that is taken to be the hallmark of this socioeconomic position. In effect, a couple's inability to enact this particular gender ideal serves to mark their failure to achieve a certain class ideal—at least in cultural, if not economic terms. So close is the mapping of one set of values upon the other that families look for ways to signal their adherence to class and gender ideals, even when social circumstances do not bring them into direct conflict. Thus, an Iranian immigrant family divides their Silicon Valley house into gendered spaces, despite the fact that the young adult couple who live there are not torn between competing labor obligations inside and outside of the home (see Montgomery, this volume). Representing a growing trend among white-collar workers, members of this extended family household perform some portion of their paid labor at home rather than at the workplace. With the garage converted into a home office for the husband and his father-in-law and the kitchen doubling as a study or conference room for the wife and her mother, domestic space is used to symbolically reaffirm a normative division of labor in which men work "outside" the home and women work "within" it. Although there are no children in this household, we can imagine that their access to these gendered "work" spaces would be restricted. However—not unlike this family's dog, who enjoyed the run of the house after the dot-com bubble burst—a child's ability to cross such boundaries would be a barometer of the economic value of the work done at home.

Despite advances in telecommunications technologies that underwrite the oft-touted benefits of "telecommuting," the relocation of paid labor from office to home does not, in itself, signal a transformation of gender roles. We need only look at the predicament of household labor on the family farm to appreciate the fact that work-family conflicts are not solved simply by incorporating productive work into the domestic sphere. That is, although the conceptual line that divides private and public spheres may be elastic—contracting to designate rooms within a house or expanding to include thousands of acres beyond it—the cultural logic of the distinction does not change. When farmers complain about the "world coming in" to their homes and communities, they gesture toward the social forces that threaten to destroy their way of life (see Fricke, this volume). The notion that danger lies in a profane public realm outside of a sacred private sphere permits farmers to affirm the dignity of the division of labor that characterizes their male-dominated households, even as they recognize that many farms could not survive economically without the additional income provided by a spouse's off-farm job. Moreover, as attested to by farmers who cannot assume their own children will take over the farm, a moral premium is still placed on the presumed "character-building" nature of growing up on the ancestral land or home place. Thus, at a time when changes in the global economy have made this kind of intergenerational project increasingly less viable, farm families face the dilemma of raising their children to value a social world that is disappearing, in the hope of preparing them for the one taking its place.

Were it only farmers who lamented the depredations of modern society, we might see their complaints as a case of sour grapes—an instance of how those on the losing side of history attempt to "save face" by decrying the rules of the game. As it happens, however, we hear a similar complaint from those who can be considered the avatars of this brave new world. Indeed, corporate managers who reject the stultifying demands of bureaucratic organizations regularly invoke the ideal of the family farm in spirit, if not in practice. Thus, the manager who leaves a lucrative career in the defense industry to open a pie shop in a bucolic tourist town chooses a lifestyle in which he can work side-by-side with his wife and children in a family-owned business (see Hoey, this volume). Although the financial prospects of this undertaking and others like it may be more auspicious than those of the family farm, these enterprises share a common vision of the family—one in which the household economy, by virtue of its imagined freedom and independence, is thought to shield the domestic unit from forces beyond its control. In this regard, it is no coincidence that there has been tremendous upheaval and uncertainty in the national labor markets from which "corporate refugees" are fleeing. They are the latest casualties in the economic restructuring that followed the collapse of the post-World War II social contract—the hard-won agreements between American corporations, labor unions, and policy makers that underwrote blue- and white-collar job security and the capacity of male workers to support a family on their income alone. Confronted with workplace contingency, "lifestyle migrants" adopt a survival strategy predicated on the belief that a balanced work and family life can be found by going into business for themselves. But is this strategy really "new"? And to what extent is a "rethinking" of gender roles actually involved?

From the ethnographic evidence presented in this volume, I see little support for the idea that "the American family," as a cultural ideal, is changing. What *is* apparent are the variety of ways that American families are finding to deal with a changing socioeconomic landscape, one in which technological innovation and global competition have altered structures of opportunity for members of different social groups. Some, such as gays and lesbians or African-American professionals, have seen barriers to their economic mobility begin to lower, opening up options for marriage and childrearing practices that did not exist before. Others, such as unionized factory workers, farmers, and corporate managers, have seen their economic status and security erode, reducing options for domestic divisions of labor they once enjoyed. Yet, through it all, the ideal of the nuclear family—a domestic unit comprised of a married couple and children that is able to support itself— has remained remarkably resilient. In part, this ideal survives because its institutionalized expressions are *functional* in a market society, and therefore reinforced by political, legal, and religious sanctions. Locating primary responsibility for the care of the young, infirm, and elderly in the domestic sphere functions to preserve a public sphere in which economic exchange operates according to a radically different logic—that of market capitalism. And in equal part, the nuclear family ideal endures because it is *symbolic* of hopes and aspirations that are central to a market culture and the American character. Yearnings for freedom, independence, and self-sufficiency leavened by longings for security, compassion, and community find their ultimate expression in what Americans want their family to be: a "haven in a heartless world," able to protect them from turbulent times while also nurturing their individual quest for self-fulfillment.

With such powerful interests and desires concentrated on this singular family form, it should not surprise us that considerable anxiety attends the wish to safeguard it. Although families may be threatened in myriad ways— most notably by economic hardships that compromise a household's capacity to care for its members—these threats are usually visualized in terms of their *effects* rather than their cause. That is, when Americans think about the forces that endanger "the family," they focus intently on the rupture of interpersonal bonds within the domestic unit—as taken to be evidenced by divorce, child abuse, or abortion, for example—while tending to blame nebulous causes like a "breakdown of moral values" or "the world coming in." In this way, the domain of dangers is conceptually circumscribed by what is presumed to be within a person's control: maintaining a protective boundary around the domestic unit and claiming responsibility for the health and well-being of those within one's kin group. Thus, the expectant mother who says she "wouldn't be a good mommy" if she didn't publicly display images of her fetal ultrasound is keenly aware of the cultural expectation that she should demonstrate maternal attachment to her baby well before it is born (see Han, this volume). Her capacity to perceive a "child" in a grainy black and white image is a claim to motherhood and all that it entails. The ultrasound as a social ritual is therefore less of a medical examination than it is a test of affective bonds within the domestic sphere. Likewise, the nuclear family ideal is less a measure of social reality than it is a cultural Rorschach test: an actively apprehended form of moral obligation that allows us to claim kinship with one another.

# About the Contributors

**Riché Jeneen Daniel Barnes** is a lecturer in the department of Afro-American Studies at Smith College, Northampton, Massachusetts, where she studies the intersection of race, class, and gender in the lives of African American middle-class families. Riché is completing her dissertation "Race, Class and Motherhood: How Professional Black Wives Negotiate Career and Family," in the department of Anthropology at Emory University, Atlanta, where she is a graduate fellow with the Sloan Center for Myth and Ritual in American Life. She has published essays on the challenges of marriage and family in the black community in several news outlets including the *Atlanta Journal-Constitution*.

**Carolyn Chen** is an assistant professor of sociology and Asian American studies at Northwestern University. Her book, *Getting Saved in America: Taiwanese Immigration and Religion*, is forthcoming by Princeton University Press.

**M. Eugenia Deerman** is an assistant professor at Eastern Illinois University. She has research interests in social movements and political storytelling. Through historical and archival research, she has studied the role of narrative in the politics of the Christian Right, the New Right, and the back-to-the-land movement. Her current research explores the role of think tanks in the American conservative movement and the historical trajectories of conservative gender and family ideology. She is working on a series of articles exploring the place of conservative ideology in popular culture and in policy making.

**Lara Descartes** is an assistant professor in the department of Human Development and Family Studies at the University of Connecticut. She is an anthropologist with interests in identity, community, and family: how race, class, gender, and sexual orientation intersect with work and home in shaping family possibilities. She has published in *Community, Work, and Family*, the *Journal of Family and Consumer Science Research*, and, with Conrad Kottak, is completing a book on media, work, and family.

**Kathryn M. Dudley** is professor of American studies and anthropology at Yale University. Her publications include *The End of the Line: Lost Jobs, New Lives in Postindustrial America* and *Debt and Dispossession: Farm Loss in America's Heartland*. She is the recipient of the 2000 Margaret Mead Award.

**Tom Fricke** is professor of anthropology at the University of Michigan where he is also founding director of the Center for the Ethnography of Everyday Life. His ethnographic research and writing is in the areas of kinship, family, work, cultural morality, and documentary methods and covers materials from research in North Dakota, Nepal, Taiwan, and Pakistan. He is currently working on a book about the North Dakota community and families discussed in his essay in this volume. An earlier account of these farmers and ranchers appeared as "Next Year Country" in the Spring 2003 issue of *DoubleTake Magazine*.

**Todd L. Goodsell** is assistant professor of sociology at Brigham Young University, where he studies family solidarity and neighborhood revitalization. His publications include research on community solidarity in *Rural Sociology* and fatherhood narratives in the edited volume *Situated Fathering: A Focus on Physical and Social Spaces*. His article "Diluting the Cesspool: Families, Home Improvement, and Social Change" is forthcoming in the *Journal of Family Issues*.

**Sallie Han** is an assistant professor of anthropology at SUNY College at Oneonta. Her forthcoming publications include an analysis of fetal ultrasound images as family photography in the edited volume, *Imagining the Fetus*, and a study of American men and pregnancy in the edited volume, *Reconceiving the Second Sex: Men, Masculinity, and Reproduction*. She is writing a book on "belly talk" (communicating with an expected child in utero) as an American cultural practice.

**Brian A. Hoey** is an associate professor of anthropology at Marshall University of Huntington, West Virginia. His research and teaching emphasize a number of themes including personhood and place, migration, narrative identity and life-transition, community building, and negotiations between work, family, and self in different social, historical, and environmental contexts. In addition to contributions to reports in print, radio and television media, Hoey publishes in the *American Ethnologist*, the *Journal for Anthropological Research*, the *Journal for Contemporary Ethnography*, and *Ethnology*. You may learn about his work at www.brianhoey.com.

**Conrad P. Kottak** is professor and former chair (1996–2006) of anthropology at the University of Michigan. He has done ethnographic field work in Brazil, Madagascar, and the United States. He is the author of *Prime-Time Society: An Anthropological Analysis of Television and Culture* (1990)—a comparative study of the nature and impact of television in Brazil and the United States. Other books include *Researching American Culture* (1982) and (with Kathryn A. Kozaitis) *On Being Different: Diversity and Multiculturalism in the North American Mainstream* (3rd ed., 2008).

**Alesia F. Montgomery** is assistant professor in sociology at Michigan State University, where she studies spatial practices, urban sociology, work/family intersections, and technology use. Montgomery's articles include "Virtual Enclaves: The Influence of Alumni Email Lists on the Workspaces of Transnational Software Engineers," forthcoming in *Global Networks* and "Living in Each Other's Pockets: The Navigation of Social Distances by Middle Class Families in Los Angeles," which was published in *City and Community*. Her projects evidence a concern with the ways in which the structure and import of socio-spatial practices change as demographic, economic, and technological developments transform the possibilities for association.

**Diana M. Pash** is a doctoral candidate in the department of anthropology at UCLA and graduate student fellow at the Center on Everyday Lives of Families, a Sloan Center for the Study of Working Families at UCLA. Her dissertation research examines community and extended kin relationships in gay co-father families. Her publications include, "Gay Fathers Define Family in Neighborhoods and Communities" in *Anthropology News* (May 2004), and her working papers include "Gay Co-father Families and their Extended Female Kin" (2006) and "Establishing Ties to Community: Gay Fathers and the Work of Alliance Building in Everyday Family Life" (2004).

**Lawrence S. Root** is a professor in the School of Social Work, director of the Institute of Labor and Industrial Relations and co-director of the Labor and Global Change program at the University of Michigan. His research focuses on employment and social welfare, personnel practices for an aging workforce, services for workers experiencing personal problems, joint labor-management programs, and work-family issues. Professor Root has directed action-research projects focusing on employee assistance programs, education and training, and distance learning in the auto industry. He chairs the University of Michigan's Committee on Labor Standards and Human Rights.

**Elizabeth Rudd** is a research scientist at the University of Washington, Seattle, where she studies globalization in doctoral education and intersections of gender, work, and family in Ph.D. careers. She has published papers on gender in German postsocialism in *Gender & Society* and *Ethnos*; her article, "Equality and Illusion: Gender & Tenure in Art History Careers," is forthcoming in the *Journal of Marriage and Family*.

**Erin N. Winkler** is an assistant professor in the department of Africology at the University of Wisconsin-Milwaukee, where she teaches courses on racial identity development and the psychology of racism. She is currently researching the racial socialization experiences of African American children in Detroit, as well as the comparative racial socialization practices among African American, Latino, and white families in the Milwaukee area.

**Alford A. Young, Jr.** is Arthur F. Thurnau Professor, and associate professor of sociology, and in the Center for Afro-American and African Studies at the University of Michigan. He has conducted research on low-income, urban-based African Americans, employees at an automobile manufacturing plant, and African American scholars and intellectuals. Professor Young is author of *The Minds of Marginalized Black Men: Making Sense of Mobility, Opportunity, and Future Life Chances* (Princeton University Press 2004) and co-author of *The Souls of W.E.B. Du Bois* (Paradigm Publishers 2006). He has published articles in *Sociological Theory, The Annual Review of Sociology*, and other journals.